The Survey Research Handbook

THE IRWIN SERIES IN MARKETING

Gilbert A. Churchill, Jr., Consulting Editor
University of Wisconsin, Madison

The Survey Research Handbook

Second Edition

Pamela L. Alreck
Robert B. Settle

Both of the

Perdue School of Business
Salisbury State University
Salisbury, Maryland

IRWIN

Chicago • Bogotá • Boston • Buenos Aires • Caracas • London • Madrid • Mexico City • Sydney • Toronto

IRWIN
Concerned About Our Environment

In recognition of the fact that our company is a large end-user of fragile yet replenishable resources, we at IRWIN can assure you that every effort is made to meet or exceed Environmental Protection Agency (EPA) recommendations and requirements for a "greener" workplace.

To preserve these natural assets, a number of environmental policies, both companywide and department-specific, have been implemented. From the use of 50% recycled paper in our textbooks to the printing of promotional materials with recycled stock and soy inks to our office paper recycling program, we are committed to reducing waste and replacing environmentally unsafe products with safer alternatives.

Sponsoring editor: Nina McGuffin
Developmental editor: Heather McCammond-Watts
Marketing manager: Jim Lewis
Project editor: Waivah Clement
Production manager: Laurie Kersch
Designer: Larry J. Cope
Cover designer: Joshua Paul Carr
Cover photographer: John Thoeming
Art coordinator: Mark Malloy
Compositor: University Graphics, Inc.
Typeface: 10/12 Bembo
Printer: R. R. Donnelley & Sons Company

The Library of Congress has catalogued the Irwin edition as follows:

Library of Congress Cataloging-in-Publication Data

Alreck, Pamela L.
   The survey research handbook / Pamela L. Alreck, Robert B. Settle.
     p. cm. — (The Irwin series in marketing)
   Includes index.
   ISBN 0-256-10321-6   ISBN 0-7863-0358-1
   1. Social surveys—Handbooks, manuals, etc.   I. Settle, Robert B.
   II. Title.   III. Series
HN29.A46   1995
301'.0723—dc20   94-7619

Printed in the United States of America
3 4 5 6 7 8 9 0 DO 1 0 9 8 7 6 5

Preface

Survey research is one of those activities that cut across a dozen different boundaries. Those in business and public administration, the social and behavioral sciences, professional and family studies, journalism and communications, education and health services, politics and law, and many other diverse areas all find an increasing need for information based on survey research. Fortunately, the same basic tools, skills, and activities for doing surveys apply, regardless of the particular purpose or topics for any one survey research project.

As active survey research consultants for many years, we've designed and conducted projects in several areas for many different types of clients. Invariably, during the initial meeting with a potential new survey sponsor, those seeking the information will explain, with a good deal of sincerity and conviction, that their own particular organization, industry, or profession is unique—probably not much like any other we've encountered. This sometimes troubles potential survey sponsors because they wonder if they should seek out a survey research consultant or agency that has worked in their own area of activity and has substantial experience with the special nature of their information needs. Their concerns are genuine, but they're also unfounded. It's certainly true that the institutions and organizations that depend on survey information are often very different from one another in their goals, objectives, and operations. Yet, by applying the same basic principles and techniques described in this handbook, we've surveyed many thousands of different types of respondents for dozens of very diverse clients with uniformly positive and valuable results. Perhaps you're wondering if you should seek a research book devoted exclusively to your own discipline, profession, or activity to guide you in a survey project. You need not be concerned because you'll find what you need here.

Fortunately, survey research *applications* cut across many institutional and disciplinary boundaries. Unfortunately, however, survey research also slices across many *technical* boundaries as well. If you're going to do a complete survey project, from beginning to end, you'll find the diversity of skills rather demanding. You'll be working with people one minute and computers the next. At one time you may be concerned with how to phrase a question or word some instruction. A few days later you may be a little puzzled about some statistical method. You may have to deal with a printer who keeps telling you your work will be ready tomorrow or a computer that just doesn't seem to want to talk to you at all. Fear not! One of our main purposes in writing this handbook is to bring together all of the various techniques and principles, skills, and activities that are required to conduct a really effective survey project. As university instructors, we've both been faced with an all too familiar situation far too many times. The typical situation is simply this: A student comes to the office or approaches one of us after class and declares with considerable gravity that he or she has decided to conduct a survey. Then comes the question: "*Where can I find a book that will tell me what to do?*" Often these same students have taken one or more university courses on research methods in their own area of study. Occasionally, they'll have a research text-book in their hand at the time. Yet we and they both know very well that neither the training they received nor the textbook they acquired would guide them through an entire survey research project from start to finish. We sincerely believe that with this handbook, we and they and you have the answer. This handbook isn't devoted to any one, specific area, but it provides comprehensive coverage of the wide variety of things you'll need to know to conduct effective survey research.

We've been guided by two criteria when judging whether or not to include material in the handbook: Is this *sufficient* and is this *necessary?* We feel that satisfying both criteria is important. When using a handbook, there's nothing quite so frustrating as finding it covers every conceivable situation except *your own.* Consequently, the breadth and scope of the handbook is, by necessity, very wide. It must be, in order to meet your own needs, whether you're a student who will conduct a single survey project to meet your academic require-ments or a seasoned survey research professional seeking some new ideas or tools of the trade.

We've also avoided or eliminated a substantial amount of material often found in research textbooks. If we had never once used or seen the need for some technique, computation, or procedure in either academic or pragmatic survey research over many years of experience, we felt you probably wouldn't need it either, and it could safely be excluded. Perhaps there will be some who feel the handbook lacks dignity because the practical and technical aspects of survey research take precedence over the conceptual and the theoretical aspects. To us, that's the whole idea, and it's a small price to pay for a handbook that's understandable and useful.

Over 300 special exhibits are included to help you refer quickly and easily to the infor-mation you'll need to conduct a survey. They cover virtually every aspect of the survey process, from initiation to final report. Each of the six distinct types of exhibits has a special purpose and type of information:

- **CHECKLISTS** contain a series of questions followed by instructions on how to proceed, depending on the answer.

- **GUIDELISTS** provide a series of instructions or directions, in sequence, to perform some task or to follow a procedure.

- **EXAMPLES** contain typical elements or formats to use as models for creating various components of a survey.

- **FIGURES** portray verbal or graphic information, showing quantities or relationships according to their relative position.

- **SUMMARIES** at the end of each chapter provide a sketch or outline of the most important things covered in the chapter.

- **TABLES** of coefficients or probabilities are contained in Appendix B to assess statistical significance.

As you examine the handbook, you should find there's little that's likely to get in the way of understanding. Some aspects of survey research, especially those involving computers and statistics, traditionally use a lot of buzzwords and obscure terminology. In our experience, that kind of vocabulary is intimidating and inhibiting rather than helpful or enlightening. So we've deliberately avoided them in favor of plain, ordinary words and phrases. If you find more here than what you need, at least it will be understandable. To the degree that we've been successful, you'll find everything you need for survey research and very little else.

Pamela L. Alreck
Robert B. Settle

Brief Contents

Contents

Checklists

Guidelists

Examples

Figures

Summaries

Tables

PART 1

Planning and Designing the Survey

Chapter 1

Initiating a Survey

WHY SURVEYS ARE CONDUCTED

Surveys are often conducted simply because it's the only way to get the information needed. Even when the information is available through other means, survey research may be an easier, quicker, less expensive, or more accurate way to get the required information.

Individuals or organizations usually sponsor surveys for one of three basic reasons: (1) They want to influence or persuade some audience. (2) They want to create or modify a product or service they provide for a particular public. (3) They want to understand or predict human behavior or conditions because it's the focus of their academic or professional work.

Surveys of an Audience

Many who sponsor surveys would ultimately like to influence the beliefs or behavior of their audience—to persuade some group of people to think in a certain way or act in some particular fashion. Virtually everyone tries, at times, to influence and persuade others. There's nothing wrong with that, because ordinarily the people they're trying to influence aren't being exploited or harmed in any way. Parents try to influence their children, spouses seek to persuade one another, employees attempt to influence their supervisors, and buyers try to convince sellers to reduce their prices. When ordinary people try to influence others, those doing the persuading can tell easily from observation or conversation whether or not they've been successful. It's far more difficult for organizations or institutions that are trying to influence or persuade large audiences to gauge the effects.

Business firms promote their goods or services. Political parties and organizations promote their candidates and issues. Government bureaus and agencies promote their positions. Social service institutions devoted to education, public health and medicine, religious belief, or social welfare promote their doctrines and services. All of these organizations communicate with their publics in a variety of ways. Yet promotion is one-way communication. The persuasive message goes out from the sender to the audience, but how does the audience respond? Are the messages effective? Is there resistance? Do those in the audience understand the message? Is the information what they need to know? Do the messages "touch a nerve" or evoke a need?

When messages are directed to a large audience, survey research can be the other half of the conversation, so there's two-way communication between the message sender and the audience. Those who receive the messages ordinarily don't take the initiative to provide feedback. Even if they wanted to, there's often no convenient way for them to respond. Those who sponsor a survey of their audience are taking the responsibility for both halves of the conversation. They're providing a medium through which their audience can talk to them. They're not imposing on the respondents because nobody can be forced to respond if they don't wish to take the time or effort to do so. In fact, most people welcome the opportunity to respond, to record their opinions and reactions, and to have some effect on the sponsor.

Surveys of a Clientele

Most people's occupations involve doing or making something for others. So do the operations of most companies, organizations, and institutions. Individuals and organizations often seek survey information to discover the needs, wants, and desires of the people they serve. They often want to know the underlying human conditions that make their goods and services useful and valuable to others. The better the providers of goods and services know and understand their clients, the more they'll be able to serve them economically and effectively. Commercial and industrial firms, political parties and candidates, governmental agencies and units, hospitals and clinics, schools and colleges, churches and religious groups, and those in professional practices all provide goods and services to their own publics. In almost every case, there are many alternatives concerning *what* they provide, *who* they provide it to, *when* and *where* it will be offered, *how* it will be produced, and the cost or charges for the goods or services. Survey research is often used to furnish information for making these decisions.

The producers of goods and services ordinarily have to take the responsibility for learning the needs and desires of their particular clientele. They usually have a fairly clear picture of what could be produced and delivered, but they're often uncertain about the needs and desires of the public. Similarly, the clients know what they need or want in a general way, but they don't usually know what goods or services could be produced or who might produce them. It's often desirable for the producers who sponsor surveys to learn about their clienteles. Such surveys typically benefit the clients or customers who respond to the surveys as well as the producers who sponsor the research. The better the producers understand their clientele, the more effectively they will be able to serve them.

Surveys of Other Populations

The reasons for surveys identified above are *practical* ones. The results are directed toward decision making and executive actions. Sponsors may also be motivated by a desire for knowledge about people, in and of itself. People, themselves, are the subject matter—the focus of attention—for many academic and professional disciplines. Students, professors, researchers, and professionals in the social and behavioral sciences, the humanities and arts, business and public administration, and a wide variety of other professional studies focus partly or entirely on the behavior and conditions of the people in the society. This kind of survey information is sought not so much to assist in decision making as to enhance the body of theoretical and conceptual knowledge of the discipline. Rather than information to be applied to practical problems and actions, *theoretical* research seeks information to answer research questions and to test hypotheses about the propensities and predispositions of people. This type of survey information may not apply directly to existing conditions or potential actions at the moment. Instead, it's used to enhance the literature and the state of current thought within the discipline or area of the sponsor.

The criteria for judging information needs differ between the two types of survey research. Nevertheless, the survey procedure itself is fairly standard, regardless of whether the purpose is practical or theoretical. Measurement tools are largely indifferent to what they're measuring. Those in many different occupations often use the same measurement tools. Carpenters, plumbers, and masons may all use a tape measure for lumber, pipe, or concrete, respectively. Similarly, surveys are measurement tools that can be used effectively by those in many occupations and for a wide variety of purposes and topics. However, it's important to identify the general purpose of the survey project, not so much to indicate *how* the survey should be conducted as to show *what information* needs and survey topics should be considered.

EXPECTATIONS OF SURVEY RESULTS

Those who consider conducting a survey may wonder what results they can and should expect. It may be difficult to assess the capabilities and limitations of survey research. Some prospective sponsors have overly ambitious expectations, while others think surveys are much more limited than they really are. A survey's value depends on both the amount of resources devoted to the survey and the care and expertise that goes into the work. It's impossible to say exactly what should or shouldn't be expected of a particular set of survey results or to predict precisely what will or won't be accomplished in a given instance. Yet some broad guidelines may be helpful to compare surveys with other techniques for gathering information.

Survey Attributes

Survey research is an extremely popular form of inquiry today. It would probably be difficult to find anyone who hasn't been asked to respond to some form of survey in the past few years, and many people are frequently approached by survey researchers. Surveys are used so often today because they offer so many advantages to those seeking information.

Flexibility and versatility

Surveys can be designed to measure things as simple as respondents' physical or demographic characteristics or as complex as their attitudes, preferences, or lifestyle patterns. They may cover only one, small aspect of the respondents' mentality or situation, or they may include dozens or even hundreds of questions about almost every aspect of the respondents' lives. Surveys can be designed to capture the respondents' personal history, their present life circumstances, their intentions and expectations for the future, or the entire scope of the time spectrum.

Survey data can be collected by personal interview, telephone interview, or direct mail. Respondents can be reached with only visual contact, only audible stimuli, or both. They can be reached in their homes, at work, while shopping, or even during their recreation. They can be presented with a response task that requires only a few seconds or one that takes an hour or more. Survey research isn't confined to a single mode of inquiry.

The volume of data collected and the degree of complexity are a matter of choice, depending on information requirements and resource availability. Simple surveys can be designed requiring only a few tally sheets and a pocket calculator to tabulate, perhaps generating only a one-page report. Complex and exhaustive surveys may use highly sophisticated computer systems and data analysis routines, making it possible to do computations and generate large volumes of precise information that was completely impossible to obtain only a decade or so ago.

Specialization and efficiency

When considering a survey, three questions quickly arise: (1) How much will it cost? (2) How long will it take? (3) How much will be learned? They often can't be answered accurately at first. Much more specification is required, because survey research isn't at all homogeneous. This is an important advantage of survey projects, because it means they can usually be customized to fit both the needs and the budgets of those seeking information. A survey could cost only a few hundred dollars or hundreds of thousands of dollars, take only a single day or extend over many months, and generate only a single piece of data or cover a huge range of information. To answer the three big questions above, the project must be matched to the needs and resources of the sponsor.

Because survey research uses sampling, information about an extremely large population can be obtained from a relatively small sample of people. Rarely do surveys sample more than about a thousand people, even when the results are to be generalized to many millions. The vast majority of surveys include only a few hundred respondents, and there are some projects where a sample of only a few dozen respondents is completely adequate. The use of well-designed and well-organized instrumentation also contributes to the efficiency of survey research. It isn't at all unusual for survey questionnaires to capture answers to a hundred or more different questions or items in only a few minutes of each respondent's time. Without this careful and often artful instrument composition, that many individual questions asked in random order and ad hoc fashion might take several hours to answer.

Survey Limitations

Despite the positive features of this type of research inquiry, survey research methods have some intractable disadvantages and limitations. Perhaps the most serious limitation is that it's difficult or impossible to measure *causality* using survey research. Surveys almost always involve *asking questions* and obtaining *self-reports* by respondents. Unfortunately, survey respondents are notoriously bad at assessing *causality*, either because they actually *don't know why they do or others behave in a certain way* or because they say why. *Experimentation* is ordinarily a much more effective method of measuring causality for behavior.

Threatening and sensitive questions

Respondents won't answer some questions because the information is so sensitive that they're too embarrassed or threatened to give the information. For example, it's difficult to learn about issues associated with social taboos, such as sexual behavior, drinking habits, and drug abuse. Some such information may be obtainable with considerable expertise, effort, and ingenuity. However, it's usually impossible to get such information from survey research if the questions or issues seriously threaten a large part of the respondent group. For instance, questions about earnings and the amount of income listed on their tax returns are likely to elicit more heat than light from respondents. Other forms of inquiry, such as *behavior audits* or *systematic observations*, are often better means for measuring such things.

Cost, expertise, and error

Surveys should and often do generate information that's worth several times more than the cost of the project. Yet surveys take time, cost money, and require intelligent, well-directed effort. Survey research is extremely demanding in one respect: It requires complete planning and careful execution at virtually every step in the process. *One person* must take responsibility for the survey project. That person does not need to do all the work or make all the decisions. Rather, the person in charge has to monitor and supervise the project continually and diligently. The survey process consists of a series of interactive steps or phases that must ordinarily be done in sequence. The researcher may sometimes have to anticipate later phases and make decisions or commitments about them before completing the earlier steps. Unless the researcher has a clear picture of the entire process, there's always the potential to do something at an early phase that will take the process down a dead-end street or have disastrous consequences at a later phase in the process.

As with any other kind of work, there will inevitably be mistakes, errors, and oversights along the way. These aren't reasons to forgo a survey project until it can be done perfectly. It never will be. The objective of complete planning and careful execution is to avoid the *major* errors and oversights. So long as there's no serious jeopardy to the value of the survey information, minor mistakes can and must be tolerated. If minor errors show up during or after completion of the survey, they should be examined to see what effect they have on the survey information. It's never advisable to denigrate or discard survey results simply because some small mistakes were made during the process. Minor errors and inadequacies shouldn't be allowed to throw a dense shadow of doubt over the entire range of survey results. Rather, they should be treated for what they are: things that may require some modification in the interpretation of and reliance on the survey findings.

Surveys Don't Dictate Decisions

Even if no errors or omissions are discovered and the survey project goes precisely as planned, the results won't be definitive. They won't dictate decisions or contain the ultimate answers. Instead, survey results should be treated as another body of evidence or set of indications.

Survey results have to be evaluated in the light of experience, common sense, and other information. Human perception and judgment will always be required. The reason that survey results aren't definitive is simple but compelling: Respondents' answers are merely stand-ins for actual conditions or actions. It's typically important to know the answers to survey questions and understand the things they represent. Actions usually follow thoughts. On the other hand, survey responses are never precisely indicative.

THE ROLES OF THE PARTICIPANTS

Surveys that are relatively limited in scope may be initiated, sponsored, designed, and conducted by the same individual, but that's not usually the case. Survey research often involves several people, and large surveys may require the services of a hundred or more people. Different aspects of the work may have special roles and responsibilities to be performed by different people. During survey planning and initiation, the major focus is on the roles of (1) those who sponsor the survey, pay for it, and seek the information it will generate, and (2) those who actually design and conduct the research.

The Sponsor's Role

Often those who sponsor a survey are unfamiliar with the survey process. They may be executives, managers, or professionals whose area of expertise lies elsewhere. They're likely to be quite familiar with the problems, decisions, actions, conditions, and perhaps the "conventional wisdom" of their own discipline, industry, or institution. Their understanding of the survey process may range from fairly accurate perceptions to only rather vague notions. Their role is to explain both what information is needed and why it is needed. Some sponsors may expect the researcher to operate in a vacuum of information about the purpose for the survey. They may feel it's satisfactory merely to provide a few basic questions to be addressed by the survey and fail to provide sufficient background or prove reluctant to discuss frankly and openly the fundamental nature of the information needs or specific purposes to which the results will be devoted. Such a relationship between sponsor and researcher isn't advisable. The sponsor should indicate the ultimate purpose for the survey and provide the researchers with clear guidelines concerning the time requirements for the survey. They should also be prepared to indicate the general level of funding or resources that are allocated to the project. The role of the survey sponsor is outlined in Guidelist 1–1.

The Researcher's Role

Those who are to conduct the survey must be thoroughly familiar with the capabilities and limitations of the survey research process. In most cases, the researcher shouldn't try to *educate* the sponsor about the survey process. Instead, the researcher should inquire thoroughly about the information needs, the nature of the decisions and actions to be based on the research results, and the overall operation of the institution, organization, or unit sponsoring the survey. The researcher can then portray the alternatives and point out the survey procedures that might be used.

The sponsors must have a sense of trust in those conducting the survey. They should feel free to provide the information the researcher seeks from them. The researcher may have to explain that those conducting the survey stand in a fiduciary relationship with the sponsor. The researcher is ethically bound to do nothing to harm or endanger the sponsor. This relationship is no different from that of physician and patient or attorney and client.

Unless it's otherwise stipulated in writing, the survey data, the information, the instruments, and even the knowledge that a survey is being conducted are all *proprietary* to the sponsor. In short, everything belongs to the sponsor. It would be highly unethical for those conducting a survey to discuss it with outsiders; to reveal the sponsor; to share the data, reports, or information; or to dispose of these *properties* in any way that might prove undesirable to the sponsor. If the researcher intends to publish the results or promulgate the information in any form, it's the researcher's obligation either to obtain approval in advance and include it as a provision of the contract or to obtain written permission later, but *before* releasing the information. These and other aspects of the researcher's role are outlined in Guidelist 1–2.

The researcher also has ethical obligations toward respondents. Reputable researchers respect and maintain the privacy of respondents, as well as their anonymity if they're promised it. When the respondents are promised they won't be individually identified, that promise must be carefully kept. Sometimes sponsors may request that individual respondents be identified. If this identification is to be provided to the sponsor, the respondents have to be advised of it in advance, so that they're free to decline participation if they prefer. If the respondents are to be assured of anonymity, only aggregate data or unidentified individual responses should be provided to the sponsor.

There may be occasions when the sponsor will seek the identity of the respondents after learning the results of the survey. For example, an employer who sponsored a survey of employees may seek the identity of individual respondents for the purpose of reprisal for negative attitudes or behavior, or a company may wish to identify potential customers, based on their survey responses, and solicit them to purchase goods. When the respondents have

---

GUIDELIST 1–1

For Sponsors Initiating a Survey

1. Furnish the researchers with sufficient background information about the setting and operations.
2. Provide a description of the issues, problems, or uncertainties that lead to consideration of a survey.
3. Indicate the type of information that would solve the problem or reduce the uncertainty.
4. Describe what decisions, choices, or actions will be based on the survey results.
5. Estimate the value of the information, based on potential risks or opportunity costs.
6. Specify the time requirements and level of funding and other resources allocated to the project.

been assured of their anonymity, the researcher is bound by ethical principles to keep that promise and to refuse the sponsor the information, even though the sponsor has initiated and funded the survey. If sponsors are so informed in advance, they have no legitimate claim to the identity of respondents.

Occasionally a potential sponsor will approach a researcher and propose a survey that's specifically designed to obtain certain results. In other words, the project is to *appear* to be an actual survey, when in fact the process is *rigged* to yield specific findings—the items are worded in such a way that they will obtain certain results, the sample is designed to obtain responses from those who are most likely to be favorable to the position of the sponsor, or the results are to be analyzed to generate a positive picture. Ordinarily such motives and intentions become clear during specification of the information needs. They're totally uneth-ical, and the prudent researcher will both refuse the proposed project and also avoid any working relationship with the sponsor in the future. These ethical considerations are outlined in Guidelist 1–3.

Often a sponsor will want a survey to be conducted by an independent researcher because the sponsor doesn't want to be identified to the respondents or to others. If the respondents know who is sponsoring the survey, that may bias the results. If customers, competitors, vendors, or others know about the survey, that may have adverse effects on the sponsor. It's completely legitimate to conduct a survey without identifying the sponsor to respondents or to others. If potential respondents don't want to participate because the sponsor isn't identified, they can refuse. The researcher is under no obligation to reveal the sponsor to the respondents or to explain the nature or reasons for the survey if it's against the sponsor's wishes.

GUIDELIST 1–2

For Researchers During Survey Initiation

1. Know the capabilities and limitations of survey research and indicate them to sponsors when appropriate.
2. Obtain background information about the operations, policies, and procedures of the sponsor.
3. Inquire about the nature of the uncertainty, problems, or issues to be the focus of the survey.
4. Ask what decisions, choices, or actions are to be based on the results of the proposed survey.
5. Make a preliminary assessment of the approximate value of the survey information for the sponsor.

6. Seek indications of the time requirements for the survey and the approximate funding and resources available.
7. Describe the type of cooperation and participation that will be required of the sponsor.
8. Explain what ethical responsibilities regarding the survey the researcher has to the sponsor and respondents.
9. Encourage the confidence and trust of the sponsor through candor and professional conduct.

POTENTIAL SURVEY TOPICS

Surveys can be designed to capture a wide variety of information on many diverse topics. Eight basic topic categories are described here: attitudes, images, decisions, needs, behavior, lifestyle, affiliations, and demographics. These categories aren't completely distinct from one another. Some may overlap, and some issues or topics don't fit perfectly into one category. Yet the topics do differ in many ways, and they're often measured by different types of survey items. The most common methods for measuring the topics are listed here to guide survey planning.

Attitudes

Attitudes are often the subject of surveys. They predispose people to act in a certain way toward the object of the attitude. Attitudes come *before* behavior and affect the way the person will act. They're fairly enduring and usually last for weeks, months, or even years. People change their mind when they receive additional information, or experience or perceive the object of the attitude differently.

An attitude always focuses on some object. It can be a physical or material thing, a person or group, or an idea or issue. Attitudes have three parts: (1) what the individual *knows* or *believes* about the topic, (2) how the person *feels* about the topic and how it's *valued*, and (3) the likelihood that the individual will take *action* based on the attitude. When attitudes are measured, the survey questions should include all three attitude components. For example, it would be necessary to ask if respondents *know* about the object, how much they *liked* or

---

GUIDELIST 1-3

For Maintaining Professional Ethics

1. Maintain a fiduciary relationship, always seeking and protecting the best interests of the sponsor.
2. Treat all survey information, including the process and the results, as the sole property of the sponsor.
3. Obtain prior permission or approval before releasing, publishing, or using any survey information or data.
4. Refuse any project or relationship with a sponsor who seeks to bias the survey to get certain results.
5. Protect the privacy and anonymity of respondents if they're promised their identity won't be revealed.
6. Never permit the sponsor to identify individual respondents for reprisal for adverse survey results.
7. Don't identify respondents for solicitation unless they know in advance they may be solicited later.
8. Recognize the legitimacy of withholding sponsor identification to respondents and others when appropriate.
9. Return all data, reports, or other materials purchased by sponsors to them on completion of the project.

disliked, and how they intend to behave toward it. The basic recommendations for measuring attitudes are contained in Guidelist 1–4.

GUIDELIST 1–4

For Measuring Attitudes

1. Be sure to include all three components of the attitude: knowledge, feelings, and action tendencies, in that order.

2. Begin with awareness and knowledge. Ignore feelings and action tendencies if knowledge is insufficient.

3. Use unaided recall to measure awareness, if possible, to avoid false reports of recognition.

4. Measure depth of knowledge with an index of the number of correct statements about the topic.

5. Use ratings scales to measure feelings, so that both direction and distance from neutral are revealed.

6. Consider a comparative scale where relative, rather than absolute levels of feelings are appropriate.

7. Don't ignore the intensity of feelings or assume intensity is the same as distance from neutral.

8. Measure intensity by asking how strongly respondents feel or how sure they are of their position.

9. Measure past, present, and future behavior to assess the strength of the behavioral component.

10. Specify hypothetical conditions and ask intentions if respondents lacked opportunity to act in the past.

Knowledge component

Because people base their feelings and actions on what they *know* about an object, it's important for researchers to learn what they know or believe about the topic. Respondents should be asked about their knowledge of the topic *first*. If they've never heard of it, there's no reason to ask about their feelings or actions. People often give an opinion, even though they've no notion whatsoever of what the thing is. Nobody likes to admit they don't know, so they pretend to know. To measure the knowledge component, begin by measuring *awareness*. There are two ways to ask about awareness: *aided* and *unaided recall*. With aided recall, the respondents are asked, ''Have you ever heard of _____?'' The problem with this kind of question is that many people will say they've heard of it, even though they haven't. To avoid this problem, ask for more detail concerning the characteristics of the object or use the unaided recall method.

With the unaided method of measuring awareness, the respondent is asked to name all the objects in a given group or to identify the object based on a description of its position or attributes. For example, people might be asked to name all the brands of a product they could recall. If they named the brand in question, they'd have awareness. Or respondents might be asked, ''Do you know the name of the member of Congress from this district?'' Naming the representative correctly would indicate awareness. Another way to get information about the knowledge component is to ask a series of true/false questions about the topic. The number of correct answers is an index of each respondent's level of knowledge.

Asking about the manner in which respondents learned of the object and the experience they've had with the topic is yet another indication.

Feeling component

People are seldom completely neutral about anything. The feeling component develops in one of two ways: through *reward* or through *evaluation*. In the first case, people learn to like or dislike the object because their experience with it was rewarding or unrewarding (punishing). For example, many people have a negative attitude toward some food because they find it distasteful (unrewarding). The second way people develop feelings about objects is by evaluation. People automatically and often unconsciously compare what they know or believe about a topic with their own personal values. If their knowledge fits their values, they develop positive feelings, and if it's contrary to their values, their feelings are negative toward the topic. For example, if a person knows that a particular brand is expensive and values economy highly, this would lead to a negative attitude toward the brand.

To measure the feeling component of an attitude, two sets of things often need to be measured: *position* on the positive/negative spectrum and *intensity* of feelings. The two aren't the same. One person may feel the object is very good but may be unsure of this, while another may feel slightly negative about the object but may hold that feeling with great intensity. It would be easy to change the first person's mind but difficult to persuade the second one to take another view. Measuring the *position* of feelings requires measuring the *direction* and the *distance* of the feelings, to know if respondents *liked* or *disliked* the object and *how much* so. Either an absolute or a relative scale might be used. A linear, numeric scale with the extremes labeled "good" and "bad" could be used to give an absolute rating. For a relative rating, a comparative scale could be used, with some other object as the standard for comparison. Both types of scales are described in Chapter 5, and the choice depends on the situation. Neither method is universally more effective or less effective.

It's easier to measure the direction and location of feelings than it is to measure intensity. Asking respondents to rate how certain they are of their good/bad or comparative rating provides a direct measure. Asking why they feel as they do or asking the likelihood of changing their opinion are indirect measures.

Action component

Even though two people have similar knowledge about the topic of an attitude and share much the same feelings, they may behave differently toward the topic. For example, two shoppers who have the same knowledge and feelings about a certain brand may both find that the brand was out of stock at their favorite store. One may simply choose another brand, but the other may postpone purchase until the brand is available or seek that brand at another store. Why the difference in behavior? Because the action components of their attitudes toward the brand differ. Perhaps the best way to measure the action component is to ask respondents about past, present, and intended future behavior toward the object. This assumes that they've had or will have the opportunity to act. If not, it may be necessary to specify a set of hypothetical conditions and ask questions about how the respondents would act under those circumstances. (See Guidelist 1–4.)

Images

People's images of something are exactly what the name implies: the mental *pictures* of the object they have in mind. But no picture is perfect. It may be blurred, as though the lens of the camera were not focused, or it may be sharp and resolute. It may be a close-up, showing every detail, or it may show only the most salient features of the object. It may be accurate and precise, showing everything exactly as it is, or it may be badly distorted, as the image in the curved mirrors of a carnival fun house. It may be complete, including the entire object, or it may show only a portion of it. And it may be a blowup or a reduction, showing the object bigger or smaller than it really is. Each person tends to see things differently from others. Thus, no two images are apt to be exactly alike, although some may be very similar and others distinctly different. But an image is likely to take on a different form from the "real thing," and when people lack some information, they tend to fill in the picture.

Image dimensions

To get a verbal picture of people's images, they might be asked how they'd describe the object. They would be likely to name several characteristics and indicate their magnitude or the quality. These characteristics would be the dimensions of the image—the features that define the image in the mind of the individual. There will be some variation from person to person, but many features will be included by nearly everyone, while some characteristics that might apply will be ignored by everyone. The tendency for most respondents to define images with about the same attributes allows researchers to measure and compare images. The first step is to ascertain what attributes or characteristic features (dimensions) are most common and important to *respondents*. That can be done precisely the way described earlier, by asking for a description of the object from several typical respondents. The researcher mustn't be the *exclusive* source of ideas for identifying attributes because respondents may actually use a different set of dimensions. The image profile is accurate only when it includes all attributes important to the respondents and no others.

The image profile

The *configuration* of several attributes or characteristics defines a complete image profile. It's the constellation of ratings, rather than any single attribute, that's of interest. The individual attributes don't stand in any set pattern with one another, and the researcher determines the order in which the items are listed. They may be in random order or according to some other system. The most important ones should be in the middle of the list, rather than first or last. When some or all features have a good/bad connotation, about half should express *virtues* and half *vices*. The two types should be scattered among one another. This controls for the tendency of some people to be globally positive or negative. Images can be measured with an adjective checklist, a semantic differential scale, or a semantic distance scale, all described in Chapter 5.

Image comparisons

Image profiles often differ among respondents with different characteristics, such as men versus women or people in different occupations. The images for one or more objects can

---

GUIDELIST 1-5

For Measuring Images

1. Use image profiles when several attributes or characteristic features of an object are to be measured.
2. Question some typical respondents about the objects to determine the attributes they use to define the image.
3. Don't depend on the sponsor to identify the relevant image dimensions.
4. Limit the number of items to only the attributes most meaningful to respondents.
5. Randomly order the items, being sure that about half can be seen as positive and half as negative.

6. Obtain ratings of more than one object in a class if comparisons of image profiles among objects are of value.
7. Have respondents rate an *ideal* object if there's uncertainty about positivity or negativity for some items.
8. Compare ideal image profiles for different respondent groups to reveal differences in preference patterns.
9. Plan to subtract ideal from actual ratings for each respondent to provide a *difference* profile.
10. Compare profiles of differences between ideal and actual object ratings to assess positive or negative valences.

---

be compared among different groups or subsamples to reveal such differences in people's perceptions and evaluations. It's also often desirable to compare images of different topics or objects in the same general class, such as different companies in an industry or opposing political candidates. When the information needs call for comparison, each object must be rated separately by each respondent. This allows the researcher to compare the profiles with one another after the data have been compiled. There may be several items that can't be readily identified as positive or negative. If so, respondents may be asked to rate their *ideal* entity. The ratings for the actual object(s) can be subtracted from those for the ideal object for each respondent. The closer the actual ratings are to the ideal, the more positive are the ratings. Negativity can be judged by the absolute value of the difference between actual and ideal. These differences between actual and ideal for each of the actual objects can also be compared. This indicates which are more positive and which are more negative. Measuring both the perceptions of objects and the positive or negative valences makes the image measurement scales powerful devices. The guidelines for measuring images are summarized in Guidelist 1–5.

Decisions

When decisions are the topic of research, the focus isn't so much on the results of decisions in the past as it is on the *process* of making decisions. Often people's choices require evaluation of alternative courses of action. Their choices depend in part on their *information sources* and

GUIDELIST 1–6

For Measuring Decision Making

1. Use when information requirements focus on the process of evaluation, not the results.
2. Determine how much the decision was based on preexisting information and how much was directly sought.
3. Classify information sources as direct experience, social influence, or media effects.
4. Measure the appropriate level of media effects: exposure, attention, content, or impact.
5. Measure abstract, global values only when information is required about decisions about many different objects or those of profound importance to respondents.
6. Expect to identify only a very limited number of evaluative criteria for any one individual.

the *evaluative criteria* they use for judgment. Those seeking survey information are often keenly interested in these aspects of the decision process that people use to choose actions. Guidelist 1–6 outlines the main considerations for measuring decisions.

Information sources

Decisions are conscious choices based in part on information. In some cases, the decision maker already has all of the information required for the decision. In others, the person will need more information, and that will require an *information search*. Survey research can measure both the information content on which a decision was based and also the nature of the information search process. Information can also be measured in terms of the source from which the decision maker obtained it. Generally, three different categories are useful: direct personal experience, social influence, and media sources.

Personal experience resulting from *behavior* and social influence resulting from *affiliations* are discussed later in this chapter. Information obtained from nonpersonal sources is called *media* information. A survey inquiry might focus on several different levels of media effects. Respondents might be asked about *exposure* to some medium, such as whether they subscribe to a particular publication or listen to a certain radio station. They might also be asked how much *attention* they paid to a medium, such as whether they actually saw or read a particular advertisement. They can also be questioned about their comprehension or recollection of *content* of a message presented through the medium. Lastly, the most detailed inquiry would measure the *impact* the message had on choices or actions.

Although valuable data on information acquisition can be obtained through surveys, a note of caution is needed. The history of survey research indicates that most people are only vaguely aware of the information they actually apply to a decision and where they obtained it. Generally, direct experience is *overstated* and media influence is *understated*. In general, people are likely to recognize that media influence other people's decisions, but they often won't admit they, themselves, are influenced.

Evaluative criteria

When someone evaluates something, the person is assigning a value to it. It's judged according to the attributes the decision maker feels are relevant. Any object of evaluation can be viewed as a "package" of different characteristics. Ordinarily, the object to be judged has many more attributes or characteristics than people actually consider. Thought processes are limited to consideration of only a handful of things at one time, usually about seven at most. There is seldom the necessity for judgment of more than a few attributes, and research has indicated that people typically use only a few features to judge and select among alternatives, even for very important decisions.

The identification of the evaluative criteria people use to select among alternatives is a major task of survey research. One of the most common ways to do this is simply to question respondents about why they made the choice they did. This requires composing a list of attributes of the chosen object and asking respondents to rate the importance of each. Another method of detecting evaluative criteria is to present respondents with a hypothetical choice situation and ask what information they'd seek about the alternatives. The attributes for which they seek information are those they'd use for evaluation. This method doesn't require previous choice experience.

Needs

Sponsors are often concerned with why people behave as they do. Most behavior is directed toward the satisfaction of one or more human needs. Thus, the answer to the question of *why* is often obtained by measuring the relationship between actions and needs, desires, preferences, motives, and goals. People generally act with intent. This doesn't imply that they know, consciously, what personal motives and needs lie beneath the surface of their actions. Consequently, it can be a difficult job to dig out the needs that underpin behavior and the motives that prompt action. The picture may be complicated further because (*a*) many different actions can serve the same motive or provide satisfaction for the same need and (*b*) several needs or motives may be served by one action or behavior pattern. To cope with these problems, the researcher must be willing to recognize the difficulties and to understand the nature of needs, desires, preferences, motives, and goals.

The terms

Needs can be viewed as categories of things that most or all people require for existence and contentment. They can be specified in terms of basic things that must be provided to sustain human life, such as food, shelter, and clothing. Needs can also be classified according to the requirements for psychological and social conditions, such as the need for love, prestige, or power. Finally, needs can be viewed in terms of specific categories relating directly to different types of activity. These needs might include such things as play, nurturance, achievement, or recognition.

Desires are closely related to needs. When a person consciously focuses on some object, activity, or state of being that might provide satisfaction of a need, the person has a desire for that thing. The individual may not be aware of exactly what need is beneath the desire. *Preferences* are often treated as desires that have less drive or energy behind them. While both preferences and desires imply a conscious focus on something, desires are stronger and preferences indicate less urgency regarding the object.

Motives are also related to needs, but they're more closely associated with actions. Motives arise from unsatisfied needs, and they trigger behavior or energize the person to perform some action to get satisfaction. They might be seen as a *push* away from some negative condition or a *pull* toward some desirable situation. *Goals* or objectives are also related to needs. A person's goals represent some *end state,* some destination or condition that the person seeks to reach through behavior. Goals are related to needs because the objective is often the satisfaction of one or more needs.

Measurement techniques

Several types of scales are commonly used to measure needs, desires, preferences, motives, and goals because they fit the nature of the concepts being measured. Needs are often measured by first deciding on the types of needs that are relevant to the information requirements. Respondents may then be asked to rank them in their order of importance or to rate them using a fixed sum scale. The researcher needs a way to obtain their *relative* importance. An ordinary, linear, numeric scale of importance isn't advisable because many will rate most or all of the needs as equally important. The forced ranking scale, the fixed sum scale, and the linear, numeric scale are all described in Chapter 5.

Desires and preferences are often measured by identifying and listing the possible categories of things that might be desired or preferred. Linear, numeric scales can be used because respondents are less likely to see all of them as equally important. To be safe, forced rankings or fixed sum scales can also be used to measure desires and preferences.

Motives are relatively simple and easy to measure when they're obviously conscious and the respondents have no reason to conceal them. For example, they might be measured by a multiple-choice item that listed the likely motives. Motives concerning sensitive behavior or opinions are more difficult to assess, and rather than using direct questioning, respondents might be asked to identify a close friend with similar views. Then the respondent might be questioned about how this person would feel or behave and why he or she would feel or act that way. This allows respondents to project their own motives onto another person.

Goals or objectives are less sensitive than many motives. They can be measured simply by listing alternative goals and having them ranked or rated in the same manner as for assessing desires or preferences. Again, the researcher must take care to avoid obtaining equal ratings for all goals or objectives that might be regarded by the respondents as generally or socially desirable. Summary recommendations for measuring needs and related concepts are provided in Guidelist 1–7.

Behavior

The measurement of behavior involves four related concepts—what the respondents did or did not do, where the action takes place, the timing of the behavior, and the frequency or persistence of behavior. In other words, it often means assessing "what, where, when, and how often." When research is used to establish which actions were taken by respondents, the alternative courses of action can be listed in categories to be sure the responses are

GUIDELIST 1–7

For Measuring Need-Related Concepts

1. Determine the needs, desires, preferences, motives, or goals that are relevant to the information requirements.
2. Specify the items or categories in terms that will be easily understood by all respondents.
3. Use a fixed sum, comparative, or forced ranking scale to avoid most or all items being rated as equally important.
4. Remember that multiple needs and related variables can be served by the same behavior, and different actions can serve the same need.
5. Use projective methods when measuring or assessing motives that are likely to be sensitive.

comparable. Simple multiple-choice items can then be used, with either a single or a multiple response permitted.

The location of some particular form of behavior is often of interest. The places might be designated as geographic areas or by some other means, such as at home versus away from home. If only a few, specific locations can be identified, a multiple-choice question can be used. Maps, graphs, or displays can also be shown to respondents to obtain their indication where the action takes place. It's best to provide the respondents with a specific set of possible locations, rather than depending on them to indicate a place in their own words. That's because each respondent tends to use different terms to describe a location, and probably no two respondents will use exactly the same phrase to describe any one place.

Respondents may be able to indicate a location by using a designation that has been assigned to the places, such as ZIP codes or political jurisdictions. Maps are often available to show such geographic areas. The researcher may have to translate these numbers indicating geographic areas into different categories from those used by the source of the designations. This is an effective means of measuring location, provided that the individual designations apply to areas that are about equal to or smaller than those required by the survey information needs. Areas can be combined, if necessary, but they can't be divided into smaller increments or blocks than those specified when the data are collected.

Respondents are often questioned about *when* they performed a certain action and whether they're presently engaged in such behavior. Future intentions to act can also be the subject of survey inquiry, but of course these predictions by respondents may not be completely accurate. Individual predictions of future actions are less reliable than the collective or aggregate predictions of the proportions who say they will act in a certain way. Some may change their mind and do something else, but others may elect to do so when they had no such intention. So aggregate predictions are often more reliable than any one expression of intent.

The *persistency* of behavior may be important to measure. Many actions are habitual,

---

GUIDELIST 1–8

For Measuring Behavior

1. Identify information needs in terms of "what, where, when, and how often."
2. Specify the actions and locations in categories to make responses comparable.
3. Determine if respondents might have engaged in only one or several categories of action, and use single or multiple-response items accordingly.

4. Remember that frequency of behavior is often best expressed in terms of time, such as times per day or week.
5. Keep in mind that *individual* intentions or predictions are ordinarily not as reliable as they are in aggregate.
6. Be sure to use such items as verbal frequency or fixed sum scales when proportions or behavioral policies are to be measured.

---

while others are performed routinely because a single decision has led to continuity until something changes the routine. Respondents' habitual or routine behavior is often of great interest to sponsors. People might be questioned about their policies or practices concerning some action, such as their favorite place, their political party, or religious preference.

Sometimes people change patterns or deviate from their former or usual actions. It's often important to determine just what proportion of the time they act in a certain way, *given the occasion to act*. In such cases, the researcher is often less interested in the *absolute* number of times the action is taken as in the frequency, *relative* to the number of occasions or opportunities to act. If so, it's inappropriate to ask how often the action is taken because it yields absolute values. One respondent may have had twice as many opportunities to take the action or perform the behavior as another. So the same number would represent half the time for the first and all the time for the second. When the focus is on the proportion of behavior, based on the number of opportunities, or when the general policy of the respondents over time is sought, a fixed sum scale or a verbal frequency scale, described in Chapter 5, can be used to obtain the proportion. Rarely can respondents be asked the percentage of times because they must know the exact proportion to respond accurately, and they usually won't. It's often best to show proportions on scales with only a few scale points, rather than many. The main issues regarding measurement of behavior are listed in Guidelist 1–8.

Lifestyles

Surveys can be used to determine the lifestyles of respondents. Lifestyles consist of the *pattern* or *configuration* of things people do, believe, and own. Groupings of the population by lifestyle can be used to identify an audience, constituency, target market, or other collectivity of interest to the sponsor. Often, those with different lifestyles will react differentially toward issues of key interest to sponsors. Different lifestyle patterns can be identified by four kinds

---

GUIDELIST 1–9

For Measuring Lifestyle Patterns

1. Seek out lifestyle libraries of items or compose items that are directly relevant to the information requirements.
2. Use multiple items to identify individual lifestyle patterns among respondents.
3. Choose questions about activities, interests, opinions, or possessions that are indicative of a particular lifestyle.

4. Keep in mind that lifestyle measurement requires many variables or items and may increase questionnaire size and response task time and difficulty.
5. Remember that lifestyle analyses focus on clusters and require substantial analysis to identify patterns.

---

of variables associated with respondents: (1) activities, (2) interests, (3) opinions, and (4) possessions. Researchers interested in the measurement of lifestyles can obtain lists of lifestyle items from the literature on the subject. Most such libraries of items have been used successfully in the past and often define meaningful lifestyle segments or groups. Another alternative is to compose a family of lifestyle items to define the lifestyle segments most meaningful and relevant to the information needs. Such lists must contain enough items to ensure that patterns are fairly reliable. No single item will define a lifestyle adequately.

In summary, a given lifestyle is a collective or conglomerate factor. The objective is to identify a pattern or profile. Consequently, respondents must be questioned about many items that relate to a given lifestyle or pattern of living. While this can be a potent method of identifying and distinguishing groups or segments, the measurement will often require many questions. In terms of questionnaire space and response time, this may be costly and, in some cases, uneconomical. Guidelist 1–9 outlines the main points to be considered when measuring lifestyles.

Affiliations

Social contact and interaction are often the focus of survey research or bear heavily on other issues relevant to the survey. Thus, the family setting, memberships, social contacts, reference groups, and communications of respondents are frequently measured or assessed within the survey research process. The main issues regarding the measurement of affiliations are listed in Guidelist 1–10. People within the same nuclear or extended family often think, behave, and live similarly. Of all social groups, the family probably exerts a stronger influence on individuals than that of other groups or units to which the person belongs. The most simple measurement is specification of family status, including marital status and children in the home. This method is discussed in the next section on demographics. Other family issues, including the roles played by various family members, group decision making, and authority

---

GUIDELIST 1–10

For Measuring Affiliations

1. Consider membership in both formal and informal groups as sources of influence for respondents.
2. Define groups clearly and concisely for respondents (e.g., such terms as "family" might include only parents and siblings, or more distant relatives as well).
3. Select the appropriate type of reference group for identification, either comparative, normative, or informative.
4. Consider both opinion leaders and key influentials when determining sources of influence on respondents.
5. Remember that identification of sources of influence is only approximate because people are often unwilling or unable to provide precise data.

---

relationships within the family, can also be measured by surveys. The types of questions asked and scales used depend on what data are being sought. The researcher must select from among the available items and scaling techniques to obtain the most appropriate device.

Both formal and informal affiliations and relationships are often the subjects of surveys. Their measurement ordinarily consists of the specification of the groups in terms that can be easily understood by the respondents, who are then asked to indicate any groups to which they belong. The importance of the group to the individual and the importance of the person to the group are also assessable through survey questioning. Other frequent topics of inquiry are leadership or officer status.

Social integration can be measured by indications of the frequency and duration of contact and interaction with others. The propensity to interact with others can be assessed directly or indirectly. Direct measurement requires specification of the groups, and respondents are asked to indicate those with whom they interact. Such indirect measures as a series of statements accompanying a Likert scale, described in Chapter 5, might be used to reveal the importance of affiliation. Alternatively, the importance of affiliation and interaction might be measured with a comparative, fixed sum, or forced ranking scale and then compared with the importance ratings of the value of other activities.

The *individual referents* or *reference groups* used by respondents may be of interest to the sponsor. These terms refer to an individual or group that serves one or more of three major functions: normative, comparative, or informative. A *normative* reference group is one that establishes or provides norms of conduct or behavior that the individual is expected to follow. Normative reference groups tell an individual *what* should and shouldn't be done.

By contrast, a *comparative* reference group provides a standard or benchmark to show *how* an individual is doing in some respect. People often comment about "keeping up with the Joneses," and the Joneses are obviously the comparative reference group. Surveys often identify just who the Joneses are and why they serve as a referent. Comparative reference

---

GUIDELIST 1–11

For Measuring Demographic Status

1. Include all demographic items that may be systematically associated with other items of importance in the survey.
2. Specify categories clearly and concisely for respondents.

3. Choose categories and items that will be comparable with other, external, secondary data or information.
4. Use sample demographic items where possible and make only necessary modifications to avoid risk.

---

groups are often used whenever people lack an absolute, concrete standard by which to judge their own standing.

An *informative* reference group conveys information about alternatives and conditions to respondents without suggesting a pattern of appropriate behavior or showing relative standing. For example, sports enthusiasts or auto experts may constitute informative reference groups for someone unfamiliar or less familiar with athletic or automotive equipment or services.

Reference groups can be identified by using several techniques. The most common and direct method of identifying reference groups is to ask the respondent to identify them. A less direct means is to question respondents about affiliations with those in similar conditions or with similar opinions, so reference groups are specified only by inference.

Surveys may be used to identify opinion leaders and those within their sphere of influence. An *opinion leader* is one who has special expertise, experience, or credibility in the eyes of others. The attitudes of the opinion leader are often amplified and extended to many others. Those known as *key influentials* occupy a special position or have special recognition that permits them to influence the attitudes of many others within a specific social setting. If key influentials can be identified prior to the survey, based on their position or office, the degree of influence or impact they exert can be measured. Respondents may rate the importance of the key influential in relation to other sources of information or influence. These data are useful, but they're never very precise because people are unwilling or unable to express influence patterns with much precision.

Demographics

Demographic factors often used in survey research include such variables as age, sex, marital status, family status, family life cycle stage, education, employment, occupation, income, and residential location and type, among others. Such data are often valuable to sponsors because (*a*) demographic groups often differ significantly on the issues of importance and (*b*) demographics can be used to identify segments, groups, audiences, or constituencies of people who are both identifiable and behave in similar ways. Guidelines for measuring demographic status are contained in Guidelist 1–11.

The key to accurate measurement of demographic status is the clear, concise statement of the categories or dimensions. This depends on clarity and meaningfulness to respondents and the degree of precision required by the information needs. Several examples of demographic items are shown in Chapter 6. They include some items that are broad and comprehensive and others that are relatively precise and fine-grained. Researchers should select from among these items and modify them as required. Previously tested items have less inherent risk than newly composed items, scales, and formats.

Conclusion

The list of topics discussed here isn't comprehensive or all-inclusive. Other topics might arise that could not easily be classified into the categories provided. This doesn't preclude their use. There are two purposes for including this outline of topics: (1) They help those seeking survey information to recognize the range and type of information that can be obtained from survey research. (2) They assist the researcher in classifying information needs and in making tentative, preliminary plans for the survey process that follows.

SUMMARY

Survey Sponsorship and Potential Topics

    A. Evaluate survey potential. The same measurement methods are useful for many occupations and needs.

    B. Maintain realistic expectations. Survey research is neither impossibly difficult nor precisely definitive.

    C. Expect and evaluate errors. Minor mistakes may affect some results, but they seldom ever invalidate all results.

    D. Recognize the potential topics. They indicate what can be measured and suggest ways to obtain information.

    E. Allow for other topics. The list provided here isn't all-inclusive, and others might be used productively.

    F. Consider suggestions carefully. The methods of measurement identified here are thoroughly tested.

Chapter 2

Planning the Project

THE SURVEY PROCESS

A survey project is a process with a series of steps linked with one another. The decisions made during the early stages affect the choices open at later stages. The information needs specified at the first stage indicate what type of sample will be required, what type of measurement instruments will be needed, what data collection methods will be most appropriate, and more. This forward linkage among the steps is shown in Figure 2–1 by the solid lines running downward and to the right, on the left side of the diagram. If there were only these forward linkages, the researcher could take one step at a time, performing each set of tasks in turn. Only the effects on following steps would have to be considered at each step. But this would assume there are no limitations on the options available at the later steps. In reality, that's seldom so. There are usually limitations on data collection and data processing resources. These limitations restrict the alternatives open at the *earlier* stages. So there are *backward* linkages in the survey process. They're shown by the dashed lines running upward and to the left in Figure 2–1, on the right side of the diagram. Ignoring these limitations during the earlier steps in the process may lead the researcher to a dead end when some restraints are encountered later.

Figure 2–1 shows that the backward linkages in the survey process run from the data collection phase and the data processing phase back up to the sampling design and instrumentation steps. Major decisions concerning data collection always have to be made *before* designing and selecting a sample or composing and constructing the questionnaire and other materials. Some information needs can be satisfied more effectively with one method of data collection than with another. Yet data collection is typically the most expensive phase of the process. It would not make sense to design a sample without first selecting the data collection method and estimating the cost of collecting the data, because different data

Figure 2–1   *Linkage in the Survey Process*

collection methods will require different sampling designs and questionnaires. The availability of data processing facilities also influences the early stages of the process. The data processing method has to be planned so sampling and instrumentation will be compatible with both the capabilities and the limitations of the data processing method chosen.

SPECIFYING INFORMATION NEEDS

The sponsor's information needs are first determined in the dialog between the researcher and the sponsor described in Chapter 1. Those needs for information must now be listed in more concrete and specific terms. For example, the researcher may have determined that the sponsoring organization may be seeking information about its workers' reactions to a new benefit program. But "worker reactions" is a relatively ambiguous term. It doesn't describe precisely what's to be measured. A survey could be designed to measure the workers'

- *Attitudes*—knowledge, feelings, and expectations regarding the program.

- *Images*—the mental picture they've developed of the program or employer.

- *Decisions*—regarding whether or not they'll avail themselves of the program.

- *Behavior*—such as how the program might change their work habits.

- *Affiliations*—to indicate the group consensus and communications patterns.

- *Demographics*—indicating what type of employee wants the new program.

To specify the information needs effectively, the researcher has to learn exactly what *kind* of information the sponsor wants in terms of the survey topics discussed in Chapter 1. The specification of information needs plays a key role in the survey process. As Figure 2–1 indicates, virtually every aspect of the survey project from beginning to end is geared to the nature of the sponsor's information needs. Everything has to be tailored to satisfying them. That's the whole purpose of the project. Accurate and effective specification is one of the most difficult of all the tasks associated with a survey. It often receives too little attention and effort. Errors or inadequacies in the specification of the information required from the survey will be amplified during the later stages of the survey process.

Survey Information Value

The value of survey information to the sponsor depends on three main factors: (1) the cost of making an error, (2) the degree of uncertainty surrounding the decisions or actions, and (3) the amount of uncertainty the survey may reduce. Each of these factors should be assessed carefully to gauge the expected value of survey information. Then the *expected value* can be compared to the funds and resources available for the project and to the *expected costs* of the survey.

The potential value of the information should be *at least* two or three times the entire cost of the survey project, and preferably even greater. That's because the estimates are only the *potential,* and not the actual value and costs. Rarely, if ever, can the value of information be determined precisely. It may prove to be of greater or lesser value than estimated. The estimate of the information value will sometimes turn out to be too conservative, and sometimes it will turn out to be too liberal.

Similarly, it's almost impossible to obtain an exact estimate of the projects' actual costs. In almost every case, there will be "cost overruns." The actual costs nearly always prove to be greater than anticipated, even with an allowance or "safety factor" built into cost estimates. There are always some hidden costs associated with survey research as well. They're items that have costs which aren't measured, such as the time and efforts of sponsoring executives or managers.

The value of information from *academic* survey research can only be estimated by scholars familiar with the concepts being tested by a survey. Estimation of information value depends on expert judgments concerning the value of the potential contribution of the research to the scholarly literature. Information from those research projects that make strong contributions in critical areas of interest are more highly valued than that which has more finite implications or deals with more trivial issues.

The cost of errors

The value of information from *applied* survey research depends on its potential to avoid two types of decision errors. They might be labeled "go" errors and "no-go" errors. Go errors are more obvious—no-go errors are more obscure. A go error results when a decision maker takes a course of action that proves to be costly or unsatisfactory. A no-go error results when the decision maker either fails to take some action that would have positive results, or ignores the alternative that would be most positive, choosing instead some less positive course. (In some areas, the possibility of go errors is called *down-side* risk, while the chances of no-go errors are viewed as opportunity costs.)

For example, assume that a company is considering a new venture. The most basic question is *whether or not* to proceed with it. A go error—the most obvious kind—would result if the firm went ahead with the new venture and it failed. The potential cost of a go error includes everything the company might loose as a result of *going ahead* with the plan. Whatever funds they had expended and weren't recovered would show up as monetary losses. Other resources expended and not regained would be part of the nonmonetary costs of the failure. Most of these losses would be fairly quantifiable and obvious.

The less obvious no-go error associated with this decision would result if the company decided not to go ahead with the venture when, in fact, it would have been successful. The potential cost of the no-go error includes any benefits—monetary and otherwise—that might have been gained if they had elected to proceed with the venture. Unfortunately, if the action is not taken, it's extremely difficult to recognize, comprehend, or appreciate what might have been gained. So most sponsors are far less cognizant of the costs of no-go errors than they are of the costs of go errors. The greater the potential gains or losses inherent in a decision or set of decisions, the greater the cost of uncertainty. Surveys that promise to reduce very costly uncertainty have commensurately more value.

The amount of uncertainty

The *amount* of uncertainty is a separate issue from the *cost* of uncertainty. In some cases, the sponsors are already fairly sure about what decision to make or what action to take. They may have a large amount of existing information about the issues in question, or they may be guided in part by information from other sources—observation, experimentation, deduction, previous experience, and the like. In other situations where there is a large amount of uncertainty surrounding the issues, those seeking survey information may be highly or even completely uncertain about what decision to reach or what action to take.

The evaluation of information value comes down to two basic questions: (1) How costly might either a go or no-go error be? (2) How much uncertainty surrounds the issues in question? When a great deal rests on the quality of the decision because there's much to be gained or lost, and when there's a high degree of uncertainty about the issues, additional information would have greater value. Often, only the sponsor will know the facts about go and no-go errors. Often only those seeking the information can assess their own degree of uncertainty. The research designer may have to question them carefully to ascertain the potential value of the information.

Reduction of uncertainty

Like any other source of information, survey research doesn't provide *perfect* information. Sometimes surveys can address nearly all the issues or problems that face the sponsor. There are also situations where only some—perhaps only a few of the existing questions—can be answered by survey information. For instance, if the sponsor wanted only to know, just before an election, the proportion of voters who intend to cast their vote for Candidate A versus Candidate B, a well-conducted survey would probably reduce nearly all of that sponsor's uncertainty. By contrast, sponsors who seek to learn the relative importance potential voters place on a complex set of political issues and candidate characteristics are likely to discover that a survey will reduce only a relatively small part of the uncertainty they face.

Even when a survey can comprehensively embrace a specific set of questions, the degree of reduction in uncertainty may vary, depending on whether the survey information is *descriptive* or *predictive*. *Descriptive* survey data may sometimes be almost absolutely definitive, while *predictive* information is usually far more tentative. A survey of householders to determine what major appliances they own would be very likely to answer that question with a high degree of certainty. There would be little doubt remaining in anyone's mind about the existing situation. By comparison, a *predictive* survey to determine what major appliances they *intended* to purchase would lack the same degree of certainty. It would provide only tentative indications of what might actually transpire, since a wide variety of factors might alter intentions and sharply reduce the predictability for the survey results. Thus, a large amount of uncertainty would remain regarding what the sponsor might expect for the future.

Information value and priority

The three factors that determine the overall value of a survey to the sponsor and the justifiable level of expenditure on a survey are the *cost of errors,* the *amount of existing uncertainty,* and the *reduction in uncertainty* promised by a survey. These factors are summarized in Figure 2–2.

The specification of information needs should meet two objectives: to *include* all of the information that's genuinely required or highly valued, based on priority, and to *exclude* any

Figure 2–2 *Factors Determining Information Value*

Factors Indicating High Value

1. The cost of selecting a "bad" alternative (go error) or failing to select the best alternative (no-go error) would be relatively high.
2. There's a very high degree of uncertainty about which alternative to choose, based on existing information.
3. Survey research information is very likely to reduce a large proportion of the existing uncertainty.

Factors Indicating Low Value

1. The cost of making either a go error (selecting a "bad" alternative) or a no-go error (rejecting a good alternative) would be relatively low.
2. There's relatively little uncertainty about the decision, based on existing information or information from other sources.
3. Survey research information will remove only a small portion of the uncertainty surrounding the decision or action.

For Classifying Information by Priority

1. There are two basic objectives to be met:
   a. Obtain *all* of the essential information.
   b. Obtain *only* what is directly applicable.
2. Information can be classified into three categories:
   a. *High priority* items that are *absolutely essential* to the project.

   b. *Medium priority* items that are *highly valuable* for decision making.
   c. *Low priority* items for *supportive data* to enhance understanding.

questions that are redundant or provide information that's of little or no value. *The priority of information needs is based on the value of information items.* Items of information can usually be classified into three levels of importance: (1) *absolutely essential,* constituting the main reason for the project, (2) *highly valuable* for making important decisions, and (3) *supportive data* to enhance the understanding of decision makers and clarify the picture portrayed by the survey results. Anything of lesser value should be culled from the list.

It's essential to prioritize the information needs because time and resources are always limited. Inevitably, it will be necessary to eliminate items or reduce the number of questions. Such deletions are more readily made when there's a clear indication of item priority. The least valuable items can be discarded and all of the most valuable questions will still be retained as the plans are modified.

The priority of the survey questions has another function, as well. When those who design and conduct the survey and compose the questionnaire or survey instrument have a clear indication of the importance of the various items, they'll be able to place greater time, effort, and emphasis on the most critical and valuable items of information. When the structure and sequence of items within the survey questionnaire require compromise, the least valuable items—those with the lowest priority—are more likely to be moved or adjusted. In that way, the most crucial questions will maintain the most prominent place within the instrument, where they're likely to receive the greatest thought and attention by respondents. The major considerations for assigning priority are shown in Guidelist 2–1.

PLANNING THE SURVEY ELEMENTS

At this point, the researcher must plan the elements of the survey process and compose the project outline. The outline will guide, direct, and coordinate the tasks required to initiate and complete the survey. The sponsor should inspect and approve the outline before the project is continued. The project outline is more essential than it may seem. It's even more important for less experienced researchers than for those with considerable experience. The elements of the project outline are listed in Figure 2–3.

Figure 2–3   *Elements of the Project Outline*

1. List information needs by priority.
2. Indicate the value of the information.
3. Identify internal resource requirements.
4. Specify sample size and design.
5. Provide a mock-up of instrumentation.
6. Note the scope of the response task.
7. Describe the data collection method.
8. Outline the data processing method.
9. Describe the type of reports required.
10. Summarize final costs and the timetable.

The elements of the project outline aren't usually planned in the same sequence as they're listed. That's because the backward linkages in the survey process make it mandatory to consider some of the later phases before making decisions about those that come earlier in the process. Usually the researcher has to make several passes or iterations through the survey process, making only tentative decisions about *sampling design, instrumentation, data collection method,* and *data processing.* This circular process is shown in Figure 2–4. Data collection is typically the most expensive aspect of a survey. It often becomes the compelling factor, requiring direct modifications to the sampling design and instrumentation, as well as the data processing procedure. So data collection is often the starting point for the planning process.

Figure 2–4   *Circular Nature of Survey Planning*

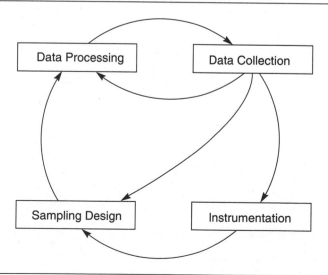

Data Collection

Because data collection is usually the most expensive (and time-consuming) aspect of the survey project, it's the logical starting place for estimating project costs. The choice of a method for collecting the data depends on the information needs and value, as well as the budget and resources available and the timing requirements. Collecting the data requires contact with respondents, and that can be accomplished by speaking with them in person, by reaching them on the telephone, or by mailing them a questionnaire to be completed and returned. Thus, personal interviewing, telephone interviewing, and direct mail surveys are the three principal methods of data collection used in survey research. The selection of the most appropriate method for collecting the data is a key decision for the researcher. Each of the three basic methods of data collection has its own special capabilities and limitations. There are some types of information that can only be obtained by one method, but often the researcher has a choice between two methods, while the third lacks the capability required.

The basic difference among the three data collection methods is the intensity of contact between the researcher and the respondents. The closest contact and the greatest opportunity for two-way interaction between those collecting the data and those providing it are provided by personal interviewing. The most remote contact is obtained by direct mail, while telephone interviewing falls between the other two methods on this spectrum. The costs and resource requirements of the three methods also differ markedly. One may require much more time than the other. One particular method may be far more or far less expensive than the others. Each demands a different type of expertise from the field data collection team. The physical facilities that are needed differ for each method of data collection. Travel and media requirements vary from one method to the next. The degree of control over data collection also differs widely.

In summary, the data collection method that's selected is likely to result in a very different survey project from that which would ensue if another method were chosen. The contact and interaction requirements, the nature of the inquiry and information sought, and the

Figure 2–5   *Comparison of Data Collection Methods*

	Personal	Telephone	Mail
Data collection costs	High	Medium	Low
Data collection time required	Medium	Low	High
Sample size for a given budget	Small	Medium	Large
Data quantity per respondent	High	Medium	Low
Reaches widely dispersed sample	No	Maybe	Yes
Reaches special locations	Yes	Maybe	No
Interaction with respondents	Yes	Yes	No
Degree of interviewer bias	High	Medium	None
Severity of nonresponse bias	Low	Low	High
Presentation of visual stimuli	Yes	No	Maybe
Fieldworker training required	Yes	Yes	No

timing and geographic circumstances of respondents are important considerations for making a choice. Figure 2–5 provides a sketch of the major factors.

Personal interviewing

The size of the survey sample may vary from a few dozen to several thousand respondents. Personal interviewing usually requires a field force of interviewers. The field workers may be recruited and trained by the researcher, or outside field data collection agencies may be hired to collect the data. If the interviewers work directly for the researcher, they must be trained in both the general procedures for selecting respondents and interviewing them and also the specific characteristics and requirements of the project. When field data collection agencies are used, they need only be instructed concerning the specific nature of the task. This data collection method requires the most interviewer training to avoid the most common sources of interviewer bias. It also requires a substantial amount of supervision in the field, and there's still a good possibility of bias because field workers may fail to adhere to instructions. The project supervisor has less control than with other methods.

Personal interviewing provides the most complete contact with respondents because face-to-face interaction permits both audible and visual communication with respondents. They can examine, touch, handle, or try objects relevant to the questions. The interviewer can present visual materials such as rating cards, pictures, or displays. Physical objects can be presented to the respondents for them to see, feel, hear, taste, smell, handle, and even consume. Personal interviewing is often able to win respondent cooperation and hold it for a long time. Nonresponse bias is minimal, and this method is quicker than mail surveys for small, geographically concentrated samples.

This method is usually the most expensive per respondent because of the travel expenses and interviewer costs, especially if the respondents are dispersed over a wide geographic area or difficult to locate. But personal interviewing can reach respondents at home, at work, or at special locations, such as intercepts at polling places, the shopping mall, or some other place close to the location of an activity that might be the topic of the survey. So the advantages may outweigh the disadvantages of this means of data collection. The flexibility of this method sometimes makes it the only choice for projects that demand direct contact, a special location, or special selection of respondents who qualify for the survey.

Telephone interviewing

With telephone surveys, the interviewers don't have to go into the field. The interviewing can either be done from one or more central locations or perhaps even from the interviewers' homes. Much depends on the location of the respondents and the toll charges for the calls, as well as the degree of trust in the interviewers and the need to supervise them. While personal interviews may take weeks or months, telephone interviewing is usually completed much more quickly. But there are some important distinctions between the two methods. Telephone interviewing allows only audible contact, not visual. The interviewer can't see the respondent and must gauge the mood and demeanor of the respondent merely by the tone of voice, vocabulary, and other audible cues. Nor can the respondent see visual material such as rating scales or the color, size, shape, and texture of some object. They can't try some device or touch, taste, smell, or handle it.

There are also important psychological differences, as well as physical. Eye contact and the physical presence of another person affect a respondent's attitude, mood, and cooperation. It's more difficult for the interviewer to build strong rapport on the telephone. Physical presence usually helps to build trust and confidence. There are also some situations and topics for which telephone interviewing leads to *greater* cooperation than personal interviewing. Telephone respondents feel they have greater anonymity, so they may be more confident and at ease if they're asked to answer personal or sensitive questions. There are also some respondents, such as the elderly or handicapped, who may be physically fragile or psychologically vulnerable. They might be threatened by the physical presence of a stranger asking questions, but they may be willing and able to respond on the telephone.

Telephone interviews usually have to be completed more quickly than personal interviews. Considerable resistance or premature termination (hang ups) by the respondent can result from interviews of more than 15 or 20 minutes. Since the interviewer can't be seen, interviewer bias may be less with telephone interviewing. Physical appearance, dress, facial expressions, gestures, and other visual aspects aren't a consideration on the phone. The interviewers ordinarily require less training and instruction. If the telephone work is done from a central location, there's a greater opportunity to monitor interviewer performance and more control by the supervisor. This method is much more limited in its ability to reach respondents at special locations. Since they must be near a telephone, respondents to telephone surveys are usually at home or at work.

Mail data collection

Mail survey data collection differs from interviewing, either in person or by telephone, in many important respects. The "cosmetic" aspects of the mailing piece must be considered carefully because its form and appearance will affect the rate of response and the quality of the data. It may also be necessary to provide an *inducement to respond,* either included in the mailing or promised and sent after receipt of a completed questionnaire. Such inducements are often effective, but unfortunately they also increase mail data collection costs dramatically.

The composition, production, printing, and mailing of the questionnaires can often be done by one researcher and a small staff or by external services. The researcher usually has much greater control with a mail survey than with interviewing. Contact with the respondents is less intense with mail surveys, and, in one respect, this method is the reverse of the telephone interview survey. The telephone provides for audible, but no visual contact, while mail provides visual, but no audible contact. Interviews often vary greatly, and any differences may be reflected in the responses as error or bias. With the mail survey, the day, time, and location where respondents complete the questionnaires may differ from one respondent to the next, but the questionnaires are identical to one another. Each respondent is presented with *exactly* the same instructions and tasks, eliminating the chance of serious interviewer bias.

Interviewing is ordinarily more expensive than collecting data by mail, although direct mail often takes longer because respondents must have time to complete and return their questionnaires. For a given budget, mail surveys usually yield a much larger sample size than interviewing, providing the response rate is satisfactory. Perhaps the greatest advantage of the mail survey is its ability to reach widely dispersed respondents inexpensively. Mailing costs are identical whether the respondent is three blocks or three thousand miles from the mailing point. The geographic dispersion of respondents is often the compelling reason for selection of this data collection method, although respondents can ordinarily be reached by mail only at home or at work, and the amount of data that can be collected from each respondent is usually more limited than it is when interviewing is used.

Mail surveys don't permit interaction with the respondents, except through the medium of the questionnaire, so the mailing piece must be constructed very carefully, the instructions must be clear to virtually all potential respondents, and the questions or sections contingent on an earlier question (known as "branching") must be kept to an absolute minimum. Normally, the questionnaire should be pretested to ensure its effectiveness and clarity, unless the researcher is thoroughly experienced and knows well what to anticipate from the particular group to be surveyed. The standardization of the communication to respondents eliminates bias due to variance among interviewers. On the other hand, the demand for covering all possible contingencies "up front" is a heavy responsibility with this form of data collection.

Survey nonresponse bias

The single most serious limitation to direct mail data collection is the relatively low response rate. Mail surveys with response rates over 30 percent are rare. Response rates are often only about 5 or 10 percent. That means that over 9 out of 10 people who are surveyed *may not respond!* If so, the cost of each completed response will be about 10 times the cost of preparation, printing, and mailing for each questionnaire originally sent. The reliability of the data depends on the size of the sample *obtained,* and not the number of surveys sent, so the researcher must make an estimate of the response rate and mail enough questionnaires to yield the approximate number of responses required. But the most important consequence of a low mail response rate is the *nonresponse bias* that's likely to result. If respondents *randomly* complete or fail to complete and return the questionnaire, there will be *no* nonresponse bias, but that's seldom the case. Whether the survey recipients complete and return the questionnaire, set it aside and forget it, or just throw it away depends in part on their characteristics, attitudes, opinions, and interest in the topic. As a result, some types of people are likely to be *over*represented and others *under*represented in the sample received, creating biased results.

Some general principles can help the researcher gauge the degree of nonresponse bias, but they don't provide a definitive solution to the problem. Ordinarily, those who are highly involved with the topic are more likely to respond than those who aren't. That includes those who feel strongly *positive* about issues or topics and those who feel strongly *negative,* as well. The more neutral the respondents or the less experience they have with the topics or issues, the more often they'll discard the questionnaire. Then, too, certain demographic groups are more likely to respond than are others. Those who are less pressured for time, such as the very young or the elderly, the unemployed, or those outside large urban areas, are more likely to respond.

Nonresponse is a *very* serious problem when there's a direct connection between the purposes of the survey and the information needs, on the one hand, and likelihood to respond, on the other. For example, if the survey is to measure the proportion of people who own a certain product, and owners are more likely to respond than nonowners are, the results will be *worse* than useless. In fact, they'll be *much* worse. The variable being measured—ownership—would directly affect the likelihood to respond. To avoid such bias, the researcher should judge the degree to which nonresponse will interact with the topics or issues of the survey. If the interaction is thought to be too strong, the data have to be collected in interviews. Even if this interaction is negligible, overrepresentation and underrepresentation of some population segments may preclude a mail survey.

Panel data collection

A few large, commercial firms, such as Consumer Mail Panels, Inc., Market Research Corporation of America, and National Family Opinion, Inc., recruit and maintain national panels consisting of individuals, families, or households among the general public. For a fee, they provide data on their panel members and access to them for survey data collection. Thus, they use an entire panel or some segment of it as an option for direct mail, telephone, and personal interview survey data collection. Typically, the panel members are recruited by the company forming the panel. They're either paid a fee for their participation on the panel or given a valuable gift to win their cooperation. Usually they're surveyed with an initial inquiry to measure and record their demographic status and other relevant background data. They may remain on a panel for a few weeks, months, or even a few years.

Such panels are especially valuable when the *same* group of respondents must be surveyed more than once, such as when the information needs require measurement of changes over time. They can also be used for a single, nonrecurring survey. They're particularly useful and economical when only a very small proportion of the public is qualified to respond to a survey. In such cases, only those qualified can be singled out from the entire file of panel members, based on either initial panel data or on data from a special qualifying question included in an earlier survey of members. Using such a panel is sometimes more economical than designing and selecting one's own sample. There are also fewer demands on the researcher, since many aspects of sampling and data collection may be simplified or eliminated. The possibility that the panel members may not be closely representative of the population is probably the major disadvantage of using a sample from a commercial panel.

Selection factors

The basic characteristics of the major data collection methods have been identified and compared. To select the most appropriate method, the researcher should decide whether or not interviews are required. If not, a mail survey is indicated. If the mail survey must be ruled out in favor of interviews, the second step is to decide whether personal or telephone interviews would be most appropriate. The factors that influence the first decision most heavily are outlined in Checklist 2–1.

If a direct mail survey proves to be less appropriate than interviewing, the researcher must choose between telephone interviewing and interviewing in person. Again, the choice is based on comparison of the information needs and interviewing task with the attributes and characteristics of the two types of interviews. Checklist 2–2 lists the major considerations in outline form. For some surveys, one method will be completely precluded and the other will be absolutely necessary. Usually the decision won't be dictated and the advantages and disadvantages of each must be weighed against one another.

While there are times when the information needs or availability of resources clearly dictate one particular data collection method, there's usually a choice to be made. Selection

---

CHECKLIST 2–1

To Choose Interviews Versus Mail

1. Does the task require interaction with the respondents? If there must be a two-way conversation, or if there are several contingencies where the question to be asked depends on a previous response, interviews will be required and direct mail collection isn't feasible.

2. Is there the likelihood of interaction between the tendency to respond and the issues or topics being measured or assessed? If such interaction is present, serious nonresponse bias precludes the use of mail and the survey requires interviews.

3. To what degree are accurate, timely mailing lists of *qualified* respondents available? Lacking one or more mailing lists that: (*a*) include a full representation of the population to be surveyed and (*b*) exclude unqualified individuals, interviewing will be necessary.

4. Must the survey be conducted in a *specific* location, such as a store or polling place, or at a specific time such as in the morning or on a particular weekend? If so, interviews are needed.

5. Can the respondents provide and *record* their own responses, or must the recording be done by a fieldworker? The more complex and intricate the recording of the data, the less likely a mail survey will provide satisfactory data.

6. Is it more important to collect a large amount of data from each of a small number of respondents, or to obtain a more limited amount of data from each of a very large number of respondents? In general, the larger the sample required, the more appropriate a mail survey becomes.

7. Are the respondents widely dispersed over a broad geographic area or concentrated in groups in a confined area? The more widely dispersed, the less appropriate interviewing becomes, because of the cost of travel or of long distance telephone calls.

8. Would respondents be more embarrassed or threatened by talking to someone than merely recording their own responses? Is complete anonymity very necessary? The higher the degree of psychological threat and need for anonymity, the more appropriate the mail survey becomes.

---

must come after specification of information needs, but there may be times when the data collection method chosen may necessitate changes in information needs. This might be either because some data can't be obtained, or because more is available than originally anticipated. Nonetheless, information needs should be the predominant consideration.

Sampling Design

The actual selection of a sample comes later in the survey process. Only the basic strategy and design must be chosen at this point and included in the project outline to guide the project. Sample size and design are discussed in more detail in Chapter 3.

Response task and sample size

Survey research strategy tends to lean in one of two directions: Obtain a large amount of data from a small sample, or obtain a small amount of data from a large sample. Usually the

---

CHECKLIST 2–2

To Choose Telephone Versus In-Person

1. Must the data be collected at some special location outside the home or workplace, such as a shopping center, polling place, meeting, or event? If so, personal interviews will be required.

2. Does the interview task require showing the respondent something? If so, telephone interviewing is precluded and personal interviews are required.

3. Must the respondents be seen to judge if they're qualified to respond? If there's a quota based on the physical appearance or observed behavior of respondents, personal interviews will be necessary.

4. Are interviewers likely to include or exclude certain types of people, based on their appearance or visible characteristics, contrary to quota specifications? If such selection bias is likely, telephone interviews are more appropriate.

5. Is there a likelihood of psychological threat or intimidation in a personal encounter with an interviewer? If so, the more remote telephone interviewing method is indicated.

6. Is contamination of responses by the respondents' companions during the interview session likely? If so, telephone interviewing is more appropriate because others are less likely to overhear the conversation or interrupt it.

7. Will the interview take an exceptionally long time? If so, personal interviews are preferred because greater rapport and cooperation can be achieved with personal presence.

8. Does the telephone directory or other telephone number list serve as an adequate sample frame? If not, telephone interviews are precluded.

9. Are the respondents spread throughout a wide geographic area? If so, time and travel costs for personal interviews are likely to be prohibitive and long distance telephone interviews are advisable.

10. Is there the necessity for very rapid data collection? If so, telephone interviews can normally be completed much more quickly than interviewing in person.

---

resources are limited while information needs are insatiable. The trade-off between the amount of data to be obtained from each respondent and the number of respondents in the sample is shown in Figure 2–6. The size of the response task and the size of the sample pivot on the fulcrum, a fixed level of funding. The more data to be collected from an individual, the greater the costs per respondent, and the larger the sample, the greater the expense. So, for a fixed level of funding, the larger the response task the smaller the sample must be, and vice versa.

The choice of which strategy to take depends on the information needs. When very precise estimates are needed, larger samples are required and that limits the amount of data that can be collected from any one respondent. When the information needs depend heavily on the relationships among the survey questions so patterns can be detected, a large amount of data must be collected from each respondent. This limits the number of respondents that can be sampled at a given cost.

It's important to estimate the amount of data required from each respondent at this point in the survey planning process. This will determine the duration and difficulty of the response

Figure 2–6 *Response Task Versus Sample Size*

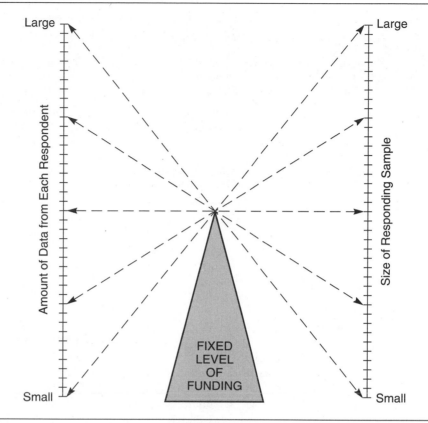

task and that will affect the estimate of cost per respondent. High cost per response will require a precise and perhaps elaborate design for a small sample. Low cost per response will permit sampling of a larger proportion of the population. The next step is to decide the approximate size of the *responding* sample; that is, the number of respondents who provide complete responses. The general considerations indicating the size of the sample and the size of the response task are listed in Figure 2–7. Once the approximate sample size and the cost per respondent have been estimated, data collection costs can be estimated and listed in the project outline. This is vital to the budgeting process, since data collection is often the single, most costly phase of the survey research project.

Population, units, and frame

The population includes all those of interest to the sponsor—the group from whom a sample will be selected. For example, a store might sponsor a survey of its *existing customers,* so only those who shopped at the store would be included in the population. Only *registered voters*

Figure 2–7   *Factors Determining Sampling Strategy*

Indications for Large Sample and Small Response Task

1. Very precise estimates of numeric values are required and there must be a high degree of confidence in them.
2. Individual survey items are of more interest than are patterns of response among many survey items.
3. The range and volume of information required from each respondent is fairly limited.
4. The data are to be collected by mail, so a simple response task is likely to increase the response rate.

Indications for Large Response Task and Small Sample

1. Estimates of numeric values for the population need only be approximate within a fairly broad range.
2. Focus of information needs is more on patterns or configurations among responses to items than on individual items.
3. The range and/or volume of information required from each respondent is relatively large.
4. The data are to be collected by telephone or personal interview rather than by mail.

---

might be included in the population if a political organization wanted to conduct an opinion poll. The actual *elements* of the population have to be defined to indicate exactly what constitutes a *sample unit* and what doesn't. For most surveys, the *sample units* will be individual people; however, sometimes *families, households, companies,* or *organizations* are surveyed, rather than just individuals. If so, the *sample units* would be defined in those terms and the *population* would consist of those sample units.

The *sample frame* is a list or set of directions that identify all the sample units in the population. For instance, a company may decide to conduct an employee survey. The *population* may be described as all existing nonunion, full-time employees. A list of them might be compiled from the personnel records. That list might serve as the *sample frame* from which a sample of a fraction of them would be chosen. But suppose the store mentioned earlier wants to conduct a personal interview survey but doesn't have a customer list to use as a sample frame. In that case, a *set of directions* that identifies the population of customers could be composed. The *sample frame* may be all those who visited the store and made purchases during a specific future period. A *sample* of them may then be interviewed.

Sampling design alternatives

The researcher typically has several options regarding the basic sampling design—*random* or *convenience, stratified* or *unstratified, clustered* or *unclustered,* in any combination. These alternatives are outlined in Figure 2–8. They need only be discussed briefly here. They're discussed more fully in Chapter 3.

Random versus convenience. When sample units are selected randomly, each unit has an equal probability of being chosen. There's a very compelling reason to strive for a random sample: With random selection, the probability of a specific amount of sampling error can legitimately be computed statistically. For instance, the report can indicate to those seeking

Figure 2–8   *Sampling Design Options*

Random

Every sample unit in the population has an equal chance of being selected. The sample represents the population well. The probability of sampling error can validly be computed statistically.

Convenience

Some sample units have a greater chance of being selected than others. The sample's representation of the population is *inferior*. It's *invalid* to compute the probability of sampling error.

Stratified

The proportion of various types of sample units in the sample is controlled by selecting a series of *subsamples* of specified sizes.

Unstratified

The proportions of various types of sample units will be approximately the same in the sample as they are in the entire population.

Clustered

A series of physical or geographic areas are selected, then a specific number of sample units are selected proportionally from each "cluster."

Unclustered

Respondents are selected randomly (or by convenience) *regardless* of their physical or geographic location.

---

the information that there's a 95 percent probability that the value in the *population* is within a given range of the corresponding value for the *sample*.

There are times when it's exceedingly difficult or even impossible to chose a sample randomly. So those who conduct surveys may sometimes have to revert to a *convenience* sample—selecting those respondents from the population that are obtainable or convenient to reach. Confidence levels and the degree of sampling error can be computed, but these statistical values are technically invalid. They'll be inaccurate to the degree that the convenience sampling deviates from random selection, including sample units that overrepresent or underrepresent that type of respondent in the entire population.

Stratified versus unstratified. It's sometimes important to be sure that a sufficient number of certain kinds of respondents or sample units are included in the sample, even though they're a relatively small proportion of the population. An *unstratified* random sample would have to be extremely large to obtain enough respondents of a certain type. A *stratified* sample can be designed to reduce the required total sample size radically. The population is divided into specific *strata* containing certain types of respondents. Then a *subsample* of the required size is obtained for each strata. The stratification procedure is explained in more detail in Chapter 3.

Clustered versus unclustered. A *clustered* sampling design is appropriate when respondents are widely dispersed in space or time. If the population is sparsely located over a wide geographic area, the entire area can be divided into sections or "clusters." The researcher can first select several such clusters (preferably at random) and then select a specific number of respondents from each cluster. If sampling is to be done over a long time, the periods during which respondents are to be interviewed can be clustered similarly. Cluster sampling may dramatically reduce data collection costs because of the savings in time and travel. The procedure for clustering a sample is discussed more fully in Chapter 3.

Sample selection methods

Regardless of the basic sampling design chosen, the researcher must decide just how the respondents will actually be selected. If a sample of 200 respondents is to be selected from a sample frame of 20,000 members of the population, exactly *how* should the 200 names be chosen? If 12 in-home interviews of urban residents are to be conducted within each of 30 neighborhood clusters, which clusters should be chosen and which homes within each cluster should be included? The most basic methods of random sample selection—N*th name sampling, random number generation, random number tables,* and *physical selection methods*—are discussed fully in Chapter 3. The choice depends on the nature of the individual survey project, and no one method is universally preferable to the others.

When the data are to be collected by telephone or personal interviewing, there are many cases where some of those originally contacted *won't* be eligible for inclusion. For example, the sampling design may *exclude* those under 18 years of age, or it might *include only* those employed full-time outside the home. Similarly, a *stratified* sample may require half the respondents to be married and half unmarried. If so, each interviewer may be assigned a *quota* of a certain number of respondents of each type. The interviewers may have to ask those they contact one or more preliminary questions to qualify the respondent before continuing. The procedures for *quota assignment* and *qualification questioning* are explained in Chapter 8. The researcher should study these issues carefully during the planning phase if it appears that *prequalification* or *quotas* may be required.

Instrumentation

The information needs are expressed in terms appropriate to the sponsor. They're also listed in the order of their priority or importance to the user of the information. Survey instrumentation involves translating the information needs into a form that will elicit data from respondents. The survey instruments, themselves, include the survey questionnaire, as well as the cover letter and mailing materials or the rating cards and display materials that might be required. Part Two of the handbook, devoted to survey instrumentation, will provide a more thorough view of questionnaire development and instrument composition.

Survey topics

Classifying the information needs into survey topics serves two purposes: It groups items that are similar to one another into the same topic categories, and it suggests the type of questions and scales needed to obtain the information. When the information needs have been classified into topic categories, the entire task of inquiry is expressed in terms more appropriate and meaningful to the researcher. This process also assembles the items into groups, so items that require about the same kind of task from the respondent are listed together. This is the first step in arriving at a sequence that will facilitate response and assure more reliable, accurate data.

To classify the information needs into topic categories, each item specified in the list of information needs must be identified as relating to one or more of the seven basic topic categories identified in Chapter 1. At times, the topic that's inherent in the question will be obvious. Where more than one topic is implied or where the identification of one particular topic is ambiguous, careful thought and judgment may be required. The translation of information needs into survey research topics should meet two important criteria: First,

CHECKLIST 2–3

To Describe the Survey Instruments

1. How will the questionnaire be organized and why? What's the main principle of organization? Will the items be congregated by topic, type of question or scale, type of response required, or some other criterion?

2. How many parts or sections will be included and in what sequence? What comes first and why? What questions will be at the end of the questionnaire and why?

3. What type and level of language will be used—technical or lay, simple or sophisticated vocabulary?

4. What kind of grammar and composition will be used—formal or casual, scholarly or colloquial wording?

5. What types of questions and response scales will be included? Will respondents answer with words, letters, or numbers? Will they choose from the specified answers or respond spontaneously in their own words?

6. What are the most sensitive or threatening questions? What will be done to reduce resistance and why will it elicit respondent cooperation?

7. What ancillary instrumentation will be used—cover letter, pictures or displays, rating cards, or other visual or audible material?

8. What's the expected size of the questionnaire? How many questions or items in total? How many parts or sections? How many pages? How much weight and physical bulk?

9. How will the questionnaire be produced?[1] What size, color, weight, and grade of paper stock? Typewritten or typeset and in what print format? How will it be reproduced and bound or attached?

10. What will be retained by the respondent and/or interviewers? What will be returned for data recording and processing?

every item of information required should be classified into one or more of the topic categories and expressed in those terms. Redundancy should be limited and deliberate, so the exact same information should not be sought more than once unless that's intentional. Second, nothing should be neglected or it won't be collected. The list of information needs should be checked against the list of topics very carefully at least a couple of times to be sure nothing has been ignored.

Instrument specification

The principal measurement instrument is the survey questionnaire. It may be necessary to compose a rough draft of the questionnaire so it can be checked and approved by the sponsor. Often, however, only a detailed description will be necessary. The description should identify the key elements of the questionnaire and other instruments listed in Checklist 2–3.

When the survey instruments have been described and perhaps drafted, the researcher should be able to estimate the size and scope of the response task. The approximate number of survey items or variables should be noted in the project outline, together with the total

---

[1]This item assumes a standard, "paper and pencil" questionnaire. If the questionnaire is to be presented on electronic media or in some other form, see Chapter 6 for detailed guidance.

time it will require of a typical respondent and the ease or difficulty of the response task. It's also important at this point to estimate the costs for composition and production of the survey instruments. Thus, it may be necessary to obtain cost estimates or bids from internal or external sources, such as typesetters, printers, and the like. When these costs have been obtained, they should be listed in the project outline, together with the other information that's relevant to instrumentation.

Data Processing

Nearly all surveys generate *quantitative,* rather than only *qualitative* data. Responses are almost always recorded in the form of numbers, rather than words. So the term *data processing* refers here to *numeric,* rather than *verbal* data processing. The product of data processing is a set of tables and graphs that portray the results of the survey. They may be presented directly to those seeking the information or incorporated into written reports.

The primary objective of data processing and analysis is to *suppress superfluous detail* and to *make the most relevant and important facts and relationships apparent.* Too much detail is confusing. It hides, rather than reveals, the meaningful information. For instance, it would be difficult to learn much about the age of the group of 1,000 people by looking at a list of their birth dates or even their individual ages. But if these data were processed to compute the average age of the group, that *information* would be more *meaningful.* A table or graph showing the *distribution* of the age of the group might be even more informative.

Some surveys may include the entire population of interest, so there's no sampling involved. If so, data analysis will reveal the *population parameters.* Their precision will be limited only by the accuracy of the reports and processing. Such surveys are exceptional.

The vast majority of surveys include only a *sample* of the entire population of interest to the sponsors. When only a sample is surveyed, another objective of data processing is to perform *statistical analysis* so that *inferences* can be made about the entire *population,* based on the survey *sample.* For example, if the group of 1,000 people mentioned earlier constituted a sample of all those in the city, their average age could serve as an *estimate* of the average age of that population. But samples are never perfect, so this sample might include a slightly younger or older group than the population as a whole. In other words, there's likely to be some *sampling error.*

Statistical analysis allows the researcher to compute the *probability* that the values obtained from the sample are within a specific range of those for the entire population. In other words, statistical analysis reveals *both* the estimated values for the entire population *and* the range of possible error at a given level of probability, as a result of sampling.

Computer hardware

Survey data of very limited scope, with a small sample and only a few questions, might be processed "by hand," so to speak. Even so, the task is likely to be extremely tedious and time-consuming. Because of the easy accessibility of computers, most survey data deserve computer processing. Computers not only save a tremendous amount of data processing time and effort, they also allow researchers to generate vastly more meaningful and valuable information.

System hardware—the computers and peripheral devices, themselves—fall into two broad categories: *desktop* systems and *central* systems. *Desktop* computers are just that. They may be linked to external input, data storage, or output devices as well as to other desktop computers or to central computers. Nevertheless, they do some or all of the processing right at the operator's desk or work station. As their name implies, *central* computer systems do the actual processing at some central location accessible by communication to several operators or *users*. They may be linked by direct cable or by telephone to remote terminals or desktop computers.

Survey data processing and statistical analysis are somewhat limited by computer hardware characteristics. Almost any garden-variety desktop computer will provide simple data description and very basic measures of association between variables, for small- to medium-size survey data files. More sophisticated analysis programs and larger databases typically require more internal computer memory, larger external data storage capacity, and perhaps faster processing speed. Most central computer systems will accommodate such programs and data. Many desktop computers won't. On the other hand, the rapid advances in computer technology have vastly increased the number of desktop computer systems that accommodate sophisticated analysis programs and process relatively large databases.

Computer software

The computer programs that can be used for survey data processing vary markedly. They range from simple, unsophisticated spreadsheet programs and database managers all the way up to highly capable and advanced statistical analysis packages and graphics programs. Spreadsheet programs, one of the staples on many desktop systems, can be used by any researcher familiar with them to make simple transformations in the survey data where necessary. Spreadsheet programs can also be used to compute simple statistics such as averages and to portray distributions of data by category in tabular form. The more elaborate spreadsheet programs may also reveal relationships between pairs of variables by cross-tabulating one variable with another or performing correlation or regression analysis. However, spreadsheet programs are "general purpose" programs. They're designed to do a wide variety of analysis tasks, not just statistical analysis. Consequently, their ability is limited to only the basic forms of survey data analysis.

Statistical analysis software comes in two forms: One kind consists of individual programs designed to do one or a few specific types of analysis—correlation and regression programs, analysis of variance programs, cluster analysis programs, and the like. The other form of statistical software is a package composed of many integrated routines that allow the analyst to simultaneously or sequentially perform a wide array of analyses using the same basic format and set of instructions. These statistical packages often reside on central computers so they can be used by any authorized user who has access to the system. However, they're no longer confined to large, central computers. Several statistical analysis packages are available for the larger, more capable desktop computer systems.

Computer graphics

The results of a survey may be reported in simple, tabular form; in reports that include numeric tables together with explanatory, narrative text; or in a format that includes graphic or pictorial information in print or for group presentation. During the project planning phase, the researcher must anticipate the requirements for graphic or pictorial reports. They often require special computer software, such as graphing and charting programs. Most desktop or central computer hardware will allow creation of simple graphs and charts. More elaborate graphic reports may require special computer hardware—output devices such as laser printers, color printers, plotters, or slide printers.

Report Generation

The nature and format of the reports to the sponsor must be specified and the costs of reporting must also be estimated in advance. A wide variety of report mechanisms and formats are used for survey projects, depending on sponsor preferences and information needs.

Written reports
The written report is both the most common report medium and the least expensive and time-consuming. The typical elements of a written survey report are described in Guidelist 2–2. The composition and production of written reports can be more expensive and time-consuming than might be anticipated. It's important to consider the size of the reports and also the number of copies of written documents when planning them and estimating costs.

Report presentations
Sponsors often prefer the researcher or research team to make a verbal presentation of the survey results and to respond to questions about the survey and its findings. If only one or a very few people are seeking the information, such report conferences may only require multiple copies of the report document. More formal report presentations, often made to larger groups, usually necessitate composition and production of visual materials—slides or overhead transparencies of bullet charts, tables, and graphs. The cost of producing such visual materials and the demands on the researcher or research team's time and efforts vary widely, depending on the sponsor's needs. Thus it's vitally important to identify the need for report presentations during the planning phase and determine the costs and timetable associated with this form of reporting.

PROJECT COSTS AND TIMING

The primary objective of the project plan is to guide and direct the entire process as the survey is conducted. The secondary objective—nearly as important as the first—is to determine in advance the cost of the project and the time schedule for the work.

Cost Estimation

Survey costs ordinarily fall into four basic categories: (1) direct labor, (2) direct materials and supplies, (3) external service fees, and (4) overhead expense allocation. The amount and proportion of each category of cost differs sharply from one phase of the project to the next. So cost estimation should be done *by stage*. One model of the stages of the survey process is shown in Figure 2–9. The data collection stage is divided into two columns because the expense items differ so markedly between mail and interview surveys.

GUIDELIST 2–2

For Composing Written Reports

1. Begin with a one- to three-page *executive summary* listing only the major highlights in telegraphic, bullet format, beginning with the material that's most important to those seeking the information.

2. Include a *response summary,* a clean copy of the questionnaire containing brief indications of the percentage distributions of response to alternatives or the average values obtained from the sample.

3. Report the most important information first in the body of the document and organize it in the *categories* or *sections* that are the most relevant to the reader seeking the information.

4. Provide attractive, clearly labeled, readily readable *tables and/or graphs* that summarize the survey results visually and portray relationships among the items or questions and patterns of response for various types of respondents.

5. Compose *narrative text* that explains the tables and/or graphs in clear, easily readable terms, avoiding technical jargon and highlighting the most important values or relationships.

6. Attach a *technical appendix* describing how the survey was conducted in detailed terms, as well as any relevant *computer print output* of statistical analyses where either or both are appropriate or requested.

Budget preparation

The budgeting process consists of estimating the cost of each of the four categories, for each stage and substage from the beginning to the end of the survey project. For example, using the model presented in Figure 2–9, the researcher would begin by calculating the *direct labor costs* for *information need determination.* It might be necessary to break that substage down into even smaller increments, identifying such tasks as *sponsor conference time, facility inspection time, travel time, telephone conference time, office work time,* and so forth. These smaller increments can then be aggregated to determine the *direct labor cost* for item 1a. The costs for direct materials and supplies, external service fees, and overhead expense allocation for *information need determination* may be estimated in a similar way. The aggregate costs for all four categories is the estimated total for that substage. Finally, the sum of 1a and 1b constitutes the total *direct labor costs* for the first stage. Example 2–1 depicts a typical, small-survey budget based on the model shown in Figure 2–9 for an *interview* survey.

Budget modification

As with other budgets, the original survey project budget is often modified after composition and inspection by the researcher and/or sponsor. While the plans for virtually every aspect of the project are subject to change at this stage of the process, the aspect that perhaps deserves the most careful consideration is the *sample size.* Figure 2–10 shows the relative cost levels for six cost categories on the vertical axis, plotted against various sample sizes shown on the horizontal axis. Over a range from 20 or 30 respondents to several hundred, the costs are fairly constant for every cost category *except data collection.* Data collection costs

Figure 2–9   *Project Costs by Stage of the Process*

1. **Survey Initiation**
   a. Information Need Determination
   b. Preparation of Project Proposal

2. **Sampling Procedure**
   a. Sampling Design
   b. Sample Selection

3. **Instrument Composition**
   a. Draft Document Preparation
   b. Questionnaire Production
   c. Ancillary Material Production

4. **Mail Data Collection**	4. **Interview Data Collection**
a. Mailing Piece Production	*a.* Training and Supervision
b. Inducement Expenses	*b.* Interviewer Compensation
c. Postage or Delivery Fees	*c.* Travel or Telephone Charges
d. Return and Receipt Costs	*d.* Return and Verification

5. **Data Processing**
   a. Editing and Data Transfer
   b. Analysis Programming
   c. Statistical Analysis

6. **Report Generation**
   a. Narrative Text Composition
   b. Table and Graph Composition
   c. Production and Duplication
   d. Report Delivery or Presentation

increase in a near-linear fashion with increases in sample size. Consequently, sample size is often adjusted, either to meet budget constraints or to take advantage of the economy of enlarging the sample.

When sample size is relatively large—perhaps several hundred respondents—decreasing sample size reduces total project cost sharply in percentage terms. That's because data collection costs represent a large part of the total project budget. Yet this sample size reduction isn't likely to increase sampling error or decrease certainty in the estimates very much at all. But a very different result occurs with relatively small samples—those of less than about 200 and especially samples of under 100 respondents. Even a large percentage reduction in sample size at this level has very little effect on *total* project costs because data collection is a relatively small part of the total cost structure. Even more important, sampling error increases dramatically when small samples are reduced even further. By the same logic, *increasing* the size of small samples adds very little, in percentage terms, to the total cost of the project. As Figure 2–10 suggests, initiation, sampling, instrumentation, data processing, and reporting

---

EXAMPLE 2–1

Survey Project Budget

Survey Initiation

Information Need Determination . . . .$ 420
Preparation of Project Proposal 500
    Total Survey Initiation . . . . $ 920

Sampling Procedure

Sampling Design 295
Sample Selection 200
    Total Sampling Procedure   495

Instrument Composition

Draft Document Preparation 710
Questionnaire Production 285
Ancillary Material Production   85
    Total Instrument Composition   1,080

Data Collection

Training and Supervision 550
Interviewer Compensation 2,100
Travel or Telephone Charges 216
Return and Verification 525
    Total Data Collection   3,391

Data Processing

Editing and Data Transfer 345
Analysis Programming 400
Statistical Analysis 500
    Total Data Processing   1,245

Report Generation

Narrative Text Composition 420
Table and Graph Composition 320
Production and Duplication 125
Report Delivery or Presentation 300
    Total Report Generation   1,165
Total Cost of Project $8,296

---

usually cost just about as much for a sample of only a few respondents as they do for much larger samples. Yet there's an important benefit of increasing the size of a small sample—sampling error drops sharply and confidence levels increase commensurately. Consequently, there's a strong tendency for survey researchers to prefer sample sizes in a range from one or two hundred to one or two thousand respondents, working most often with sizes toward the middle to lower part of that range.

Figure 2–10   *Project Cost Elasticity*

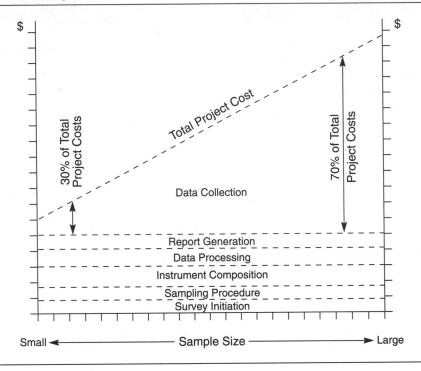

Project Timing

The time schedule for a survey project is often as critical as the budget—sometimes even more so. Just as they tend to underestimate costs, researchers and sponsors alike are prone to underestimate the time requirements. Good work takes time! When tasks have to be rushed, errors and mistakes are much more likely. Simple mistakes that occur early in the process—whether they involve timing or not—tend to be amplified with each later phase of the work. Thus, they may jeopardize the reliability and validity of the survey results. So careful timing is critical to both small and large survey projects.

Scheduling tasks

Many survey tasks have to be undertaken *consecutively*—others can be done concurrently. Because of the complexity of the survey process, it's virtually mandatory to formulate a survey *project schedule*. Graphic schedule charts, such as the one shown in Example 2–2, are vastly more effective than tabular schedules. Such schedules range in sophistication from simple calendar notations for very small, uncomplicated projects to computer project management and scheduling routines that identify critical paths and track the work as it's performed. But regardless of their simplicity or complexity, all project schedules have the same

EXAMPLE 2–2

Simple Project Schedule Chart

Task	Weeks from Start											
	1	2	3	4	5	6	7	8	9	10	11	12
Determine Information Needs	■											
Draft Project Proposal	■											
Get Sponsor Approval		■										
Design Sampling Procedure			■									
Write Respondent Selection Instructions			■									
Write Questionnaire Items and Scales			■	■								
Compose Complete Questionnaire				■	■							
Have Questionnaire Printed					■							
Prepare and Copy Rating Scale Cards	■											
Select Data Collection Agency				■	■							
Ship Materials to Data Collection Agency						■						
Train Field Supervisors and Interviewers						■						
Data Collection Period							■	■				
Receive and Sight-Edit Questionnaires							■	■				
Verify Response of Part of Sample								■				
Key Data to File and Process Edit								■				
Write Analysis Programs and Instructions							■					
Run Statistical Analysis Routines									■	■		
Inspect and Analyze Computer Output										■		
Compose Report Tables and Graphs											■	
Write Narrative Text of Report											■	
Assemble and Duplicate Report												■
Deliver Final Report to Sponsor												■

GUIDELIST 2–3

For Scheduling the Project

1. Break down each phase of the survey project into *independent* tasks if:
   a. the nature of the work is different or distinctive,
   b. they're to be done by different people,
   c. different equipment and materials are required, or
   d. the work is at different locations.
2. Estimate the *time duration* for each task, including:
   a. the actual work time on the task,
   b. time spent waiting for external materials or services, and
   c. an allowance for unexpected delays.
3. Identify the *dependency* of each task on completion of another when:

   a. the work product of one serves as input to another,
   b. the same person or people must do them both,
   c. the same facility or equipment is required for both, or
   d. approval of one task is needed before doing another.
4. On a *scheduling chart,* list the tasks in time sequence, graphing them:
   a. from the start, to determine the date of completion, or
   b. from the due date, back-timing to determine the date to begin.

---

two basic objectives: *planning* and *control*. The schedule ensures that each task will be done and done when it should be. It also serves as a benchmark or standard to compare performance with the plan and adjust the work or change the schedule when necessary. The directions for composing a simple project schedule chart are listed in Guidelist 2–3.

Monitoring and controlling

Like any plan, the project time schedule shouldn't be something that's done one time and then set aside and ignored. It's not etched in stone. It's a working document to which the researcher refers more or less constantly. Very little gets done ahead of schedule, while everything and anything is prone to fall behind. If delays extend the duration of a task, the project manager has two options: change the schedule, shifting the subsequent, dependent tasks to a later time; or *change the work* by arranging to do it or later tasks in a shorter time.

Finally, the survey project manager would be well-advised to share both the original time schedule with the sponsor and to update the sponsor periodically regarding the progress of the work. Sponsors rarely understand why a survey takes as much time as it does—they tend to want everything *yesterday!* If they "sign off" on the schedule, they're less likely to push researchers to hurry the work. Experienced researchers also work by another, iron-clad rule: *If there's a delay, notify the sponsor IMMEDIATELY!* Keep in touch. There's nothing more unnerving to those awaiting information than silence. Sponsors seem to detest a *surprise* even more than a delay. If the information seekers know there will be a delay, they may not like it but at least they can plan for it.

THE FINAL PROJECT PLAN

The important factor for the researcher to note when completing the survey project plan is the necessity for an integrated project. Each element must fit together and be compatible with the others. When inconsistencies or incompatibilities are discovered, the elements must be changed. It's always advisable to express the elements of the project plan in written form. This plan will be the basis for later decisions and choices as the work is done and the project continues to completion. It may be necessary to edit and refine the project outline and append any questionnaire drafts or other relevant materials. The project outline should be submitted to the sponsors, with whatever annotation they might require. When approved, it serves as the basis for an agreement or contract for the survey project work to be performed by the researcher. For those projects where the researcher sponsors the survey, it's advisable to submit the project outline and obtain comments and suggestions from others who might provide insight by virtue of their training or experience.

SUMMARY

Completing the Project Plan

A. Consider first things first. The survey objectives and information needs should be the basis for selecting instrumentation, data collection, and processing methods.

B. Value control very highly. The chance of catastrophic error increases dramatically with the number of people involved in survey data collection.

C. Communicate with others. Maintain a dialogue with the sponsor and obtain comments from those who can assist.

D. Evaluate options thoroughly. Questionnaire, data collection, and processing alternatives must all be identified and examined to make the best choice.

E. Choose alternatives carefully. If there's doubt about instrumentation, collection, or processing, turn to later chapters on these topics for direction.

F. Place trust in sampling. Don't use large samples when careful sampling design will obtain precise information from smaller numbers of people.

G. Budget very carefully. Most things cost more than anticipated and the budget should have a safety factor to allow for error.

H. Match costs and information value. Revise project tasks or increase the funds allocated so that there's an adequate margin of safety between costs and benefits.

Chapter 3

Designing the Sample

THE PURPOSE OF SAMPLING

Nearly every survey uses some form of sampling. The concept of sampling is easily understood. It simply means taking part of some population to represent the whole population. The alternative to sampling is enumeration—counting the entire population. The census of the U.S. population conducted each decade and political elections where all qualified citizens who register and vote are *counted* at the polls are both examples of enumeration. Sampling is much more common. Even though the Census Bureau uses enumeration for the decennial census, they generate a gigantic volume of data about citizens, companies, and other units by surveying only a sample of the population under study. The news media, political parties, and candidates generate predictive data, using sampling, before the actual election. Sampling is a key factor for virtually any survey project.

The main reason for sampling is economy. To survey every individual in a population using enumeration is ordinarily much too expensive in terms of time, money, and personnel. There's really no need to survey every individual. Only a small fraction of the entire population usually represents the group as a whole with enough accuracy to base decisions on the results with confidence. While sampling is extremely practical and economical, it has to be done correctly or it will introduce bias or error in the results. The sample must be selected properly, or it won't represent the whole. It has to be large enough to meet the requirements for reliability—but not too large, or it will waste resources.

Specification of Population

The actual specification of a sampling design begins with identification of the *population* to be surveyed. The three main tasks are shown in Guidelist 3–1. This may appear to be a

GUIDELIST 3–1

For Identifying Populations

1. Be sure the population consists of those people who actually possess the information sought by the survey.
2. Identify all the major factors that would otherwise qualify respondents and make their responses meaningful to the sponsor.
3. List the criteria for inclusion and exclusion of respondents, together with the decision rules to be used.

simple task, but it seldom is. Suppose a survey is to be conducted to measure community attitudes toward a municipal, political issue. Then the population to be surveyed would include all those within the city. Are those who are temporarily living outside the city to be included or excluded? Should only registered voters be included in the population? Must respondents be 18 or 21 years of age or older? What about those who own property in the city but live elsewhere? Should businesses and organizations be included, or only individuals?

It's important for the researcher to anticipate the decisions that are likely to arise during actual sample selection. Respondents must be qualified on the basis of two criteria: (1) they have to possess the information, and (2) they may need to have certain attributes or characteristics to make their responses meaningful.

Sample Unit Specification

A sample unit is the smallest entity that will provide one response. Ordinarily, survey sample units consist of individual people. Each person in the population might be a sample unit. This isn't always the case. For some surveys, the appropriate sample unit might be a household, consisting of all those living in one housing unit. For another, the sampling unit might be a family, consisting of parents, their children, and relatives. Some surveys may require sample units that are individual business firms or companies. Others may use organizations or institutions as sample units.

Specification of a sample unit, outlined in Guidelist 3–2, must be neither too broad nor too narrow. If it's too broad, it won't be the smallest single unit. For example, it wouldn't be appropriate to use the family as a sampling unit for a survey of political attitudes because different family members may hold different opinions about the issues. If the specification of a sampling unit is too narrow, it would produce redundancy or be misleading. For example, a survey designed to discover the methods charitable institutions use to solicit contributions could not effectively use individual employees as the sample units. Each would be reporting on the same institution, and all but one would be redundant. There's one other factor that must be considered when specifying sample units. There are times when the new

---

GUIDELIST 3–2

For Specifying Sample Units

1. The sampling unit should be specified so it's the smallest single entity from which the data can be obtained.
2. If the unit contains several individuals who might provide different data, the specification of the unit is too broad and should be narrowed.

3. If responses from individuals would be redundant or overrepresent some entities, the specification is too narrow and should be broadened.
4. If the survey data are to be compared with existing survey or secondary data, the same sample units must be used for the survey or the data won't be comparable.

---

survey data will be compared with existing survey data—secondary data from some other source. If so, it's important to be sure the specification of the sample unit for the survey is the same as for the data to which the survey results will be compared, to ensure comparability.

Sample Frame Selection

The sample frame is a list or set of directions identifying all the sample units in the population. Individual respondents will be selected from the sample frame when the survey data are collected. The sample frame might be a list of names and telephone numbers for a telephone survey, a map showing a specific residential area for in-home interviews, or a list of names and addresses for a mail survey. There are other types of sample frames used for special surveys or data collection methods. Assume that interviews will be conducted at a location such as a store. The sample frame might consist of all those who enter the store during the sampling period, even though these shoppers can't be individually identified in advance.

It's seldom possible to obtain a perfect sample frame. The more complete and accurate the sample frame, the better the sample will represent the population as a whole. There are three criteria for selecting a sample frame for a survey: the frame should be all–inclusive, it should be exclusive to the population under study, and the units identified in the frame should be defined in exactly the same way as the sampling units. An *all-inclusive* sample frame is one that includes every member of the population to be surveyed. The frame should be *exclusive* in the sense that *only* those in the population are included. Lastly, it should list or identify the entities in the population the same way as the sampling units are specified. There are times when the sample frame should contain other details as well. The basic rules for selecting the sample frame are listed in Guidelist 3–3.

RELIABILITY AND VALIDITY

The concepts of reliability and validity can be clarified by an analogy. Figure 3–1 shows four different patterns. Each of the four pictures shows a target—a *bull's eye* on a dart board.

GUIDELIST 3-3

For Selecting a Sample Frame

1. The sample frame is necessary to identify the entities or units to be surveyed.
2. The sample frame should be all-inclusive, so every unit in the population to be surveyed is included.
3. The frame for the sample should exclude any units that aren't part of the population being surveyed.
4. The entries listed in the sample frame must be specified in exactly the same way as the sampling units were specified.
5. When the sample is clustered, stratified, or both, the sample frame must indicate cluster boundaries and/or strata membership for the individual units.

Figure 3-1 *The Reliability/Validity Diagram*

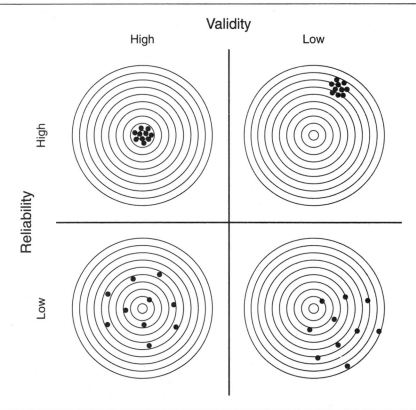

The dots on the diagram are the marks of the darts thrown at each target. Each of the rows and columns on the diagram are labeled to show what they represent. The top row shows the results when reliability is high, and the bottom row shows low reliability. The column at the left contains the patterns for high validity, and the one at the right shows low validity.

Validity and Bias

Both targets in the left column of the diagram contain marks that are *centered* on the bull's eye. Although the marks on the lower target are spread over a wider area, they're in a random pattern, *centered* around the bull's eye. Nothing is *pushing* or *pulling* all the marks in one direction. By contrast, the patterns on both targets in the right column are off the mark. All tend toward one direction. The person throwing the darts at the target at the upper right had a steady hand, but consistently threw the darts high and a little to the right of the bull's eye. The player who threw the darts at the target on the bottom right was less steady and consistent and also persistently threw too low and to the right. Thus, the effect of *systematic bias,* often called just plain *bias,* is to push or pull the results in one or another *specific direction.* The two targets in the column on the right side of the diagram represent the results of survey data with low validity.

The pattern of marks on the lower, left target of the diagram are identified as low in reliability but with high validity, because the pattern is *centered* on the bull's eye. Technically, *no data can be more valid than it is reliable. Validity* requires hitting the bull's eye. In this case, *random error* caused the dots to miss the mark, resulting in low reliability. Thus, *the degree of reliability* LIMITS *the degree of validity.*

A measurement of any kind is valid to the degree it measures *all* of that and *only* that which it's supposed to measure. To be valid it must be free of extraneous factors that systematically *push* or *pull* the results in one particular direction. If something other than what's being measured affects the results by introducing a systematic *bias,* the results are less valid. Unfortunately, the effects of sampling, as well as many other factors, can bias the results of a survey. For example, the way a question is written may bias the answers. Interviewers may bias their respondents' answers if they aren't careful. Bias can also be introduced during recording, processing, and even reporting the survey results. Later chapters will identify and discuss other sources of bias and their effect on validity. Sample validity and sampling bias will be discussed in more detail later in this chapter.

Reliability and Error

In the top row of the diagram, the marks from the darts are all closely clustered. The person throwing the darts managed to place them all in very nearly the same place on the target. Thus, there's very little *random error* in these data. By contrast, the marks on the targets on the bottom row are spread over a wider area. This dart thrower wasn't doing exactly the same thing from one throw to the next, and the darts were randomly scattered on the targets. They're not very good *replicates* or representations of one another. They lack *repeatability.* These pictures illustrate the relationship between *reliability* and *(random) error*—the more error, the lower the reliability. High reliability implies a low level of error.

Reliability means freedom from *random error.* The most fundamental test of reliability is *repeatability*—the ability to get the same data values from several measurements made in the same way. For example, if a survey question obtained the same response, time after time, from one particular respondent who was asked that same question several times in one month, that would mean there was high reliability *over time.* If the answers varied in a random pattern, the reliability over time would be low. If a survey item yielded the same data from one respondent to the next when they did actually hold identical positions on the issue, that would indicate high reliability *over respondents,* and if there were random differences, reliability over respondents would be low. Similarly, if a survey yielded the same distributions of data from one sample of a given size to the next when they were drawn in the same way, there would be relatively low *sampling error* and high reliability *over samples. The greater the random error, the lower the reliability.*

Random error can result from a host of measurement factors. For instance, if a survey item used a term that was completely unfamiliar to many respondents, they would probably guess at the meaning. Even though they don't have any idea what it really means, respondents usually give answers. If those answers were merely random guesses, the reliability of the data for that item would be reduced. Similarly, interviewers may make *random* errors in recording results. Random error might also be introduced during processing or at other phases of the project. These kinds of error will be discussed in later chapters. *Sampling error* is the focus of attention here.

It's impractical to measure the entire population, so usually the researcher knows nothing about the whole population except what's learned from the sample itself. Thus, researchers and statisticians usually think of sampling error in terms of comparisons between similar samples. Data from a sample are relatively free from sampling error—are *reliable*—if other samples of the same size selected the same way from the same population provide the same or very similar results. If different samples provided very different results, there would be a lot of sampling error and the data from the original sample would be unreliable.

SAMPLE SIZE DETERMINATION

The sample size depends on the budget and degree of confidence required. The sponsor and researcher can *buy* higher reliability, lower sampling error, and greater confidence for additional time, money, and effort. Ordinarily, though, there's some minimum sample size, below which the data are worthless. Similarly, there's a point of diminishing returns, above which additional confidence is negligible. The object of sample size determination is to find the optimum point between those two extremes for the survey project at hand.

Sample Size and Error

Smaller samples are more likely to be different from the population than larger ones. So smaller samples have more sampling error and lower reliability. Suppose only 5 people out of 10,000 were interviewed on some subject. There's a fairly good chance most or all of them would happen to hold views that aren't typical of the whole group. By comparison, it's very unlikely that a sample of 1,000 people would happen to include a high proportion of people who were very different from the other 9,000 in the population. Thus, the larger the sample, the lower the sampling error. Box A of Figure 3–2 shows that sample size and

Figure 3–2   *Sampling Factor Relationships*

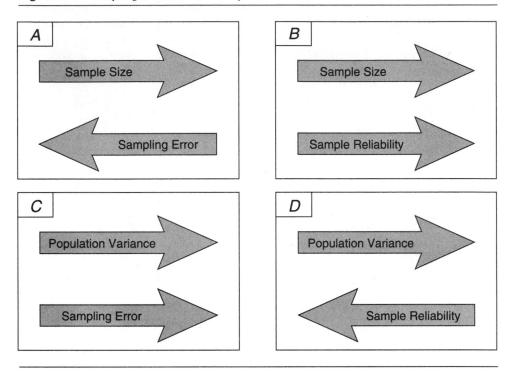

sampling error go in different directions—they're *inversely* related to one another. Box B of Figure 3–2 indicates that sample size and sample reliability go in the *same* direction—there's a *direct,* rather than inverse, relationship between sample size and reliability.

Confidence Level

Confidence level has a rather precise meaning for statisticians and survey researchers. It can be expressed as the *probability* that a value in the *population* is within a specific, numeric range from the corresponding value computed from a sample. For example, if the mean value of some variable computed from a *random* sample is 50, it wouldn't be logical or safe to assume that the mean for the entire population is exactly 50, as well. There's likely to be some *sampling error.* The pertinent question is *"How much error?"*

Standard error

If the sample was, in fact, *randomly* selected, the probability of a *certain amount* of sampling error can be computed. The value that indicates the range of error or *confidence interval* (C.I.) is called the *standard error of the estimate* (S.E.). As Figure 3–3 shows, the researcher can be

Figure 3–3   *Confidence Intervals and Probability Levels*

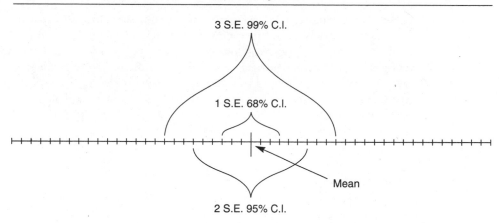

68 percent sure that the actual population value or *parameter* is within plus or minus 1 S.E. of the corresponding sample statistic. Similarly, there's a 95 percent chance the parameter value is within ±2 S.E. and a 99 percent probability it's within ±3 S.E.

Thus the value of S.E. and the corresponding breadth of the confidence intervals are quantitative measures of sample reliability and sampling error. The more reliable the sample, the lower the value of S.E. will be and the more narrow the confidence intervals will be. Conversely, the greater the sampling error, the larger the value of S.E. will be and the wider the confidence intervals will be. The determinants of confidence intervals will be discussed in more detail in the next section.

Key variable analysis

Surveys ordinarily include several items or variables, and occasionally they may have as many as a few hundred. Despite this multiplicity of variables, the specification of information requirements and assignment of priority will ordinarily identify only a few *key* variables that are the most important—those that constitute the major reason for the survey. The researcher should have a sense of the level of confidence desired for these key variables.

The confidence requirements can be assessed by asking a series of *"What if . . ."* questions about various levels of confidence and error. For example, the sponsor might be asked, "What if the average value for this item is off by 1 or 2 percent?" Usually the answer will be that it would make no real difference—that it wouldn't matter. The next question might be, "What if it were off by 5 percent?" The researcher will soon discover both the consequences of basing decisions on estimates that are somewhat inaccurate for the population, and also the *critical points, below* which the error wouldn't be important, and *above* which it would have very negative consequences. These estimates of the desired confidence level serve as target values during sample size determination.

The Outside Limits

There are maximum and minimum *practical* sample sizes that apply to virtually all surveys. Ordinarily, a sample of less than about 30 respondents will provide too little certainty to be practical. Figure 3–4 depicts a plot of the upper and lower 95 percent confidence level for samples (from the same population) ranging from 20 to 300 respondents in increments of 20. The values are expressed as a percentage of the mean. So there's a 95 percent chance the actual population mean is within about 37 percent of the sample mean for a sample of only 20 respondents. Similarly, for a sample of 300, there's a 95 percent probability of a range of error less than ten percent of the sample mean.

Minimum limit

Usually experienced researchers regard a sample of about 100 respondents as the minimum sample size for large populations, though there are exceptions. Figure 3–4 indicates that confidence intervals narrow sharply when very small sample sizes are increased, up to about 100 respondents. So small increases in sample size at lower levels yield big reductions in sampling error and big increases in confidence. In short, it's well worth it to increase the size of very small samples.

Another reason survey samples seldom contain fewer than a couple of hundred respondents is related to the cost structure for survey research, discussed in Chapter 2 and shown in Figure 2–10: Project Cost Elasticity, on page 50. The *fixed* costs will be incurred regardless of sample size. Thus, the additional or *marginal* cost of including at least 100 or so more respondents is often very small in comparison to the value of the fixed costs that will automatically result.

Maximum limit

The maximum *practical* size for a sample is about 1,000 respondents, under ordinary conditions. Contrary to popular belief, the maximum practical size of a sample has *absolutely nothing* to do with the size of the population if it's many times greater than the sample. This fact may be difficult for a novice to accept, but it's statistically sound and indisputable. A simple analogy makes this fact intuitively understandable. Suppose you are warming a bowl of soup for yourself and you want to know if it's hot enough. You would probably *sample* it by stirring the soup, then trying a spoonful. The *sample size* would be *one spoonful. Now* assume that you are to warm a hundred gallons of soup for a large crowd, and you want to test it to see if it's hot enough to serve. You would probably stir it and take a sample of *one spoonful,* even though the so-called *population* of soup was hundreds of times larger than when only one serving was sampled. Thus, the size of the population has *nothing* to do with the size of the sample that's required.

It's seldom necessary to sample more than 10 percent of the population to obtain adequate confidence, providing the resulting sample is less than about 1,000 and larger than the minimums noted earlier. Thus, for a population of 1,000 units, the experienced researcher would probably consider a sample size of about 100 or so. For a population of 5,000 units, the minimum practical sample would be 100 or so, and the maximum would be approxi-

Figure 3–4 *Sample Size and Confidence Intervals*

mately 500, or 10 percent. For populations of 10,000 or more, most experienced researchers would probably consider a sample size between about 200 and 1,000 respondents.

The futility of using extremely large samples is demonstrated by Figure 3–5. For this population, a sample of 2,000 provided a 95 percent confidence interval (C.I.) of only plus or minus two percent of the mean. A sample of 10,000, five times that size, reduced the C.I. only slightly to just over plus or minus one percent. Above a sample size of about 4,000, confidence intervals decrease only very slightly and at a decreasing rate with each increment of 1,000 respondents. So, aside from some special circumstances, discussed below, samples of more than a few hundred are seldom required. Those over one or two thousand are very rarely justified.

Figure 3–5   *Standard Error of Large Samples*

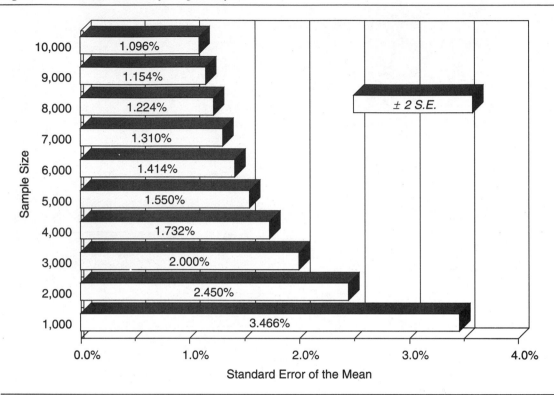

Variance in the Population

There's always a chance that a sample will include many individuals who are atypical, who are different from the most typical members of the population. The degree of sampling error is partly a function of the *variation,* from one individual to the next, within the population. The more similar the individuals in the population, the smaller the sampling error. The more they *vary* from one another, the greater the sampling error. Box C of Figure 3–2 indicates that population variance and sampling error are *directly* related to each other.

If there's more sampling error when the variance in the population is large than when it's small, then there's also *lower* sample reliability. Box D of Figure 3–2 indicates that population variance is *inversely* related to sample reliability—the *larger* the variance in the population, the *lower* the reliability of the data for a sample of a given size.

Variance and reliability

A simple example shows how variation in the population affects sampling error. Suppose the sponsor wants to know the average age of all high school students in a particular school district. If a sample of about 200 student records were randomly selected from the files, the average for the sample would probably be within only a few weeks or months of the average age that might be computed from all the records. That's because nearly all the students will be between 14 and 18 years of age—there isn't very much *variation* in the population on this variable. So the *sampling error* will be small.

Now suppose the sponsor wants to know the average age of *all* the students in the school district, from kindergarten to high school senior. The average from the same size sample of student records would probably differ from that of the entire student population by several months. There's more *variation* in age within that population. By extension, if the sponsor wanted an estimate of the average age of *all residents* in the district, from the most recent newborn to the very eldest, the range of *sampling error* would be denominated in years, rather than merely weeks or months. Again, the reason is more variation in age in the population of *residents* than in the population of *students,* just as there's more age variation in *students* than there is in *seniors*.

The *age ranges* for these three populations are plotted on the horizontal axis of Figure 3–6. The 95 percent *confidence intervals* are plotted on the vertical axis. When the variation is less than 5 years, for high school students, the 95 percent C.I. is very small, indeed. It

Figure 3–6 *Population Variance and Reliability*

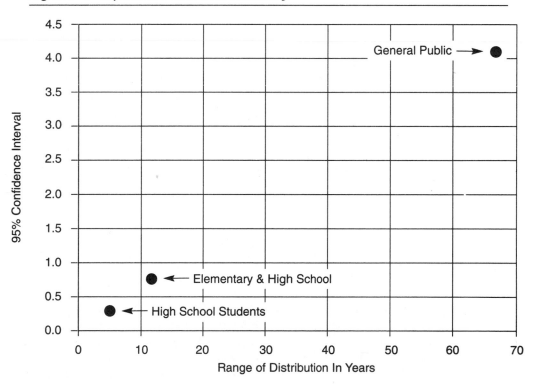

GUIDELIST 3–4

For Controlling Sampling Error

1. Sampling error results because those in the sample aren't perfectly representative of the population as a whole.
2. Any sample of less than the entire population will virtually always have some sampling error.
3. The larger the proportion of the population included in the sample, the smaller the sampling error.
4. Sampling error is *random* error, but it affects *both* the reliability and the validity of the data.

5. The greater the sampling error, the lower the reliability and validity of the sample data.
6. The greater the variation among individual members of the population, the greater the sampling error.
7. Therefore, the greater the population variance, the larger the sample size must be to attain a given level of reliability.

---

increases only slightly with an age range of just over 12 years for students from first grade to high school senior. The age range for the general public in this population was about 67 years. With that much variation, the 95 percent C.I. jumped to almost 13 times that for high schoolers and over 5 times that for all students.

Assessing variation

Since confidence level is partly a function of variation in the population, the researcher must make an estimate of the amount of variation that's likely to exist in the population for the *key* survey variables. These estimates might be based on the previous experience of the researcher or sponsor. Casual observation may also provide some indications. Data from previous surveys or from other secondary sources may be available. If there's no indication whatsoever of the population variance for some key items, a simple pilot survey on only those items for a fairly small number of respondents from the population may be necessary to obtain an estimate.

The more the respondents are likely to differ on the key items of the survey, the larger the sample must be to reach a given level of confidence. If all responses are almost identical, fewer respondents need be surveyed. If responses vary widely among respondents, there will be a greater chance of selecting people who aren't typical and a larger sample will be needed. These relationship are outlined in Guidelist 3–4.

After identifying the key variables, assessing the tolerable error for each, and making an estimate of the amount of variance among those in the population for each, the next step is to combine this information. This process will require some judgment and perhaps just plain guesswork. The objective is to identify one or, at most, two or three items that will require the *largest* sample size to provide adequate confidence. If there's one item for which there are *both* a very high need for confidence *and* a high level of variance in the population, that's obviously the determining variable for selecting the sample size. Any sample large enough to meet the confidence requirements for that item will be sufficiently large for all the others. If the key items requiring the most confidence are likely to have the least variance in the population, and vice versa, the items must be considered as a group or the researcher must make a *judgment call* and pick one or two as a guide.

Subsample Sizes

Some survey samples may be divided into subsamples and analyzed separately. When that's the case, the size of each subsample must be determined separately as well. In the vast majority of cases, the entire sample will be used for analysis and interpretation, to estimate the values and distributions in the population. Ordinarily, though, most survey data is *implicitly* divided during analysis into what might be called subsamples. So it's necessary for the researcher to anticipate the types of analysis that will be used and the size and number of the implicit subsamples that might be created.

The two most common techniques used for data analysis that implicitly create subsamples are cross-tabulation and breakdowns of averages. For example, respondent age might be broken down to show the average for men and for women, or the sex of the respondents might be cross-tabulated with their response to a yes/no question. In the first case, two subsamples would be created: males and females. In the second, four implicit subsamples would result: men responding positively, men responding negatively, women responding positively, and women responding negatively.

The reliability and confidence that result from these types of analyses depend in part on the size of the implicit subsamples. The size of the subsamples depends, in turn, on both the nature of the variables or items used for cross-tabulation or breakdowns, and also on the distributions of response obtained from the survey. Items with only two alternatives or levels create fewer and larger subsamples than those with many response options or levels. Thus, the size of subsamples or cells within the analysis is of less concern when there are fewer categories for the item, providing that respondents are about equally divided among the levels or subsamples. This is certainly not the usual case. For example, on a simple, dichotomous, yes/no question, only 10 percent or less may fall in one category. That would create a very small subsample. This problem is confounded even further because cross-tabulation creates individual cells which may become even smaller. For example, suppose the item cited above was to be cross-tabulated with another, similar variable. Assume that it also has a distribution of 10/90 as well. If there were no relationship between the two items, only 10 percent of 10 percent, or 1 percent of respondents, would reside in the smallest cell of the cross-tabulation.

Certainly the researcher designing a sample and determining the appropriate size can't fully anticipate all the breakdowns and cross-tabulations that will be used for analysis. Nor can the researcher predict accurately the distributions of response that will result for items with response categories. On the other hand, the researcher must be aware of the implicit creation of subsamples. In addition, those designing a sample must anticipate the *potential* for subsamples inherent in the survey task. If the analysis is likely to generate many, small subsamples, the total sample size must be relatively large to ensure adequate numbers within them.

Judgment and Determination

There are statistical formulas for the computation of a specific sample size to yield a given level of confidence for a single variable. Unfortunately, they're of little value, even to experienced, practicing researchers, for several reasons. The computations require fairly accurate estimates of population variance, and that's seldom known in advance. In addition, most surveys include dozens or even hundreds of items or variables, and it would be virtually impossible to complete the calculations for each. If such computations were performed for each item and the largest required sample size were used for the survey, the sample would very likely be much larger than that required for all but a few survey items. Lastly, sponsors usually know and can verbally express the degree of confidence in the data and the estimates they desire, but rarely if ever will they be able to express these requirements numerically as confidence intervals.

Most surveys don't call for a precise sample size. So it takes study and judgment of the conditions listed in Figure 3–7 to make an intelligent choice. If most or all the factors indicating a large sample size are present, the researcher would choose a sample size very near the maximum practical limit for the population, as noted earlier. By contrast, if most or all the conditions indicating a small sample size applied to the survey, the sample size selected would appropriately be very near the minimum limit noted above for the particular population to be sampled. When there are factors that indicate a large sample but others indicating a small one, the actual sample size must be in the mid-range between the maximum and minimum values suggested. It may be advisable for the researcher to consider each of the factors listed, to determine the importance of each for the particular survey task at hand. Obviously, the most salient and important factors for the project would be the determining ones to be weighed most heavily in the decision.

Figure 3–7   *Factors Determining Sample Size*

Factors Indicating a Large Sample

1. The decisions to be based on the survey data have very serious or costly consequences.
2. The sponsors demand a very high level of confidence in the data and estimates.
3. There's likely to be a high level of variance among the units in the population to be sampled.
4. The sample is to be divided into relatively small subsamples during analysis and interpretation.
5. Project costs and timing vary only slightly with increases in the size of the sample.
6. Time and resources are readily available to cover the costs of data collection.

Factors Indicating a Small Sample

1. There are few if any major decisions or commitments to be based on the survey data.
2. The sponsors require only rough estimates concerning the parameters of the population.
3. The population to be sampled is very homogeneous, with little variance among units.
4. The analysis and interpretation will be based on the entire sample or only a few, large subsamples.
5. A large proportion of total project costs are for data collection or costs increase dramatically with sample size.
6. Budget constraints and/or time requirements limit the volume of data that can be collected.

Preliminary Sampling

To make the necessary decisions concerning the appropriate sample size for a survey, the researcher must somehow anticipate at least two types of results beforehand: variance in the population for the key variables to be measured, and distributions of response for items that will form implicit subsamples during analysis. There may be cases when it's virtually impossible to anticipate one or both of these two types of results. If so, the researcher has two options—a *pilot survey* or a *sequential sampling* design. Either might provide the data necessary to the decision.

The pilot survey

One option is to conduct an informal *pilot survey* to obtain responses to only the key variables in question. These results can be tabulated to show the degree of variance and confidence intervals that might be expected from the actual survey, as well as the percentage distributions of response to categorical items. The advantages of a pilot survey are simplicity, speed, and economy. Only a small number of respondents and a few questions are required.

The pilot survey need not even use the same data collection method as that for the main survey, and such pilot surveys can often be completed easily, quickly, and inexpensively. It may also provide useful information about other aspects of the survey process. For instance, the survey instruments might be tested, the alternative data collection methods might be compared, and so forth.

Sequential sampling

Another alternative open to the researcher in doubt about the most appropriate sample size is known as *sequential sampling*. With this technique, the researcher proceeds with the project as though a sample size had been determined. Any quotas are expressed as percentages, rather than numbers of respondents. The necessary analysis routines are prepared in advance, and the survey is begun without precise determination of when it will be terminated. As the data are obtained, they're submitted to analysis, the confidence intervals around estimates computed, and the size of the implicit subsamples noted. By observing the decrement in the confidence intervals and/or the increases in subsample sizes as data are added to the file, the researcher may be able to predict quite accurately the point at which the values will be adequate. If so, that number of respondents would be set as the point at which data collection would terminate. If prediction isn't feasible, the data collection would continue until the results were satisfactory, then terminated at that point.

The disadvantage of sequential sampling, compared to a pilot survey, is that this method takes more time, effort, and resources. It's more cumbersome and complex, and requires analysis routines to be available during data collection. Nor does it permit testing of other survey decisions, such as the questions' wording or scaling techniques, while these can be tested in a pilot survey. The major advantage of sequential sampling is its precision and accuracy. As the cliché says, "What you see is what you get!" Extra data obtained after adequate certainty and subsample size have been reached will enhance the values, but they can't be less than what's required.

SAMPLE SELECTION METHODS

The simple, random sample is the most straightforward form of probability sampling. There are also *systematic* designs that yield a sample where the probability of inclusion of respondents is equal or known to the researcher. Stratified and clustered samples are the most common of these systematic sampling designs. Their advantages and applications will also be discussed here.

Random Sampling Benefits

A *random* sample is the most desirable kind for almost every survey. *Random* in this context doesn't mean haphazard. Random samples are extremely important to the reliability and validity of the data. When the respondents are picked at random, the probability of any one person being included in the sample is precisely equal to the probability of including any other. (In a technical sense, the probability of inclusion need not necessarily be equal, but the probability must be *known*. A random sample is merely a special case of a *probability sample*.) The random sample is best because it's most representative of the entire population. It's least likely to result in bias. It has statistical properties that allow the researcher to make *inferences* about the population, based on the results obtained from the sample. Random samples permit the computation of *confidence intervals* indicating the probability the population average is within a certain range around the sample average. With random sampling, the researcher can calculate and report the *statistical significance* of relationships between survey items, based on the probability that such relationships would result only from sampling error.

Without random selection, none of these statistical coefficients or values would be accurate or legitimate. This isn't to say they can't be computed. They can be. The analytical computations can be performed for *any* numeric data, regardless of how it was obtained. Unfortunately, values and coefficients would have little or no real meaning or legitimacy, and they could be very misleading, indeed. The more the sample deviates from purely random selection, the less representative it's likely to be—the less legitimate the results of statistical computation will be.

Stratified Sampling

There are times when it's useful to divide a population into two or more segments or *strata* and sample a different proportion of each. The selection of sample strata is usually based on some demographic characteristic, but other variables might also be used to divide the population into strata. A stratified sample is practical when it's desirable to sample a much larger or smaller proportion of some strata than others. Stratification is also useful if there's very *little* variance in the population *within* strata, and *great* variance *between* them. Each situation can be exemplified.

Differential confidence
Assume some company wants to measure employee preferences for several different fringe benefits that might be included in a labor contract. Some employees belong to a union whose contract will expire soon. Negotiation of a new contract is to begin shortly. Another

---

CHECKLIST 3–1

To Choose a Stratified Sample Design

1. Is there a requirement for greater reliability and a larger sample for some strata than for others? If so, stratification would be practical.

2. Are there indications of little population variance *within* strata and large variation *between* strata? In such cases, stratification is recommended.

3. Is it possible to obtain a sample frame showing strata membership for individuals? If not, stratification isn't feasible without quota sampling.

4. Can respondents' strata memberships be determined in advance by observation or questioning with a quota system? If they can't, stratification isn't possible.

---

group's union very recently signed an agreement. It will be many months before that contract could be changed. The sponsor needs to be very precise about the first group's opinions. They need only a general overview of the second group's attitudes.

If simple, random sampling—no stratification—were used, the result might be less confidence than desired for the first group and more than necessary for the second. Resources would be wasted and the results wouldn't be optimum. In this situation, the population of employees can be divided into two mutually exclusive groups or strata, based on their union affiliation. A *large* proportion of the first strata and a *smaller* proportion of the second would be surveyed. As a result, there would be an appropriate level of confidence for each group. Checklist 3–1 identifies the conditions for choosing a stratified sample.

Interstrata variance

Another situation exemplifies the use of stratification to markedly increase the reliability and confidence obtainable from survey data. Suppose a political survey will be conducted on a particular issue, and the researcher knows the population is sharply divided or *polarized* about the issue. The male voters tend to hold one position very strongly, and the female voters are likely to take an opposing view with equal vigor. There are also indications of very little variation among the men concerning the issue, and the women also tend to agree fairly closely.

With an unstratified, random sample, a very large sample of the whole population would be needed to provide the required degree of certainty about the combined views of men and women. That's because the degree of reliability is partly a function of the *variance* in the population. (This issue will be discussed in more detail later in this chapter.) In this case, the variance would be large because of the polarization. If the population is divided into male and female voter strata, the variance within each will be small, so a smaller proportion of each can be sampled. The necessary reliability and confidence intervals for the combined results would be obtained, yet the sum of the two subsamples would be much smaller than the number required for an unstratified sample.

GUIDELIST 3–5

For Designing a Stratified Sample

1. Select the variable(s) or characteristic(s) on which to base or define the strata.
2. Obtain a sample frame that shows the stratum membership of each sample unit.
3. Estimate the variance *within* strata and the variation *between* stratum.
4. Determine the confidence level needed for each stratum, based on information needs.
5. Specify the sample size for each strata to obtain the desired confidence level for each.

With stratified sampling, the sample frame must indicate strata membership on the variables used to define the strata. In the first example above, the union affiliations of employees would have to be indicated in the personnel records. The strata membership of respondents must also be identifiable in advance, or else a quota system must be used with stratification. The steps for designing a stratified sample are outlined in Guidelist 3–5.

Cluster Sampling

Sometimes the population to be surveyed is physically or geographically separated or widely dispersed. That doesn't matter to mail surveys, because postage is ordinarily the same, regardless of whether the respondent is across the street or across the country. The concentration of the population is very important for personal interview surveys because the fieldworkers can spend more time and effort traveling from one respondent to the next than on the actual task of interviewing. Toll charges for telephone interviewing can also be very high if respondents are geographically dispersed. Cluster sampling is a method for reducing cost and time requirements by surveying groups of respondents who are geographically close to one another.

Travel economy

An example of a typical situation where cluster sampling can be used effectively may clarify the technique. Suppose a company would like to survey potential buyers of their product within a single area. The sample units are households, and a detailed street map of the entire area will provide the sample frame. Fifty-two consumers are to be interviewed. Individual households might be selected at random based on their location on the map. With a design such as the one shown in the upper box of Figure 3–8, even the two respondents who are nearest to one another may be several blocks or miles apart. Some outlying respondents may require many miles of travel.

To reduce travel time and cost markedly, the researcher may decide on a clustered random sample, such as that shown in the lower box of Figure 3–8. The design might specify that

Figure 3–8   *Cluster Sampling Economy*

Unclustered Random Sample

Clustered Random Sample

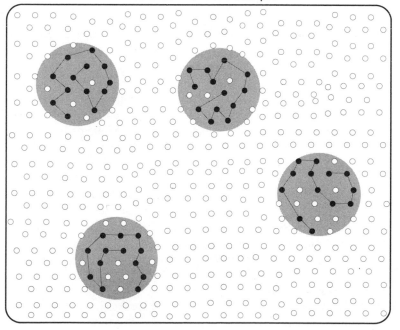

CHECKLIST 3–2

To Choose a Cluster Sample Design

1. Is the data to be collected by personal or telephone interviewing? If not, clustering isn't necessary.
2. Are the respondents spread over a wide physical or geographic area? If so, clustering may be appropriate.

3. Will travel time and costs be high, relative to the actual interviewing time? If so, cluster sampling will be economical.
4. Is the total sample size large enough to permit selecting many clusters? If not, clustering shouldn't be used.

---

each of four clusters will contain 13 respondents, all from the same neighborhood. The location of each neighborhood would be chosen at random from the map, just as an individual respondent might be selected. The interviewers would then be instructed to begin with a particular household, then move five household units in a specific (randomly determined) direction, and obtain a second interview from the sixth household. They would continue until all 13 interviews in the cluster were obtained, then travel to the next cluster location. With the use of the cluster sampling design in Figure 3–8, the driving time and travel costs would be reduced to a small fraction of those for an unclustered random sample. Checklist 3–2 identifies the conditions for selecting a clustered sample.

Telephone economy

Cluster sampling can also be used effectively to reduce costs for telephone interviewing. Rather than placing many long distance calls with relatively high toll charges, clusters can be specified within particular, randomly selected communities, area codes, or exchanges. Interviewers within those communities can then place local calls that have only small toll charges or none at all. Guidelist 3–6 outlines the steps for cluster sample specification.

Cluster sampling isn't *limited* to geographical clustering, although that's most often the reason for using such a design. Clusters might also be selected on some other basis, such as groups of consecutive records from a large computer file, rather than an *n*th name sampling design. This might be done to save time and costs associated with *passing* every individual record to select a sample from a very large file contained on different physical devices. Another situation that isn't based on geographic areas or distance is the case of cluster sampling *over time*. For example, if visitors to a certain location were to be surveyed over an extended period, the total time might be divided into clusters, such as four-hour periods, and the cluster periods during which sampling were to occur could be selected randomly. This would reduce the amount of time required of interviewers and thus might reduce data collection costs substantially.

Other economies

It's important to note those within one cluster must *not* be too close to one another or very similar to one another because they share the same location or position in space or time. If

---

GUIDELIST 3–6

For Specifying a Cluster Sample

1. Determine the degree to which those within one area are likely to be similar to one another or to interact.
2. Decide on the number of units to be *skipped* between individual units, based on similarity and interaction.
3. Consider the degree of variance that's likely to exist from one area to another.
4. Specify a minimum number of clusters that would still be large enough to sample the entire region adequately.

5. Divide the total sample size by the minimum number of clusters to obtain the number to be within each cluster.
6. Select the first or *key* unit in each cluster on a random basis.
7. Determine the procedure for moving from the key unit to others within the cluster, maintaining random selection.

---

there's strong interaction among those in the same cluster, or if those within a cluster are markedly more similar to one another than are those from different clusters, responses within a cluster would be redundant. Estimates of population variance would be erroneous and statistical inference would be illegitimate. The clusters should also be small enough so many areas are surveyed. If only 3 clusters of 100 respondents each were specified, the design would be faulty and the data likely to be biased. If 30 clusters of 10 households each were specified, there's much less chance that most or all would be atypical of the entire region than if 3 clusters of 100 were used.

Quota Sampling

There are often situations where a stratified sample would be most desirable, but the sample frame doesn't indicate the strata membership of the sampling units. If the data can be collected with interviews, a quota sample may be the best solution to this problem. When a quota sample is employed, it's advisable to use a random sampling technique and to specify a stratified sample, as described earlier. The need to *qualify* potential respondents is the major factor that distinguishes a *quota* sample from others. When the sample frame doesn't indicate strata membership, the interviewers don't know the stratum or group to which a potential respondent belongs. Thus, interviewers are assigned a *quota*—a given number of people from each stratum. The interviewers are instructed to contact potential respondents and ask *qualifying* questions before beginning the inquiry itself. If the interviewers need a respondent for the stratum to which the person belongs, they continue with the interview. If they don't need a respondent for that particular stratum, they politely terminate the interview with an explanation, then continue to contact other potential respondents until they identify one belonging to one of the strata that still requires another respondent.

Interviewers may not always need to ask qualifying questions. They may be able to

---

GUIDELIST 3–7

For Designing a Quota Sample

1. Select the variable(s) or characteristic(s) on which to base or define the quotas, just as with stratification.
2. Use combinations of variables to define quotas carefully and be sure it's economical to locate such respondents.
3. Estimate the variance that's likely to exist among individuals within each quota category and the variation to be expected between quota categories.
4. Decide on the level of confidence required for each quota category based on the information requirements.
5. Specify the sample size for each quota category to provide the desired confidence level for each.
6. Provide instructions for interviewers to qualify respondents by strata membership and assign individual or group quotas to interviewers.

---

identify membership when they see or hear the respondent. For example, if the quota is based on sex, both telephone and personal interviewers need only see the people or hear their voices. With stratification variables such as age, employment status, occupation, and the like, interviewers have to ask the potential respondents about their status before they're accepted as qualified.

Quota sampling can also be based on observation or questioning about some incidence of behavior. For example, stratification might be based on whether a shopper makes a purchase or not, or buys brand X, brand Y, or brand Z. Quota specifications may be based on virtually anything that can be observed by the interviewer or ascertained quickly with a few questions. The quota sample design procedure is outlined in Guidelist 3–7.

Economy is the principal advantage of quota sampling designs. This technique can often be nearly as economical for stratified sampling where the sample frame indicates strata membership. On the other hand, if the sample isn't designed properly, quota sampling can become exceedingly expensive. This is because it may require very many contacts to identify those in the most obscure strata. For example, telephone interviewers may have to call many thousands of people before finding "a black, Protestant woman over 70 who drinks more than a pint of sour mash whisky a day." Such a strange quota assignment may sound bizarre, but it can arise by combining quotas on race, religion, age, and consumption habits. Combined quota variables must be used with care.

Special Designs

There are many very acceptable variations of the sampling designs discussed above. Such special sampling procedures are used to cope with problems or achieve special objectives. Researchers are encouraged to handle such unusual problems by combining some of the techniques or devising new ones that will be effective. There are no hard-and-fast rules, so

> **GUIDELIST 3–8**
>
> *For Developing Special Sampling Designs*
>
> **1.** Inspect the conventional designs to determine if any might be modified or extended for the special case.
>
> **2.** Attempt to combine designs, such as clustering and stratification, to meet special needs.
>
> **3.** Remember that random sampling can be done over time, entities, or occurrences, as well as over sample units.
>
> **4.** Be certain that any special sampling design doesn't violate random selection or distort variance estimates.

long as the sample is random and sufficiently free from sampling error and bias. When selecting or creating special sample designs, the researcher should continually seek the answer to two questions: Will the design being considered violate random selection resulting in bias? Will it seriously distort the inferences and estimates of variance among the population? If either is likely to result, the design should be abandoned in favor of another or modified until these two prime requisites are met. The main considerations for choosing and creating special sampling designs are listed in Guidelist 3–8.

SAMPLE SELECTION PROCEDURE

Once the basic sampling design has been chosen and the sample size has been specified, the task of actually selecting respondents remains. In some cases, such as mail surveys and most telephone surveys, the actual selection of sampling units from the sample frame will be done entirely in the central office. In other situations, such as telephone or personal interview surveys that use *quotas,* the actual selection will be made at the point and time of contact with potential respondents. In those cases, the selection procedure should be specified and translated into a series of instructions for interviewers. The potential sources of bias and the guidelines for avoiding selection bias are identified later in this chapter. The actual instructions for telephone or fieldworkers to qualify respondents and fill their quotas during data collection are discussed in Chapter 8.

Random Selection Methods

Random sample selection sounds easy, but it's difficult in actual practice. Without careful adherence to a well-specified procedure, systematic bias is likely to creep in undetected. The procedure chosen has to be tailored to the demands of the individual survey situation. No one procedure is generally preferable to another. Guidelines for selecting random samples are shown in Guidelist 3–9.

GUIDELIST 3–9

For Selecting a Random Sample

1. For *n*th name sampling, divide the number in the population by the number to be sampled for the value of *n*.
2. Randomly pick the first unit for an *n*th name sample from the first one through *n* entries of the frame.
3. Random number generators often produce near-perfect random lists, usually without duplicates and ordered from lowest to highest.

4. When a seed number is required by a random number generator program, it should be picked at random.
5. In Appendix B, Table B–1 contains a random number table and Example B–1 contains instructions for selecting random numbers from the table.
6. When units from the sample frame can be identified on physical objects, mechanical devices can be used to create a random sampling list.

*N*th name sampling

When the sample frame consists of a list of sample units, the most common method of selecting a random sample from the list is to select every *n*th name. *N* is calculated by dividing the sample size into the number on the list. If a sample of 200 were to be drawn from a list of 10,000, every 50th name would be picked. Technically, this is systematic, rather than *pure* random sampling, but it's completely legitimate.

When *n*th name sampling is used, the researcher shouldn't begin counting with the *first* name on the list. Those who happen to be the first on a list, such as the first name on the page of a telephone directory, are contacted much more often than others, because of their position on the list. In the example, the researcher should begin with one of the first 50 names. The actual starting point should be picked *randomly*. If the number drawn happened to be 37, the first unit for the sample would be the 37th name on the list, the second, the 87th, and so on.

Random number generators

There are many computational routines and computer programs that generate lists of random numbers. When a random number generator is used, it will usually be possible to discard duplicate numbers and sort them in sequence from lowest to highest. The units to be included in the sample would then be picked from the sample frame according to the random list.

If the sample frame consists of a computer file, many database management programs and other computer routines can be instructed to select a random sample of a certain size. If so, the sample list can be printed or displayed directly and the researcher is relieved of the task of making the actual selection.

Tables of random numbers

A series of numbers can be selected from Table B–1 in Appendix B or any such table of random numbers. Example B–1 describes how numbers are chosen from a random number table. Once the list of random numbers has been selected, it's used in exactly the same way as computer-generated random numbers.

Physical selection methods

There are several mechanical devices to select numbers randomly. One such device is commonly used to select *bingo* numbers, and others use small balls, cubes, tags, and the like. These physical random selection methods are quite acceptable, providing the selection is *truly* random—that every unit has an equal probability of being selected.

Sample Selection Bias

Selecting sample units from the sample frame on a random basis may appear to be simple and easy, but it's often difficult to select them on a *purely* random basis. No systematic patterns must evolve. Extraneous sampling factors that affect survey results produce systematic bias and reduce the validity of the data. Any factors that would change the probability of any one unit or type of unit being selected must be ruled out.

Sampling bias sources

The way the sampling units are selected may lead to overselecting or underselecting respondents of a certain type. If so, their responses wouldn't accurately represent those of the entire population. For example, suppose a survey were conducted to measure how satisfied or content people are. If all the fieldworkers were quite shy and would only interview people who looked like they were very friendly, the data would reflect two things: How satisfied people in general really are, and also the *positive* effects of picking people who look friendly and happy. Selecting only friendly people to interview would produce a bias in the direction of greater satisfaction. The greater the bias, the lower the validity of the data. Eight sources of sampling bias are identified in Guidelist 3–10. The sources listed here are the most common, but they don't constitute an exhaustive list. Every survey is subject to other, specific sources of bias, as well. The sample selection process, itself, should be examined carefully to identify any additional sources of bias.

Controlling bias

If the sample is to be selected *at random,* the probability that any one respondent will be selected must be exactly equal to the probability of selecting any other. For instance, if 10 percent of the population is to be sampled, then the probability of randomly selecting any one respondent is 1 in 10, or 10 percent. Any factor that alters that probability, either increasing or decreasing it for some respondents, will create *bias* in the selection process. It's important to protect against factors that bias random selection. The statistical inferences about the population depend on random selection and the equal probability of selecting each sample unit. There's a danger the presence of serious, unrecognized biases may lead to inaccurate estimates and errors when making interpretations and drawing conclusions.

Even when a *convenience,* rather than a random, sample is to be used, it's still necessary to avoid any unnecessary sources of bias. The more closely the convenience sample selection procedure approaches a random selection, the more valid the survey results will be.

Accessibility bias. For many surveys, the actual selection of units takes place in the field,

---

GUIDELIST 3–10

For Identifying Sources of Sampling Bias

1. *Accessibility bias*. Some respondents are more readily selected or included in the sample so they're overselected.

2. *Affinity bias*. Respondents who are most attractive to the interviewer are more often selected, so they're overrepresented.

3. *Cluster bias*. The respondents selected are too closely clustered, so they're more similar to one another than to the population as a whole.

4. *Nonresponse bias*. Respondents of a certain type more often refuse to participate, so they're underrepresented.

5. *Order bias*. The order of respondent selection overselects or underselects those of a certain type because they're in a certain place.

6. *Self-selection bias*. Respondents are allowed to *volunteer* and those of a certain type more often do so, so they're overrepresented.

7. *Termination bias*. Respondents of a certain type more often prematurely withdraw their participation in a continuing task, so they're underrepresented.

8. *Visibility bias*. Some types of respondents are more easily identified or recognized than others, so they're more often selected.

---

rather than at the survey headquarters. If so, some respondents may be more easily reached than others. Fieldworkers tend to pick the most readily available respondents. When all units aren't equally accessible, controls and incentives are necessary to ensure there will be no overrepresentation or underrepresentation of some types of respondents.

Affinity bias. When the selection of individual respondents is performed in the field by interviewers, there may be affinity bias. This is especially true if the selection plan fails to identify *precisely* which individuals are to be picked, so there's some choice on the part of the fieldworkers. Interviewers tend to select certain types of respondents because they have an affinity for them. For example, they'll ordinarily ignore those who are:

— apparently very busy or hurried,

— crabby, grouchy, or unpleasant in appearance,

— in groups or in the company of others,

— adults caring for small children,

— physically handicapped or impaired,

— wearing unusual or bizarre dress, or

— otherwise different in any way.

By contrast, they may tend to approach and include people who are:

— of the same social class as they are,

— of the same age and sex as they are,

— more leisurely in their movements,

— more friendly or cooperative, or

— physically attractive.

When respondents are selected on the basis of their affinity to the interviewer, bias is introduced into the process. This affinity bias can be avoided by very precise specification of who is to be selected and contacted and by strict supervision and enforcement of the instructions to fieldworkers.

Cluster bias. Some sampling designs include clusters of respondents, rather than individuals. Cluster sampling is legitimate and often very practical. Cluster bias occurs when the clusters are specified too closely. If respondents from 10 households next door to one another were interviewed, that may lead to bias because of two things: *membership* and *interaction*. People of the same type or status tend to live and work near one another. Those who live near one another are likely to interact, sharing their attitudes and opinions with one another. This tendency for consensus formation would bias the survey results because units within one cluster would provide redundant responses and there would be less variance among those in one cluster than among the population as a whole. Respondents in geographic or sequential clusters must not be too close to one another or be directly interconnected. The responses from each individual must be completely independent of those from all others. To obtain that independence, cluster designs should specify enough distance so there's no connection between individuals within a cluster.

Nonresponse bias. Nonresponse may be *independent* of the survey content, or it may *interact* with it. If people decide to respond to a survey or not to respond, *purely* on a random basis, then the nonresponse will be independent of the survey content and there won't be nonresponse bias. In such a case, the response rate need only estimate and include a sufficient number to be contacted, so the data collection yields an adequate number of respondents to satisfy the sample size requirements. The selection of respondents would remain a random selection.

Unfortunately, nonresponse is almost never completely independent of the survey issues. Interaction between survey issues and nonresponse can be direct or indirect. With direct interaction, the very things to be measured affect whether or not people will respond to a survey. Suppose a survey were conducted to measure purchase probability for a new consumer product. Those who have a need for the product are more likely to respond to the survey than are those who see no need for it. The latter group is likely to notice the topic, conclude they have no interest, and discard the questionnaire or refuse the interview. The survey results would portray the product as much more popular and with much greater potential for acceptance than actually exists in the population as a whole.

There may also be indirect interaction, mediated by the demographic or psychographic status of some respondent groups. For example, those in some demographic categories have more time than others. Elderly, retired respondents often feel less time pressure than younger people who are fully employed. They may respond in greater numbers than others. There may not be a direct interaction between the issues measured by the survey and the willingness to respond, but there's an indirect interaction. If those who are retired are *both* more likely to respond *and* more likely to answer in a particular way, this would be a serious source of nonresponse bias.

It's almost impossible to avoid nonresponse bias entirely, and so some such bias must usually be tolerated. It's the researcher's responsibility to assess the degree of direct and indirect interaction that may exist between the survey issues and topics, on the one hand, and the propensity to respond, on the other. At times, it may be virtually impossible to predict the direction of the effect: whether a particular attitude or opinion would tend to increase or decrease the response. When there are no clear indications of the direction of the bias, it may be advisable to conduct a pretest or pilot study that focuses directly on the issue of nonresponse. Another alternative is to use dual data collection methods. Nonresponse is likely to be very high and the effects can be quite severe for mail surveys. So some survey projects use a mail survey to obtain a sufficient number of respondents within the budget or resource constraints, while also doing a limited number of interviews. By comparing the results from the two types of respondents, the mail response results can often be adjusted or modified to compensate for the nonresponse bias that's detected and measured.

Order bias. Most lists of the population that serve as sample frames contain sample units that are listed or appear in an orderly pattern. A telephone directory lists names in alphabetical order. A list of credit card holders may be in sequence from the earliest to the latest applicants. The selection routine has to take into account any such order in the sample frame. The sequential order of the units shouldn't be allowed to increase or decrease the probability that any particular unit or block of units are selected for the sample.

Self-selection bias. Some sampling designs permit the self-selection of respondents. The most common type of self-selection occurs with a mail survey, where respondents can easily refuse or fail to respond. This *nonresponse* bias was discussed earlier. Aside from that kind of bias, self-selection can occur whenever respondents have a choice of attending or participating. To avoid self-selection bias, the researcher may need to deemphasize or reduce potential respondents' perceptions that they can freely volunteer or easily decline. While they can't be coerced or forced to participate, it's often possible to give the *appearance* that participation is mandatory—that those who decline will suffer some cost or be disqualified from receiving something of benefit or value to them.

Termination bias. Some personal and telephone interviews take a lot of time to complete. The respondents who are the most cooperative, patient, or submissive will rarely terminate prematurely. By contrast, less cooperative, more impatient, or aggressive respondents may terminate the interview prematurely more frequently than others. If so, they will be underrepresented in the sample—a potential source of bias. The same precautions that are used to avoid *self-selection* also apply to this source of bias.

Visibility bias. Often some types of units in the population are more visible than others. If the telephone directory serves as the sample frame, those who have unlisted or unpublished numbers and those without telephones wouldn't be included. The researcher has to be sure that such frames or lists are complete. Similarly, some potential respondents are more visible to field interviewers than others. For instance, some shoppers exiting a store may take a different route from most others. Those conducting *intercept* interviews might easily neglect them. The researcher has to be sure the selection system doesn't pick the more visible units at a higher rate than those which are more obscure. Checklist 3–3 contains the key questions to ask to avoid all the main sources of bias.

Science and Art of Sampling

While there are scientific principles and statistical procedures associated with sampling, the task of designing a sample, choosing a sample size, and selecting respondents remains largely an art. Researchers designing survey samples should follow the guidelines and apply the recommendations, but ultimately they must be somewhat creative and willing to trust their own judgment.

CHECKLIST 3–3

To Avoid Sample Selection Bias

1. Are some units in the population more visible than others? If so, be sure the more visible units are selected in the same proportion as the more obscure units.

2. Are the units in the sample frame presented in systematic order? If so, the sequence must not alter the probability of selection of some units over others.

3. Are some respondents more accessible than others? When they are, controls and incentives must be used to obtain equal proportions of those with high and low accessibility.

4. Are sample units clustered, either deliberately or accidentally? When clusters exist, there must be no more interaction or similarity within clusters than between them.

5. Will fieldworkers have more affinity for some respondents than others? If so, incentives and controls must be used to avoid overselecting those with greater affinity.

6. Is there an opportunity for respondents to select themselves or decline? If so, the opportunity should be reduced or concealed from potential respondents.

7. Will there be a high proportion of nonrespondents? If so, there should be as little interaction as possible between nonresponse and the issues being surveyed.

8. Are some types of respondents *both* more or less likely to respond *and* likely to respond in a certain way? If so, the nonresponse bias must be reduced or controlled.

SUMMARY

Sampling Design and Size Determination

A. Strive for reliability and validity. Check each decision to determine if it will increase sampling error or introduce a systematic bias into the data.

B. Identify components quite precisely. The population, sample units, and sample frame must be described with clarity and precision.

C. Determine sample size carefully. Consider confidence required, population variance, analysis techniques, and the resources available for the project.

D. Depend upon random sampling. The greater the deviation from random selection, the less legitimate and accurate the statistical analysis and reports will be.

E. Evaluate design refinements. Use stratification, clustering, quota sampling, and special designs to increase reliability and decrease costs.

F. Use trial when necessary. A pilot survey or sequential sampling will indicate the appropriate sample size if it can't be determined in advance.

G. Identify sources of bias. Be aware of the major sources of bias, but constantly inspect the design to be sure additional sources of bias aren't introduced.

H. Be creative and confident. Sampling design and size determination are more of an art than a science!

PART II

Developing Survey Instruments

Chapter 4

Composing Questions

THE CORE OF THE SURVEY

The questions asked of respondents are the ultimate core of the survey project. The entire effort is directed toward inquiry, and the questions are the elements that perform the actual interrogation. The reliability and validity of survey results depend on the way that every aspect of the survey is planned and executed, but the questions addressed to the respondents are the most essential component. Their performance ordinarily has a more profound effect on the survey results than has any other single element of the survey. Thus, it's vitally important that this fundamental task of composing the questions be done carefully and properly.

This and the following two chapters form a trio because they're all devoted to the broad topic of asking questions and obtaining answers. The more general principles and practices regarding question composition will be discussed first in this chapter, because they apply to virtually all types of questions that might be asked in a survey questionnaire. Then, the most common mistakes and threats to reliability and validity are identified and recommendations for avoiding them are provided. Several more technical aspects of writing questions are also discussed, and a wide variety of examples are presented. The scaling techniques used with many survey questions are presented and discussed in Chapter 5. Chapter 6 contains guidelines for construction of the survey instrument, including question sequence, the questionnaire structure and format, and the introduction and instructions to respondents. While studying the material concerning question composition presented here, it may be useful to refer to the following two chapters to see how the questions relate to the scales and how they fit into the questionnaire as a whole.

Basic Attributes of Questions

Effective survey questions have three important attributes: focus, brevity, and simplicity. The questions should focus directly on the issue or topic specified in the statement of information needs. They should be as short or brief as possible while still conveying the meaning. The questions should be expressed as simply and clearly as they can be.

Focus

Every question on a questionnaire should focus directly on a single, specific issue or topic. This appears to be very obvious, but in practice it isn't as easily achieved as it might seem. Example 4–1 shows three sets of questions. The first of each set lacks focus, and the second is focused directly on the issue or topic in each case. In the first set, the researcher seeks to measure purchase preference. It would be a mistake to ask which respondents liked best, because they may *like* a very elegant and expensive brand, but be unwilling to buy it because of its price. In the second example, asking when the respondent usually goes to work also lacks the necessary focus. It doesn't indicate the point from which the respondent "goes" to work, nor does it ask for a time of day. Thus, some respondents might say, "Just as soon as I get to the shop" or "It depends on how much traffic I run into." The third example listed is supposed to determine voting preference for a particular office. The first question of the set is focused on party preference, rather than the individual choice of a candidate. The two need not be the same.

The best way to be sure that a question is focused directly on the issue at hand is to ask as precisely as possible exactly what the sponsor needs to know. Each of the correct examples shown is a direct expression of the information need; they focus directly on one issue.

Brevity

There are several reasons for keeping survey questions as brief as possible. The longer the questions, the more difficult the response task will be. Short questions are less subject to error on the part of both interviewers and respondents. When questions become too long and cumbersome, respondents are likely to forget the first part of the question by the time they read or hear the last part. Also, long questions are more likely to lack focus and clarity.

EXAMPLE 4–1

The Focus of the Question

Wrong: Which brand do you like the best?
Right: Which of these brands are you most likely to buy?

Wrong: When do you usually go to work?
Right: What time do you ordinarily leave home for work?

Wrong: Are you going to vote Democratic or Republican?
Right: Which candidate will you vote for on election day?

> ## EXAMPLE 4–2
>
> ### *The Brevity of the Question*
>
> **Wrong:** Can you tell me how many children you have, whether they're girls or boys, and how old they are?
> **Right:**   What's the age and sex of each of your children?
>
> **Wrong:** If you own one or more automobiles, please list the year and the make of each one, starting with the newest one?
> **Right:**   Please list the year and make of each car you own?
>
> **Wrong:** When was the last time that you went to the doctor for a physical examination on your own or because you had to?
> **Right:**   How many months ago was your last physical examination?

In Example 4–2, the brief form of each question is more likely to provide reliable data than is the longer form.

If a person is asked the brief form of the first question, the respondent might reply, "I have a nine-year-old boy and a four-year-old girl." The interviewer would know the age of the boy and that of the girl. If the longer version of the first example were used and the respondent could remember everything that was asked, the response might be, "I have two children. A boy and a girl. They're four and nine years old." The interviewer might either assume the boy was four and the girl nine, or else the fieldworker would have to ask which child was which age. In the second set of questions, there's no need for the respondent to put the cars in sequence because that can be done by the analyst later. The item doesn't have to be conditioned on car ownership because those who have no car will leave it blank. For the last pair, the brief form is more straightforward and the longer form would receive answers in weeks, months, years, or by date.

Clarity

The meaning of the question must be completely clear to all respondents. Clarity demands that virtually everyone interprets the question in exactly the same way. In Example 4–3, the correct version of the question in each pair has only one interpretation while the incorrect version has two or more.

In the first incorrect example shown, the phrase "What do you have to say . . ." can be interpreted in different ways. The phrase might be perceived as asking, "What do you have to say (to me, right now,) . . ." If that were the case, the respondent is likely to indicate how much he or she agreed with the selection of charities, rather than indicating his or her own degree of influence.

In the second example, the researcher intends to measure the proportion of storage space used by each head of household. The correct version of the question makes that clear, but the incorrect version doesn't. There's nothing in the wording to indicate that the proportion of each person's space should be indicated, and the respondents are likely to assume the

EXAMPLE 4–3

The Clarity of the Question

Wrong: What do you have to say about the charities that your church contributes to?
Right: How much influence do you, yourself, have on which charities your church contributes to?

Wrong: About how much of the storage space in your home do you and your spouse use?
Right: What proportion of the storage space in your home is used for your things and what's used for your spouse's?

Wrong: Ordinarily, do you take aspirin when you feel some discomfort or when you feel actual pain?
Right: Do you usually take aspirin as soon as you feel some discomfort, or only when you feel actual pain?

question concerns the use of storage space by both spouses, combined. Thus, they're likely to respond with such a statement as, "We use all of the storage space we have!"

The third example is supposed to present a dichotomy. It assumes that the respondent does use aspirin, and that the individual *either* takes aspirin at the first sign of discomfort *or else* waits until there's the perception of actual pain. The dichotomy is lost in the unclear version of the question, and respondents might simply respond, "Yes, I do." The researcher wouldn't learn at which point the aspirin was consumed, and such data would be useless.

When constructing questions, the researcher must ask again and again: Does this question *focus* precisely on the issue? Is this as *brief* as the question can be stated? Is it completely *clear* what's being asked? If the researcher returns several times to questions that were written earlier to consider the issues outlined in Checklist 4–1, he or she will ordinarily detect some defects and find several questions that can be improved. It's also advisable to have one or more other people check each question for focus, brevity, and clarity. Checking one's own work is difficult because the writer knows what's intended, but others can only approach the questions strictly on their content and wording.

Expressing the Questions

Survey questions are, of course, expressed in words. To obtain meaningful answers, questions must be expressed with the appropriate words. In addition, the words must be combined and arranged in a way that's appropriate to the respondents. Thus, both vocabulary and grammar are important when forming survey questions.

Vocabulary

If the words used in a question aren't in the vocabulary of some respondents, they won't understand what's being asked. This will introduce error or bias in the data. Individuals have three levels of vocabulary. Respondents have a *core* vocabulary of words with which they're very familiar. These are words they use in common speech. They also have a wider vocabulary of words that they recognize when they hear or read them. They seldom, if ever, use

---

CHECKLIST 4-1

To Construct Effective Questions

1. Does the question focus directly on the issue or topic to be measured? If not, rewrite the item to deal with the issue as directly as possible.
2. Is the question stated as briefly as it can be? If the item is more than a few words, it may be too long and should be restated more briefly.

3. Is the question expressed as clearly and simply as it can be? If the meaning won't be clear to virtually every respondent, the item should be restructured.

---

such words in common speech, but they have a fairly good understanding of what they mean. Then, of course, there are many other words in the language that individuals don't recognize or understand. Such words have little or no meaning for them.

The researcher should use words that are in the *core* vocabulary of virtually *all* respondents. The reason can be explained very logically. *Comprehension of very pedestrian vocabulary is universal, while that of sophisticated vocabulary is peculiar to the elite.* The reader may well understand the last sentence, but most respondents from the general public wouldn't! Nor would anyone use such a sentence in common speech. The sentence should have been expressed this way: *Everybody understands common words, but only very well-educated people understand words that are seldom used in speech.* The conclusion is obvious. If common words from the core vocabulary of the least sophisticated respondents are used in the questions, everyone will understand. If bigger words or words that are seldom used in speech are used in the questions, many won't know what they mean or what's being asked. The researcher has everything to gain by using simple, core vocabulary and avoiding difficult wording, as shown in Example 4-4.

EXAMPLE 4-4

The Use of Core Vocabulary

Wrong: Are you cognizant of all the concepts to be elucidated?
Right: Do you know about all the ideas that will be explained?

Wrong: With what frequency have you experienced this of late?
Right: How many times have you had this happen recently?

Wrong: What emotions were evoked by perceiving the spectacle?
Right: What kinds of feelings did you have when you saw it all?

EXAMPLE 4–5

The Use of Compound Sentences

Wrong: What would you do when you had only a few things to buy and there were a lot of people in the checkout line?

Right: Suppose you have only a few things to buy. There are a lot of people in the checkout line. What would you do?

Wrong: How do you work it out when you want one thing and your spouse wants another and you both feel very strongly about it?

Right: How do you settle disagreements with your spouse when you both have strong feelings about it?

Wrong: If you didn't have a reservation ahead of time and you found out that the only seats that you could get were at the very top of the upper balcony, what would you do?

Right: What would you do if the only seats available at show time were at the top of the upper balcony?

Sometimes people who write survey questions unconsciously want to appear well-educated or sophisticated, so they use fancy words and complex sentences. Also, many people were taught as students to use a special vocabulary or sentence structure for writing, one different from their speech. In either case, there's a temptation to use a vocabulary that's beyond the core vocabulary of many respondents. The researcher should keep firmly in mind that the ultimate measure of sophistication in survey research is to generate data that are reliable and valid—data that are free from error and bias. That can best be done by using simple, core vocabulary.

Grammar

When writing survey questions, arranging the sentences in the right way is as important as using the right vocabulary. There are four basic kinds of sentence structure: simple, compound, complex, and compound-complex. Simple sentences have a subject and predicate, and sometimes an object or complement. Compound sentences are just two simple sentences linked together by a conjunction. Complex sentences are simple sentences with a dependent clause taking the place of a word, and compound-complex sentences are a combination of the two. The most effective questions are simple sentences. When a simple sentence can't be used, a complex sentence may be required. Compound sentences and compound-complex sentences should be broken down into simple and complex sentences. Three examples of effective and confusing questions are shown in Example 4–5. The correct phrasing in the first example broke the compound sentence into three simple ones. In the second pair, the correct expression of the question uses different wording to avoid the compound-complex sentence structure. The third correct example eliminated several superfluous words.

The choice of both vocabulary and grammar for expressing survey questions should be based on what the *least sophisticated* respondents will understand. The basic rules are contained in Guidelist 4–1.

GUIDELIST 4–1

For Expressing Questions Correctly

1. Use only core vocabulary—the words and phrases people use in casual speech.
2. Limit the vocabulary so the least sophisticated respondent would be familiar with the words.
3. Use simple sentences where possible, and complex sentences only when they're actually required.
4. Use two or more short, simple sentences rather than one compound or compound-complex sentence.
5. Change long, dependent clauses in sentences to words or short phrases where possible.

INSTRUMENTATION BIAS AND ERROR

The way questions are expressed can all too often introduce systematic bias, random error, or both. Even questions expressed with focus, brevity, and clarity may jeopardize reliability and/or validity. Use of the proper vocabulary and grammar doesn't guarantee that they'll be free from bias or error. Consequently, several specific types or forms of instrumentation bias and error and the means of avoiding them must be noted.

Unstated criteria

If the criteria by which respondents must judge some issue or respond to some question aren't completely obvious, the criteria must be stated in the question. If an item might be judged by multiple standards and the criteria aren't explicitly stated, some respondents will use one set of criteria and others will use another.

In Example 4–6, there's no clear indication of the criterion in the incorrect question. Thus, some people may respond based on their own needs and others may consider what the stores need to do to win customers in general. The correct question clearly indicates the criterion to be the personal preference of the respondent only.

EXAMPLE 4–6

The Use of Unstated Criteria

Wrong: How important is it for stores to carry a large variety of different brands of this product?
Right: How important is it to you that the store you shop at carries a large variety of different brands?

EXAMPLE 4–7

The Use of an Inapplicable Question

Wrong: How long does it take you to find a parking place after you arrive at the plant?
Right: If you drive to work, how long does it take you to find a parking place after you arrive at the plant?

Inapplicable questions

The questions must be applicable to all respondents in the sense that they can reply, based on their own experience or condition. In Example 4–7, those who walk to work, ride a bike or motorcycle, or take a bus or cab would often indicate that parking was no problem to them. The researcher in this case wants to include only those people who drive to work. Thus, to include those who don't drive would provide biased results. The data obtained from the incorrect question would indicate a less severe problem or need than actually existed among those who drive.

Example containment

When the question contains an example that consists of a response alternative or identifies a class or type of response alternative, it's likely to interject bias. Many respondents may choose or include the example but fail to include others because the example brings that particular response or type of response to mind. In Example 4–8, the incorrect question would lead many to identify toasters, mixers, or blenders. They're likely to exclude such appliances as vacuum cleaners, power tools, and hair dryers. It's important to identify the entire class of alternatives and avoid examples that are among the possible choices for the respondents.

Overdemanding recall

The researcher must not assume that respondents will recall their behavior or feelings over an extended period. Often the topics or issues of the survey are very important to those conducting the project, so the researcher assumes they're equally important and memorable to respondents. That's rarely the case.

EXAMPLE 4–8

The Use of Examples in Questions

Wrong: What small appliances, such as countertop appliances, have you purchased in the past month?
Right: Aside from major appliances, what other smaller appliances have you bought in the past month?

EXAMPLE 4–9

The Use of Overdemanding Recall

Wrong: How many times did you go out on a date with your spouse before you were married?
Right: How many months were you dating your spouse before you were married?

The first question in Example 4–9 assumes that respondents would remember the actual number of times they had gone out with their spouse before their marriage. Very few would recall that. Yet, many wouldn't want to admit that they did not remember, so most respondents would probably estimate the number. Thus, there would be a large amount of error in the data. By contrast, most married respondents are likely to have good recollection of both the day when they met their spouse and the date of their marriage. These are fairly important anniversaries for most married couples. Thus, virtually all could report the number of months they were dating before their marriage.

Overgeneralizations

There are times when it may be appropriate and acceptable to ask respondents for generalizations. When a survey question seeks a generalization, it should represent a policy, strategy, or habitual pattern of the respondents, rather than specific behavior. Whenever specific incidents can be identified, the survey question should be specific. In Example 4–10, the incorrect item asks the respondents to generalize about their behavior. The question is much too general, as well. It doesn't state whether the respondent is to use the immediate past as a frame of reference, go back well into the distant past, or indicate expectations for the future. By contrast, the proper wording of the item includes the past 10 incidents of the action. They would ordinarily be easily recalled by virtually all respondents, and the data are far more precise and accurate, so error is reduced and reliability is improved greatly.

Overspecificity

A survey question is overly specific when it asks for an actual or precise response that the respondent is unlikely to know or unable to express. In Example 4–11, virtually all respondents will be able to indicate their *policy* concerning the action in broad terms. Few respondents could report an exact number of times they had behaved in that way. In addition, the incorrect example would be of little value in many cases, because there's no *base* number of opportunities. Two people might both report they read 30 such explanations. One may have visited only 30 exhibits and read the plaque on each, while the other may have visited 300 and only read 1 in 10. They would appear from the data to be identical, yet their policies toward this issue would be very different, indeed. If the information needs were concerned with the policies, the data would lack validity.

EXAMPLE 4–10

The Use of Overgeneralizations

Wrong: When you buy "fast food," what percentage of the time do you order each of the following type of food?
Right: Of the last 10 times you bought "fast food," how many times did you eat each type of food?

Overemphasis

If the wording of a question is overemphatic, it's likely to introduce bias by calling for a particular type of response. When it's necessary to describe some condition in the question, it's advisable to use words that lean toward understating, rather than overstating, the condition. Respondents are then free to reach their own conclusions about the degree of severity. If the condition is described in overemphatic terms, a judgment or conclusion is imposed on the respondents. Such words as *catastrophe* or *tragedy* suggest that a potent remedy is required, while words such as *predicament* or *mishap* don't. An example of such a case is presented in Example 4–12.

The correct and incorrect examples are identical except for the last word in each: *crisis* versus *problem*. The use of the word *crisis* implies a conclusion on the part of the researcher. In addition, it's always desirable to avoid or to end a *crisis* as quickly and completely as possible. On the other hand, a *problem* isn't something that necessarily requires immediate or dramatic action. Each question must be examined carefully to avoid wording that overemphasizes or overstates the condition. Words that are overly dramatic or constitute a conclusion must be avoided.

Ambiguity of wording

Many words and phrases designate different things for different people. Often those who write questions are totally unaware that others may have a completely different understanding of the term. In Example 4–13, the researcher is referring to the evening meal. Those from the eastern or western areas of the country eat breakfast, lunch, and *dinner*. In many areas

---

EXAMPLE 4–11

The Use of Overspecificity

Wrong: When you visited the museum, how many times did you read the plaques that explain what the exhibit contained?
Right: When you visited the museum, how often did you read the plaques that explain what the exhibit contained? Would you say always, often, sometimes, rarely, or never?

EXAMPLE 4–12

The Use of Overemphasis

Wrong: Would you favor increasing taxes to cope with the current fiscal crisis?
Right: Would you favor increasing taxes to cope with the current fiscal problem?

---

of the Midwest, people eat breakfast, *dinner,* and supper. A researcher native to New York or Los Angeles might be shocked and surprised by the results if the incorrect example were used in a national survey. To avoid such ambiguity, virtually every questionable word or phrase must be checked carefully to be sure that it has a common meaning for everyone in the survey sample.

Double-barreled questions

When two questions are contained within one item, the item is known as a double-barreled question. In Example 4–14, the incorrect item actually asks two questions: Do you take vitamins, and, if so, do you take them to avoid sickness? Those who take vitamins regularly but for some reason other than to avoid sickness would be in a quandary as to *how to* respond. To obtain the required data, the researcher should first ask if the respondents take the action. A second question might be expressed as in the correct example, or it might be *conditioned* on an affirmative response to the first item. Thus, it might be stated: "If so, why do you do so?"

Probably the most common form of the double-barreled question includes both the action and the reason or motive in the same item. This is certainly not the only form of double-barreled question, however. Simply asking about two things at one time also creates a double-barreled item. For example, "Do you often get headaches and stomachaches?" Those who get one but not the other would be puzzled by that item. Consider the question, "Do you and your family often go to the movies?" Singles who enjoy the movies could not answer accurately, nor could respondents who do one thing when their family does another. The key to detecting double-barreled questions is to determine if part of the item might be true and part false.

EXAMPLE 4–13

The Use of Ambiguous Words

Wrong: About what time do you ordinarily eat dinner?
Right: About what time do you ordinarily dine in the evening?

EXAMPLE 4–14

The Use of Double-Barreled Questions

Wrong: Do you regularly take vitamins to avoid getting sick?
Right: Do you regularly take vitamins? Why or why not?

Leading questions

When questions lead the respondents to a particular answer, they create a very strong bias and often result in data that are completely invalid. The incorrect question in Example 4–15 would result in the identification of much greater danger than would the use of the correct form. Respondents are actually being led to identify dangers, while the information requirements seek only to measure the degree to which respondents, themselves, perceive danger.

In many situations, those conducting the survey are hired by a sponsor. Some sponsors may underwrite the survey to prove a point or obtain certain kinds of results that are in their own best interests. Such sponsors may try to insert leading questions or insist on such wording to produce data that are favorable to their position or in their own best interests. Survey data that purport to be "independent and objective" when such leading questions are used are actually fraudulent. This applies as well to other deliberate sources of bias, such as the use of "loaded" questions. Thus, the researcher who maintains an honest reputation through ethical behavior must not allow the deliberate "rigging" of survey results. When sponsors insist on such unethical practices, the researcher is best advised to resign from the project, no matter how attractive it might otherwise appear.

Loaded questions

While leading questions direct the respondents' attention to a specific type of response or suggest an answer, loaded questions are less obvious. The loaded question includes some wording or phrase that constitutes a more subtle form of influence. Often loaded questions take the form where a "reason" for doing something is included in the item. Notice the

---

EXAMPLE 4–15

The Use of Leading Questions

Wrong: Don't you see some danger in the new policy?
Right: Do you see any danger in the new policy?

EXAMPLE 4–16

The Use of Loaded Questions

Wrong: Do you advocate a lower speed limit to save human lives?
Right: Does traffic safety require a lower speed limit?

---

phrase "to save human lives" in the incorrect question shown in Example 4–16. Saving lives is, of course, a very desirable goal. The question is phrased in such a way that those who would respond in the negative would appear not to value human life. The correct version of the question in this example is more objective. It deals directly with the issues and avoids weighting one response with the feelings or emotions associated with "life-saving" policies.

The most common sources of bias and error resulting from the composition of questions are summarized in Checklist 4–2. Some introduce a systematic bias, "skewing" the answers in one particular direction. Others lead to random error because they result in answers that might "go in any direction." Some create both bias and error. The greater the amount of error or bias that's introduced, the lower the reliability and/or validity of the survey results will be. Probably no survey question is completely free of error and bias, but the goal is to approach that as closely as possible.

SOURCES OF RESPONSE BIAS

When the questionnaire instructions, questions, scales or response options introduce bias, it's called *instrumentation bias.* The major forms of such bias were discussed in the preceding section. When bias is introduced because of the mentality or predispositions of respondents, it's called *response bias.* Those composing survey questions must consider this type of bias as well, because it can be reduced or controlled in part by the wording and sequence of questions. The many different sources of response bias can be classified in a variety of ways. Ten of the major types are listed and identified in Figure 4–1. Each of them will be discussed briefly below.

Social desirability

When personal preferences, opinions, or behavior deviate from what's socially prescribed, respondents are very prone to report what's socially acceptable, rather than their true answers. This is a serious problem, and even the most experienced researchers find it a difficult problem to overcome. Some issues, such as sexual deviation, drug or alcohol abuse, or tax evasion, may require some other form of investigation because survey data would be useless.

The wording and the format of the question may increase or decrease the degree to which it will evoke a socially desirable response, rather than the true answer. For example, if the spouses of working women were asked, "Do you earn more than your wife?" nearly all would respond that they do, because of the social role prescription that the male be the

CHECKLIST 4–2

To Avoid Instrumentation Bias

1. Does the question state the criterion for answering? If not, the criterion must be clearly indicated.

2. Is the question applicable to all respondents? If not, it must be reworded or some respondents exempted by using a detour around it for those to whom it doesn't apply.

3. Does the item contain an example that's also a possible answer? If so, change or discard the example.

4. Does the question require respondents to remember too much detail or recall distant events? If so, it must be modified or generalized to make recall easier.

5. Is the question as specific as it can reasonably be? If the item is too general, state it more specifically.

6. Is the item more specific than the way respondents think? If so, it should be expressed in more general terms.

7. Does the question overemphasize some condition? If so, it must be stated in less dramatic terms.

8. Are some of the words in the item ambiguous? If so, reword it using more commonly recognized phrasing.

9. Is the question as free from threat to respondents as possible? If not, change it to reduce the threat.

10. Does the question include only one issue? If it's a double-barreled item, it must be split or modified.

11. Will yea-sayers or nay-sayers always choose one answer? If so, revise the item to include both "yes" and "no."

12. Does the question lead respondents toward a particular answer? If so, the leading phrase must be removed.

13. Is the question *loaded* with a reason for responding in a particular way? If so, the reason must be deleted.

Figure 4–1   *Sources of Response Bias*

1. *Social desirability.* Response based on what's perceived as being socially acceptable or respectable.
2. *Acquiescence.* Response based on respondent's perception of what would be desirable to the sponsor.
3. *Yea- and nay-saying.* Response influenced by the global tendency toward positive or negative answers.
4. *Prestige.* Response intended to enhance the image of the respondent in the eyes of others.
5. *Threat.* Response influenced by anxiety or fear instilled by the nature of the question.
6. *Hostility.* Response arising from feelings of anger or resentment engendered by the response task.
7. *Auspices.* Response dictated by the image or opinion of the sponsor rather than the actual question.
8. *Mental set.* Cognitions or perceptions based on previous items influence response to later ones.
9. *Order.* The sequence in which a series is listed affects the responses to the items.
10. *Extremity.* Clarity of extremes and ambiguity of mid-range options encourage extreme responses.

main "breadwinner." The same question can be expressed in a way that's less likely to obtain a socially desirable response: "Are your wife's monthly earnings usually somewhat more, about the same, or somewhat less than your own?" The first version states the social norm and, in effect, asks if the respondent conforms. Most will indicate they do. The second version provides all three alternatives without stating the norm, and it "softens" the phrasing by using the words *somewhat* and *about*.

Acquiescence

People are usually cooperative. Their agreement to respond to a survey indicates their tendency to cooperate. If they feel that a certain response will be more welcome to the sponsor, researcher, or interviewer, then many will almost automatically provide it. There are two things the researcher can do to reduce such bias: (1) Assure respondents that candid, honest answers are much more helpful than purely favorable ones. They must understand that cooperation requires honesty, not flattery. (2) Provide no indications of which answer is *positive*. If questions are worded so the respondents can't detect what answer is positive in the eyes of the sponsor, researcher, or interviewer, their tendency to cooperate won't affect their responses.

Yea- and nay-saying

Some people have a more or less global tendency to agree or answer positively and others to disagree or respond negatively. When an entire series of survey items or scales seek responses on a positive/negative dimension, yea-saying or nay-saying may become a source of bias. One method of controlling such bias is to avoid yes/no or positive/negative options. For example, rather than asking the question, "Would you prefer to go?" it might be expressed, "Would you prefer to: (a) go to that place, or (b) remain where you are." In the second version, there are no positive or negative options. When many questions must be answered on a positive/negative basis, this form of bias can be partially controlled by "reflecting" roughly half of the items. For example, if attitudes toward some issue were to be measured by listing a series of statements and asking about agreement or disagreement, then half the statements might be negative toward the issue and half positive. Thus, yea-saying or nay-saying would, in effect, automatically compensate or "equal out."

Prestige

Virtually everyone likes to "look good" in their own eyes and in the eyes of others. When respondents inflate their income, shave a few years off their age, or amplify the importance of their job on a survey questionnaire, their desire for prestige becomes a source of bias. If every aspect of the survey shows respect and admiration for people of all walks of life, the likelihood of this type of bias will be reduced. This bias can be reduced further by avoiding questions that invite respondents to seek prestige. Asking "How would you rate yourself on self-reliance?" would invite a high rating and introduce serious bias. The same information could be obtained by seeking a rating along the continuum from "Depend entirely on myself" to "Depend mostly on others." Assigning the lower numbers to self-reliance and the higher to dependency would also help to compensate for the remaining bias from the pursuit of prestige.

Threat

Survey questions can constitute a psychological threat to respondents when they deal with issues and outcomes that have very negative consequences for them. Most people don't like to think about such things as their own death, disease, serious accidents, the loss or separation of a loved one, and the like. When the survey requires information concerning such issues, it's important to avoid the more graphic words and phrases, using euphemisms instead. It's less threatening to speak of having a "hearing impairment" than to talk about being "partially or totally deaf." Other means of reducing threat bias are either to "depersonalize" the issue either by referring to it in the abstract or by "projection," referring to the experience or condition of some other person. For example, rather than asking what the *respondents* would do if they lost their job, it may be necessary either to ask about how people might cope with unemployment (the abstract) or what they might suggest if a friend (another person) were temporarily unemployed.

Hostility

There are some situations where either the topics or issues included in the survey or the response task itself may engender strong hostility or resentment in some respondents. Once these strong feelings have been evoked, respondents won't focus exclusively on the thing that evoked their feelings or be able to dissipate their feelings very quickly. In such cases, the respondents who feel hostile may generalize these feelings to other questions that follow. They are, in effect, responding more to a previous item than to the ones that follow. One way to avoid this form of bias is to word questions in a manner that's less likely to create feelings of hostility. When it isn't possible to avoid evoking some hostility or where these negative emotions must be measured by the survey, there are two ways to keep them from contaminating the items that follow. One way is to allow the respondents to dissipate these feelings as fully as possible directly on the issues that created them. If respondents are allowed adequate opportunity to express these feelings before continuing, they're more likely to "get them out of their system," and then to relax and continue. Another helpful technique is to provide some means of separating one section very distinctly from the next. If respondents clearly understand that the next set of items deals with an issue or topic that's completely separate, they're less likely to carry their hostile feelings over to this new area.

Auspices

When respondents know in advance who is sponsoring the survey, their feelings toward the sponsor may bias their answers to the questions. For example, a survey of employees sponsored by the company may generate very different answers than if it were sponsored by the labor union. To avoid such auspices bias, many surveys are conducted by an independent agency or research team. There's often no necessity to tell respondents in advance who is sponsoring the survey. When information about the sponsoring organization must be obtained or when respondents might easily infer the identity of the sponsor from the questions, such questions should come as late in the questionnaire as possible. Such bias can also be avoided by "clouding" or "smoke-screening" the identity of the sponsor. For example, if the survey focused on the sponsoring company's brand of products, the same questions might also be asked concerning some other brands as well. That way, respondents wouldn't be sure which company was seeking the information and auspices bias would be controlled.

Mental set

When respondents are asked to perform some mental task, they develop a set of perceptions and assumptions that serves as a frame of reference for responding. Usually, they'll maintain that same frame of reference or mental set until they realize it no longer applies. For example, the survey might include two questions: "How many times have you moved in the past five years?" and "How many times have you owned the home in which you lived?" Their frame of reference for the first question would cover only the past five years. When responding to the second question, many would use the same frame of reference, considering only the past five years when they answer, even though the question doesn't limit the history to that period. If the researcher intended the second question to include the entire residential history of the respondents, rather than only the past five years, the obsolete mental set of the respondents would create a bias. This bias can be avoided or controlled by making it perfectly clear to respondents when they're to shift their frame of reference or make a new set of assumptions to respond to the next item. That can be done by beginning a new section with new instructions or by stating the new assumptions or frame of reference as a preface to the next question.

Order

The order or sequence in which survey questions or scaled items are listed will often affect the response, even though respondents are to respond to each in turn. There are three things that might induce order bias in these cases: *initiation, routine,* and *fatigue.* With the first item or so, initiation requires that respondents learn how to handle the response task. Samples or items of little importance should be listed first, so any bias from initiation won't affect the most important items.

When several similar items appear in sequence, the routine nature of responding may lead to a response strategy or policy. If that happens, each item won't be viewed or evaluated independently, as they should be. Bias from routine response can be reduced by varying the list to make individual items distinct and to require separate consideration of each. Rather than composing all items on a list to ascend in one direction, the list should be composed so some items ascend in one direction while others descend in that direction. For example, a list of statements might consist of a random mix, so some are positive about the issue and others are negative. Recognizing this, respondents would then have to read and evaluate each statement independently, rather than developing a "policy" of agreeing or disagreeing with all of them.

When respondents must rate or respond to a long list of items, the rote nature of the task may cause fatigue. In short, they get tired of the process. If that happens, they may respond carefully to the earlier items and carelessly to the later ones on the list, causing error, bias, or both. This form of bias can be controlled by keeping any one list or sequence short enough so even the least motivated respondents won't be affected by fatigue when responding to that section.

When responses are required for each item on a list, initiation, routine, and fatigue may cause order bias. Two kinds of order bias apply when respondents are given a list of alternatives and asked to pick one from the list: *primacy* effect and *recency* effect. People often remember the first items of any list, simply because they're first. This is called a primacy effect. They also recall the last items more readily than others because they have been

---

CHECKLIST 4–3

To Control Response Bias

1. Is the question subject to any of the 10 sources of response bias listed in Figure 4–1? If so, consider each of the methods for control noted below.

2. Can the question be reworded to reduce or eliminate the bias? Compose a few alternative forms of the question and select the version that's least likely to be subject to bias.

3. Might the instructions be changed so the item isn't subject to the bias? Examine and substitute instructions for the question, section, or scale to reduce bias.

4. Does the source of bias arise from the choice or form of a scale? Consider alternative scales from the examples in the following chapter or modify the scale to reduce bias.

5. Does the structure of the section or questionnaire induce or encourage bias? Try reforming the section or moving it to another location in the questionnaire.

6. Do the presence or nature of preceding or following questions or items make the question subject to bias? Tentatively rearrange the items in the section or move the question to another section to control the bias.

7. Do the modifications in the question or questionnaire to reduce one form of bias make it more subject to another? Check the revised item against the sources of response bias to be sure the changes have not created another problem.

---

presented more recently. Thus, this is called a recency effect. Usually, both apply for any long list, but not always with equal strength. In any case, the general principle indicates that people are more likely to recall the first and last things that are presented in sequence than they are those which come between. Consequently, there's a bias toward respondents picking the first or last alternatives from a group, simply because they're more easily remembered. There are two methods for reducing or controlling order bias from primacy and recency effects. One way is to be sure lists are fairly short. This is especially important for interview surveys, where respondents are read the list and must keep the whole set of alternatives in mind while they choose one. Ordinarily, only four or five options can be recalled at one time. When a longer list of alternatives must be evaluated relative to one another, it's usually advisable to provide a scale and have *each* item rated. Ratings can be compared during analysis, and the most preferred option can be identified by its highest rating.

Another method of controlling order bias resulting from primacy and recency effects is to vary the order or sequence of items from one respondent or subsample to the next. This is ordinarily not feasible for mail surveys, because more than one form of questionnaire would be required and that would be costly. It may be more feasible to instruct interviewers to read a list in random order (checking off each as it's read) for each respondent. This method should be used only when order bias is regarded as a serious threat to the validity of the data, because it puts a burden on the interviewers and requires that they be instructed and monitored carefully.

Extremity

This form of bias is similar in some respects to primacy and recency effects. When scales are used, respondents sometimes tend to "dichotomize" the scale by picking only the extremes. Thus, if a scale contained numbers from 1 to 10 with the extremes labeled "Extremely good" and "Extremely bad," some people may answer only with a 1 or a 10. In effect, they're refusing to make a more fine-grained discrimination. It's easier to think in terms of black and white than it is to distinguish between shades of gray. (Ironically, the result is the exact opposite of "fence-riding," or picking a neutral, middle value, so the respondent actually avoids making a choice entirely.)

The careful choice and composition of scales will help to reduce or control extremity bias. Such bias may result because the scales have too many numbers or points. The number of scale points should be about the same as the number of categories in the respondents' mind. For example, when looking at a product, buyers may think in such terms as: terrible, unacceptable, poor, fair, good, and excellent. A scale of five, six, or even seven points would be appropriate, but one with a hundred points isn't. It's also important to label the ends of the scale with the *ultimate extremes*. In the example above, if the extremes were labeled "poor" and "good" rather than "terrible" and "excellent," a bias would result because the mid-range would cover only products that were viewed as fair.

Controlling response bias requires checking and rechecking the survey questions and items again and yet again. Sometimes correcting for one source of bias inadvertently causes the introduction of another. Checklist 4–3 outlines the process for controlling response bias.

QUESTION FORMAT

There are two basic formats for survey questions: unstructured and structured. Unstructured questions are sometimes called "open-end" questions because only the question is expressed and no alternative answers are listed for the respondent. Structured survey items do two things: they ask a question and they list the alternative answers the respondent might choose. Experienced researchers prefer to use structured questions whenever they're feasible because they have many important advantages.

The dimension of answers

Unstructured questions often don't clearly indicate the dimension along which respondents are supposed to respond. In Example 4–17, an unstructured item is listed in the top section together with seven verbatim answers from different respondents. Notice that some respondents are selecting reasons for visiting *that* particular store, while others are indicating why they visited *today,* rather than another time. The unstructured version of the item doesn't indicate the range along which respondents should answer, while the structured version clearly indicates it.

In the structured form of the item used in the example, the list of alternatives clearly indicates to respondents that they're to base their answer on the attributes or characteristics of the store. In effect, they know more precisely what's being asked or what information is sought. The researcher with considerable experience probably knows through some unpleasant experiences that respondents seldom answer the way they're expected to respond when they're free to provide any answer they wish. Even when it appears to the researcher that the dimension along which respondents are to answer is plainly evident, respondents are likely to be in a different frame of mind and, therefore, will respond along some completely different dimension.

Comparability of data

Unstructured items often produce data that aren't directly comparable from one respondent or group to the next. When structured items are used, the data are comparable among respondents. Thus, data processing and analysis can compare and contrast the answers of various individuals or subsamples.

The unstructured question in Example 4–17 may produce as many different verbatim responses as there are respondents in the sample. It would be necessary to "group" answers into categories when editing and postcoding the data, after the information was collected. This can be a laborious and time-consuming process. In addition, the editor or analyst must make many judgments about the meaning or intent of the respondents when grouping the responses into categories. On the other hand, when a structured item is used, this process of selecting categories is done in the field, at the time the information was collected. Furthermore, the judgments are made by the respondents, themselves, rather than by another person who must interpret their meaning or intentions.

EXAMPLE 4–17

Structured Versus Unstructured Questions

Unstructured Item

Q. Why did you visit this store?

A1. _____ "I happened to be in the neighborhood."
A2. _____ "I didn't have anything better to do."
A3. _____ "I like the merchandise they have here."
A4. _____ "I have an account at this store."
A5. _____ "I always shop on Wednesday."
A6. _____ "A friend recommended the store."
A7. _____ "It's fun to shop. I enjoy it."

Structured Item

Q. What's the one *major* reason you visited this store?

A1. _____ The price of the goods.
A2. _____ The selection of merchandise.
A3. _X_ The location of the store.
A4. _____ Friendly, helpful staff.
A5. _____ Availability of credit.
A6. _____ Some other reason. Specify what: ———
A7. _____ No particular reason; don't know.

Often an interviewer may be instructed to read only the question, but not the alternatives, and then select the category to check. Even in such cases, when the selection of the category can be done while the interview is in progress, the fieldworker can question the respondent further if there's uncertainty. If, on the other hand, the categories are to be selected during editing and postcoding, there's no way to obtain additional information if it's needed.

Recording accuracy

It's difficult and time-consuming for either the interviewer or the respondent to record verbatim responses to questions. The answers listed in the top section of the example are quite short, but in actual practice respondents might provide two or three sentences to explain why they visited the store. If the structured version of the same item listed in the bottom of the example were used, the respondent or fieldworker would only have to check the appropriate category. Thus, there's much less likelihood of error in recording.

The response task

When a self-administered questionnaire is being used, or when the alternatives are listed for the respondent, the response task is much quicker and easier with structured items. Thus, there's likely to be greater cooperation, a higher response rate, less missing data, and fewer "random" responses when structured items are used.

Inappropriate reasons

There are several reasons why unstructured survey questions are often used when structured items would be superior. It takes time and effort in the beginning to compose structured questions effectively. It takes only a few minutes to write an unstructured question. There's a tendency for the researcher to hurry the composition task and worry about the editing and coding later, after the data have been collected. Thus, the work is both amplified and procrastinated.

Another reason for the frequent and inappropriate use of unstructured questions comes from the sponsor. Often those who sponsor a survey feel that the use of structured items will limit the "richness and variety" of people's answers. This is, of course, quite true. Such untrained and inexperienced sponsors fail to recognize the enormity of the task of interpretation. Invariably, when presented with several hundreds or thousands of verbatim responses, they're overwhelmed by the volume and abandon the data by necessity. The researcher has the responsibility to explain the problems associated with verbatim answers and provide assurance that structured items will obtain the required data. The guidelines for using (or if possible, avoiding) unstructured questions are provided in Guidelist 4–2.

Composing Categorical Items

When a structured question is used, it's often necessary to choose the categories or response alternatives to be used by respondents. Such items are called "discrete, categorical" items because all responses must fall into a particular category. (Alternative forms of structured items using conventional categories or numeric scales are presented in the following chapter.) It takes considerable time and effort to compose a categorical question and select the proper categories. On the other hand, if the task is done carefully and thoroughly, it will save time and effort later and increase the reliability and validity of the data.

GUIDELIST 4–2

For Using Unstructured Questions

1. Structure the question whenever it's possible to do so, even though it requires time and effort.
2. Resist requests by sponsors for verbatim responses, explaining the difficulty of interpretation.
3. Be sure the dimension or range of alternatives is crystal clear to respondents when an item is unstructured.
4. Be sure the interviewers or respondents can record verbatim responses to unstructured items accurately.
5. Estimate the degree to which using an unstructured question will increase the response task.
6. After all is said and done, go back and see if it may not be possible to use a structured item, anyhow.

Stating the question

Typically, a categorical item asks a question, followed by a series of alternative answers. When composing the question itself, all the principles and guidelines discussed earlier apply. Thus, the same things are required of the question itself, whether it's structured or unstructured. The only important difference between the two is that structured questions receive some *help* when the alternatives are listed for respondents. Aside from that, the task of expressing the question remains the same.

An all-inclusive list

The categories used form what's sometimes called a *taxonomy,* or system of classification. The responses are classified into categories. There are three rules or principles to observe when choosing the categories for an item: (1) the list must be all-inclusive, (2) the categories must be mutually exclusive, and (3) there should be more variance in the meaning *between* categories than within them.

The first rule is that the list must include every possible response. Every answer a respondent might possibly give must fit into a category, and there must be no conceivable answer that doesn't fit into a category.

In Example 4–18, the incorrect classification scheme shown in the top section doesn't meet the requirement of an all-inclusive set of categories. Suppose some respondents had actually seen the new clinic building. There's no category for recording that means of learning about the clinic. By contrast, the correct version shown in the lower section of the example includes an "other" category, so those responses that don't fit into any of the first six categories can be recorded and identified in the seventh. It's very advisable to include an open, "other" category in such lists. Even though the questions are pretested in a pilot survey, there are likely to be a few exceptional or unusual responses that won't fit into any category listed.

When an "other" category is used, the nature of the "other" may or may not be specified, depending on the information requirements. There are times when those seeking infor-

---

EXAMPLE 4–18

Structured Category Questions

Incorrect Classification

Q. How did you *first* learn about the new clinic?

A1. _____ From a friend or co-worker.
A2. _____ From a relative or family member.
A3. _____ From a newspaper or magazine.
A4. _____ From the radio or television.
A5. _____ From a news story.
A6. _____ By seeing a sign, billboard, or poster.
A7. _____ By some other announcement or advertisement.

Correct Classification

Q. How did you *first* learn about the new clinic?

A1. _____ From a relative or family member.
A2. _____ From an associate or acquaintance.
A3. _____ From a newspaper or magazine *advertisement*.
A4. _____ From a radio or television *advertisement*.
A5. _____ *Read* a news story in some publication about it.
A6. _____ *Heard* a *news* story about it on radio or TV.
A7. _____ Some other way. *Specify how:* _____

---

mation may be interested *only* in a few certain categories, but answers might range widely beyond them. When that's the case, the answers that don't fit into the categories of interest may all be lumped into an "other" category without specification of just what the other things are. For some situations, the nature of the "other" responses may be useful or required by those seeking the information. When they are, they should be specified so they can be identified, categorized, and postcoded when the completed questionnaires are being edited.

A mutually exclusive list

There must be a *unique* association between any given answer and one category or alternative. No response should fit into two or more categories. In Example 4–18, the incorrect version of the item has overlapping categories.

Those respondents who first learned of the clinic through a news story could be recorded in that category and/or as having gained awareness from newspapers or magazines or from radio or television. The correct version of the item in the lower portion of the example not only makes a distinction between broadcast and print media, but also between paid advertising and publicity through news articles. Thus, no answer would fit into more than one category, and the requirement for a mutually exclusive list has been met.

Meaningful clusters

When answers are recorded in categories, the alternatives used should cluster responses similar to one another. Answers substantially different from one another should fall into separate categories. Lacking such a classification system, the data wouldn't be especially meaningful, or at least some value will be lost. In Example 4–18, the categories used in the improper example don't make a distinction between print media publicity and broadcast media publicity. "News stories" consist of one category, and both types would be clustered together, although they might be regarded as having significantly different meanings for the sponsors. Also, the incorrect version makes a distinction between "signs, billboards, and posters," and "some other announcement or advertisement." Such a distinction doesn't appear to be valuable or meaningful.

The incorrect list of alternatives in the example would result in too much variation in meaning in the category for news stories and too little meaningful variation in the last two categories. There are no set rules for forming categories with more variance in meaning between than within them. The task requires a thorough understanding of what distinctions will and won't be meaningful to the sponsors. The choice also depends on what would be meaningful to *respondents*. Thus, the task is something of an art, requiring judgment and perhaps a pilot test.

Size and number of categories

The researcher composing a structured, categorical item must also decide the number of categories to be used and how broad or narrow each should be. The simple, dichotomous question with only two categories is the lower limit on the number of categories. The upper limit is ordinarily about six or eight categories. With more than that, the response and recording task increases greatly, and it's seldom necessary or advisable to exceed that limit. The choice of the number of categories between these two extremes depends on how "fine-grained" the sponsor would like the data to be. The general rule should be to have no more categories than are actually required. The reason for minimizing the number of categories lies in statistical processing. When the analysis seeks to measure the relationships between survey items, it's often necessary to cross-tabulate two items or break down one item by the various levels of another. If the categories are quite narrow and there are several of them, some are likely to contain very small numbers of responses. Thus, they may have to be combined with others during analysis to obtain adequate "cell" sizes, which defeats the purpose of using many, narrow categories.

There's one *very important* precaution when determining the size and number of categories for a discrete, structured item. If there's doubt in the mind of the researcher composing the item about how precise or fine-grained the data must be, the researcher should elect to use the larger number of more narrow categories. The reason is simple, but compelling: categories can easily be *combined* during processing, if necessary. On the other hand, if they prove to be too broad, so a large majority of respondents fall into only one or two categories, there's *no way* to disaggregate the broad categories into smaller ones after the data have been collected. Once clustered, the answers must remain so.

Categorical items are sometimes the backbone of the survey questionnaire. Sometimes they're only a small part, but some categorical questions are almost always included. The recommendations for composing effective categorical items are summarized in Guidelist 4–3.

GUIDELIST 4–3

For Composing Categorical Items

1. For composing the question itself, the same rules and principles apply to structured, categorical items as to unstructured questions.
2. The categories must be "all-inclusive," so there's an appropriate category for any conceivable response.
3. If all possible answers can't be anticipated or when some types are of no interest, exceptional responses should be clustered into an "other" category.
4. The categories must be mutually exclusive, so no answer would fit into more than one category.
5. There should be more variance in meaning between categories than within them, so answers are clustered into categories on a meaningful basis.
6. Ordinarily, there should be no more than six or eight categories for any one question.
7. Categories should be broad enough to capture a sufficient number of responses and to provide adequate frequencies during processing and statistical analysis.
8. The categories shouldn't be more "fine-grained" than required by the sponsors.
9. When in doubt, choose the more narrow categories because they can always be combined later but they can't be split after data collection.

Verbal and Numeric Scaling

The discrete, categorical, structured survey item is only one type of verbal "scale." Several thoroughly tested and commonly used verbal and numeric scales are presented and discussed in the following chapter. They should, of course, be used where appropriate. It's *always* advisable to use an ordinary *numeric* scale when feasible to do so. Less experienced researchers sometimes tend to use categorical items in place of numeric scales. They may feel that categorical items will facilitate the analysis, or they may hold the mistaken notion that respondents would prefer the categorical type. Neither is so, and the question should seek a number, not a category.

In Example 4–19, discrete categories are used in the incorrect example. The categories are inappropriate because the data can readily be obtained in numeric form, as shown in the correct item. In addition, the categories are too broad and the data can't be disaggregated after data collection. Ordinarily, it's important to distinguish between those who had "some high school" or "some college" and those who completed the course of study and obtained a degree or diploma. That discrimination is forever lost with the categorical form of the item.

By contrast, the numeric data can easily be grouped into categories if required by those who seek the information. Those with 8 years of school or less could be grouped into the "elementary only" category, those with 9 to 11 years into "some high school," those with 12 years into "high school graduate," and so forth. In addition, the correct version of the item is less threatening and presents the respondents with a much simpler and easier task than does the categorical item.

EXAMPLE 4–19

Numeric Versus Categorical Items

Incorrect Categorical Item

Q. What level of education have you attained?

A1. _____ Elementary school only.
A2. _____ High school only.
A3. _____ College education.
A4. _____ College postgraduate.

Correct Numeric Item

Q. What's the last year of education you have completed? [For example, high school graduate equals 12 years.]

A. _____ years of formal education.

SUMMARY

The Composition of Survey Questions

    A. Focus very precisely. Every item should zero in very directly on one, specific issue or topic.

    B. Keep each item brief. The longer the question, the greater the response task and the more error and bias.

    C. Strive for clarity. Every respondent must know exactly what's being asked.

    D. Use "core" vocabulary. Use the same words as the least sophisticated respondents would use in common speech.

    E. Use simple sentences. Two or more simple sentences are far preferable to one compound sentence.

    F. Avoid specific sources of bias or error. Be sure items are free from the factors that create bias and error.

    G. Use structured questions. Unstructured items ordinarily provide large quantities of poor quality data.

    H. Classify answers carefully. Observe the three rules for an effective classification system.

    I. Choose appropriate categories. Be certain they're neither too broad nor too narrow, too many nor too few.

    J. Use scaling effectively. Refer to the following two chapters for guidance on numeric and verbal scales and to combine survey items into groups.

Chapter 5

Creating Item Scales

WHY SCALES ARE USED

Answers to survey questions are typically a choice of *position,* either within some category or along some continuous spectrum. A response scale is merely a representation of the categories or continuum along which respondents will arrange themselves. When scales are used, reports describe the *distribution* of respondents along the scale or in the categories. The positions of various individuals or groups can then be compared with one another. Scales can be coded with numbers. The numeric codes that represent answers to questions are more easily manipulated than words. The use of a numeric database saves time and money and helps to ensure accuracy, reliability, and validity. Scales can be arranged so they capture answers to many questions quickly and in very little space. They're both *efficient* and *practical.*

Specificity of Scales

Scales are used to obtain responses that will be comparable to one another. All responses should be expressed in the same terms. Sometimes the scale will be obvious to the respondent, and sometimes it will be necessary only to name the scale. There are also times when the scales will have to be clearly portrayed.

Implicit scale dimensions

For some questions, the scale already exists in the minds of the respondents. For example, when someone is asked their age, they'll respond with the number of years. There's a common understanding between the questioner and the respondent about the scale to be used. This is an *implicit* scale because it's *implied* by the question. Other examples include weight, height, eye color, distance between cities, and simple, dichotomous questions such as yes or no.

Explicit scale dimensions

At other times, there is no common understanding between the questioner and the respondent. If people were asked, "How long has it been since your last visit to a physician for treatment?," some might respond in days, some in months, and some in years. A few may even say, "Oh, it's been a long time" or "I go whenever I'm sick." Such answers are difficult to manipulate or compare to one another. It would be better to ask, "How *many months* has it been since . . ." rather than, "How long has it been since . . ." That way, the scale is *explicit*. All responses will be expressed in calendar months and they're comparable.

For common denominations, such as months, pounds, dollars, degrees of temperature, or the number of a certain thing, such as trips taken during a given time, virtually everyone will be familiar with it if it's named in the question. When this is the case, and the question can be asked by merely specifying the scale in the question, it should be done that way, so long as the respondents understand the scale specified.

Depicted scale dimensions

When scales can't be specified within the question, they must be *depicted* as response options, verbally, numerically, or graphically. For example, if the question were, "Where are you going when you leave here?", answers wouldn't be comparable. There's no scale that can easily be specified within the question, so the response options must be listed or depicted following the question: home, work, shopping, recreation, and so forth. When seeking qualitative evaluations, preferences, images, perceptions, or judgments, the scale dimensions may be depicted in the form of rankings, ratings, graphic figures, or some other set of response alternatives. In the examples that follow, several of the most popular scaling devices are shown.

The scale should be depicted only when necessary. Implicit scales should be used when respondents are sure to understand them and are as willing to respond to an implicit scale as to a depicted one. This is usually the case. When specification is required, common, simple dimensions should be used. Some researchers inappropriately specify age *groups* when it would be more simple and accurate to ask, "What's your age?" Three words in the question and one number for the answer—what could be simpler? No specification is necessary, and the scale is implied.

The question concerning level of education is another example. Here, the scale must be explicitly specified, but many researchers will list an elaborate set of categories, including: elementary only, some high school, high school graduate, some college, college graduate, some postgraduate school, or postgraduate degree. A simpler way to ask would be, "How many years of formal education have you completed?" The researcher can safely assume that 8 years means elementary school, 12 means high school, and so on. Where an underlying dimension is commonly understood by both questioner and respondent, it should be used without elaboration. Checklist 5–1 lists the main considerations when selecting scale categories.

CHECKLIST 5–1

To Select the Scale Category

1. Will the respondents clearly understand the dimensions they're to use? If so, dimensions need only be *implied*.
2. Will the respondents be familiar with the scale dimensions if they're named, such as years, times,

or miles? If so, the dimensions need only be *explicit*.
3. Will the respondents be uncertain or unfamiliar with the scale? If so, the scale must be *depicted*.

MULTIPLE-CHOICE QUESTION

Multiple-choice questions are very common because they're simple and versatile. They can be used to obtain either a single response or several. Multiple-choice questions of both single response and multiple response are shown in Example 5–1.

Multiple-Response Items

In the multiple-response case, the respondents can indicate one *or more* alternatives, and they're instructed to check *any* within the question, itself. In this case, *each* alternative becomes a *variable* to be analyzed. Thus, this one item actually asks seven questions. They could be expressed individually, one at a time: "Do you regularly read the paper for business news?" for each of the six, and "What other papers do you regularly read for business news?" That would take much more time and space, and so this one item is very economical.

Single-Response Items

When only one alternative is to be singled out from among several by the respondent, the item is a multiple-*choice,* but a single-*response* item. No "ties" are allowed, and the respondent is supposed to pick only one. Respondents don't always follow instructions if they're unclear. Consequently, single-response items can be used only when: (1) the choice criterion is clearly stated and (2) the criterion actually defines a single category. Notice that the words, "most often" and "one" are italicized in the item shown in the lower section of the example. This clearly states that only one option is to be designated. Note also that few if any respondents are likely to read two or more publications with exactly the same frequency, so ties are unlikely and there's a *unique* answer to the question. The selection of a single-response, rather than a multiple-response item, depends on the researcher's needs and the respondents' ability to identify one answer.

It's important to note again that the multiple-choice item is ideal for responses that fall into *discrete* categories. On the other hand, multiple-choice items shouldn't be used for numeric data. When the answers can be expressed as numbers, a direct question should be used, and the number of units should be recorded. If it's desirable to *group* responses into

```
                        ⟨  EXAMPLE 5–1  ⟩
```

The Multiple-Choice Item

Multiple Response

Please check *any* type of newspaper you regularly read for business news.

_____ Local, morning paper		11
_____ Local, evening paper		12
_____ Local, weekly paper		13
_____ Regional, weekly paper		14
_____ National, daily paper		15
_____ National, weekly paper		16
_____ Other (What kind?_____)		17–18

Single Response

What kind of newspaper do you *most often* read for business news?
(Check only *one*.)

(1) _____ Local, morning paper		
(2) _____ Local, evening paper		
(3) _____ Local, weekly paper		
(4) _____ Regional, weekly paper		19
(5) _____ National, daily paper		
(6) _____ National, weekly paper		
(7) _____ Other (What kind?_____)		20

categories within certain ranges, that can easily be accomplished during computer processing. The guidelines for writing effective multiple-choice items are presented in Guidelist 5–1.

CONVENTIONAL SCALE TYPES

The types of scales that are most commonly used in surveys are described below. While all of them have been thoroughly tested and used extensively, some are much more common than others. Nearly every information need or survey question can be scaled effectively with the use of one or more of the scales described in this chapter. Some special scales, less conventional than these, are presented in the following chapter. Thus, the researcher's scaling decisions are more a matter of *choice* among the conventional scales than of invention of scaling devices.

The Likert Scale

There are times when it's necessary to obtain people's *position* on certain issues or conclusions. This is a form of opinion or attitude measurement. An unstructured or *open-ended* question might be used for this purpose, but that type of question has many problems associated with analysis and interpretation. Answers are seldom comparable. The Likert scale,

---

GUIDELIST 5–1

For Using Multiple-Choice Items

1. The entire range of response should be classifiable into a few discrete categories. About 8 or 10 are usually the maximum.
2. The category names should define a set of discrete alternatives, so there's a clear distinction between them in the minds of interviewers and/or respondents.
3. The named categories should be mutually exclusive, so no possible answer could fit into more than one of the categories used.

4. There should be certainty that the labeled alternatives will capture over 90 percent of all answers that are likely to be given to the question.
5. An "other" category should be listed last to include any answers that don't fit into the named categories, unless there's no possibility of other answers.

---

named for its creator, states the issue or opinion and obtains the respondents' degree of agreement or disagreement. This scale provides answers in the form of coded data that are comparable and can readily be manipulated.

When a Likert scale is used, the question is stated in the instructions, above the scale. The question becomes, "How much do you agree with this statement?" The actual items aren't questions, but statements that represent particular opinions. Respondents indicate their agreement or disagreement to each, so responses are on a single dimension or continuum. The instructions for such a scale, the scale itself, and 10 item statements are shown in Example 5–2.

Likert scaling is very popular with researchers because of the power and simplicity of the format. The principal advantages of this type of scale include flexibility, economy, and ease of composition. The procedure is flexible because items can be only a few words long, or they can consist of several lines. Vocabulary can be technical and sophisticated or it can be very simple and primary, depending on what's appropriate to the population to be surveyed. The method is economical because one set of instructions and scale can serve many items, and once the respondent understands what's required, he or she can complete the items very quickly and easily. Likert scaled items can often be composed by the researcher quickly and easily, especially when the issues have been articulated in advance as statements.

A major advantage of this scale is the ability to obtain a summated value. In the example, the research is measuring attitudes toward sex role prescriptions. Some of the statements prescribe something for one sex but not the other, and some others state that no distinctions should be made between the sexes. Besides obtaining the results of each item, a total score can be obtained from this set of items. Some of the items would have to be reflected by reversing the numeric scores, so all items ascend toward either pro or con. Then, the total value would be an index of attitudes toward the major issue, as a whole. This ability to measure a more general construct is a major advantage of the Likert scale. Guidelines for using Likert scales are provided in Guidelist 5–2.

EXAMPLE 5–2

The Likert Scale

Please pick a number from the scale to show how much you agree or disagree with each statement and jot it in the space to the right of the item.

Scale

1 Strongly agree
2 Agree
3 Neutral
4 Disagree
5 Strongly disagree

A man should never cry in public . . . . ———	11
Higher education is more important for men than women . . . . ———	12
Women should receive equal pay for equal work . . . . ———	13
A man shouldn't resent a woman supervising his work . . . . ———	14
A woman's place is in the home . . . . ———	15
A man should help and protect a woman in public . . . . ———	16
Women should pay their share when dating . . . . ———	17
The husband should make the major family decisions . . . . ———	18
Women should never put career before family . . . . ———	19
Men should always take the lead in sexual matters . . . . ———	20

The Verbal Frequency Scale

The format of the verbal frequency scale is fairly similar to that of the Likert scale, with a couple of important exceptions: Rather than strength of agreement, the verbal frequency scale contains five words that indicate *how often* an action has been taken. Rather than statements about issues, the items of the verbal frequency scale indicate some action the respondents might have taken. Example 5–3 contains 10 items to measure the degree of political activism of respondents.

There are times when it might be necessary to know the frequency of some action or behavior by respondents. Under some conditions, the question to measure this might simply ask, "How many times in the past have you?" Such a simple, straightforward question is recommended when the *absolute* number of times is appropriate and required. However, there are many occasions when the absolute number is of little use, or when the respondent would be unable to specify an absolute number. In the example provided, the absolute number of times wouldn't be of very much interest or value. Suppose there had been three or four elections in the districts of some of the respondents, and none in the districts of others. In that case, some groups would *appear* to be very inactive, based on the absolute level of participation. In fact, this inactivity wouldn't be the *choice* of the respondents. It merely reflects a *lack of opportunity* to participate. In this case, the researcher wants to know the proportion or percentage of activity, given an opportunity to perform it. The verbal frequency scale provides this more meaningful measure.

GUIDELIST 5–2

For Using Likert Scale Items

1. The Likert scale should be used for several items, rather than just one or two, to obtain the inherent economy.
2. The researcher should be able to identify or compose statements that are opinions *typical* of a global issue.
3. The items should be sufficiently diverse, so they represent an adequate range of the global issue.

4. There must be reasonable certainty that many respondents won't pick only a neutral value.
5. If a summated score is to be computed, about half the items should be inclined toward the pro side of the issue and half toward the con side, to avoid *yea-sayer* or *nay-sayer* bias.

For some measurements, the respondents might not be able to say with any precision of recollection exactly how many times they have behaved in a certain way. For example, respondents could be asked, "What percentage of the time did you vote for a political candidate who was a member of your own political party in the past six elections in which you voted?" Besides the protracted length of this question, there are other difficulties. To answer accurately would require remarkable powers of recollection. Most respondents would be reluctant to try to recall each election and to complete the tedious computations to obtain an accurate percentage. With the use of the verbal frequency scale, this difficulty is avoided.

In the example and in many real situations, the focus isn't on the actual number or percentage of performances. Instead, it's on the respondents' *policies* concerning the frequency of certain actions. Thus, the item that seeks to measure how often the respondent votes along strict party lines provides an overall measure of loyalty to a political party. The general policy and underlying motivation are more important and valuable than the actual number or percentage of times the respondent has voted in that way in the past.

Guidelines for using verbal frequency scales are contained in Guidelist 5–3. The advantages of the verbal frequency scale include the ease of assessment and response by those being surveyed. The number of opportunities to perform the action is automatically assumed within the question. It serves as the basis for picking the frequency category. There are two strong incentives for using the verbal frequency scale: (1) The ability to array activity levels across a five-category spectrum for data description, and (2) the ease of making comparisons among subsamples or among different actions for the same sample of respondents.

Perhaps the major disadvantage of this type of scale is that it provides only a *gross* measure of proportion. For example, "sometimes" can mean anywhere from about 30 to 70 percent of the time. Also, different groups may assign different *breakpoints* between categories. In the example shown, the research could *reflect* all items, so the values ascended toward political activism, and then sum the values for all 10 items. This would provide an overall index of political involvement. In this case, the researcher would be *assuming* that seeking information about a candidate is as much a contribution to overall political action as contributing money

EXAMPLE 5–3

The Verbal Frequency Scale

Please pick a number from the scale to show how often you do each of the things listed below and jot in the space to the right of the item.

Scale

1 Always
2 Often
3 Sometimes
4 Rarely
5 Never

Seek out information about candidates and issues . . . . _____	11
Actually vote during a strictly local election . . . . _____	12
Actually vote during a state and national election . . . . _____	13
Vote along strict party lines . . . . _____	14
Contribute money to a local political campaign . . . . _____	15
Contribute money to a state political campaign . . . . _____	16
Contribute money to a national political campaign . . . . / . . . . _____	17
Volunteer to work on a local political campaign . . . . _____	18
Volunteer to work on a state political campaign . . . . _____	19
Volunteer to work on a national political campaign . . . . _____	20

or volunteering to work on a campaign. To the degree that this assumption is appropriate, such an overall index has considerable value in many research areas. Thus, the ability to obtain an overall measure of a construct is an advantage that the verbal frequency scale shares with the Likert scale, but individual weighting of items may sometimes be necessary.

The Ordinal Scale

The ordinal scale is actually a multiple-choice item that shares some of the arithmetic characteristics of a Likert or verbal frequency scale. Yet there's an important difference in the response categories. With a multiple-choice item, the response alternatives don't stand in any fixed relationship with one another. With the ordinal scale item, the response alternatives define an ordered sequence. So, the choice listed first is less than the second, the second less than the third, and so on. The scale might be reversed so each choice alternative is greater than the one that follows. The item is ordinal because each time category listed comes *before* the next one.

Example 5–4 contains two items intended to measure when in the day the family first turns on the television set. They might have been phrased, "About what time do you or someone in your family *first* turn on the television set in your home on weekdays?" Then, the respondent would simply record a time of day. While the simple, direct question would obtain an absolute time of day, it wouldn't indicate the time *relative* to waking or eating.

GUIDELIST 5-3

For Using Verbal Frequency Scale Items

1. The verbal frequency scale should be used for several items, not just one or two, to obtain the economy.
2. The researcher should be able to compose items that assume the opportunity to perform the action.
3. The items should be used when only an approximation of percentages is required, with limited precision.
4. These scales are most appropriate when respondents are unable or unwilling to compute exact percentages.
5. If a summated score is to be computed, each item should have approximately equal *weight* in determining the overall index, or a weighted average should be computed in place of a *total* score.

Thus, if this relationship between TV viewing and other daily activities were important, the typical time for each of the other activities would also have to be obtained.

The principal advantage of the ordinal scale is the ability to obtain a measure *relative* to some other benchmark. For example, the position of a child *relative* to his siblings within the family is often regarded as more important than just the child's age. The assumption is that a child of a certain age will be treated differently if he or she is the first child of the family than if there are older siblings. The *order* is the major focus, not merely the chronological age.

Note that in the example provided here, if two respondents both indicated they turn on the television a little while after awakening, they would appear as identical on this question. They would be seen as the same, even though one individual or family may arise at five o'clock in the morning and the other not until nine o'clock. Thus, the item obtains a *relative* measure, but some information is lost concerning the distance or span between categories. The ordinal scale shouldn't be used when an absolute, numeric value can be easily obtained and when it's most meaningful. Thus, there's no reason to use the less economical and more complex ordinal scale when a direct question concerning a quantity will serve as well. Guidelist 5-4 summarizes the requirements for using ordinal scales.

The Forced Ranking Scale

Forced rankings of items produce ordinal values, just as the verbal frequency scales and the ordinal scales do, only the items are *each* ranked relative to one another. In Example 5-5, the brand most preferred is ranked first. The forced ranking scale obtains not only the most preferred, but also the sequence of the remaining items.

With forced ranking scales, the *relativity* or relationship that's measured is among the items. This is one of the main advantages of this scaling technique. People are often faced with choices among goods, services, ideas, individuals, institutions, or actions. They're constantly making choices among a limited set of options. The forced ranking scale indicates

EXAMPLE 5–4

The Ordinal Scale

Ordinarily, when do you or someone in your family first turn on a television set in your home on a weekday?
(Please check only one.)

(1) _____ The first thing in the morning
(2) _____ A little while after awakening
(3) _____ Mid-morning
(4) _____ Just before lunch
(5) _____ Right after lunch   11
(6) _____ Mid-afternoon
(7) _____ Early evening before dinner
(8) _____ Right after dinner
(9) _____ Late evening
(0) _____ Usually don't turn it on.

Ordinarily, when do you or someone in your family first turn on a television set in your home on Saturdays?
(Please check only one.)

(1) _____ The first thing in the morning
(2) _____ A little while after awakening
(3) _____ Mid-morning
(4) _____ Just before lunch
(5) _____ Right after lunch   12
(6) _____ Mid-afternoon
(7) _____ Early evening before dinner
(8) _____ Right after dinner
(9) _____ Late evening
(0) _____ Usually don't turn it on.

what those choices are likely to be, from an *ever-shrinking* number of alternatives. While the parallel between the actual life choice situation and the measurement format is an advantage of forced ranking, this scale has several disadvantages. The major limitation is the failure to measure the *absolute* standing and the *interval* between items.

Suppose two respondents to the sample item both rank Coca-Cola first and Pepsi-Cola second. This suggests they would choose Coca-Cola if they were given a choice among all four. It also suggests that if Coke were not available and the others were, they would both select Pepsi. This may or may not be the case, however. While the two appear identical, they may differ. One of the two hypothetical respondents may regard Coke and Pepsi as almost equally preferable. The other may see Coca-Cola as far preferable to any of the others, including Pepsi. Thus, the first individual may substitute Pepsi with little sacrifice, if Coke were not available. The second person may refuse a cola beverage if his or her favorite were not available. In effect, then, the forced ranking reveals the *order* of preference, but the

---

GUIDELIST 5–4

For Using Ordinal Scale Items

1. The ordinal scale should be used when a direct question concerning a quantity or value wouldn't be sufficient.

2. This scale is appropriate when the researcher seeks to include some benchmark to obtain a relative measure.

3. The researcher should be aware of the statistical limitations of ordinal versus interval or ratio data.

4. The response alternatives must stand in a meaningful sequence, based on some order of magnitude.

5. The interval between categories must be of little or no interest, and the order should be of major concern. In that sense, the researcher must be willing to sacrifice some information.

---

distance or *interval* between ranks for different respondents or between different pairs may differ markedly. That information is lost with ranking, but direct ratings of each item could obtain it. If ratings of items are obtained, the absolute value, interval between items, and relative standing are all easily computed and reported.

The number of entities or items that can be ranked is also a limitation with this type of scale. Respondents must first go through the entire list and identify their first choice. They must then go through the list again, eliminating their first choice, and selecting the alternative they would rank second, and so on. To rank 20 items, respondents would have to make 19 *passes* through an ever-decreasing list of alternatives, until only the last choice remained. Consequently, forced ranking scales are limited to only a few items. If too many are included, the response task becomes too tedious and time-consuming. This problem can also be avoided by using ratings, rather than rankings. Ratings don't require several *passes* through the list, and each item need be considered only once. Guidelines for using forced ranking scales are listed in Guidelist 5–5.

EXAMPLE 5–5

The Forced Ranking Scale

Please rank the colas listed below in their order of preference. Jot the number 1 next to the one you prefer most, number 2 by your second choice, and so forth.

_____ Pepsi-Cola		11
_____ Coca-Cola		12
_____ Royal Crown Cola		13
_____ Like Cola		14

GUIDELIST 5–5

For Using the Forced Ranking Scale

1. The number of things to be ranked should be less than 10, to avoid making the response task too difficult.
2. The major focus should be on the *relative* standing of the entities, not their absolute position.
3. The researcher must be willing to forgo measurement of the *distance* between ranks.

4. A single judgment criterion must be clearly stated, so all entities are arrayed on the same dimension.
5. As with other scales yielding ordinal data, analysis is confined to a limited set of statistical procedures that don't require equal intervals.

The Paired Comparison Scale

At times a researcher may want to measure simple, dichotomous choices between alternatives. The paired comparison scale is appropriate to such a need. The same basic assumptions apply to paired comparisons as to forced ranking scales. The focus must be almost exclusively on the evaluation of one entity *relative* to another. In this sense, paired comparisons can be regarded as a special case of ranking, where only two items are ranked at a time. The same brands of cola beverages used to exemplify the forced ranking scale are also used in Example 5–6. In this case, each brand is compared with each other brand.

There's a major problem with paired comparisons when several pairs are ranked, known as *lack of transitivity*. Logically, if a respondent prefers A to B and prefers B to C, then he or she should obviously prefer A to C. It isn't unusual when paired comparison scale data are analyzed, to find that many respondents fail to provide this transitivity.

If "ties" or equal rankings can be tolerated, and especially if the determination of absolute distance or interval between pairs is useful, it's advisable to use a numeric rating scale. Virtually all the limitations and problems inherent in paired comparisons are avoided by using ratings, rather than rankings, of items taken two at a time.

Guidelist 5–6 contains recommendations for using paired comparisons. Despite their limitations, paired comparisons can be useful when only certain comparisons are sought and the relative distance between rankings is unimportant. When only *one* item must be compared with several others, and no direct comparisons among the others are required, a simple comparative scale can be employed using the one item as the standard by which all the other items are judged.

The Comparative Scale

In those situations where the researcher is most interested in the comparison(s) between one object and one or more others, the comparative scale is most appropriate. With this type of scale, one entity can be used as the standard or benchmark by which several others can be judged. In Example 5–7, the previous management group is the standard by which respondents are to judge the new management group.

EXAMPLE 5–6

The Paired Comparison Scale

For each pair of soft drinks listed below, please put a check mark by the one you most prefer, if you had to choose between the two.

(1) _____ Pepsi-Cola   11
(2) _____ Coca-Cola

(1) _____ Royal Crown Cola   12
(2) _____ Pepsi-Cola

(1) _____ Royal Crown Cola   13
(2) _____ Like Cola

(1) _____ Royal Crown Cola   14
(2) _____ Coca-Cola

(1) _____ Coca-Cola   15
(2) _____ Like Cola

(1) _____ Like Cola   16
(2) _____ Pepsi-Cola

There are two very important advantages of using a comparative scale. Note that with this method, no *absolute* standard is presented or required, and all evaluations are made on a *comparative* basis. Ratings are all *relative* to the standard or benchmark used. Thus, where a relative measurement is of greatest interest, or where no absolute standard exists, the comparative scale approach is applicable. Researchers are often most interested in comparisons of only their own sponsor's store, brand, institution, organization, candidate, or individual with that of others that are competitive. The comparative scale meets the requirements for such measurement.

Unlike such methods as ranking or paired comparisons, the comparative scale doesn't produce ordinal data, even though a relative measure is obtained. The scale consists of a *rating,* rather than a ranking of items. The results indicate the *interval* between the standard and the item being compared to it. The *rank* or position of an item relative to other items rated on the same scale can also be determined by comparing the values of the ratings.

Another advantage of the comparative scale is its flexibility. The simple example shown here can be extended in two ways: The same two entities can be compared on several dimensions or criteria, and several different entities can be compared with the standard. For example, by listing several scales with different labels beneath them, such as "Much more progressive" and "Much less progressive," and so forth, an entire *profile* of the new management could be obtained, with the perceptions of the previous management team serving as the standard for judgment.

A second type of modification is to list the same scales but include several different entities.

GUIDELIST 5–6

For Using Paired Comparisons

1. The number of things to be compared should be less than 10, to avoid making the response task too difficult.

2. The method is most effective when actual choices in the real situation are always between two things.

3. The researcher must be willing to forgo measurement of the *distance* between items in each pair.

4. A single judgment criterion must be clearly stated, so all entities are arrayed on the same dimension.

5. The less sophisticated and careful the respondents, the greater the lack of transitivity will be, and the researcher must always expect some failure of transitivity.

Each would be judged against the same standard. In the example, the question would read, "How would you rate each management group, compared to the present one? Compared to the present one *this group is . . .*" Then, each management group would be listed with a scale beside or below it. Each group could be compared with the present and, indirectly with one another.

Rankings are used much too often, and the comparative scales aren't used as much as they should be. The comparative scales are more powerful in several respects: They present an easy, simple task to the respondent, ensuring cooperation and accuracy. They provide interval data, rather than only ordinal values, as rankings do. They permit several things that have been compared to the same standard to be compared with one another, and economy of space and time are inherent in them. Guidelines for using comparative scales are contained in Guidelist 5–7.

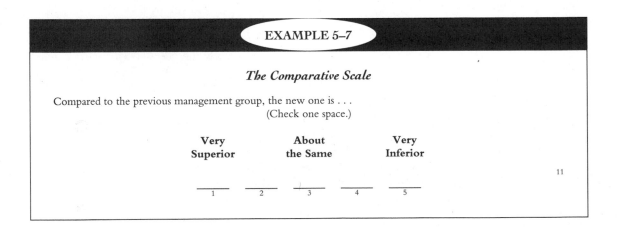

EXAMPLE 5–7

The Comparative Scale

Compared to the previous management group, the new one is . . .
(Check one space.)

Very Superior	About the Same	Very Inferior
__ __	__ __	__ __
1 2	3	4 5

11

GUIDELIST 5–7

For Using Comparative Scales

1. The major research emphasis should be the comparison of a single, standard entity with one or more others.
2. The actual rating scale should have an even number of alternatives, if *fence-riding* is likely.
3. The researcher must be sure the respondent is very clear about which is the standard and which is to be rated.

4. This method is advisable only if all or nearly all respondents are very familiar with the standard.
5. The method is particularly applicable when interval data are desired, but a relative measure is required. Both ranking and distance between entities are generated.

The Linear, Numeric Scale

When items are to be judged on a single dimension and arrayed on a scale with equal intervals, a simple, linear, numeric scale with the extremes labeled appropriately is the most advisable method of scaling. Example 5–8 provides a sample of the way this common scaling method is used.

In the example, the question is listed first, and the indented instructions are quite detailed, perhaps more so than would be necessary for most adult respondents. If those in the responding sample are fairly sophisticated, the instructions might simply say: "Pick a number from the scale to show your opinion and jot it in the space beside each item below."

In the example provided, the researcher seeks to measure the *importance* of 10 public issues. In effect, the respondents' values are being tapped and compared. Notice that this scaling technique is very economical, since a single question, set of instructions, and rating scale apply to many individual items. It's also important to note that the linear, numeric scale provides *both* absolute measures of importance and relative measures, or rankings, if responses among the various items are compared. (Of course, there's the possibility of identical ratings, yielding "tied" ranks.) Yet, even though ranking is available, the rating scale is an equal interval scale and provides data that are relatively unrestricted compared to ordinal data from forced rankings or paired comparisons.

There has been considerable controversy among researchers about whether the intermediate points on the scale should be labeled with words, such as "Somewhat important" or "Slightly important." Usually, it isn't advisable to label the intermediate levels of the scale. There are several reasons: First, consensus concerning the meaning of such words as "very" or "slightly" is less likely than for the interpretation of only a series of numbers. Second, the graphic spacing and the common understanding of the equal *distance* between numbers form a conceptual *mapping* of the underlying evaluation. Third, with only numbers, there's no possible mistake about there being only a single dimension or continuum. The bulk of the research on this issue indicates that labeling of intermediate values is no more effective. Doing so can sometimes produce undesirable results—for example, scale points

EXAMPLE 5-8

The Linear, Numeric Scale

How important to you is each of the public issues listed below?
If you feel the issue is extremely important, pick a number from the far right side of the scale and jot it in the space beside the item. If you feel it's extremely unimportant, pick a number from the far left, and if you feel the importance is between these extremes, pick a number from someplace in the middle of the scale to show your opinion.

Scale

| Extremely Unimportant | 1 | 2 | 3 | 4 | 5 | Extremely Important |

The protection of endangered species of animals . . . . ____	11
The improvement of the quality of the air . . . . ____	12
The discovery of additional petroleum reserves . . . . ____	13
The development of *renewable* sources of energy . . . . ____	14
The reduction or elimination of water pollution . . . . ____	15
The development of additional nuclear power . . . . ____	16
The protection of overall ecological balance . . . . ____	17
The industrial and technical growth of the nation . . . . ____	18
The provision of social services to those in need . . . . ____	19
The improvement of national defense and security . . . . ____	20

that aren't separated by equal intervals. Extensive experience indicates that most surveys don't require labeling of intermediate points, and there's practically no confusion or misunderstanding using only numbers.

Simplicity, clarity, economy, and productivity are all certainly among the major advantages of the linear, numeric scale. The format is clean and straightforward. Respondents have little or no difficulty understanding the task they're to perform. The same question, instructions, and scale can be used for many items. Rankings can be computed with the use of this scale, but it provides equal interval data for statistical analysis and an absolute level of measurement. Guidelines for using linear numeric scales are listed in Guidelist 5–8.

The linear, numeric scale has few limitations, compared to other scaling methods. Of course, it isn't applicable to all situations. For example, it's less effective than the verbal frequency scale for measuring approximate frequency, and not applicable when direct comparison with a particular standard is required. This scale is a powerful device, and it has become very conventional and popular among many researchers.

The Semantic Differential Scale

Researchers would often like to learn the *image* of an entity in the minds of the public. The most commonly used device for measuring such images is shown in Example 5–9. Using this scaling device, the image of a brand, store, political candidate, company, organization, institution, or idea can be measured, assessed, and compared with that of similar topics.

GUIDELIST 5–8

For Using Linear, Numeric Scales

1. This method is most applicable where evaluative responses are to be arrayed on a single dimension.
2. The scale is most economical where several items are all to be rated on the same dimension.
3. Scale extremes should be labeled "Extremely" to define the dimension, and the words used must be bipolar opposites.
4. In the vast majority of cases, the intermediate scale values shouldn't be labeled with words, and only numbers spaced at equal intervals should be used.

To use the semantic differential scale, the researcher must first select a series of adjectives that might be used to describe the topic object. This can be a difficult task. It's very important to select the adjectives specifying attributes important to the respondents. The attributes used in the survey should be the major ones actually used by respondents to judge and evaluate the topic rated. The actual attributes and adjectives most relevant in the minds of respondents are seldom obvious to the researcher. If there's any uncertainty, a preliminary inquiry can be used to identify the most appropriate terms. If important attributes are neglected, an incomplete picture is developed. If unimportant attributes are included, some aspects of the profile that result will be irrelevant.

Once the attributes and the adjectives associated with them have been selected, the polar opposites of each adjective must be determined. This, too, can be a major problem, and some substitutions to the list may be necessary. For example, is the opposite of "good" the word "poor" or the word "bad?" Once the attributes have been identified and descriptive adjectives and their polar opposites have been chosen, the semantic differential scale can be composed. About half the items should list the more positive adjective first and the others should list the more negative first. Items are ordinarily listed in random order on the actual scale.

The major advantage of the semantic differential scale is its ability to portray images clearly and effectively. Since several pairs of bipolar adjectives are used, the results provide a profile of the image of the topic that's rated. When a series of semantic differential scales is used to measure the image of several topics or entities, entire image profiles can be compared with one another. Still another advantage of the semantic differential scale is the ability to measure *ideal* images or attribute levels. In the example provided here, the researcher seeks to measure the image of pizza served at a particular restaurant. If another semantic differential scale were used to measure the image of a competing establishment, the two could be compared. Yet, additional information might be extremely helpful.

For most items used in the example, the *positive* and *negative* adjectives can be identified easily. Obviously it's better to be "good" than "bad" and "fresh" than "stale." Suppose, however, the sponsor's pizza is more moist or more spicy than a competitor's. Is that good or bad? Where several scales can't be identified as positive or negative, respondents can be

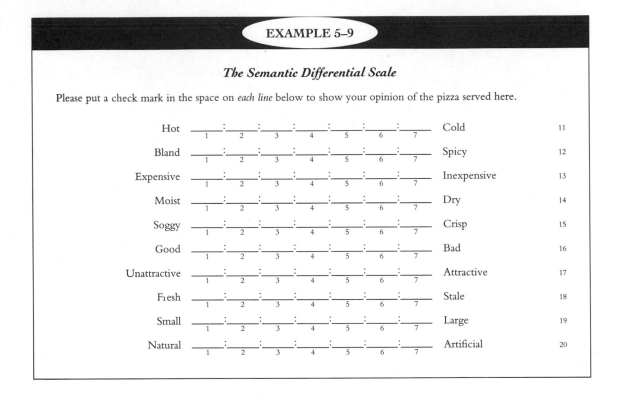

EXAMPLE 5–9

The Semantic Differential Scale

Please put a check mark in the space on *each line* below to show your opinion of the pizza served here.

Hot	___:___:___:___:___:___:___	Cold	11
	1 2 3 4 5 6 7		
Bland	___:___:___:___:___:___:___	Spicy	12
	1 2 3 4 5 6 7		
Expensive	___:___:___:___:___:___:___	Inexpensive	13
	1 2 3 4 5 6 7		
Moist	___:___:___:___:___:___:___	Dry	14
	1 2 3 4 5 6 7		
Soggy	___:___:___:___:___:___:___	Crisp	15
	1 2 3 4 5 6 7		
Good	___:___:___:___:___:___:___	Bad	16
	1 2 3 4 5 6 7		
Unattractive	___:___:___:___:___:___:___	Attractive	17
	1 2 3 4 5 6 7		
Fresh	___:___:___:___:___:___:___	Stale	18
	1 2 3 4 5 6 7		
Small	___:___:___:___:___:___:___	Large	19
	1 2 3 4 5 6 7		
Natural	___:___:___:___:___:___:___	Artificial	20
	1 2 3 4 5 6 7		

asked to rate their *ideal,* whatever the topic. To determine differential preference patterns, it's often very useful to compare only ideal images among respondent groups. Images of real and ideal topics can also be compared, and the closer a real image corresponds to the ideal image, the more positive the profile.

Guidelines for using semantic differential scales are presented in Guidelist 5–9. The requirement for bipolar adjectives presents a serious limitation to the use of the semantic differential. The adjectives must be on the ultimate extremes of the spectrum and they must define a single dimension. It's sometimes difficult to identify antonyms. For example, is the opposite of spicy "bland" or "mild" in the minds of potential respondents?

The Adjective Checklist

It's sometimes necessary to ascertain just how a topic is viewed by respondents and what descriptive adjectives or phrases apply to it. This can, of course, be measured with the semantic differential scale, but such an application may not be appropriate. The semantic differential technique is limited in the number of items that can be used and requires the specification of bipolar opposites. The adjective checklist is a very straightforward method of obtaining information about how a topic is described and viewed.

In Example 5–10, the instructions ask respondents to check any of the adjectives that

---

GUIDELIST 5–9

For Using the Semantic Differential Scale

1. This method is most effective for measuring image profiles, people, things, organizations, or concepts.
2. Adjectives must define a single dimension, and each pair must be bipolar opposites labeling the extremes.
3. Precisely *what* the respondent is to rate must be clearly stated in the introductory instructions.
4. No more than about 20 items should be used, and about half should begin with the most positive word.
5. If the same scale is used for several topics and/or for rating an *ideal* entity, image profiles can be compared among real entities and between real and ideal ones.

---

describe their jobs. There are 24 adjectives listed, but because of the economy of space and time and the ease with which respondents can complete the task, many more could have been included. Simplicity, directness, and economy are the major virtues of the adjective checklist. The adjectives listed can be many and varied. Short, descriptive phrases can even be used. This is especially valuable for exploratory research work. The greatest disadvantage of the adjective checklist is the dichotomous data it yields. There's no indication of *how much* each item describes the topic. Recommendations for using adjective checklists are provided in Guidelist 5–10.

EXAMPLE 5–10

The Adjective Checklist

Please put a check mark in the space in front of any word or phrase that describes your job.

_____ Easy	_____ Safe	11-12
_____ Technical	_____ Exhausting	13-14
_____ Boring	_____ Difficult	15-16
_____ Interesting	_____ Rewarding	17-18
_____ Low-paying	_____ Secure	19-20
_____ Strenuous	_____ Slow-paced	21-22
_____ Routine	_____ Enjoyable	23-24
_____ Dead-end	_____ Rigid	25-26
_____ Changing	_____ Pleasant	27-28
_____ Important	_____ Satisfying	29-30
_____ Demanding	_____ Degrading	31-32
_____ Temporary	_____ Risky	33-34

For Using the Adjective Checklist

1. This method is appropriate for measuring images.
2. The instructions and response task are quick and simple, and many adjectives can be included.
3. Precisely *what* the respondent is to rate or judge must be stated very clearly in the instructions.

4. The scale yields a profile, but only in the form of discrete, nominal, dichotomous data.
5. If several topics and/or an ideal entity are rated using more than one adjective checklist, profiles among real entities and between real and ideal can be compared.

The Semantic Distance Scale

The major advantages of the adjective checklist, discussed above, are simplicity and economy, but the *profiles* it provides are only nominal data. The values only name categories indicating whether the item was checked. It doesn't show how *well* or how *poorly* the adjective described the topic. By comparison, the semantic differential scale does measure this *distance* between the descriptive adjective and the thing rated. Yet, the semantic differential requires bipolar adjectives and is limited in the number of items that can be used because the response task is more difficult than with the adjective checklist. Example 5–11 shows a scale that combines the best of both.

The semantic distance scale is very similar in appearance to the adjective checklist. The major distinction is that the semantic distance scale includes a linear, numeric scale below the instructions and above the descriptive adjectives or phrases. Rather than merely checking or not checking an item to indicate whether or not it applies to the topic, the semantic distance scale requires that the respondent provide a *rating* of *how much* each item describes the topic. In that way, the data generated by the scale is interval *distance* from the item to the topic. The interval data are similar to that obtained by the semantic differential scale.

The semantic distance scale can be used to portray an image, just as the semantic differential scale and the adjective checklist can. The major advantage of the semantic distance scale over the semantic differential is that the adjectives or descriptive phrases used need not have *polar opposites*. The researcher could specify "dry" without being concerned if the opposite is "wet" or "moist." The advantage of the semantic distance scale, compared to the adjective checklist, is the quality of the data provided by the former. Semantic distance scale data are interval data, rather than nominal data indicating only discrete, yes-or-no categories. Consequently, it can be manipulated and statistically processed with all the facility associated with any other interval scale data. Greater complexity is the major disadvantage of the semantic distance scale, compared to the semantic differential or adjective checklist. The respondent task is more difficult to explain.

Guidelist 5–11 summarizes the main points to be observed when using semantic distance scales. All the same capabilities inherent in the semantic differential and the adjective check-

EXAMPLE 5–11

The Semantic Distance Scale

Please pick a number from the scale to show how well each word or phrase below describes your job and jot it in the space in front of each item.

Scale

Not at all	1	2	3	4	5	6	7	Perfectly

_____ Easy	_____ Safe	11–12
_____ Technical	_____ Exhausting	13–14
_____ Boring	_____ Difficult	15–16
_____ Interesting	_____ Rewarding	17–18
_____ Low-paying	_____ Secure	19–20
_____ Strenuous	_____ Slow-paced	21–22
_____ Routine	_____ Enjoyable	23–24
_____ Dead-end	_____ Rigid	25–26
_____ Changing	_____ Pleasant	27–28
_____ Important	_____ Satisfying	29–30
_____ Demanding	_____ Degrading	31–32
_____ Temporary	_____ Risky	33–34

list are included with the semantic distance scale. Profiles can be compared among real topics, an ideal entity can be rated, and ideal profiles of preference can be compared among different respondent subsamples or respondent groups. Of course, real entity profiles can be compared with ideal profiles, by subject, if computer analysis is used, and the degree of correspondence will indicate the overall *favorability* of the ratings of actual objects.

The Fixed Sum Scale

There are times when it's important to learn what *proportion* of some resource or activity has been devoted to each of several possible choices or alternatives. The fixed sum scale is an excellent device for this purpose. It would be possible simply to ask, "What percentage of the time do you do each of the following?" However, the respondent is likely to have great difficulty with such a question. The data from many respondents aren't likely to total to 100 percent. Example 5–12 shows a more effective format. The scale is most effective when it's used to measure actual behavior or action in the *recent* past. Ordinarily, about 10 different categories are the maximum, but as few as 2 or 3 can be used. The number to which the data must total has to be *very* clearly stated.

Recommendations for using the fixed sum scale are listed in Guidelist 5–12. The major advantage of the fixed sum scale is its clarity and simplicity. The instructions are easily understood and the respondent task is ordinarily easy to complete. It's important to list an *inclusive* set of items for this type of scale. If there are several options missing, respondents

---

GUIDELIST 5–11

For Using the Semantic Distance Scale

1. This method is appropriate for measuring images.
2. Many words or phrases can be included.
3. Precisely what the respondent is to judge and rate must be stated very clearly in the instructions.
4. The scale yields a profile indicating *how much* each phrase describes the topic, with continuous data.

5. If several topics or an *ideal* entity are rated with multiple semantic distance scales, profiles among real entities and between real and ideal can be compared.

---

would have to list several "other" alternatives. There would be no way to know how many times each was exercised.

SCALE COMBINATIONS

Many of the scales described thus far have been shown in *listed* form. By listing items together in the same format, they can share a common scale. This saves valuable questionnaire space, but that's not the most important reason for using scale lists. Listing scales together reduces

---

EXAMPLE 5–12

The Fixed Sum Scale

Of the last *10 times* that you ate lunch or dinner at a casual or fast food restaurant, how many times did you have each of the things listed below?

(Please be sure to make the total equal 10.)

_____ Hamburgers	11
_____ Hot dogs or sausage	12
_____ Chicken	13
_____ Pizza	14
_____ Chinese food	15
_____ Fish or seafood	16
_____ Deli sandwiches	17
_____ Hot sandwiches	18
_____ Mexican food	19
_____ Other (What?_____)	20–21

Total = 10

GUIDELIST 5–12

For Using the Fixed Sum Scale

1. The scale is used to measure proportions, rather than absolute values.
2. The occurrences must be apportioned into not more than about 10 categories.
3. The instructions must state very clearly the value to which the responses must total.
4. The scale provides continuous data so proportions can easily be compared among alternatives.
5. The data can be converted to percentages by dividing each value by the actual total, so every case will total a hundred percent and be comparable.

---

the response task and facilitates recording, and that's the greatest benefit of this format. Once the respondents have read the instructions and learned how to respond to the first item or so, they can do the rest on the list very quickly, easily, and accurately. They don't have to stop and study the item. They can just answer it and move on to the next. They mentally carry the same frame of reference and judgment criteria from one item to the next, so the data are closely comparable.

The Multiple-Rating List

The multiple-rating list shown in Example 5–13 is a commonly used variation of the linear, numeric scale described earlier, but there is an important distinction. With the linear, numeric scale list shown in Example 5–8, the respondent has to pick a number from the scale shown above the item and then *write the number* beside the item. The multiple-rating list has the labels of the scale extremes at the top. The scale, itself, is *listed beside each item.* This has two advantages: (1) all the respondent has to do is circle a number, and that's easier than writing it; and (2) the responses form a *visual pattern,* so the juxtaposition of the responses on a horizontal spectrum is a closer mapping to the way people actually think about the evaluations they're making. For instance, "safe" is to the *left* and "risky" is to the *right* in Example 5–13. The actual numbers have very little to do with the evaluations. Guidelist 5–13 contains the directions for composing multiple-rating lists.

The Multiple-Rating Matrix

The multiple-rating matrix shown in Example 5–14 is a very *condensed* format for using a combination of linear, numeric scale items. The scale, itself, is the same as the linear, numeric scale discussed earlier. The distinction between it and the matrix lies in the way the items are listed in a *matrix* of rows with *multiple columns.*

The multiple-rating matrix has two important advantages: First, it saves questionnaire space. The multiple-rating list in Example 5–13 obtains only data points. The multiple-rating matrix in Example 5–14 takes less questionnaire space, yet it captures 36 data points.

EXAMPLE 5–13

The Multiple-Rating List

Several savings or investment vehicles are listed below. Please indicate how safe or risky you feel each one is by circling a number beside it. If you feel it's very safe, circle a number toward the left. If you feel it's very risky, circle one toward the right, and if you think it's someplace in between, circle a number from the middle range that indicates your opinion.

	Extremely Safe					Extremely Risky		
Bank savings account	1	2	3	4	5	6	7	11
Savings and loan savings account	1	2	3	4	5	6	7	12
Money market account	1	2	3	4	5	6	7	13
Certificates of deposit	1	2	3	4	5	6	7	14
Treasury bills	1	2	3	4	5	6	7	15
Corporate common stocks	1	2	3	4	5	6	7	16
Corporate preferred stocks	1	2	3	4	5	6	7	17
Corporate bonds	1	2	3	4	5	6	7	18
Municipal bonds	1	2	3	4	5	6	7	19
U.S. government bonds	1	2	3	4	5	6	7	20
Foreign government bonds	1	2	3	4	5	6	7	21
Credit union shares	1	2	3	4	5	6	7	22
Commodity futures	1	2	3	4	5	6	7	23
Corporate stock futures	1	2	3	4	5	6	7	24
Precious metals	1	2	3	4	5	6	7	25
Precious gems	1	2	3	4	5	6	7	26

GUIDELIST 5–13

For Using a Multiple-Rating List

1. The scale, itself, is similar to the linear, numeric rating scale and it's used in much the same kind of measurements.
2. The listing format is most applicable where evaluative responses are to be arrayed on a single dimension.
3. The list is most economical where many, very brief items are all to be rated on the same dimension.
4. Scale extremes are at the top and they must define a single, bipolar dimension on which all items can be rated or *placed*.
5. The intermediate scale values shouldn't be labeled with words, and only numbers, spaced at equal intervals, should be listed beside each item.

In addition, the objects and their characteristics that are rated are all very close to one another. So the respondents are readily able to *compare* their evaluations from one rating object to another. Each item is more likely to be rated using the same criteria and frame of reference as those of the others. Ratings obtained in this format are very comparable.

The principal handicap of the multiple-rating matrix—often a prohibitive one—is its *complexity.* The instructions are complex and the task is a bit difficult. There's a good chance some respondents will be confused and make mistakes—both obvious ones and errors that aren't so obvious. Some may refuse the section and skip it because it looks too hard to do. Others may fill in only one space in each column or each row. Such data are useless. Even more serious is the likelihood that some respondents will work *down the columns* while others will work *across the rows!* If that happens, there's no way to tell who did it one way and who another way, and the data would be less reliable than it should be. The main considerations for using a multiple-rating matrix are summarized in Guidelist 5–14.

The Diagram Scale

Diagram scales can be used for many special situations. They're especially useful for measuring *configurations* of several things, where the *spacial relationships* convey part of the meaning. Example 5–15 shows one type of diagram scale to capture a *complete picture* of the family. Asking the respondent to circle his or her own age after listing it in the diagram has an additional advantage. Respondents are *less likely to lie* about their age because they ordi-

---

EXAMPLE 5–14

The Multiple-Rating Matrix

The table below lists four types of PRO brand baseball equipment along the top, and several characteristics of sports equipment along the left side. Please take *one product at a time!* Working down the column, pick a number from the scale indicating your evaluation of each characteristic and jot it in the space in the column below the product label and to the right of the characteristic. Please fill in *every space,* giving your rating for each product on each characteristic.

Scale

Very Poor	1	2	3	4	5	6	Excellent

	Bats	Balls	Gloves	Shoes	
Price . . . . _____		_____	_____	_____	11–14
Design . . . . _____		_____	_____	_____	15–18
Selection . . . . _____		_____	_____	_____	19–22
Durability . . . . _____		_____	_____	_____	23–26
Appearance . . . . _____		_____	_____	_____	27–30
Availability . . . . _____		_____	_____	_____	31–34
Service . . . . _____		_____	_____	_____	35–38
Packaging . . . . _____		_____	_____	_____	39–42
Construction . . . . _____		_____	_____	_____	43–46

GUIDELIST 5–14

For Using a Multiple-Rating Matrix

1. The scale, itself, is identical to the linear, numeric rating scale and it's for exactly the same kind of measurements.
2. This format is applicable only if evaluative responses are to be arrayed on a single dimension.
3. The matrix is effective only where a few items are to be rated on the *same* set of several *criteria* or *attributes*.

4. The rating matrix is most useful when closely comparable objects are to be rated with exactly the same judgment criteria and frame of reference.
5. This complex, difficult format should be used *only* when respondents are expected to be both bright and cooperative.

narily list the correct age with the others in the family and they're reluctant to change it afterward.

NONVERBAL SCALES

The survey items and scales discussed and shown in examples earlier have all contained verbal and numeric content. There are some situations where *nonverbal scales*—pictures or

EXAMPLE 5–15

The Diagram Scale

Please list the ages of all those in your family living at home in the spaces below. Jot the ages of the men and boys in the top circles—the ages of the women and girls in the bottom circles. Use as many as you need, listing them in order from oldest to youngest in each row.

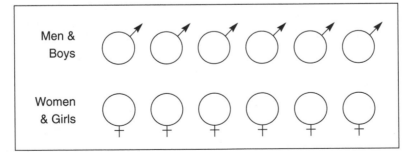

Now draw a big circle around the space with your own age in it.

EXAMPLE 5–16

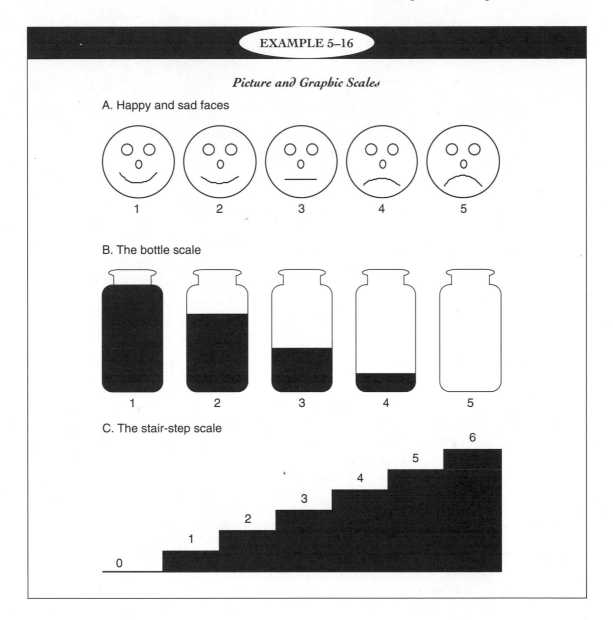

Picture and Graphic Scales

A. Happy and sad faces

B. The bottle scale

C. The stair-step scale

graphs—must be used to obtain the data. For example, with a survey of young children, the respondents' ability to read or to understand numeric scales may be very limited. In other, special situations, the survey might include respondents who are illiterate or who aren't literate in the language of the survey. It may not be feasible to measure the evaluations or reactions of children or others who don't read well with the scales described earlier. These situations require *nonverbal* scaling.

GUIDELIST 5–15

For Creating Pictorial Scales

1. They must be very easy for respondents to understand.
2. They should show something respondents have often seen.

3. They should represent the thing that's being measured.
4. They should be easy to draw or create.

The Picture Scale

Section A of Example 5–16 shows happy and sad faces that are very familiar to very young children. Even though they may have very little experience with letters, numbers, and other symbols, they have learned to recognize facial expressions very early in life. The interviewer would first ask the child to point to the face that's very happy, then to the one that's very sad, to be sure the child understands the pictures. Then the children would be asked to point to the face that shows how they feel when they do each of the things listed in the items, such as going to school or watching TV cartoons.

The Graphic Scale

For older children or adults in special situations, the Bottle Scale, shown in Section B of Example 5–16, may be more acceptable. It provides somewhat more useful measurement data because the extremes visually represent *none* and *all* or *total*. The Stair-Step Scale, shown in Section C, works effectively both for older children and for adults with little education or with impairments that limit their ability to respond to verbal and numeric scales. As with the bottle scale, space or distance represents numeric values that can be coded and recorded. Other types of diagram scales or items include simple line drawings depicting geographic areas, buildings, housing complexes, malls, or shopping centers. They can be used to measure traffic patterns or the locational patterns or preferences of respondents.

These are only a few of many such pictorial or graphic scales that might be created and used when a nonverbal instrument is required. Other possibilities include pictures of ladders or thermometers, or geometric figures of various size or height. Guidelist 5–15 lists the main requirements for pictorial scales. Any picture or graphic scale should be easy for the respondents to understand. They should be based on some phenomenon with which the respondents would be *very* familiar. Picture and graphic scales are most often typically used only for personal interview surveys.

SCALE SELECTION CRITERIA

There's seldom a single, clear-cut choice of a scale for any given question or information requirement when composing a questionnaire. Thus, it's impossible to list a set of rules that dictate exactly what scale should be used in each situation, even if every circumstance could be anticipated. Yet clearly, some scales are easily identified as potential tools for some common information needs and questions, and there are often other scales that are clearly inappropriate.

The criteria and considerations listed in the summary are merely guidelines. There are no ironclad rules that would limit the creativity and effectiveness of the researcher. While the conventional scales are nearly always adaptable, others should be invented for special needs and circumstances when they're required.

SUMMARY

How to Create Effective Scales

A. Keep it simple. Given a choice between a very short, concise scale and a more elaborate, sophisticated one, the less complex scale should be used. Even after identifying a scale to be used for an item, ask, "Is there an easier, simpler scale or way of asking this question?"

B. Respect the respondent. While respondents are ordinarily cooperative and helpful, response is a favor. They have little involvement with the task. Select scales that will make it as quick and easy as possible for them. That will reduce nonresponse bias and improve accuracy.

C. Dimension the response. In what dimensions do respondents and sponsors think about the issue? They'll not always be the same, so some commonality must be discovered. The dimensions along which the respondents are to answer must not be obscure or difficult, and they should parallel respondents' thinking.

D. Pick the denominations. Always use the denominations that are best for respondents. The data can later be converted to the denominations sought by information users. Feet and inches can be changed to metric or time converted to a 24-hour clock during processing.

E. Choose the range. Categories or scale increments should be about the same breadth as those ordinarily used by respondents. Normally, respondents classify things into a range from about 2 to about 7 or 8 categories, and seldom more than 10. Respondents often can't be as precise as researchers would like.

F. Group only when required. Never put things into categories when they can easily be expressed in numeric terms. People think in years, not decades or centuries. Data can always be grouped during processing, but if obtained in broad categories, it can't be desegregated later, no matter how desirable that might be.

G. Handle neutrality carefully. If respondents *genuinely* have no preference, they'll resent the forced choice inherent in a scale with an even number of alternatives. If feelings aren't especially strong, an odd number of scale points may result in *fence-riding* or piling on the midpoint, even when some preference exists.

H. State instructions clearly. Even the least capable respondents must be able to understand. Use language that's typical of the respondents. Explain exactly what the respondent should do and the task sequence they should follow. List the criteria by which they should judge and use an example or practice item if there's any doubt.

I. Always be flexible. Scaling examples provided here are only that. They can and should be modified to fit the task and the respondents. The instructions, format, vocabulary, and number of scale points can all be changed to suit the needs of the survey. Scales should fit the task, not conform to the original author's specifications.

J. Pilot test the scales. When there's any doubt about the ability of respondents to use the scales, a brief, informal pilot test is quick, inexpensive insurance. Don't wait until the entire questionnaire is written. Individual parcels can be checked with a few typical respondents.

Chapter 6

Building Questionnaires

FUNCTION OF THE QUESTIONNAIRE

The composition of individual survey questions and the scaling techniques used with them were discussed in the two previous chapters. It's time to bring these elements together into a complete, finished survey instrument. When the survey is self-administered, such as mail surveys are, the instrument is called a questionnaire. Technically, the measurement and recording instrument for surveys using interviewing is called an *interview schedule*. All survey instruments will be called *questionnaires* here, as they ordinarily are by research practitioners. The same principles and practices apply to construction of both types of instruments. In those few instances where interviewing versus self-administered data collection methods affect the questionnaire construction, the differences will be noted.

The questionnaire has several functions or objectives. It's the *package* that presents the questions and later contains the record of response for one respondent. The first section of the questionnaire introduces the survey to the respondents. The internal sections contain the items and scales to measure the survey topics, in a logical and necessary sequence. The final section ordinarily has questions to measure the respondents' characteristics, so they can be grouped and compared. The questionnaire also includes several other elements that facilitate data handling. These include the spaces to record the data and the codes that identify particular responses. The questionnaire may also show the record and line position of the computer file into which each data point will be keyed.

This chapter also identifies and discusses other instrumentation devices to accompany the questionnaire. They include such things as the mailing piece for mail surveys or rating scale cards for interviewing.

Survey Introduction

Research surveys usually depend very heavily on the *voluntary* cooperation of respondents. Research experience consistently shows that nearly all who refuse to cooperate do so within the first few *seconds* after initial contact, whether that contact is in person, on the telephone, or by mail. The principle is simply this: If the prospective respondent agrees to participate immediately when the survey is introduced, only a very small percentage will withdraw their cooperation later. Once they *begin,* they nearly always continue. They're very likely to complete the response task, except under the most unusual circumstances. Consequently, it's essential that the introduction be composed and delivered effectively. If the survey is introduced properly, the response rate will be increased and the reliability and validity of the survey will be enhanced. If it's done poorly, refusal and nonresponse will increase data collection time and expense. Error and bias will result and the reliability and validity of the data will be diminished.

A Sample Questionnaire

Example 6–1 contains a seven-page questionnaire to exemplify many of the principles and techniques discussed in this chapter. It is designed to illustrate how the various survey questions, scales, elements, and sections are organized and combined into a single, integrated, smooth-flowing questionnaire. It's substantially longer and more comprehensive than one would ordinarily expect such a questionnaire to be, so that all the various survey questions and scale types could be included. Consequently, it presents respondents with a somewhat more daunting response task than it would ideally be, even with a substantial inducement for survey participation.

This questionnaire would be used to survey guests departing from a luxury hotel. While it's meant to be illustrative, rather than completely practical and usable, it closely parallels an actual survey instrument of this type. The various elements of the sample questionnaire will be referenced throughout the discussion of questionnaire construction in this chapter.

Questionnaire Organization

The cover letter or interviewer greeting is the introduction to the questionnaire and response task. It's useful to view the questionnaire, itself, in three main parts: the introduction, the body of the questionnaire, and the conclusion. Each plays a different role. The composition of cover letters is discussed in Chapter 7. In Chapter 8 the initial greeting is considered in detail.

The first part of the questionnaire initiates the task for the respondent. It sets the stage and suggests what kinds of questions will follow. It indicates the type of information sought and provides an indication of the response task. Usually, this first part contains the most general questions that will be asked of respondents. It's important to include only questions that apply to all respondents and are fairly quick and easy to answer in the introductory part of the questionnaire. It's especially important to avoid any questions or issues that may be threatening to respondents. This isn't the place to ask *delicate* questions or seek *sensitive* information.

The sample questionnaire in Example 6–1 begins with an Adjective Checklist—perhaps the quickest, easiest type of item there is. The respondents get the feeling they've done a lot very quickly and easily. Once started, they're likely to continue.

The body of the questionnaire is the middle part. It's ordinarily much larger than the introduction or conclusion. It contains questions or items that deal with the substance and detail of the survey topics. The specific organization of the body of the questionnaire is

---

EXAMPLE 6–1

Sample Questionnaire

A Please put an **✗** in the space before *any* and *all* words you feel describe your stay at this hotel.

◇ Active	◇ Aggravating	◇ Amusing	11-13
◇ Boring	◇ Busy	◇ Costly	14-16
◇ Delightful	◇ Disappointing	◇ Disgusting	17-19
◇ Disturbing	◇ Entertaining	◇ Exciting	20-22
◇ Fantastic	◇ Frustrating	◇ Healthy	23-25
◇ Informative	◇ Invigorating	◇ Lazy	26-28
◇ Memorable	◇ Painful	◇ Pleasant	29-31
◇ Productive	◇ Recreational	◇ Regretable	32-34
◇ Relaxing	◇ Restful	◇ Sensational	35-37
◇ Stimulating	◇ Tantalizing	◇ Terrible	38-40

B Please check *any* of our services you used during this visit?
(Please check (✔) *all* boxes below that apply.)

☐ Inside Self-Parking	☐ MiniBar in the Room	41-42
☐ Valet Parking	☐ Laundry or Cleaners	43-44
☐ Wake-up Call	☐ Business Center	45-46
☐ Bellman or Doorman	☐ Health Club or Pool	47-48
☐ Lobby Coffee or Breakfast	☐ Room Service	49-50

C Please pick a number from the scale to show how important *each* of these factors is *to you* when you're CHOOSING A HOTEL and jot it in the space to the right of *each item*.

Scale									
Extremely Unimportant	1	2	3	4	5	6	7	**Extremely Important**	

Convenience of the location of the hotel within the area you're visiting.	_____	51
Safety and security of the hotel and neighborhood in which it's located.	_____	52
Knowledge or experience with other hotels in the same chain.	_____	53
Recommendations or suggestions of travel agents or representatives.	_____	54

EXAMPLE 6–1

Sample Questionnaire (continued)

D

If **THIS** is your *favorite* hotel, please skip to **E** below.

Please check *one* space on *each line* to show how *this hotel* compares to YOUR FAVORITE HOTEL.
Compared to my favorite hotel, THIS ONE IS . . .

	Much Less			The Same			Much More	
Expensive	1	2	3	4	5	6	7	11
Convenient	1	2	3	4	5	6	7	12
Comfortable	1	2	3	4	5	6	7	13
Neat, Clean	1	2	3	4	5	6	7	14
Spacious, Roomy	1	2	3	4	5	6	7	15
Attractive	1	2	3	4	5	6	7	16

E

Please pick a number from the scale to show how much you *agree* or *disagree* with each statement and jot in the space to the right of the item.

SCALE
1 = Strongly Agree
2 = Agree
3 = Neutral
4 = Disagree
5 = Strongly Disagree

I'm very concerned about safety and security when I stay at a hotel. ········· ____	17
The size of a hotel room is more important to me than how it's furnished. ·· ____	18
I like hotels that have elegant, unusual lobbies and open areas. ··············· ____	19
If it cost the same, I'd much prefer a suite to just one hotel room. ············· ____	20
When I travel, I like to stay in a different kind of hotel at each place. ·········· ____	21
Even if some hotels in a chain are very nice, others might be terrible. ········ ____	22
I like newer hotels much more than older ones, even if they're well-kept. ·· ____	23
When picking a hotel, the most important thing to me is its location. ·········· ____	24
I don't like to decide to stay at a hotel until I visit it first. ····························· ____	25
I like to see what the rooms are like before I agree to stay at a hotel. ········ ____	26

EXAMPLE 6–1

Sample Questionnaire (continued)

F

How important to you is each of these hotel facilities or services?
Please circle one number on each line.

	Don't Know	Extremely Unimportant				Extremely Important	
Gym or health club	0	1	2	3	4	5	27
Laundry or cleaning service	0	1	2	3	4	5	28
Mini-bar in the room	0	1	2	3	4	5	29
Business center facilities	0	1	2	3	4	5	30
Inside parking	0	1	2	3	4	5	31
Valet parking	0	1	2	3	4	5	32
Doormen and bellmen	0	1	2	3	4	5	33
24-hour restaurant or cafe	0	1	2	3	4	5	34

G

Please pick a number from the scale to show how often you do *each* of these things *when you stay at a hotel* and jot it in the space to the right of *each* item.

SCALE
1 = Always
2 = Often
3 = Sometimes
4 = Rarely
5 = Never

Have a rental car delivered and/or picked up at the hotel?	____	35
Take early morning coffee when freely served in the lobby?	____	36
Obtain information from the concierge or tour desk?	____	37
Visit the hotel bar or lounge?	____	38
Order pizza from outside the hotel to be delivered?	____	39
Swim or sunbathe at the hotel pool (when available)?	____	40
Eat one or more meals at the hotel restaurant?	____	41
Use the physical fitness or exercise facilities (if available)?	____	42
Have drinks or "set-ups" from the hotel bar served in the room?	____	43

EXAMPLE 6–1

Sample Questionnaire (continued)

H When you plan and go on a trip, *at what point* do you *usually* decide what hotel you'd like to stay at?   (Please check [✔] only *one* space.)

Before I know I'm going. (I have a favorite I always prefer.) ························· _____ 1

As soon as I know the destination. (Before I make travel arrangements.) ·· _____ 2

After making travel arrangements or reservations. ································ _____ 3

Sometime before I leave on the trip. ··· _____ 4

While I'm traveling. (Along the way.) ·· _____ 5   44

When I arrive in the city where I'm staying. ·································· _____ 6

Just before it's time to go to a hotel and check in. ···························· _____ 7

Only after visiting one or more hotels to see which I like. ····················· _____ 8

I How well does each of these words or phrases describe your impressions of *our hotel staff?*

	Don't Know	Not At All		*Please circle one number on each line.*			Perfectly So	
Unfriendly ··········	0	1	2	3	4	5	6	7	45
Prompt ··············	0	1	2	3	4	5	6	7	46
Capable ·············	0	1	2	3	4	5	6	7	47
Discourteous ······	0	1	2	3	4	5	6	7	48
Caring ···············	0	1	2	3	4	5	6	7	49
Too busy ···········	0	1	2	3	4	5	6	7	50
Helpful ··············	0	1	2	3	4	5	6	7	51
Greedy ··············	0	1	2	3	4	5	6	7	52

J Which *one* courtesy bath product do you find *MOST useful* and enjoyable?
(Please put an ✘ in only *one* circle below.)

1 ◯ Shampoo
2 ◯ Cream Rinse
3 ◯ Bath Oil
4 ◯ Moisturizer
5 ◯ Sun Lotion

Which *one* courtesy bath product do you find *LEAST useful* and enjoyable?
(Please put an ✘ in only *one* circle below.)

1 ◯ Shampoo
2 ◯ Cream Rinse
3 ◯ Bath Oil   53-54
4 ◯ Moisturizer
5 ◯ Sun Lotion

EXAMPLE 6–1

Sample Questionnaire (continued)

K Please indicate below what type of hotel RECREATION and ENTERTAINMENT you like best?
(Put an ✗ in space before the *one* you *most* prefer for *each* of the *six pairs* listed below.)

RECREATION	ENTERTAINMENT	
❑ Tennis or Golf ❑ Swimming Pool or Gym/Health Club	❑ Vocal or Instrumental Music ❑ Comedy, Magic or Pantomime	11-12
❑ Golf ❑ Tennis	❑ Continuous by Various Soloists ❑ Periodically by Performing Groups	13-14
❑ Swimming Pool ❑ Gym or Health Club	❑ In the Bar, Lounge, or Restaurant ❑ In the Atrium Lobby	15-16

L Please *rank* each kind of music below in your order of preference.

(Please put a 1 in the space before the kind you like best, 2 in the space before your second favorite, and so forth.)

_____ Classical

_____ Country

_____ Easy Listening

_____ Jazz

_____ Rock

Please *rank* each type of performer below in your order of preference.

(Please put a 1 in the space before the type you like best, 2 in the space before your second favorite, and so forth.)

_____ Ventriloquists		17-18
_____ Mimes		19-20
_____ Magicians		21-22
_____ Jugglers		23-24
_____ Comedians		25-26

M Please check [✔] *one* space on *each line* to show your overall, general opinion of this hotel as a whole.

	1 2 3 4 5 6 7		
Expensive		Inexpensive	27
Ugly		Beautiful	28
Old		New	29
Immaculate		Filthy	30
Elegant		Commonplace	31
Prestigious		Debasing	32

EXAMPLE 6–1

Sample Questionnaire (continued)

N Please rate *each* area of the hotel listed below on *each* factor—*cleanliness, attractiveness, comfort, and convenience*—by picking a number from the scale and jotting it in *each square.* (*Fill in every square, recording a zero if you don't know.*)

Don't Know	SCALE						
	Very Poor					Excellent	
0	1	2	3	4	5	6	

	Cleanliness	Attractiveness	Comfort	Convenience	
Main Lobby	☐	☐	☐	☐	33-36
Guest Rooms	☐	☐	☐	☐	37-40
Halls and Foyers	☐	☐	☐	☐	41-44
Pirate's Lounge	☐	☐	☐	☐	45-48
Ship's Galley Restaurant	☐	☐	☐	☐	49-52

O Of the *last ten times* you stayed at a hotel, *how many times* did you stay at. . . .

This particular hotel?	____	times	11-12
Another hotel in *this* chain?	____	times	13-14
A hotel that's part of *some other national chain*?	____	times	15-16
An individual, *independent* hotel?	____	times	17-18
Some other kind of hotel? (What kind? _____)	____	times	19-20

(*Please make the TOTAL = 10*)   **Total =   10**   times

P Please list the ages of all those who shared your room or suite during this stay with us in the spaces below, including *yourself.* Jot the ages of all the men and boys in the top circles and the ages of all the women and girls in the bottom circles.

Men & Boys	♂ ♂ ♂ ♂ ♂	21-30
Women & Girls	♀ ♀ ♀ ♀ ♀	31-40

EXAMPLE 6–1

Sample Questionnaire (concluded)

Q Please put an ✗ in the box to indicate which head of household you are, then check or fill in the items below for *each* head of household in your home.

I am the . . .

▢ **MALE Head of Household**	▢ **FEMALE Head of Household**	41
Age ···················· _____ years	Age ···················· _____ years	42-45
Formal education ·· _____ years *(For example, High school graduate=12 years)*	Formal education ·· _____ years *(For example, High school graduate=12 years)*	46-49

EMPLOYMENT STATUS:	*EMPLOYMENT STATUS:*	
1 ▢ company employed	1 ▢ company employed	
2 ▢ government employed	2 ▢ government employed	
3 ▢ self-employed	3 ▢ self-employed	
4 ▢ seeking employment	4 ▢ seeking employment	50-51
5 ▢ military	5 ▢ homemaker	
6 ▢ retired	6 ▢ retired	
7 ▢ student	7 ▢ student	

OCCUPATIONAL STATUS:	*OCCUPATIONAL STATUS:*	
1 ▢ professional [med, law, etc.]	1 ▢ professional [med, law, etc.]	
2 ▢ managerial, executive	2 ▢ managerial, executive	
3 ▢ administrative, clerical	3 ▢ administrative, clerical	
4 ▢ engineering, technical	4 ▢ engineering, technical	52-53
5 ▢ marketing, sales	5 ▢ marketing, sales	
6 ▢ skilled craft or trade	6 ▢ skilled craft or trade	
7 ▢ semiskilled occupation	7 ▢ semiskilled occupation	

ANNUAL INCOME:	*ANNUAL INCOME:*	
Approximately $ ___ ,000.00	Approximately $ ___ ,000.00	54-59

THANK YOU FOR COMPLETING THIS GUEST QUESTIONNAIRE. PLEASE TAKE IT TO THE REGISTRATION DESK WHERE YOUR V.I.P. BONUS GIFT IS WAITING FOR YOU TO CLAIM IT.

discussed below. Generally the items should be in a sequence that's logical and meaningful to respondents. There should be a smooth transition from one issue or topic to the next, with no sudden breaks or dramatic changes in the respondents' frame of reference.

Figure 6–1 lists the sections, by identifying letter, in the introduction and body of the sample questionnaire, preceding the demographic section. Each section contains just one type of survey question, item, or scale. This organization will be discussed more completely later in this chapter.

The final or concluding part of the questionnaire is reserved for two kinds of questions: those that deal with the most sensitive or delicate issues or topics, and those that measure the attributes or characteristics of the respondents. The *demographic* or *biographic* questions are almost always at the very end of the questionnaire. The reasons for putting these questions last are compelling. First, the respondent has become familiar with the inquiry and rapport should be maximum at this point. They have more trust and are less likely to be skeptical or uncooperative than at an earlier point. Second, some respondents may terminate at this point or refuse to answer some of the items. Nevertheless, they have provided the bulk of the data and their responses to the earlier items in the body of the questionnaire may still be usable.

The sample questionnaire in Example 6–1 concludes with the demographic questions— a very conventional method of closing. The most sensitive of the demographic questions, those on income, are reserved for last. Basic guidelines for organizing questionnaires are listed in Guidelist 6–1.

Figure 6–1 *Sample Questionnaire Item Types*

Section	Question or Scale Type
A	Adjective Checklist
B	Multiple-Choice, Multiple-Response
C	Linear, Numeric Scale
D	Comparative Scale
E	Likert Scale
F	Multiple-Rating List
G	Verbal Frequency Scale
H	Ordinal Scale
I	Semantic Distance Scale
J	Multiple-Choice, Single-Response
K	Paired Comparisons
L	Forced Rankings
M	Semantic Differential Scale
N	Multiple-Rating Matrix
O	Fixed Sum Scale
P	Diagram Scale
Q	Demographic Items

GUIDELIST 6–1

For Organizing the Questionnaire

1. Picture the questionnaire in three main parts: introduction, body, and conclusion.
2. Begin with the most general questions and avoid those that might be threatening or difficult to answer.
3. Remember the introductory part sets the stage and influences the respondents' expectations about what's to come.
4. Be sure the body of the questionnaire flows smoothly from one issue to the next.
5. Organize items in the body in a sequence that's logical and meaningful to respondents.
6. Save the most sensitive issues and threatening questions for the concluding portion, when rapport is greatest.
7. List demographic or biographic questions last, so if some respondents decline most data are still usable.

CREATING QUESTIONNAIRE SECTIONS

For most surveys, the questions can be grouped into smaller sections than the three main parts just described. Some surveys may include only a dozen or so questions, but typically a survey will have 50, 100, or more individual items. Grouping them into sections simplifies the task of asking and answering the questions. It makes the task *appear* simpler and easier for respondents, and actually makes it so. The more effectively the items are grouped into sections, the more efficient the questionnaire will be.

Grouping Items by Topic

The most common way to group items is by topic. For example, a marketing research survey may contain questions about three different topics: purchase *behavior,* the *image* of one or more retail stores, and the *lifestyles* of the respondents. One section of the questionnaire might be devoted to each of these topics. Each section might contain all the items devoted to that particular survey topic. This would be an effective way to organize the items, providing that it appears logical or makes sense to the respondents. For example, it would make sense to ask all about the products they bought from various stores in one section, then, in another, to ask about their perceptions or images of several different stores. This might be followed by a section with several items to define their lifestyle based on their activities, interests, and opinions. This would be a much more meaningful organization than if all the various topics and kinds of questions were intermixed with one another.

A survey of employees may provide another example of grouping questions or items by topic. For such a survey, it would make sense to the respondents if all the questions about job satisfaction were asked in one place, all items about relationships with co-workers were contained in another, and all questions concerning occupational history were listed together in a third section. It wouldn't be appropriate to *jump around* from one to another of these areas of inquiry. After the first question or so about a particular area, the respondents' minds will have turned to that issue. They can easily respond to additional items about the same basic issue, but it would be difficult to shift abruptly to another, entirely separate issue, then turn their attention again to the first.

Grouping Items by Scaling Technique

Often the same scaling technique can be applied to many questions or items. When that's the case, it's very practical and efficient to list them together in one section of the questionnaire. For instance, all the items composed as statements and using a Likert scale (Strongly agree, Agree, Neutral, Disagree, or Strongly disagree) can be listed in one place and the scale shown only once at the top of the section. Another section might contain all the items that use a verbal frequency scale (Always, Often, Sometimes, Rarely, or Never). Such grouping by scale type saves time and space and makes the response task easier. The respondents need only to read the instructions and get familiar with the scale one time. They can then continue through the list of all the items that use that type of scale.

Grouping Items Both Ways

Items can often be grouped by both topic and scale type. A set of items devoted to the same topic may also use the same scaling method. That's the ideal situation because there are both a logical sequence and a high degree of time and space economy. Several examples of scaling techniques in the previous chapter contain items grouped by both scale type and topic. Sometimes special scaling methods can be devised to apply to many items dealing with a

Figure 6–2 *Sample Questionnaire Topics by Section*

Section	Issue or Topic of Items
A	General impression and image profile of the guests' visit to the hotel.
B	Experience and use of various hotel services during this visit.
C	Importance of four common evaluative criteria for choosing a hotel.
D	Comparison of guests' perceptions of this and their favorite hotel.
E	Measurement of common guest beliefs, values, and opinions.
F	Profile of the importance of eight ancillary hotel guest facilities.
G	Assessment of guests' general policies and practices while traveling.
H	Timing of hotel choice during the travel planning process.
I	Measurement of the guests' image profile of hotel staff personnel.
J	Identification of most and least preferred courtesy bath product.
K	Comparisons of hotel recreation and entertainment options.
L	Rank ordering of music and entertainment alternatives.
M	Measurement of the guests' image profile of the hotel as a whole.
N	Guest evaluations of five internal hotel areas on four criteria.
O	Profile of guests' experience and use of various hotel types.
P	Picture of the individual, family, or group occupying the room or suite.
Q	Demographic profiles of male and female heads of household.

GUIDELIST 6–2

For Grouping Items into Sections

1. Group items into sections to save interviewer time or to save space on a self-administered questionnaire.
2. Always group items in a way that's meaningful to the respondents or facilitates answering questions.
3. Items that deal with the same survey topic or issue can often be clustered into meaningful sections.
4. Items that use the same scaling technique may be grouped together into a coherent section.
5. Special scale formats may be devised to apply to many items dealing with the same basic issue or topic within one questionnaire section.
6. It's very efficient and practical to group items so that many of them share the same scale and instructions.

---

single topic. Then they can be grouped into one section, reducing the time and effort required to answer the questions.

The survey questionnaire for hotel guests shown in Example 6–1 is organized by topic and scale type, simultaneously. The broad topics or issues addressed by each section of the questionnaire are identified in Figure 6–2. Each section covers a fairly distinct set of topics or issues and each just one type of item or scale.

A questionnaire should be seen as the outline of a *conversation* between the researcher and the respondents. The respondents don't expect the conversation to switch abruptly from one topic or format to another. Each section should be integrated and consistent. There should be a *bridge* leading from one section to the next, to ensure the proper flow of the dialogue. Guidelist 6–2 contains recommendations for grouping questionnaire items into sections.

DIRECTING RESPONSE FLOW

For many surveys, every respondent will be asked every question in the questionnaire. But in some surveys, only certain questions apply to some respondents while other items do not. For instance, a survey might have some questions addressed only to men or only to women, even though both sexes are included in the sample. Similarly, the questionnaire may contain items or sections that apply only to people who respond a certain way to previous questions. In such cases, the *flow* of the questions has to be governed or directed carefully. That's typically done by *branching* the flow of the conversation according to specific criteria. The principal factors to consider when organizing and grouping questionnaire items are listed in Checklist 6–1.

Conditional Branching

Often there are survey items that apply to some respondents but not to others, depending on their answers to a previous question. When that's the case, the questionnaire writer can

---

CHECKLIST 6–1

To Organize and Group Items

1. Does the initial section set the stage for respondents? If not, only general, nonthreatening items that apply to everyone should be retained in the first section.
2. Is each section in the body of the questionnaire organized around one topic, set of issues, or scaling technique? If not, items must be regrouped into meaningful sections.
3. Does the *conversation* flow smoothly from one section to the next? Rearrange the sections or insert a *bridge* between sections when necessary.

4. Have threatening or *sensitive* questions been retained for the latter sections of the questionnaire? If so, they'll more often be answered because rapport is greater.
5. Are the demographic or biographic items contained in the concluding section? Placing them there increases response and obtains the most data in case of refusal.
6. Does the entire dialogue flow smoothly in a manner meaningful to respondents? If not, any abrupt shifts or discontinuities should be identified and removed.

---

use *conditional branching* or a "go to" statement so those for whom the items don't apply will skip them. This is called "*conditional* branching" because the branch in the flow of questions is made *on condition* that a certain answer is given to the preceding question.

Four slightly different methods of conditional branching within a questionnaire are shown in Example 6–2. The instructions might be expressed a little differently, depending on whether the questionnaire was used for a self-administered, mail survey or by a personal or telephone interviewer. In either case, the basic concept is the same. The examples assume the researcher intends to ask one or more questions about the Sunday newspaper. It wouldn't make sense to ask such questions of those who didn't subscribe. So the questionnaire must *first* ask whether the respondent subscribes. If so, the question(s) would be asked. If not, they wouldn't, and the process would move on to other issues and questions.

The first example is an *implied* branch because there are no specific branching instructions. The second question begins with the phrase, "If so, . . ." indicating that *if not,* the question need *not* be answered. This is the most simple form of conditional branching around a question that may not always apply. It's often used in self-administered questionnaires because it's simple, quick, and easy for the respondent to understand. Even if some respondents who need not answer the question do so anyhow, little time and effort is lost. The data for such cases can be ignored when it's transferred and processed.

The second example is very typical of an *explicit* branch. It contains instructions directing the interviewer or the respondent to go to a particular question, and any items between the instruction and that point would be ignored or skipped. Alternative forms of the instruction might specify a different page of the questionnaire, or some other mark or indication can be used in place of question numbers. For example, interviewers might be instructed: "If **NO,** go to the **X**, below," or some similar designation.

EXAMPLE 6–2

The Use of Conditional Branching

Implied Branch or Subquestion

Do you subscribe to the Sunday newspaper?   _____ yes _____ no
  If so, do you read it regularly?   _____ yes _____ no

Explicit Branch with a Single "Go To"

Do you subscribe to the Sunday newspaper?   _____ yes _____ no
  [If not, go to Question 30]

Explicit Branch with "Skip"

Do you subscribe to the Sunday newspaper?   _____ yes _____ no
  [If not, skip Question 20]

Explicit Branch with Multiple "Go To's"

What Sunday newspaper do you *most* often read, if any?   _____ yes _____ no

      _____ *Times* . . . .(Go to Question 30)
      _____ *Tribune* . . . .(Go to Question 35)
      _____ *Dispatch* . . . .(Go to Question 40)
      _____ *Chronicle* . . . .(Go to Question 45)
      _____ none . . . .(Go to Question 50)

The third section of the example shows a similar branch with an *explicit* instruction, but rather than directing the interviewer or respondent to a particular place, it says what must be skipped. It's ordinarily advisable to use this form when only one or two items are to be skipped. This format gets too complex and difficult when several items must be skipped. The question(s) to be skipped must also immediately follow the instruction. The interviewer or respondent won't remember to skip the items if they come later in the questionnaire.

The last example consists of an explicit, multiple branch. In this case, a different set of questions are asked, depending on which paper is most often read. (Note that the item seeks only one newspaper. If it asked about subscription, more than one might be identified and the branching would become extremely complex and intricate.) This type of branching instruction is acceptable for interview surveys, but it's ordinarily too complex for mail surveys that are self-administered by respondents. Notice, also, that this format will require a second branch after the set of five questions about any one newspaper. Presumably, an unconditional branch instruction would be used to direct the questioning process to item 50, where a new set of questions or issues would be addressed.

As with the single "go to" branch statement example, the designation of where to go need not be listed as a question number. The instruction might refer to "Part A, B, C, etc.," to "Section I, II, III, etc.," to a page number, or to any other meaningful designation. The questionnaire writer may use color coding or shading of pages or sections, or any other device that would help make the place to which the process should move distinct and clearly identifiable, as it is in Section D of Example 6–1.

Unconditional Branching

An *unconditional* branch directs the questioning process to another place for *all* respondents who reach that particular location on the questionnaire. In the example of a branch with multiple "go to" instructions used in Example 6–2, some respondents might indicate they most often read the Sunday *Times*. The interviewer would then move to Question 30, shown in Example 6–3, and ask the next five questions. Since Questions 35 through 49 apply to other newspapers, the process would then branch *around* them and go to the next section, beginning with Question 50. A similar branch instruction would follow Questions 39 and 44. (Obviously, if the branch was to Question 50, none would be required after Question 49.) As in the case of conditional branch instructions, *unconditional* branches need not always use a question number. Any other clearly identifiable means of designating the location to which the questioning process should move would be acceptable.

Branching Limitations

The main considerations for using branching instructions are identified in Checklist 6–2. Branching instructions within the questionnaire can be very useful and helpful, and at times, some form of branching is inevitable. On the other hand, the use of branching is *strictly limited*. Each branch adds greatly to the complexity of the interviewing or response task. Too many branches may introduce bias and error, reducing the reliability and validity of the results. In self-administered mail surveys, the least sophisticated respondents often become confused or bewildered by the instructions and fail to follow them correctly. The respondents are voluntarily doing the task for the researcher. If it becomes too complex or difficult, many will give up and discard the questionnaire, rather than completing and returning it.

EXAMPLE 6–3

The Use of an Unconditional Branch

30. Do you regularly read the:	Magazine section?	_____ yes	_____ no
31.	Sports pages?	_____ yes	_____ no
32.	Editorials?	_____ yes	_____ no
33.	Religious news?	_____ yes	_____ no
34.	Home directory?	_____ yes	_____ no

(Go to Question 50)

CHECKLIST 6–2

To Use Branching Instructions

1. Are the data to be collected with a self-administered questionnaire? If so, branching must be strictly limited.
2. Does only one question immediately following another need to be skipped by some respondents? In that case, use an implied branch, such as "If so . . ."
3. Must some respondents skip an entire set of questions? If so, a conditional branch with "go to" should be used.
4. Do several different answers to an item require going to several different sections that must be completed? If so, a multiple, conditional branch and an unconditional branch after each such section will be needed.
5. Is the location to which each branch is to be made clearly designated and easily identified? If not, shading, color coding, or some other designation should be included.
6. Is it absolutely certain that the least sophisticated or least motivated interviewers or respondents can and will branch correctly? If not, modifications are necessary.
7. Are there more than a few branches required within the questionnaire? If so, multiple forms of the questionnaire should be considered.
8. Are there several branches that are based on the same basic *condition* or response? If so, the conditioning question should be used as a *qualifier* in the greeting and multiple forms of the questionnaire used.

While branching can be used a little more liberally for personal or telephone interview surveys, it's still very limited. The people who *construct* questionnaires often, if not always, overestimate both the *ability* and the *willingness* of the interviewers to follow their instructions. It's also difficult for questionnaire or interview schedule writers to appreciate the conditions under which the fieldworkers or interviewers must ask the questions and record the responses. It's extremely difficult to hold the respondents' attention and maintain their interest while simultaneously recording answers, reading branching instructions, and finding the correct location of the next question. An occasional branch over one or a very few items is usually okay. When many branches are required and the task is very complex, it would be better to *prequalify* respondents and use *alternative forms* of the questionnaire for different groups of respondents.

Unlimited Branching

There's a notable exception to the restrictions and limitations on branching noted earlier. Some commercial data collection agencies have special telephone interviewing facilities where the questionnaire is presented on a computer display. But rather than merely a static display of a questionnaire page, the machine is programmed to present the questions *dynamically,* one question or item at a time. The interviewer/operator also records the response to each item directly on the keyboard.

With this kind of dynamic questionnaire, there's virtually no limit to the amount and complexity of branching, because it's all done by the computer, rather than the interviewer or respondent. The program "looks at" each answer as it's recorded, or looks back at the record of earlier responses, then chooses the next item based on earlier answers. Neither the interviewer nor the respondent need be concerned or even aware of the branching.

There are a few, similar, personal interview situations where dynamic computer-generated questionnaires are also used. Field interviewers may be equipped with laptop or notebook computers that present the questions and on which the responses are recorded. In other, special cases, respondents may be induced to sit down at a computer or terminal that will present the questions and allow them to respond on a regular or special keyboard or perhaps a touch-sensitive display screen.

Computer-generated survey interrogation allows the questionnaire writer to devise a highly complex, dynamic flow of questions. In addition, data input is edited "on the spot," so that errors can be noted and corrected immediately. These innovative computer applications are currently used mainly by only a relatively few data collection firms, but their popularity is certain to grow dramatically in the next few years. Yet most of those who conduct surveys infrequently will probably continue to depend on traditional paper-and-pencil methods.

Composing Instructions

Whether the questionnaire is self-administered or administered by an interviewer, *instructions* will be required or helpful in many places. Instructions aren't really part of the actual questions or items. Rather, they tell the interviewer or respondent how to present or respond to the questions. Most often the instructions apply to a *set* of items or questions. For example, several items may use the same response scale, and the instructions indicate how to use that scale.

The indented paragraphs above the items listed in examples of scales, shown in the previous chapter, are typical instructions. They apply to all the items listed below them. Most scaling techniques require some instruction, at least for the first time they appear in a questionnaire. Instructions for using scales are the most common instructions found in questionnaires. Yet this is only one type of questionnaire instruction. Several other types may also be required or useful.

Instructions for using scales

The more complex the scaling technique and the less sophisticated the responding population, the more elaborate the instructions must be. For example, the very common Likert scale with five categories ranging from "Strongly agree" to "Strongly disagree" ordinarily requires very simple instruction. Typically, it's sufficient merely to say, "Please pick a number to show how much you agree or disagree and jot it in the space beside each statement below."

The semantic differential scale, shown in Example 5–9 in the previous chapter on page 130, requires very brief instruction because of its visual or graphic nature. On the other hand, the semantic distance scale, shown in Example 5–11 on page 133, needs a little more elaboration because it's less graphic and depends on a linear, numeric rating scale from which numbers are selected and recorded. The fixed sum scale shown in Example 5–12 on page 134 of the previous chapter is even more complex because the answers should total to a given, constant sum. Thus, that example provides the basic instruction at the top, an additional, parenthetical note just above the items, and yet another *cue* at the bottom indicating the total to which the numbers should sum.

The degree to which instructions should be simple and brief or elaborate and complete depends as much on the sophistication of the respondents as on the complexity of the scales. In Chapter 5, Example 5–13 on page 136 contains very thorough and complete instructions. It assumes that the respondents are relatively naive or unsophisticated. If this same scaling technique and set of items were to be used for a survey of certified public accountants, rather than the general public, the instructions might simply say: "Please circle a number for each investment vehicle to show your perception of financial risk." The rule is to compose instructions that meet the requirements of the *least* sophisticated respondents.

Elements of instructions

Instructions on how respondents from the public should use scales usually contain several elements: (a) what items or elements to rate; (b) what criterion or standard to use; (c) how to use the scale, and (d) exactly how and where to report or record the responses. In Example 6–4, the correct version contains all elements while the incorrect version contains none.

The incorrect example doesn't indicate that respondents should rate each and every item. Many respondents would rate only some of them and ignore others or would rate all of

---

EXAMPLE 6–4

Correct and Incorrect Scale Instructions

Wrong: Please rate the importance of the following.

Scale

Unimportant 1 2 3 4 5 Important
- _____ Dishwasher
- _____ Kitchen range
- _____ Refrigerator
- _____ Washing machine
- _____ Clothes dryer

Right: Please rate how important it's for you to own **EACH** of these household appliances. If it isn't at all important to own it, pick a low number from the scale and jot it in the space in front of the item. If it's very important, pick a high number, and if it's somewhat important, pick a number from the middle range and jot it in the space.

Scale

Unimportant 1 2 3 4 5 Important
- _____ Dishwasher
- _____ Kitchen range
- _____ Refrigerator
- _____ Washing machine
- _____ Clothes dryer

GUIDELIST 6–3

For Composing Scale Instructions

1. Clearly indicate which items are to be rated and if only one is to be picked or an answer recorded for all items.
2. Say what criterion or standard should be used to judge the items or answer the questions.
3. Describe how the scale is to be used and include an example if the task is complex or difficult.
4. State how the responses are to be reported or recorded, such as a check mark, number, circle, etc.
5. Use brief instructions for simple, easy tasks and more elaborate instructions for more difficult response tasks.

6. Make the instructions clear and complete enough to be sufficient for the least sophisticated respondents.
7. The less sophisticated the responding sample, the more complete and thorough the instructions must be.
8. Write instructions so the most sophisticated respondents need only read the first part and can skip the remainder.

---

them collectively, as a set. More importantly, this version of the instructions doesn't indicate the basis, standard, or *criterion* to be used when rating the items. The correct version indicates that importance of *ownership* should be rated. Many, if not most, respondents would agree that it's vitally important to have a refrigerator or a kitchen range available, and, in the incorrect version, these appliances would almost always be rated as highly important. On the other hand, many who rent homes where such appliances are provided wouldn't regard it as important to own those appliances.

The incorrect version doesn't indicate how the scale is to be used. Take note that there are five points on the scale and five items to be rated. Many respondents would probably *rank* the items, when the researcher's intention was actually to obtain ratings, so that two or more may be rated the same.

Lastly, the incorrect version doesn't indicate how or where the answers are to be recorded. Thus, some respondents are likely to check a space, others to circle scale numbers, and still others to write in the words "unimportant" and "important." To the inexperienced researcher, such responses might sound like absurdities that are highly unlikely. They aren't. Extensive experience demonstrates all too well that a surprisingly large proportion of respondents will provide very bizarre responses if the instructions aren't crystal clear. Guidelines for writing clear instructions are contained in Guidelist 6–3.

It's ordinarily better to err in the direction of providing instructions that are too thorough rather than too brief. If the instructions are well written, the more sophisticated respondents who quickly understand will need only read the beginning, while others have complete direction when needed.

Special instructions

There are times when the respondents must be given special instructions on how to respond to one or more survey items. The need for such special instructions depends on the particular

---

EXAMPLE 6–5

Special Respondent Instructions

A. Please read each item one time, then indicate your opinion. Remember, it's your first impression that counts.

B. Please answer the following questions about your favorite brand, even though you may sometimes buy others.

C. Please pick a number from the scale to show how often your spouse does each of the following things.

D. Please rate how satisfied or dissatisfied you are with each appliance that you now own. Leave the space beside the item blank if you don't now own one.

E. Let's assume that you have decided to buy a new car in the next few weeks. What brand would you be most likely to consider first?

F. If one of your children suddenly needed emergency medical treatment during the daytime, where would you be most likely to take the child?

---

situation. Some examples of them are shown in Example 6–5. In Section A, respondents are instructed to read each item only once and not to study or compare the items. The instructions in Section B of the example list an *unconditional inclusion*. The favorite brand is to be rated, *regardless* of whether or not other brands are sometimes purchased. In Section C, the respondent is instructed to respond for his or her spouse, rather than for him- or herself.

The instructions in Section D list a *conditional exclusion*. Since the respondents don't rate appliances they don't own, these are *implied*, miniature branches around such items. The last two sections list *assumptions* that the respondent is to make when answering the questions. In Section E, the assumption is explicitly listed in the first sentence. The example in Section F implies an assumption with the use of the conditional clause, "If one of your children . . ."

These are but a few special instructions that might be needed for some survey items. Special instructions such as these are needed whenever the respondents are to make an assumption, answer for another person, base their responses on a special criterion, or otherwise act or respond in some *extraordinary* way. The same rules of grammar, vocabulary, and style for composition of survey items, themselves, also apply to the composition of special instructions. They must be crystal clear, and the key words or phrases should be underlined or highlighted to make them clearly recognizable.

Interviewer instructions

For telephone or personal interview surveys, instructions for the interviewers, listed within the survey instrument, are often needed. They're designed for the interviewers only. They aren't read or shown to the respondents. Several such instructions are shown in Example 6–6.

Sections A, B, and C are samples of branching instructions for interviewers. Branching

---

EXAMPLE 6–6

Instructions for Interviewers Only

A. [If yes:] What store did you purchase it from?
B. [If respondent is male, *skip* to page 5.]
C. [If respondent is married, return to ★ above and ask each question about his or her spouse.]
D. [Hand respondent the *pink* rating card.]
E. [Check appropriate category below but DON'T read alternatives to respondent.]
F. Are there any other reasons? [*Probe* for all others.]
G. [Record ethnicity of respondent below. DON'T ASK!]

_____ White	_____ Black
_____ Oriental	_____ Hispanic
_____ Other (Specify what: _____)	

---

was discussed in detail earlier in this chapter, but it's important to note here the exceptions that apply for an interview survey. First, the instructions should be enclosed in brackets or parentheses, written in uppercase letters, or otherwise distinguished from the items, themselves. The questionnaire writer should use one convention throughout the instrument to indicate to the interviewers that these phrases are *not* to be read to respondents. Any easily recognizable markings will do, so long as the *same* ones are used throughout and all interviewers know what they mean.

It's also important to note that branching must be limited and very clearly indicated. Some researchers are inclined to assume that the fieldworkers are more sophisticated and better motivated than they actually are. The branching can be *somewhat* more elaborate or slightly more complex for interviewers than if the questionnaire is self-administered, but not much. Interviewers receive training and instruction before going into the field. They can examine the questionnaire thoroughly before using it. Nevertheless, it's best to assume they're no more sophisticated than respondents.

Section D of the example is merely an instruction to give the respondent a visual display of a rating scale. Such supplementary materials will be discussed more fully later in this chapter. In Section E, the fieldworker is instructed about recording the responses and reminded not to list the alternatives for the respondent. Similar instructions can be used to indicate that the alternatives should be read to respondents, when that's required. Notice that the word DON'T is both entirely uppercase and underlined, to be sure the interviewer sees this is a prohibition.

Section F of Example 6–6 shows a question followed by a general instruction for the interviewer to probe for more reasons. The use of probing is discussed more fully in Chapter 8. Interviewers are instructed on the methods for probing when they're trained or before going into the field. The questionnaire needs only to tell them when to do so, but they don't need to be told exactly how to do it each time a probe is required.

In the final example, Section G, the interviewers are conducting a personal survey so they can visually identify the respondents' ethnicity. They're instructed to record it without

---

GUIDELIST 6–4

For Composing Special Instructions

1. Keep the instructions as clear and simple as possible.
2. Use uppercase letters, boldface type, italics, or underlining to highlight important words or phrases.
3. Set instructions slightly apart from actual items.
4. Use some convention, such as brackets or parentheses, for instructions to interviewers only.

---

asking the respondent, to avoid any potential threat. Note the use of uppercase letters and underlining, so interviewers won't fail to see that part of the instruction.

These are only a few special instructions for interviewers. Many other types might be used, as they're needed. The same rules about clarity and simplicity apply to these instructions as to all others. Guidelines for writing special instructions are provided in Guidelist 6–4.

Interview rating cards

Surveys often require respondents to rate items using a scale. With self-administered questionnaires, the scales can be printed directly on the survey instrument. If personal interviewing is used, the various scales must be printed on cards that can be handed to the respondents, so they can see the scale and select their choice for each item as it's read. Three such samples are shown in Example 6–7.

In each case, the questionnaire would contain an instruction to the interviewer to hand the respondent the rating card. The cards should be color coded by printing each on a different color card stock, or they can be labeled with a name, letter, or number to distinguish the various types. When such identification is used, the labels should be printed on *both* sides of each card, to facilitate their recognition and use. It's usually not advisable to include more than one such scale on the same card. Ordinarily, the contents of the cards are printed in large typeface, so they're clearly readable to all respondents, including the elderly or those with poor vision.

In the first two examples, Sections A and B, two frequently used scales are shown. They're basically the same as those used for a self-administered questionnaire, shown in Example 5–8, page 128, and Example 5–3, page 121 in Chapter 5. The same type of instructions are given respondents, and they're used in the same way as described earlier. The last example in Section C shows a rating card for obtaining an indication of annual family income. This is a *sensitive* item. Many respondents are likely to refuse; those with high incomes tend to understate and those with low incomes tend to overstate income if asked the dollar amount. Thus, using random letters obtains more reliable data. Respondents are asked simply to report what letter indicates their annual family income. The basic guidelines for composing rating cards are listed in Guidelist 6–5.

GUIDELIST 6–5

For Creating Respondent Rating Cards

1. Put only one rating scale on each card to make identification easier and facilitate handling.
2. Color code the cards or label them with a name, letter, or number on *both* sides so they're easily recognized.
3. Have the cards computer-printed in a large type-face or use a copy machine that will enlarge the image.
4. Compose instructions using the same rules as for scales on self-administered questionnaires.

EXAMPLE 6–7

Respondent Rating Cards

A.
                    Linear, Numeric Scale Card

> Scale
>
> UNIMPORTANT   1 2 3 4 5   IMPORTANT

B.
                    Verbal Frequency Scale Card

> 1 = Always
> 2 = Often
> 3 = Sometimes
> 4 = Rarely
> 5 = Never

C.
                    Annual Family Income Indicator

> R = Under $10,000
> G = $10,000 to $19,999
> L = $20,000 to $29,999
> W = $30,000 to $39,999
> F = $40,000 to $49,999
> Q = $50,000 and Over

CHECKLIST 6–3

To Identify Threatening Questions

1. Does the question ask about financial matters? This society judges people by what they earn and own, and most people fear the IRS above all else.
2. Does the question challenge mental or technical skill or ability? People often fear looking stupid or inept in their own eyes or to others.
3. Will the question reveal self-perceived short-comings? People are highly sensitive to their inability to accomplish personally or socially desirable goals.
4. Is the question about *social status* indicators? Those with low-level educations, jobs, neighborhoods, and the like may be defensive about such questions.
5. Does the question focus on sexuality, sexual identity or behavior? Sexuality is a very private topic and many are embarrassed by even the mention of sex.
6. Does the question refer to consumption of alcohol or illegal drugs? Many will deny or understate such consumption or be insulted by the suggestion of use.
7. Are personal habits the topic of the question? Most people don't like to admit their inability to form or to break personal habits.
8. Does the question address emotional or psychological disturbance? Such illnesses are far more threatening to people than physical ailments.
9. Is the topic of the question associated with the *aging process?* Indicators of aging arouse fear and anxiety among many people of all ages.
10. Does the question deal with death or dying? Morbidity is often a forbidden topic and many refuse even to think about their own or their loved ones' death.

CONCLUDING THE QUESTIONNAIRE

The conclusion of the questionnaire is reserved for two kinds of questions: (1) Items that are *delicate* or *sensitive*—those that are potentially *threatening* or *intimidating,* and (2) questions about the respondents' *demographic status.* Often the latter are *inherently* threatening to some respondents—especially those that fear they'll be identified or those who are reluctant to reveal facts about themselves.

Minimizing Threat or Intimidation

Checklist 6–3 lists ten categories of questions that many respondents find threatening. Financial information heads the list because income and wealth are important status indicators and because almost everyone fears the IRS and other tax agencies. Some of the other sources of threat may not be as easy for the questionnaire writer to identify. For instance, any instruction, question, or scale that's unclear to respondents may suggest they're ignorant or incompetent. Questions that deal with failure to attain certain goals (e.g., losing weight, learning to play a musical instrument, or even keeping the house clean) may be threatening.

Some respondents—especially, but not exclusively those at lower levels of the social hierarchy—may be defensive about common social status indicators. That might include anything from the car (or truck) they drive to the fact that their spouse was a high school dropout. People also get highly resistive and defensive about questions concerning sex, alcohol, or illicit drugs. Inability to form socially desirable personal habits—healthy diet, exercise, cleanliness, orderliness, promptness, and the like—is a sensitive issue for many. Similarly, the inability to *break* socially undesirable personal habits—smoking, nail-biting, knuckle-cracking, fidgeting, and other such habits or mannerisms—evokes strong, defensive feelings and reactions among some people.

This culture and society also encourage people to hide, avoid, or retreat from other issues as well. Survey questions about mental or emotional illness often elicit resistance from respondents. Factors related to aging—such as the use of bifocals, hearing aids, or dentures—may yield a negative reaction or a response that's less than truthful. Lastly, death and dying are forbidden topics to many.

If the survey questionnaire includes questions dealing with any of these potentially sensitive or threatening issues, they should be worded very carefully to avoid bias, as suggested in Chapter 4. During construction and organization of the survey instrument, such sensitive items or sections should be identified, earmarked, and inserted near the end of the questionnaire. That way, rapport is at its highest, and respondents are less likely to lie or resist. Even if they do refuse to continue, the data they provided earlier may still be usable.

The Demographic Section

Almost every survey contains items indicating the status of the respondents. These are called *demographic* items. They're used in three ways: First, the profiles portray the nature of the sample. Second, the demographic profile of the sample can be compared to that for the population as a whole, when these parameters are known. Third, the items can be used to divide the sample into subsamples by age, sex, and so on. The data for the other survey items can then be compared among the demographic groups to determine the effect of demographic status on other responses.

Figure 6–3 contains a fairly comprehensive list of demographic items. Not all of them will be required for any given survey, and some other items, such as travel history or residential history, might also be included with demographics. For some surveys, demographic data for only the respondent would be necessary. For others, it may be valuable to obtain demographic data for both heads of household. (In years past, surveys sought data for *the* head of household, assuming the person was a male. That might create resentment today. Obtaining data for *both* heads of household is also more valid for many households.)

The age of the youngest child is often included because it can be used with marital status and occupation to determine the stage in the family life cycle. There are several different classifications of family life cycle, but one of the most common schemes is described in Figure 6–4. Often, the stage in the family life cycle is more likely to influence response than merely the age of the respondent. For example, a 35-year-old single male may respond in a manner more similar to a 20-year-old single male than to a 35-year-old who is married and has children in the home.

Demographic items are ordinarily clustered together in a single section and included at the end of the questionnaire. That way, respondents are less likely to refuse or terminate the process, since they've been cooperating for some time. Notice that income, ordinarily the most sensitive and threatening demographic item, has been listed last. Similarly, if racial

Figure 6–3   *Commonly Used Demographic Variables*

    A Sex of respondent.
    B Sex of family members.
    C Age of respondent.
    D Age of each head of household.
    E Age of family members.
    F Age of youngest child in the home.
    G Education of respondent.
    H Education of each head of household.
    I Employment of respondent.
    J Employment of each head of household.
    K Occupation of respondent.
    L Occupation of each head of household.
    M Annual income of respondent.
    N Annual income of each head of household.
    O Annual family income.
    P Racial or ethnic identity of respondent.
    Q Race or ethnicity of each head of household.
    R Religious preference of respondent.
    S Religion of each head of household.
    T Type of family dwelling.
    U ZIP code or location of residence.
    V Time of residence at present location.
    W Self-designated social class membership.

or ethnic identity or religious preference is to be included, that should be listed just prior to annual income. Even if a small proportion should decide to refuse further cooperation, the data obtained earlier in the questionnaire may still be usable and valuable.

    A typical demographic page is shown in the last page of Example 6–1. In the example, age, education, and income are to be obtained in continuous, numeric form. They can be grouped into appropriate categories during data processing if that's required. Employment and occupation are listed in categories. Different categories and more or fewer of them

Figure 6–4   *Family Life Cycle Stages*

Stage	Description
1. Young Single	Under 45, not married or living with a spouse, no children in the home.
2. Young Couple	Under 45 years of age, married, no children in the home.
3. Full Nest I	Single or married parent, youngest child under six years old in the home.
4. Full Nest II	Single or married parent with youngest child in the home from 6 to 15.
5. Full Nest III	Single or married parent, the youngest child in the home between 16 to 23.
6. Empty Nest I	Over 44, married, no children in the home, one or both in the work force.
7. Empty Nest II	Over 44, married, no children in the home, retired, neither in the work force.
8. Single Elder I	Over 44, not married, no children in the home, still in the work force.
9. Single Elder II	Over 44, not married, no children in the home, retired, not in the work force.

might be used, depending on the nature of the survey and the information requirements. The categories listed have proved to be both meaningful and easily understood in many surveys of the adult public.

The format in the example is typical of one for a self-administered questionnaire. Respondents can complete it quickly and easily. If there's only one head of household, the other column is simply ignored. This or a similar format would, of course, work effectively for an interview survey, with appropriate interviewer instructions included.

PRECODING THE QUESTIONNAIRE

When a questionnaire is *precoded,* it contains a number (or letter) code for each alternative response to each structured question. They're called "response codes." Guidelines for precoding response alternatives are provided in Guidelist 6–6. Notice that in Example 6–1, Section Q, the employment and occupation categories are numbered from one to seven with tiny numerals to the left of each box. These are the code numbers that will later be keyed to a data file. Listing such codes on the questionnaire *before* the questionnaire is printed avoids the extremely laborious, time-consuming task of *postcoding* each item on each completed questionnaire after the data are collected. One of the major reasons for using structured questions is to make precoding possible.

Notice that in the example, *age, education,* and *income* aren't and can't be precoded. Nor do they need to be. The numeric values that respondents record will be keyed directly to file. No precoding is required for these and other numeric items recorded by respondents. Similarly, some scales, such as those in Example 6–1, Sections F and I, have no precodes because the codes are a part of the scales, themselves. Where the scale is formed by categories, such as in Example 6–1, Sections E and G, the categories must be precoded with a letter or number. Similarly, when respondents check a *position* on a scale, such as in Example 6–1, Sections D and M, the individual positions should be precoded so there's no confusion about what value to key for each response. Numbers are far preferable to letters because they can be keyed and handled more easily during data transfer and processing.

It's ordinarily desirable to precode virtually every response alternative on the questionnaire, with one notable exception—dichotomous response categories. For such choices as yes/no, checked/not checked, male/female, and so forth, no precoding is required. Instead, the code value to be applied to each of the two alternatives is merely specified before data entry if it's not obvious to those keying the data. For instance, in Example 6–1, Sections A and B, the operator keying the data to file might be instructed to enter the number 1 for any item that's checked and a zero for those that aren't.

Precoding Record Formats

Another type of code number also should be listed on the questionnaire before it's printed. These are the numbers that show the position where the data for each item will be keyed to the computer record. They're called "format codes," rather than *response* codes.

The response codes for item categories can be listed as the questions or scales are written. By contrast, the record format codes in the far right-hand column should *never* be done until the *entire* questionnaire has been assembled. When the questionnaire is laid out, it's important

GUIDELIST 6–6

For Precoding Survey Items

1. Use numbers for response codes, rather than letters, because they're more easily processed.
2. Response codes aren't required for *dichotomous* items that are checked only if they apply.
3. Numeric items, and scales containing numbers to be checked or circled, require no response precoding.
4. Enclose response codes in brackets or parentheses, or print them in very small typeface, or both, so respondents will ignore them.

to allow space in the margin for format codes, but the actual numbers should *not* be listed until the questionnaire is completely finalized. That's because any changes, such as adding or deleting an item or even changing an item, may require changes in *all* the record format codes that follow the change.

Record format precoding—listing the record format codes on the questionnaire—may appear to be a difficult task. Actually, it's quite simple and easy, but it must be done *precisely*. If there are any errors, they'll be *very* difficult to correct after the questionnaire is printed or duplicated. Errors usually aren't discovered until the questionnaires have been printed and the data collection completed. If there's an error, a new set of record format numbers may have to be listed *on each completed questionnaire,* from the point the error occurred to the end of that particular record or to the end of the questionnaire itself. That's a very tedious and time-consuming process.

The way the format is precoded depends on the type of data format to be used by the data file and analysis programs. The same data in three different formats are depicted in Figure 6–5.

Precoding spreadsheet formats

Survey data can be analyzed by a spreadsheet and/or charting program on a desktop computer. Spreadsheet analysis is usually limited to relatively small, simple surveys. If there are a large number of variables (questions or items), it would be cumbersome to manipulate and analyze the data with a spreadsheet. Nor do these programs provide a full range of statistical tools. Spreadsheets are usually capable of some statistical analysis, and they can often provide charts or graphs of the results. So spreadsheet analysis is effective when there are relatively few variables to be analyzed and when only the most conventional statistical analysis will be required.

The spreadsheet with data from 10 respondents might look similar to the example shown in the upper section of Figure 6–5. Usually each row of the spreadsheet is numbered and each column is designated either by numbers or letters of the alphabet. If the data from the survey will be entered and analyzed with a spreadsheet, the column letters or numbers are the record format code values. The letters or numbers for the column where each variable will be entered in the spreadsheet should be listed beside each question or item on the

Figure 6–5   *Three Data File Formats*

Spreadsheet Format

	1/A	2/B	3/C	4/D	5/E	6/F	7/G	8/H
	Rating 1	Rating 2	Miles	Ownership	Dollars Spent	Sex	Age	Marital Status
1	3	3	8	1	77.50	1	28	2
2	5	1	22	1		1	35	1
3	4	2	40	1	.45	1	61	1
4	4	2	119	1	145.80	2	44	1
5	5	1	27	1	22.50	1	41	1
6	3	3	48	1	11.87	2	50	1
7	2	4		2	9.16	2		2
8	4	2	31	1	81.40	1	64	1
9	3	3	4	1	35.55	2	27	1
10	3	3	60	1	6.25	1	21	2

Free-Floating Format

```
1 , 3 , 3 , 8 , 1 , 7 7 . 5 0 , 1 , 2 8 , 2
2 , 5 , 1 , 2 2 , 1 , , 1 , 3 5 , 1
3 , 4 , 2 , 4 0 , 1 , . 4 5 , 1 , 6 1 , 1
4 , 4 , 2 , 1 1 9 , 1 , 1 4 5 . 8 0 , 2 , 4 4 , 1
5 , 5 , 1 , 2 7 , 1 , 2 2 . 5 0 , 1 , 4 1 , 1
6 , 3 , 3 , 4 8 , 1 , 1 1 . 8 7 , 2 , 5 0 , 1
7 , 2 , 4 , , 2 , 9 . 1 6 , 2 , , 2
8 , 4 , 2 , 3 1 , 1 , 8 1 . 4 0 , 1 , 6 4 , 1
9 , 3 , 3 , 4 , 1 , 3 5 . 5 5 , 2 , 2 7 , 1
1 0 , 3 , 3 , 6 0 , 1 , 6 . 2 5 , 1 , 2 1 , 2
```

Fixed Format

```
0 1 3 3 0 0 8 1 0 7 7 5 0 1 2 8 2
0 2 5 1 0 2 2 1 0 0 0 0 0 1 3 5 1
0 3 4 2 0 4 0 1 0 0 0 4 5 1 6 1 1
0 4 4 2 1 1 9 1 1 4 5 8 0 2 4 4 1
0 5 5 1 0 2 7 1 0 2 2 5 0 1 4 1 1
0 6 3 3 0 4 8 1 0 1 1 8 7 2 5 0 1
0 7 2 4 0 0 0 2 0 0 9 1 6 2 0 0 2
0 8 4 2 0 3 1 1 0 8 1 4 0 1 6 4 1
0 9 3 3 0 0 4 1 0 3 5 5 5 2 2 7 1
1 0 3 3 0 6 0 1 0 0 6 2 5 1 2 1 2
```

questionnaire. Notice that only *one* column is assigned to each variable (item or question), regardless of whether the value to be entered is one digit, two digits, or more.

The upper section of Example 6–8 shows how a questionnaire is precoded with spreadsheet column letters. Only the first three items from the demographic page of the questionnaire contained in Example 6–1 are shown here. The first item is the sex of the respondent, and the code value of 1 for male or 2 for female is to be entered in column JJ. The age of the male head of household is to be entered in column JK, and so on.

Precoding free-floating formats

The middle section of Figure 6–5 displays the data as it appears in a *free-floating* format. Each variable—each piece of data from one item or question—is separated from the next by a comma *delimiter*. So each variable doesn't occupy a particular column or horizontal position in the record. Instead, each variable is identified only by its place in the *sequence*. In the *spreadsheet* format, the age of the respondent is always entered in the column 7/G. In the *free-floating* format, age is always entered *seventh* in order, preceded by six commas or delimiters.

Data can be entered into raw data files or word processing programs in free-floating format. Most spreadsheets and data analysis programs allow data to be entered or transferred into them in this format if the variables or data field are separated by an appropriate delimiter, such as a comma, tab character, or some other special character that's designated by the program. With this format, the data record format is precoded on the questionnaire by listing the variable number for each piece of data—each question or item. The format codes in the middle section of Example 6–8 show the sex of the respondent is the 39th variable in the sequence, the age of the male is the 40th, and so on. With a free-floating format, it doesn't matter whether the piece of data for an item is one digit or character, or several. Only the *sequence* of values and delimiters matters.

It's fairly easy to precode the record format on the questionnaire with this type of data format. It's only necessary to be very careful not to skip an item. Each and every individual piece of data—each variable—must be identified and assigned a sequence number. Yet, despite the ease of precoding the questionnaire with this data format, it's neither highly recommended nor often used. That's because data entry in a free-floating format is very tedious and highly prone to errors. If the person entering the data gets confused about which variable to enter next, or if a mistake must be corrected, the only way to identify the right piece of data is to *count the delimiters and fields* from the beginning of the case to the point in question. Thus, either a spreadsheet format or a *fixed* format is highly preferable to a free-floating format, especially when there's a substantial amount of data to be entered and analyzed.

Precoding fixed formats

The bottom section of Figure 6–5 depicts the same data set as that in the two sections above, but this time it's in a *fixed format*. With a fixed format, one horizontal position on each line or record is assigned to *each digit, character, or space*. Consequently, the data for any one variable—question or item—is identified strictly by its *physical place on the record*. Each such place or spot on the line is called a "position," and each position can hold only one digit, character, or blank space.

EXAMPLE 6–8

Record Format Precoding Methods

Spreadsheet Record Format Precodes

Q Please put an ✗ in the box to indicate which head of household you are, then check or fill in the items below for *each* head of household in your home.

Spreadsheet Column Letters

I am the . . .

☐ *MALE Head of Household*   ☐ *FEMALE Head of Household*   JJ

Age ···················· _____ years   Age ···················· _____ years   JK-JL

Formal education ·· _____ years   Formal education ·· _____ years   JM-JN
(For example, High school graduate=12 years)   *(For example, High school graduate=12 years)*

Free-Floating Record Format Precodes

Q Please put an ✗ in the box to indicate which head of household you are, then check or fill in the items below for *each* head of household in your home.

Item – Variable Numbers

I am the . . .

☐ *MALE Head of Household*   ☐ *FEMALE Head of Household*   39

Age ···················· _____ years   Age ···················· _____ years   40-41

Formal education ·· _____ years   Formal education ·· _____ years   42-43
(For example, High school graduate=12 years)   *(For example, High school graduate=12 years)*

Fixed Record Format Precodes

Q Please put an ✗ in the box to indicate which head of household you are, then fill in the items below for *each* head of household in your home.

Record Position Numbers

I am the . . .

☐ *MALE Head of Household*   ☐ *FEMALE Head of Household*   41

Age ···················· _____ years   Age ···················· _____ years   42-45

Formal education ·· _____ years   Formal education ·· _____ years   46-49
(For example, High school graduate=12 years)   *(For example, High school graduate=12 years)*

With a fixed format, each variable is assigned a data *field* of a given size. For instance, if the maximum value a variable might take on is 9, it would only need a one-position field. If the maximum was 999, it would need a three-position field, and so on. The bottom portion of Example 6–8 shows how the record format precoding would appear if the data were in a fixed format. The one-digit field for the sex of the respondent will be keyed to the 41st position on the record. Similarly, the formal education of the female head of household will be entered in the 48th and 49th position of the record. If she had only eight years of education, a zero or blank would precede the number 8.

Each line in a fixed format data file may contain as many as two or three hundred positions. Ordinarily, though, lines or records that exceed about 80 positions (digits, characters, or spaces) are difficult to read and manipulate on a computer display. Most displays show a maximum of about 80 positions on each line, so it's advisable to limit the length of a record to only about 60 to 80 positions, so that an entire record can be viewed at once.

If the questionnaire contains a relatively large number of questions or items, there may be too many data codes to "fit" onto a single record of 80 or less total positions. For instance, a total of 179 positions would be required for all of the data obtained from the questionnaire shown in Example 6–1. A record that long would be too difficult to manipulate. The record format diagram for the sample questionnaire, shown in Figure 6–6, specifies a maximum record size of 60 positions. So the data were "broken" into four records per questionnaire or *cases* for analysis, so that none exceeded the maximum.

Questionnaire and case numbers

Each questionnaire should be assigned a unique number, either before or after data collection. This *case number* will be keyed to the data file. Then, if an error is discovered or a problem encountered after the data have been transferred, the case number identifies the completed questionnaire from which the data were keyed. The researcher can return to the completed questionnaire and make any corrections needed. The researcher should decide if the case number is to be listed at the beginning or at the end of each line or record in the data file. It's always advisable to list the case number in the same position on each record, preferably at the beginning of each record, as shown in Figure 6–6. That way, it's quick and easy to sort the data file, to put it in correct order, and to identify any missing or extra records.

In this example, each questionnaire was assigned a three-digit case number followed by a one-digit record number. Note that it's *always* advisable to allow too many, rather than too few, positions for this or any other data field, if there's any doubt. If too many are assigned, one or two positions may remain blank and won't be used. If too few are assigned, there's no way to *shrink* the number of digits needed for a number, and serious problems are likely to result.

In the example shown in Figure 6–6, six positions following the case and record numbers were left blank to facilitate reading and handling the records. Thus, the first actual data point on each record will be entered in position 11 and the last data point will never be beyond position 60.

In Section A of the example, each item requires only a single digit to indicate whether it was checked, but there are three items on each line across the page. So the data for the first row of three items were assigned to positions 11–13, those for the second row to 14–

Figure 6–6 *Record Format Diagram*

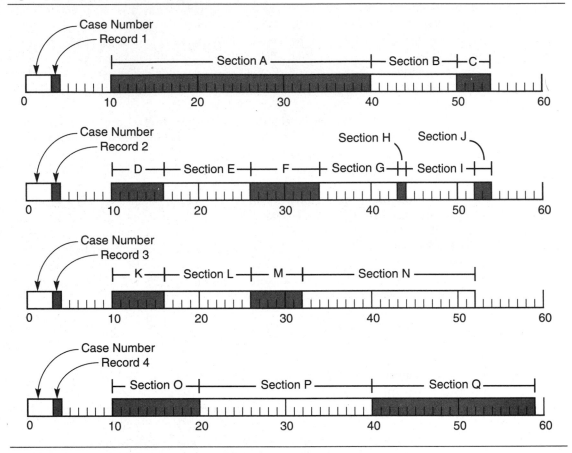

16, and so on. In Section B, there are only two items per horizontal row, requiring two positions per line. Similarly, Section C calls for only one digit (1 through 7 or blank) per item, and there's only one item on a line.

Notice that the data for the first three sections of the questionnaire required 54 positions and a maximum of 60 was specified in advance. Rather than going to a new record in the middle of the data for Section D, the questionnaire writer precoding the instrument merely left the last four positions of the first record blank and began a new record at the start of Section D. Compare the diagram in Figure 6–6 with the record format precode values on the questionnaire in Example 6–1. Notice that each record begins with a new section, and each section is contained on a single record. It isn't absolutely necessary to begin each new record at the start of a page or section, but it's often desirable to do so. It makes data entry quicker, easier, and more accurate.

It's important to note that a single data field—the data for one question or item—must *never* be *split* between two records. For instance, if the answer to a survey question to be entered near the end of a record is a three-digit number, the entire number must either be assigned to the end of one record or the beginning of the next. There's really no need to assign one or two digits to one record and the remaining digit or two to the next record, and it would create serious data handling and analysis problems. Computer programs virtually always recognize that each new record will begin with a new field of data.

Experience indicates that it's all too easy to make mistakes when listing the record format in the margin of the questionnaire. One common mistake is to fail to recognize *multiple responses* to an item and allow positions for *each alternative*. To clarify this point, refer to Example 6–1 and compare Section B with Section J. Both of these sections contain *multiple-choice* questions. Thus, they look very similar at first glance. Yet the amount of data they provide is *very different* because Section B contains two *multiple-response* items while Section J has two *single*-response questions. Notice that in Section B the alternatives aren't precoded. That's because respondents can check any or all alternatives. *Each alternative becomes a survey item or variable.* The number 1 would be keyed for that item if it were checked, and a zero if it were not. Notice also that *each* alternative has been assigned a position on the record. The problem is that it's extremely easy to glance at the item, assume it's a single-response item, and assign only *one* position to it. If the mistake were not discovered until it were too late to correct it, all of that remaining record, and perhaps the following records as well, would be "off" by four positions.

In Section J of Example 6–1, each of the two items allows for only one response; one alternative must be selected. So, only one position is required for each. If the person precoding the record format made a mistake and assigned one alternative position, five positions would be "wasted" and data transfer would be a little less convenient, but no serious harm would be done. Again, the basic rule, "better too many than too few," holds true.

Precoding for any format

There may be times when the questionnaire writer doesn't know what data format will be required. If that's the case, there is a way to precode the record format so that it's acceptable to any of the three alternatives discussed here. The record format codes would be assigned and listed exactly as they are for the *fixed record* format, with *one important exception*—ONE POSITION MUST BE "SKIPPED" BETWEEN EACH, INDIVIDUAL VARIABLE OR DATA FIELD. For instance, in Section A of Example 6–1, the precode values would be 11–16, rather than 11–13 as they are shown now. That way, the code for the first item would be entered into position 11; a comma, tab, or other special character to serve as a delimiter would be entered in position 12; the value for the next item in position 13; and so on.

Data formatted and entered in this fashion would be acceptable to a spreadsheet, but it would also be readable as either a free-floating or a fixed field record. While that's a definite advantage, the price is denominated in terms of efficiency. Data entry and data handling would be somewhat more cumbersome and difficult. Guidelines for listing the record format are provided in Guidelist 6–7.

The acid test

Testing the codes and record formats is absolutely mandatory for inexperienced researchers and highly recommended for even the most experienced. It takes only a few minutes to do

---

GUIDELIST 6–7

For Listing the Record Format

1. Don't begin listing the format until the entire questionnaire draft is complete.
2. Specify the maximum record size or number of positions to be used.
3. Determine the maximum number of digits needed for the case numbers.
4. Assign the required number of positions at the beginning of each record for the case and record number.
5. Determine the first position in which actual data will be keyed and begin listing with that number.
6. Determine the maximum number of positions required for each item, in turn, and list the positions for the variable in the right margin.

7. Remember that each alternative of a multiple-response item constitutes one variable and each requires a separate field.
8. Allow a field of sufficient width for any "other" or open-ended items to be postcoded.
9. Never *split* a single variable or data field between two records.
10. Begin a new record at the beginning of a new section to facilitate data transfer, even if some records are shorter than others.
11. Always perform the acid test, filling in maximum values, checking all options, and keying to a test file.

---

so, and the testing usually returns many, many times its cost in time by catching errors before the data are collected. To test the codes and record formats, the questionnaire writer should make a copy of the final questionnaire draft. Then, the researcher should complete the questionnaire, listing the *maximum* value for each item. *Every* alternative on each multiple response item should also be checked. When that has been done, the data from the test questionnaire should *actually be entered* to a computer file. More often than not, one or more errors will be discovered.

Pretesting the Questionnaire

When the entire questionnaire has been completed—when all the items have been organized, the sections arranged, the instructions inserted, and the responses and record format precoded—when it's all done and everything is complete, DON'T SEND IT TO BE PRINTED! Not yet. Instead, duplicate 20 or 30 copies and administer it to as many typical respondents. See how it goes when they fill it out or when they're interviewed. See if they understand the questions, the scales, and the instructions. Observe how accurately they follow the branching, if there is any. See how long it takes them and how easy or difficult they find it. Ask them about their reactions and suggestions when they've finished. Then, actually try entering the data into a computer file. Maybe everything will work beautifully and the instrument is nearly perfect. Maybe. But very often—very often, indeed—even well-trained and highly experienced researchers find some changes that will improve the performance of the questionnaire. And sometimes the pretesting of the questionnaire will reveal very serious errors, oversights, or problems that would have spelled disaster if they hadn't been detected and corrected before going into the field or the mail.

SUMMARY

The Construction of the Questionnaire

  A. Emphasize the introduction. Most refusals will come immediately, and, once respondents begin, they seldom terminate prematurely.

  B. Check sequence carefully. Simple, interesting, informative items should come first and sensitive or threatening items as late as possible.

  C. Group items into sections. Combine items that use the same scales or put the same topics into sections to facilitate response and simplify the task.

  D. Limit and control branching. Make branch instructions simple, clear, and concise and avoid complex branching or multiple branches as much as possible.

  E. Use ample instructions. An instruction should be included if there's any doubt and they must be simple enough for the least sophisticated respondents.

  F. Don't overestimate interviewers or respondents. Sophistication and motivation are always less than the researcher is likely to expect.

  G. Make good use of rating cards. For personal interview surveys, good rating cards will simplify the response task and increase reliable, valid responses.

  H. Be sure to precode responses and record formats. Precoding must be done very precisely and accurately and submitted to the "acid test."

  I. Always pretest the entire questionnaire on a pilot sample of 20 or 30 respondents, observing closely as they respond to the instrument.

PART III

Collecting and Processing Data

Chapter 7

Mail Data Collection

MAIL SURVEY CHARACTERISTICS

Mail surveys are distinct from interview surveys in several ways. Many aspects of data collection for the mail survey don't apply to interview surveys. Even those tasks or attributes common to both types of surveys typically require more or less emphasis for one type of data collection than for the other. Because of these distinctions, mail surveys and other self-administered surveys are discussed in detail in this chapter. Surveys that collect data through telephone or personal interviews are considered thoroughly in the next chapter. Those who intend to conduct several survey projects should study both chapters to compare the unique capabilities and limitations of each type of data collection. Those who intend to conduct only a single study using one type of data collection will find complete guidance in the chapter on the type of data collection to be used for the project at hand.

The mail survey is self-administered. Interview surveys ordinarily are administered entirely by the field or telephone worker. Thus, the "cosmetic" aspects of the mail survey are much more important. The mailing piece is the only contact respondents will have with the researcher and the project. Consequently, it must perform effectively on its own. It has to be completely self-contained. It must "stand on its own" and do the entire job—winning cooperation, capturing the data, and returning it to the survey headquarters. Once the questionnaire and mailing piece are complete and the survey is mailed, there won't be an opportunity to make changes or corrections. At that point, the researcher is "locked into" the instrument and data collection process. Thus, the preparation and mailing of the survey must receive very careful attention, so that every detail will be handled properly and mistakes or inadequacies kept to an absolute minimum. This usually requires substantial testing and revision, and perhaps a "pilot" data collection project, to be sure the mailing will do the job reliably.

MAILING PIECE PRODUCTION

The relatively high percentage of *nonresponse* is by far the most important shortcoming of mail survey data collection. It's obviously important to do as much as possible to reduce nonresponse and encourage an adequate response rate. The appearance and quality of the mailing piece and its contents have a very important effect on mail survey response rates. Consequently, the technical aspects of the survey mailing piece and its production will be discussed here in substantial detail. It certainly isn't necessary for those conducting a mail survey to become a printing or publishing expert. However, it is essential that they understand the alternatives from which they may choose and appreciate the importance of intelligent decisions.

It's always best to plan and create a mailing piece that's consistent in quality. If some components of the mailing are to be done very inexpensively, it's wasteful to do other parts lavishly. On the other hand, if most of the components are of very high quality, one or two parts that are obviously done cheaply will diminish or eliminate any advantages of the higher-quality parts. The researcher must assess the budget and estimate the response rate, then choose the level of quality for the mailing. Usually the mailing piece is composed entirely of printed material. Before considering each individual component of the mailing piece, those aspects that apply to all of the components deserve attention. These include the paper, color, size, print, layout, attachment, and envelope.

The Paper Stock

Paper is the *vehicle* for mail inquiries, while the *printing* is the voice of the interrogator. Before turning to the printed words themselves, it's important to consider the vehicle on which they're carried.

Paper

The quality of the paper used in a mailing will affect the general impression the recipients have of the project. It isn't advisable to use very light paper stock to save postage costs. The paper should be 20-pound stock or heavier, so the paper is opaque and the print on the back of a page or on the following page won't show through the paper. The least expensive paper has a very low cotton fiber content, but it's quite acceptable for economical survey projects. Only the most elegant survey mailing piece uses 100 percent cotton rag bond paper.

Paper with a *smooth* surface, such as regular typing paper, is advisable for almost all surveys. *Slick* surface paper, such as that used for many magazines, isn't advisable for survey mailings. It tends to give the impression that the mailing piece is an advertisement, rather than a research questionnaire. Paper with a textured surface is appropriate only for very high quality mailings. When distinctive, textured paper stock is used, the cover letter and the mailing and return envelopes should also be of the same paper.

It's most effective to use matching envelopes and paper stock for a survey mailing. Custom formed and folded envelopes are very expensive when they're purchased in lots of less than several thousand. So, for most mail surveys, it's advisable to use paper and matching envelopes purchased "off the shelf" from a paper supply house, stationer, or printer. Such paper and envelopes all should be purchased at the same time and from the same source, to ensure a good match.

Color

Inexperienced mail survey researchers are sometimes tempted to use bright or unusual colors in the hope of gaining more attention from the recipients. While it's true that such colors do stand out and attract more attention, this isn't a good policy for survey research. Using bright, garish colors will have a negative rather than a positive effect. Such colors give the mailing the appearance of a direct mail advertisement or solicitation. Many recipients discard such materials out of hand as soon as they pick up their mail.

White paper is *always* perfectly acceptable. Off-white or *very light* gray, beige, olive green, or cream may sometimes be appropriate for high-quality mailings. Pink, blue, and yellow paper should be avoided. They detract from the businesslike seriousness of purpose a good survey mailing piece should have.

Size

The cover letter and questionnaire for a mail survey should ordinarily be on standard, 8-1/2-by-11-inch (letter-size) paper. Smaller sizes aren't usually advisable for *mail* surveys because they don't allow enough space. Smaller sizes may be appropriate for other kinds of self-administered survey questionnaires—product insert questionnaires, customer questionnaires, and the like. These special, self-administered instruments will be discussed in more detail later in this chapter.

Some less-experienced researchers may consider using 8-1/2-by-14-inch (legal size) paper to get more content on fewer pages. That's usually *not* a good idea. Almost everyone except the legal profession is used to handling and filing letter-size paper. Legal-size paper too often presents problems. It's usually advisable merely to include another page on the questionnaire rather than attempt to reduce page count by using larger paper.

The standard number 10 business letter envelope is quite satisfactory for nearly all surveys. It can contain several sheets of letter-size paper. The return envelope should be a *number nine* reply envelope, so that it will fit inside the mailing envelope without folding. Some mail survey researchers attempt to economize by using number 10 envelopes for both mailing and return. The difficulty is that the return envelope must be folded twice and inserted sideways into the mailing envelope, creating an unattractive mailing piece. Whenever the mailing piece is large, a larger envelope is far preferable to multiple folding and a thick, bulging mailing piece.

Print Characteristics

The least impressive typeface for a survey mailing piece, or any other printed material, is dot-matrix type. The letters are formed by combinations of dots. The newer, high-quality dot-matrix typewriters, dot-matrix computer printers, and inkjet printers may produce type that's very clean, crisp, and resolute. Older dot-matrix and inkjet printers typically produce copy that isn't very sharp and clear. Laser printers generate print copy of excellent quality, and laser printing is widely available. So, even when the working drafts are printed with low-quality dot-matrix or inkjet type, it's usually not difficult to have the final, camera-ready copy printed on a laser printer.

Color

Black ink is always acceptable for mail surveys. Very high quality mailings may use blue or brown ink that's color-coordinated with the paper. Red ink should be used only for headings or highlighted items in a two-color printing, but never for the entire questionnaire.

Two-color printings are only very rarely needed. When questionnaire sections have to be highlighted or set apart from others, screening to produce a gray background or using line borders will usually work as effectively as color coding. Corporate or institutional letterhead and printed envelopes can be used for the cover letter and mailing, even though they may be multicolor. The return addresses on the envelopes should then also be printed in the same colors.

If the cover letter for the survey will be individually hand-signed by the sender, the signer should use a *blue* pen rather than black. After expending the time and effort to individually hand-sign each, it's important to make that effort perfectly obvious to recipients.

Typeface

Many electronic typewriters, nearly all computer word processing and page processing programs and printers, and all desktop publishing systems offer a variety of typefaces or "fonts" from which to choose. They range from extremely conventional to extremely novel. Generally, the more conventional the typeface chosen, the better. It's very important to avoid the more novel or unusual typefaces in favor of one that's totally unremarkable. The goal is to have the reader notice and pay attention to the *content* of the words, not the printing of the document.

Conventional typefaces vary from completely *sanserif* to heavily *seriffed*. The *serif* is the small stroke used to finish off the main lines of a letter. For instance, this is an example of sanserif type, while this is an example of seriffed type. There are no strict rules, but many researchers prefer using a lightly seriffed or completely sanserif typeface used for the questionnaire in Example 6–1. Seriffed type is often a little easier to read on the pages of a book or newspaper, but sanserif type on a self-administered questionnaire lends a more *technical, scientific* tone to the document's appearance. It also has a very clean, uncluttered appearance that may make the response task look a little quicker and easier to the respondent.

Type size

Space is always at a premium on a self-administered questionnaire. Many questionnaire writers try to save space by using smaller print. Most people outside the fields of advertising and publishing don't realize that almost everyone over about 45 or 50 years of age needs reading glasses or bifocals. Almost everyone that age *needs* them, but they don't always *have* them or *use* them. Even when they do, small type can be very difficult and tedious to read. The alternative, of course, is to discard the questionnaire or at least set it aside, where it will probably be forgotten.

This is a serious problem because this kind of nonresponse is *systematic!* In effect, it systematically screens out those of a certain age group. That not only increases sampling error, it also creates *systematic bias*. In other words, it decreases both the *reliability* and the *validity* of the results.

Type size in the printing and publishing fields is denominated vertically in *points*. There are 72 points per inch. So 12-point type is one-sixth of an inch high, and 9-point type is only one-eighth of an inch high. It's perfectly acceptable to print such things as response precode and format precode values as tiny as only 7-point or even 5-point type. That way, they're less noticeable to respondents. By contrast, 12-point type will be easier for all respondents to read, and especially those with less than perfect vision. It may be okay to use 10-point type for some questionnaires where space is really lacking, but the printing shouldn't be any smaller than that.

Page Layout

The manner in which the print is organized on the paper is just as important as the type itself. The recipient will glance at the entire envelope or page and gain a general impression of what's there immediately—*prior* to reading even the first word. So the page layout actually "says" something to them before they begin to read the printing.

Format

The format of a self-administered questionnaire is also important because it affects the general appearance of the instrument and the likelihood that the respondent will complete and return it. A highly capable electronic typewriter or a computer word processor or page processor provides much more versatile formatting features than less sophisticated methods. Some features, such as full left-and-right paragraph justification, make the questionnaire more attractive, presentable, and inviting to complete. Proportionally spaced letters, so that the space for a broad letter such as m is wider than that for a narrow letter such as j, also improve the appearance. When both full justification and proportional spacing are used, the type looks nearly as attractive as the professional typesetting used for publications.

Other formatting features play an even more important role. If they're available, they should be used wherever appropriate. Boldface, italicized, and/or underlined type will highlight words or phrases so that respondents are sure to recognize key words. Boxing items in cells of a table helps to avoid confusion and errors by respondents. So do "leaders" on tabs that run from the end of an item or line to the space where the response should be recorded. The questionnaire shown in Example 6–1 contains many such special format features to simplify the respondents' task and reduce mistakes and errors.

Layout

The appearance or "cosmetic" aspects of the entire mailing piece are extremely important for mail surveys because they affect response rate and bias. The first principle is to use a conventional layout. The address on envelopes should begin at the point about midway between top and bottom and between the sides. All envelopes should have a return address in the upper left corner, and nothing should be printed on the back. The cover letter should have ample margins and be typed in simple, "block" style without indentation. It should be single-spaced, with a double-space between paragraphs and elements, in typical business style and format. The layout of the questionnaire should also be as simple, clean, and conventional as possible.

It's very important that every page of the questionnaire for a mail survey has an ample amount of "white space." The appearance should be clean and simple, rather than dense and cluttered. It's always advisable to use more pages than to fit the content too tightly. Thus, it's best to use one-and-a-half-spaced or double-spaced type rather than single-spaced, and sections should be double- or triple-spaced, to set them apart. This makes the response task appear much easier and simpler for the respondent, so the response rate and the reliability and validity of the data are increased.

Assembling the Piece

Up to this point, we have been considering the features of each individual element of the mailing piece. But the mailing piece for a survey is an *integrated* vehicle or conveyance. It's time to put the individual parts together into a well-organized whole.

Attachment

Most questionnaires require more space than merely the front and back of a single, letter-size page. When multiple pages are required, they should be attached to one another so that they won't become separated or the questionnaire completed in the wrong sequence. Ordinarily, the cover letter need not be returned, so it doesn't need to be attached to the questionnaire, although it could be.

Multiple questionnaire pages can be printed on both sides and stapled together in the upper left corner. This is the least impressive and least expensive method of attachment. A more elegant alternative is to have the questionnaire printed on larger stock and folded down to letter-size pages. Thus, 11-by-17-inch paper stock can be folded once to produce two letter-size sheets on which four pages are printed. It's usually not advisable to use larger stock, folding twice or more, because the sequence of the pages won't be clear to respondents. A six-page questionnaire might be constructed by using a folded, 11-by-17-inch sheet for the "outside" pages, with a single, letter-size sheet inserted between them. Then, no stapling is likely to be necessary.

The most impressive method of attaching a multiple page questionnaire would be to use a "booklet" format. Several 11-by-17-inch sheets are printed and folded together once down the middle. They're "saddle" stapled two or three times in the binding crease with a special stapler. This creates a small booklet that won't separate, and the sequence of pages is obvious. The entire booklet can then be mailed in a large envelope or, if there are only a few pages, folded twice for insertion into a number 10 envelope.

Enclosure

The manner in which the components are enclosed or inserted into an envelope affects the appearance of the mailing piece when it's received by the recipient. The general principle is to pick an envelope size that's appropriate to the content and to avoid very thick or bulging mailing pieces. For example, the use of number 9 reply envelopes was recommended. If the mailing and return envelopes are the same size, the return envelope must be folded twice to insert it, and this produces a thick, bulky mailing piece.

It's usually advisable to fold the cover letter with or into the questionnaire. Both should then be inserted to the front or the back of the envelope, with nothing else inserted inside them. When possible, arrange the insertions so that the cover letter is the first thing those who open the mailing will encounter, followed by the questionnaire itself. When a mailing house or specialist is used to insert and mail the survey, it's *very important* to check the finished pieces before mailing to be sure it was done correctly. Guidelist 7–1 contains descriptions of good, fair, and poor characteristics of each element of a mailing piece.

GUIDELIST 7–1

For Mailing Piece Construction

Paper

Good: Twenty-pound or heavier, 100 percent rag bond.

Fair: Twenty-pound or heavier, part cotton rag stock.

Poor: Light paper that's not opaque, so print shows through.

Color

Good: White, off-white, light gray, or beige paper, black ink.

Fair: White paper and black ink.

Poor: Bright, dense, or unusual colors, pink, blue, or yellow.

Size

Good: Letter-size panels, #9 and #10 envelopes, or special sizes.

Fair: Letter-size sheets, #9 and #10 envelopes.

Poor: Legal-size or oversize paper, envelopes small or folded.

Print

Good: Typeset, multisize, proportional, justified, bold, italics.

Fair: Typed, single-size ribbon, 12-pitch.

Poor: Typed, old ribbon, smaller than 12-pitch.

Layout

Good: Ample white space, use of graphics and shading.

Fair: Ample white space, well-separated sections.

Poor: Cramped, dense, narrow margins, sections too close.

Attachment

Good: Large, folded stock, saddle stapled multiple pages.

Fair: Single sheets, stapled in upper left corner.

Poor: Pages not attached or multifolded and complex.

VENDORS AND SERVICES

Everyone has had a great deal of experience preparing and mailing letters in the normal course of organizational or personal life. So, preparing and mailing a survey may not appear, at first glance, to be a difficult or time-consuming task. On the other hand, very few organizations or individuals have had the experience of preparing and mailing hundreds or perhaps thousands of identical mailing pieces to recipients with whom they have never before communicated. The sheer size of the task and volume of material can come as a surprise for those who haven't had such experience. Also, the fact that the mailing pieces are identical creates additional problems. The effect of any mistakes or inadequacies are automatically multiplied by the number of mailing pieces. Consequently, virtually every detail of the task deserves much greater attention and care than what's required for preparation of a single letter or a small group of mailing pieces.

The researcher or sponsoring organization doesn't have to do all the tasks associated with the preparation and mailing of a survey. Fortunately, there are service organizations and individuals who specialize in doing various tasks required for a survey mailing. They vary greatly in many respects—their range and level of expertise, the quality of their work, the minimum volume they're prepared to handle, the range of goods or services offered, their costs or prices, and the time required for delivery or performance. It's the researcher's responsibility to assess the need for such external assistance and to check their qualifications, and the quality and performance of the firms that might be used to prepare and mail the survey material.

Namelist sources

The listing of people to whom the survey is to be mailed is known as a "namelist." For some mail survey projects, the researcher or sponsor may have a namelist already. In other cases, internal accounting or personnel records may contain the information necessary to compose a namelist. These "in-house" lists make it unnecessary to obtain a list from an outside source. For example, a retail store wishing to survey its credit card customers could assemble the namelist from credit applications in the accounting department. A political candidate may wish to survey those who have recently volunteered their time and efforts or contributed to the campaign. Again, the sponsor should have the list in-house in that case. In these situations, the namelist may have to be transformed in some way, but there's no necessity to seek a list from an independent source. Guidelines for using an in-house namelist are provided in Guidelist 7–2.

There are many mail survey research projects that require mailing to the general public or some subsection of the general public, such as those in a certain geographic area or people with certain demographic characteristics. Other projects may require a mail survey of a special population, such as those engaged in a certain occupation, those in a certain position, or those with some particular condition or attribute. In these cases, the sponsors aren't likely to have the namelist in advance, and it must be obtained from those who specialize in assembling and providing such lists.

Namelists can be purchased or rented from firms who specialize in the management and sale of namelists. Some of these firms may have accumulated a namelist as the result of their principal business, such as a magazine that sells (or more correctly, rents) its list of subscribers. There are also many firms whose principal business is the creation, management, and brokerage of namelists. These firms have elaborate computer facilities, and they obtain namelists together with other coded information about those on the list. They may merge lists, match names and overlay additional information, purge duplicates, make address corrections, and update the list to keep it current and timely. Some firms are strictly namelist brokers. They don't "own" the lists in which they deal. They merely serve as a source of lists for those who require them. They maintain records and relationships with a variety of firms who own and manage namelists. They're often able to locate and provide special lists, and they're paid for doing so on a commission basis.

The principal market for namelists consists of those who use direct mail advertising to market their goods or services directly to buyers. Nevertheless, the firms specializing in namelists provide a rich and varied source of names for mail surveys. Rarely is the population so specialized that a namelist isn't available from some commercial source. Namelist brokers and managers are ordinarily listed in the yellow pages of any metropolitan telephone book. Mailing houses who specialize in doing large mailings are also listed. They're very likely to be brokers or to know of several brokers in the community. Standard Rate and Data Service, Inc., 5201 Old Orchard Road, Skokie, Illinois 60076, publishes a special directory semian-

---

GUIDELIST 7–2

For Using an In-House Namelist

1. Use the specification of the population and sample frame as a guide standard when selecting a source of names.
2. Use an existing in-house namelist if one is available and it meets the sample frame requirements.
3. If there's no existing list, see if a namelist can be assembled from accounting, personnel, or sales records.
4. See if it would be feasible for the survey sponsor to gather a namelist in the process of regular business.
5. Check existing directories and public records to see if a namelist can be composed from available records.

---

nually called *Direct Mail List Rates and Data.* Those who can't find a local namelist broker or who are looking for a highly specialized list may refer to that directory for extremely thorough and complete namelist information.

Namelists may cost as little as $50 or $60 per 1,000 names, but most firms have a minimum order quantity of 5,000 or 10,000 names. This minimum covers the cost of initiating the job and picking the names from the master list, which may contain many millions of names in total. The namelist selected will probably contain many more names than the actual sample size. When it does, the supplier can usually use the *n*th name sampling procedure described in Chapter 3 to select the number needed plus a small surplus as a backup.

Usually, a commercial namelist takes a week or two to get, but sometimes it may take several weeks. So it's advisable to shop for a list, select one, and buy it well in advance. The supplier may require that the buyer provide a copy of what's to be mailed. Ordinarily, a preliminary draft of the mailing piece will suffice, so there should be no delay.

Namelists vary greatly in quality, measured in terms of recency, proportion of nondeliverable mailing pieces, correctness of names and addresses, and duplication of names on the list. Either the list supplier or the broker may be able to provide information about such list characteristics if they're questioned carefully about them. Perhaps the most important protection is to deal only with a highly reputable source.

The post office

Mail surveys are delivered by the postal service, and the post office personnel are valuable sources of information and assistance. They'll provide the necessary information about permit fees, postage costs, and mailing restrictions, but they also offer much more. Postal authorities are familiar with the details of metered postage, precanceled stamps, formats for printing permit information on mailing and return envelopes, size and shape requirements for mailing pieces, bulk mail regulations and preparation, presorting and addressing requirements, and mail box facilities for receiving returns.

The main postage considerations are discussed later in this chapter. It's important to note here that those who anticipate conducting a mail survey should check with the local postal authorities well in advance. All the necessary information should be gathered and all the required approvals should be obtained *before* any component of the mailing piece is finalized and produced. By doing so, potential obstacles and expensive, time-consuming corrections can be avoided.

Stationers and paper suppliers

Stationery stores and suppliers and paper supply houses offer a variety of paper and envelope stock. If a printer is to be used, the printing firm may also provide the paper stock. Thus, it may not be necessary for the researcher to purchase paper separately for printing. Nevertheless, it's advisable to compare both cost and availability of paper between printers and paper suppliers. Printers would, of course, often prefer to provide the stock themselves because they buy at a discount and sell at retail cost, retaining the margin between the two. On the other hand, most printers are willing to print on stock provided by the customer.

Stationers and other paper and office products suppliers are also sources for other materials and supplies that may be required when preparing a mailing. For example, most stationery or graphic art supply stores carry "dry transfer" lettering sheets, stencils, lining and shading materials, and the like, which can be used in place of typesetting or graphic art services. Simple, inexpensive devices for affixing stamps, sealing envelopes, and other such routine tasks are also readily available from these outlets.

Desktop publishing services

There are many small shops—independents and chain members—that provide computer graphics design and desktop publishing services, based on an hourly fee, charge per page, or job estimate. The questionnaire writer may give them a computer disk in the proper format for laser printing. Alternatively, they may only be given a rough draft of the questionnaire, which they then refine through subsequent drafts until the finished product is approved by the researcher. Of course, the time and cost involved depends on how much or how little they do.

Graphic art shops and desktop publishing shops may provide very valuable services for mail survey researchers who don't have their own capability in these areas. Yet it's important to interject a note of caution regarding their work. The largest customers or clients of such firms are usually local advertisers and small advertising agencies. So they're often very familiar and well experienced with print advertising, whether it's published in print media or sent by direct mail.

The trouble is that the requirements for an effective print advertisement are *very* different from those for an effective survey questionnaire. Advertising is designed to capture attention and to convey information. Questionnaires are designed more to *obtain* information than to convey it—to *inquire,* rather than to persuade. It's the mail survey researcher's responsibility to ensure that the questionnaire and other mailing piece components are designed for and meet the requirements of an effective survey inquiry. The graphic artist or designer may suggest or recommend what he or she feels is more *aesthetically pleasing* or *attractive,* or what's more likely to *gain attention* and *get results* in terms of advertising. The researcher should politely but firmly reject those criteria in favor of the technical requirements for a survey mailing piece.

Printing companies

Printers often provide a variety of services besides the actual printing of the survey materials. Most have a variety of paper stock and envelopes available. Many offer layout and typesetting services as well. At times, the entire "package," including paper and envelopes, layout and typesetting, printing, and folding may cost less from a printer than when each task is performed separately. This is especially likely when the mailing is small—including only a few hundred or fewer mailing pieces. In other situations, considerable savings may be realized by using separate vendors, especially for large mailings. Thus, it's important to check and compare both the cost and the time requirements and to assess the degree of expertise and quality of the work that might be obtained from various alternatives. There are two very real advantages to using a "full service" printing company: The research staff doesn't have to spend as much time and effort delivering, picking up, and dealing with several different vendors. The coordination is also likely to be better when a single firm does several tasks. These factors have to be balanced against any savings that might be obtained by using several different vendors.

Mailing houses

Direct mail advertisers and marketing companies are the principal customers of mailing houses. A mailing house is a service firm that specializes in assembling all the printed materials, then folding, inserting, sealing, affixing postage, presorting, and delivering the mailing to the post office. Many also provide additional services, such as namelist acquisition, graphics, typesetting, paper stock, envelopes, and printing. The chief service offering of mailing houses is, of course, the preparation of the mailing.

Mailing houses are typically geared for very large mailings—tens of thousands, hundreds of thousands, or even millions of pieces. So, using them may not be practical for small mailings of less than 1,000 pieces. On the other hand, it may be advisable to use a mailing house for larger survey mailings. Without special mailing preparation equipment, folding, inserting, sealing, metering, stamp affixing, and label affixing by hand may require hundreds of hours of individual labor.

MAILING PIECE COMPONENTS

The mailing piece for the typical survey consists of four or five different components: the mailing envelope, the cover letter, the questionnaire, the return envelope, and perhaps an inducement. Decisions about any one component can't be made independently of the others. The mailing piece has to be an integrated package, and the components must be consistent and compatible with one another. Thus, the researcher must constantly be aware of the effects of a decision about one component on the requirements for the others.

The Mailing Envelope

The typical survey questionnaire would be mailed in a standard number 10 business envelope. Nothing should be printed on the back of the envelope, and the front should contain only three elements: the name and address, the return address, and the stamp or metered postage imprint.

The address

The mailing envelope can be addressed either by typing or printing directly on the envelope, or by affixing labels containing the names and addresses of the potential respondents. When personalized letters are used for the survey, "window" envelopes can also be used. They have a transparent window through which the name and address typed on the letter can be seen.

When an in-house namelist is used, the names and addresses may be typed directly onto envelopes from the source documents, such as a manufacturer's file of completed warranty cards. They may also be typed onto preprinted, letter-size sheets and then transferred to pressure-sensitive label sheets by a copy machine that will accommodate the special forms. This is often useful when the same list is to be used two or more times. With the wide availability of desktop computers, namelists may also be keyed or transferred to a computer file and envelopes or labels printed with a dot-matrix, inkjet, or laser printer.

Commercially obtained mailing lists are usually available in several different label formats. Labels can easily be removed by hand or machine and attached to the envelopes. Sometimes the namelist can be obtained on a computer diskette. If so, either the labels or the envelopes can be printed directly by a computer printer.

The return address

The mailing envelope must *always* contain a return address. Postal regulations require it, and without it the researcher wouldn't be able to determine the number of mailing pieces that were not deliverable. The return address should be printed in the upper left corner of the envelope. The printing of the envelope is relatively inexpensive, and labels should never be used for the return address. In most cases, the return address on the mailing envelope should be the same as the address and return address on the reply envelope. The exception is if the sponsor's letterhead and envelopes are used, but the survey is to be returned to an independent researcher for analysis, to maintain the anonymity of respondents.

The postage

The type and amount of postage will affect the response rate. The response rate will be greatest when first class postage stamps are affixed. It's least with a bulk mail permit, and metered postage falls somewhere between the other two. Bulk mailing requires a bulk mail permit from the post office. The permit number and required indication are then printed directly on the mailing envelope. An alternative is to acquire a bulk mail permit and purchase "precanceled" stamps, to enhance the response rate a little. Bulk mail is slower than first class mail, but it costs about half as much per piece and each can be over three ounces without extra cost. For large mailings with many pieces going to the same ZIP code, bulk mail preparation provides additional savings. This requires sorting by ZIP code and bundling the mailing pieces for each ZIP code or state. That's fairly easy to accomplish if the namelist is sorted by ZIP code before the letters are addressed. The researcher should check with postal authorities *well in advance,* to allow time for printing and production. Guidelines for selecting the type of postage are listed in Guidelist 7–3.

The Cover Letter

The letter that introduces a mail survey or other self-administered questionnaire to respondents is usually called a "cover" letter. It's technical name is a "letter of transmittal." In the

---

GUIDELIST 7–3

For Selecting Postage for Mailing

1. Regular, first class postage stamps on the mailing envelope will result in the highest response rate.
2. Precanceled stamps at the bulk mail rate are second most effective in obtaining response.
3. Metered postage on a mailing, even though first class, provides lower response rates than do postage stamps.
4. Using a bulk mail permit printed on mailing envelopes obtains the lowest response rate.
5. Bulk mailing is less expensive and allows for heavier mailing pieces than first class mailing.

---

absence of personal contact and conversation, the cover letter must explain the project and win the cooperation of the recipient, and it must do so entirely on its own. Thus, it must contain several elements and accomplish multiple goals.

Figure 7–1 lists a dozen questions that will ordinarily be in the mind of the recipient of a mail survey. The items are listed in the same sequence they're likely to arise in the mind of the person who receives the letter. So it's often advisable to include the answers to each in the same order within the actual cover letter. Example 7–1 includes the answers to each of the 12, in this same sequence. Briefly study the list of questions and the sample cover letter together. Notice that Questions 1 and 2 are answered in the first sentence of Paragraph A in the example. Questions 3 is answered in part by the fact that the survey was sponsored by a manufacturer, and the exact reason why is contained in the latter part of Paragraph D. The second sentence of Paragraph A answers Questions 4 and 5. The answers to Questions 6, 7, and 8 are contained in Paragraph B of the letter, and the response to Questions 9 and 10 are contained in Paragraph C. Questions 11 and 12 are answered in Paragraphs D and E, respectively. Thus, every one of the dozen most likely questions that might arise in the mind of the recipient is anticipated and answered within the model cover letter.

Figure 7–1   *Questions a Cover Letter Must Answer*

---

1. What's this about?
2. Who wants to know?
3. Why do they want this?
4. Why was I picked?
5. How important is this?
6. Will this be difficult?
7. How long will this take?
8. Will it cost me anything?
9. Will I be identified?
10. How will this be used?
11. What's in it for me?
12. When should I do it?

EXAMPLE 7–1

The Mail Survey Cover Letter

Dear Respondent:

A. The manufacturers have asked us to conduct a brief survey of a sample of hot tub owners. You were selected from those who have purchased a hot tub, and it's very important to learn your opinions because you represent many other owners who have similar experiences.

B. The questionnaire has been designed so that you can complete it very quickly and easily. It takes only a few minutes, and you need only check off your answers or jot down a number. A postpaid return envelope has been included for your convenience.

C. You can be absolutely sure that all of the information you provide is strictly confidential, and no individual hot tub owners will be identified. Your answers will be combined with those of many others and used only for statistical analysis.

D. As a token of the company's appreciation, we have included a gift to enhance your enjoyment of the hot tub. We genuinely appreciate your valuable assistance. Your honest impressions and opinions, whether favorable or unfavorable, are very necessary to be sure that the company serves the public as effectively as possible. We do appreciate your candid opinions.

E. Please complete and return the form right away. Again, thank you for your help.

Aside from the information content of the cover letter, the form and style are also important. The letter should be geared to the nature of the responding sample. The same general rules concerning vocabulary, grammar, and style that apply to question composition also apply here, with one exception. Survey questions should be as "conversational" as possible, but a cover letter can be too informal. People hold certain expectations about how a business letter should read, and they shouldn't be disappointed. Thus, the general conventions for a business letter should be observed. This does *not* mean that it's advisable or appropriate to use such trite phrases as "Herein enclosed please find . . ." or "With your kind permission, . . ." It does require the use of a conventional format and a *slightly* more formal style in the cover letter than in the questionnaire itself.

A good cover letter shouldn't be too stiff, formal, and demanding. Neither should it beg the recipient to respond. It shouldn't be "over the head" of the least sophisticated respondents, but it shouldn't appear to be patronizing or condescending to the most sophisticated respondents. Guidelines for composing an effective cover letter are listed in Guidelist 7–4.

Bulk printed cover letters

The type of cover letter that's least expensive and most easily produced is the bulk printed cover letter. The letter has been written and typed in final form, with a salutation such as "Dear Respondent:". It's then printed on letterhead stock. Each letter is identical, and respondents aren't individually addressed on the letter.

Personalized cover letters

When the cover letter for each respondent is individually typed, including the individual's name and address and a salutation that greets the person by name, they're called "person-

GUIDELIST 7–4

For Composing a Cover Letter

1. Remember the respondent is likely to accept or reject the response task within the first few seconds.
2. Anticipate the 12 questions that recipients might ask and answer them in the cover letter.
3. Use a conventional business letter style format for the cover letter to meet respondent expectations.
4. Avoid an overly formal style and trite or hackneyed words and phrases in the cover letter.
5. Keep the vocabulary and sentence structure within the limits of comprehension of the least sophisticated reader.
6. Show respect for the readers, their time, and effort, and avoid being too demanding or presumptuous.
7. Don't beg the reader to respond or grossly overstate the importance of the information.
8. Keep the letter friendly and cordial and be confident that nearly all recipients are likable, cooperative people.

alized" letters. The recommendations provided above regarding cover letters apply equally to those printed in bulk and to personalized letters. Personalized cover letters require additional tasks and decisions. Respondents are more likely to read a letter that's addressed directly to them and appears to be hand typed and signed than to read a "general" letter that's unaddressed and obviously printed. They're also more likely to do what the personalized letter asks of them. So response rates can be increased by including a personalized letter. The disadvantage of such a strategy is the cost of the letters.

Personalized letters are created by first composing the body of the letter itself. When it has been edited thoroughly, it's keyed to a computer file. It's often called a "boiler plate" letter or "shell document." It contains everything except the name, address, and the salutation. When personalized letters are used, the names and addresses must also be keyed or transferred to a namelist file on the same system.

The letter and the names may have to be coded in a certain way to show what portions of the name and address are to be printed in particular locations in the shell document. These codes depend on the processing system being used to produce the letters. During processing, the program performs a routine called a "list/merge" function. The program typically takes the first name on the list, inserts it into a copy of the letter, and then routes it to another file or to a printer. The result is a letter for each name that includes the name and address of the individual and a salutation using the person's name, followed by the letter itself. Personalized letters should always be produced with a correspondence-quality printer rather than a dot-matrix printer. Any advantage to the personalization would be lost by the knowledge that the letter was produced in bulk.

There are many word processing and desktop publishing firms in every metropolitan area. Most of them can also produce personalized, laser-printed letters. If researchers want to use personalized letters but don't have the equipment, they need only to refer to the telephone directory. It's always advisable to get cost and timing estimates from several sources, because they vary widely from one to the next. As an alternative to using a service firm, the researcher may want to check with the firm or organization sponsoring the survey. Businesses, schools, hospitals, and government departments often have desktop computer systems that can merge the letter with the namelist and personalized letters. This may require a few conversations with those in the organization who are familiar with the system, but the use of sponsor-generated personalized letters may prove to be both feasible and economical.

The Questionnaire

When potential respondents receive the mailing, the first thing they're likely to do is read the cover letter. The second thing (and sometimes the first) is likely to be a quick examination of the questionnaire itself. The more professional and important the questionnaire appears to be, the more likely the respondents will complete and return it. The easier and quicker they perceive the task to be, the more likely they'll begin answering the questions. Thus, the "cosmetic" aspects of the questionnaire and its appearance to recipients at first glance are vitally important to an adequate response rate. Checklist 7–1 identifies the main considerations for finalizing the questionnaire.

The questionnaire is the core of the mailing. It's the instrument that will both present the questions and capture the responses. While the quality of the survey depends in part on every aspect of the mailing, the questionnaire itself is clearly the most important component. The need to examine every aspect of the final questionnaire draft can't be overstated. With interview surveys, the researcher can often make modifications in the questionnaire, provide additional instruction for fieldworkers, or extra coaching for respondents after data collection begins, if such changes are absolutely necessary. When the data are collected by mail, there's no opportunity for any form of modification after the questionnaire has been mailed to the respondents. If there's any uncertainty about the questionnaire's effectiveness, then additional testing and trial are surely warranted.

Some key aspects and essential elements of the questionnaire discussed earlier deserve reiteration here. The questionnaire should be inserted into the mailing envelope so it will be the first thing the recipient sees after reading the cover letter. The first page or front of the questionnaire should be especially attractive. It should look very quick and easy to complete. If the questionnaire has several pages, the sheets should be attached. It's usually advisable to print the page number in the upper right corner of each page. A note in parentheses at the very bottom of each page should be worded, "Please continue on page . . .", with the next page number noted.

The questionnaire should have a title printed at the top of the first page, or at the top of each page. It should also have a note at the end of the last page, thanking the respondents for completing the task and urging them to return the questionnaire promptly. The entire questionnaire should comprise an integrated "package" that's obviously one document. If one part of the questionnaire has to be modified, the change will often require changes in several other parts of the questionnaire as well. This may discourage the researcher from making what might be viewed as minor changes. The temptation to ignore modifications that tend to "cascade" into several changes should be resisted vigorously. The ultimate criteria for deciding whether a modification is required or not consist of clarity and ease of

---

CHECKLIST 7–1

To Finalize the Questionnaire

1. Does the questionnaire appear, at first glance, to be quick and easy to complete?

2. Does the first page of the questionnaire contain only easy, nonthreatening questions?

3. Is there any uncertainty about the questionnaire's effectiveness that might be reduced by testing?

4. Will the questionnaire be the first thing recipients see after reading the cover letter?

5. Are the pages attached so they won't be lost or separated from one another?

6. Are all the pages clearly numbered and arranged so respondents can follow the sequence easily?

7. Does each page have a note at the bottom, directing respondents to the next page?

8. Is there a title at the beginning of the questionnaire and a note of thanks, urging a quick reply, at the end?

9. Do the sections within the questionnaire form simple steps or subtasks to be completed one at a time?

10. Does the questionnaire have ample white space, with an open, uncramped, uncluttered appearance?

11. Has all work done by others been checked thoroughly?

---

response, not the convenience of the researcher. Additional time spent on the final preparation and checking of a questionnaire often pays for itself many times over when the data have been received and processing begins.

The internal part of the questionnaire should consist of clearly defined sections. That way, the total response task is divided into a series of short, simple subtasks. This encourages response, since the recipient isn't faced with one, large time-consuming task. It's very important that the pages don't look crowded or too dense with type. Ample white space makes the task appear simpler and easier. Any layout or construction that would further simplify and clarify the response task should be sought and examined thoroughly. When a questionnaire draft is to be prepared by a typesetter or graphic artist, the work must be checked very carefully. Those who perform such technical services may be experts at their work, but they seldom compose survey questionnaires. Consequently, they're apt to make decisions based on criteria other than ease and simplicity of response. If aesthetic or artistic principles are at odds with the requirements for clarity and simplicity, they must give way and the latter must take precedence. The researcher must *never* fail to examine the "proofs" and drafts of the work of others. Failure to do so is the single most common source of errors in questionnaires that receive final preparation from others.

There are some special situations where the researcher may want to identify individual subsamples of respondents to whom the survey will be sent, without asking respondents to identify themselves as group members within the questionnaire. They may not know the group or subsample to which they belong, or the question may be threatening to them. In such cases, the questionnaire should be "coded" to indicate group membership, and the code value used as data during analysis. The respondents need not even be aware of such codes, and, in any event, the subsample codes have no meaning to respondents.

To produce two or more different questionnaires with separate codes adds significantly to printing or copying costs. The simplest and most economical way to code the groups is to print an odd number of asterisks, centered, with a few spaces between them, at the very end of the questionnaire. The printer or copy machine operator can then be instructed to stop the machine after the appropriate number of copies of that page has been printed, and mask or "wipe out" one asterisk on each end of the line. This is often required, and printers are likely to be familiar with the process. Copy machine operators may have experience with this coding technique. If not, they should be instructed carefully to be sure they understand the procedure.

The respondents wouldn't know that their questionnaire contained a different number of asterisks, a different code, than others. When the data are keyed to file, the operator can be instructed to count the asterisks and key in the number that are on each questionnaire. This number serves as an indication of the group membership when the data are processed and analyzed.

The Return Envelope

As noted earlier, the return envelope should be smaller than the mailing envelope so that it can be inserted into the mailing without folding. Nothing should be printed on the back of the envelope, and the front contains the same three elements as those on the mailing envelope. The return envelope should contain *both* an address and a return address, although they're usually the same. Both should be printed rather than on labels affixed to the return envelope.

Guidelist 7–5 identifies the return postage options for the reply envelope. The manner in which postage is attached to the return envelope will affect response rate significantly. Affixing regular, first class postage stamps results in the highest response rate. Some people question the use of a postage stamp on the return envelope. They suspect that some respondents will remove the stamps to use for their own mail, and fail to return the questionnaire. That only very rarely happens. The typical recipient is reluctant either to remove the stamp or to discard it because of its obvious value. Many feel a little obligated to return the questionnaire.

Using first class postage stamps on return envelopes is a costly technique. It isn't recommended unless it's important to maximize response rate *in every way possible*. A business reply permit is an acceptable alternative for most surveys. With a business reply permit on the return envelope, postage is charged for only those surveys that are returned. On the other hand, the fee per return is almost twice the rate for first class mail. So if the response rate is expected to be very high, a business reply permit may not accomplish appreciable savings. On the other hand, if a low response rate is anticipated, the business reply permit would be by far the most economical choice, and that's usually the case.

INDUCEMENTS TO RESPOND

Ordinarily, response rates for mail surveys are rather low. This has two negative effects: It increases costs because the number of mailing pieces must be several times the number of respondents required. It also increases the likelihood of nonresponse bias, reducing the survey's validity. Mail surveys often include a gift or premium for the recipients: an *inducement*

GUIDELIST 7–5

For Selecting Postage for the Reply

1. Use of postage stamps on return envelopes *encourages* rather than discourages response.

2. Metered postage on return envelopes is inadvisable because it's both too expensive and ineffective.

3. Business reply permits printed on the return envelopes are satisfactory for most mail surveys.

to respond to the survey. Inducements to respond need not be of great value. They don't have to pay recipients for their time and effort or compensate them for responding. Rather, they're just a token of appreciation. The inducement shows goodwill on the sponsor's part. Inducements tend to catch the recipients' attention and put them in a more positive frame of mind. For some, they can also create a sense of *obligation* to respond if the inducement is sent with the original mailing on the assumption that recipients will complete and return the questionnaire.

Inducements that are contingent on receipt of a completed questionnaire are rarely recommended. There are several reasons: First, they require a second mailing or later delivery to all those who respond. Second, such an inducement is often seen by recipients as "pay" for completing the questionnaire, and so it must be fairly valuable or it may actually *inhibit* response. Third, the inducement is more likely to influence the *manner* in which people respond, introducing a serious source of bias. For example, some people may feel they have to be positive toward the issues in order to get their gift. Thus, except for a few, very special cases, inducements shouldn't be contingent on response. Instead, they should be sent with the original mailing, if possible. The range of premiums or gifts that might be used for a survey is practically limitless. Yet, all the various alternative inducements won't have an equal effect on response rates.

Selecting Inducements

Six major criteria for selecting an inducement are listed below. Obviously, an effective inducement need not necessarily meet all the criteria exactly, but the closer it conforms to the criteria, the more effective it's likely to be.

Economy

When hundreds or even thousands of people are to be included in the mailing, the cost of an inducement becomes a very important factor. It's important to select an inexpensive item. The objective is to find something that the recipients will value highly, but that won't cost much for the sponsor to provide.

Nonreactivity

The inducement must not influence the nature of the responses to the survey questions. It shouldn't be directly associated with the topics, issues, or sponsor, so that recipients "react" to the items in a certain way. To the degree that an inducement affects the *way* that people respond, it will create bias. For example, if the survey dealt with the way people evaluate a particular brand or product, it would be extremely inadvisable to use a sample of the same brand or product as an inducement.

Uniqueness

Inducements that aren't otherwise obtainable by the respondents tend to be more attractive. Such gifts may be relatively inexpensive, but they may be seen by recipients as quite valuable because they can't easily be purchased or acquired in some other way or from some other source.

Value

Even as a token of appreciation for cooperating, an inducement must be of sufficient value so that it doesn't demean the importance of the survey. Giving something obviously worth only a few cents for performing a task that requires considerable time and effort might serve to diminish rather than enhance goodwill and cooperation. Yet, the value doesn't have to be monetary. The monetary value is irrelevant if the inducement has personal, social, psychological, or emotional value to recipients.

Luxuriousness

Gifts which respondents would probably love to own but wouldn't be likely to purchase for themselves are the most potent and effective inducements. As with any gift, utilitarian items are less welcome or valued than are little luxuries or treats the recipients wouldn't otherwise obtain for themselves.

Individualization

While they may be expensive to obtain or produce, gifts and premiums that are individualized are more effective. If the inducement is "personalized" with the individual's name or otherwise directly related to the individual, such as referring to their occupation or some other attribute or characteristic the recipient is known to have, it tends to have greater value.

Types of Inducements

Without attempting to include an exhaustive list, it might be helpful to discuss a few, common forms of inducement. Studying the experience of others is a good way to avoid missed opportunities or repeating the mistakes of others.

Cash payments

The use of cash as an inducement fails to meet most of the criteria listed above, yet unfortunately, it's often used as an inducement to respond to mail surveys. The disadvantages of using money are several, but the most important is the fact that it "disappears" into the individual's pocket without a trace. In other words, currency is homogeneous, and so the recipient is likely to forget about the gift very quickly. Also, with the use of money as an inducement, there's danger it may appear the person is being "paid" for participation, yet the amount isn't likely to compensate them very adequately for their time and effort.

The disadvantages of using money as an inducement to respond don't preclude the use of a cash inducement. As with any potential inducement under consideration, much depends on how creatively the researcher communicates with potential respondents. Even money can be used very effectively, with a clever approach, as Example 7–2 indicates.

Certificates or passes
Many service organizations have very high fixed costs and very low variable costs for creating their services. For example, it costs little or nothing for a movie theater to serve additional patrons by giving away tickets. The only "cost" would be the lost revenue if recipients would have otherwise purchased them or if there were a "full house," so that tickets could have been sold for the seats occupied by the guests. Service providers (e.g., theaters, restaurants, airlines, public transportation, and so forth) who sponsor surveys can provide certificates or "passes" for free services as inducements to respond. These inducements cost the sponsor little or nothing, yet they're very valuable to the recipients.

Drawings or sweepstakes
Some mail surveys use the *chance* to win a drawing prize as an inducement to respond. Recipients must complete and return the questionnaire to be eligible for the drawing. There are some important advantages to this kind of inducement: Only *one* prize has to be delivered rather than hundreds or perhaps thousands of inducements for each and every recipient or respondent. When the budget is limited, the total amount available may constitute a substantial prize for the lucky winner, but only a pittance if divided among all the respondents.

Perhaps most important of all, this kind of inducement requires the respondents to identify themselves. They have to provide their name and address so they can be contacted if they win the drawing. So they have an incentive to relinquish their anonymity. But that's a two-edged sword. Knowing the identity of respondents may allow the researcher to redrop a mailing to only those who haven't responded, to avoid getting duplicate responses from the same people. It may also be useful to combine the responses to the survey with other data about individuals that's already on file.

Despite the advantages, there are some very serious disadvantages to using drawings or sweepstakes as a form of mail survey response inducement. Some people will absolutely refuse to reveal their identity, especially if the survey topics or issues are controversial or confidential in nature. So asking them to relinquish their anonymity may *decrease* rather than increase the response rate. But there's an even more serious danger—the potential for introducing systematic bias. If those who love to enter drawings and those who don't also hold *systematically different* views on the issues or topics of the survey, the inducement will cause *nonresponse bias,* discussed in Chapter 2. Even more serious is the possibility that recipients will go ahead and respond because they want to enter the drawing, but will actually lie or distort their answers because they won't be anonymous. That would increase *response bias,* discussed in Chapter 4, and that's a far more serious threat to the validity of the survey.

Reports of results
For surveys of people in their occupational role, offering a report of some of the results of the survey may be a powerful inducement to respond. For some surveys, it may also be

EXAMPLE 7–2

Novel Inducements to Respond

Worthless Money That Paid Off

A survey of U.S. residents sponsored by a Mexican bank included as an inducement a one-peso coin. One peso has so little value the coins aren't even used in circulation in Mexico. In U.S. monetary value, it was worth only an extremely small fraction of a cent. Yet recipients appreciated the gift and responded well to the survey because this little story of the peso and dollar sign was included. The gift had psychological rather than monetary value.

Your Souvenir Peso . . .		
. . . while valued at just a few cents, it is rich in history. On the coin itself is the Mexican national seal, consisting of an eagle eating a rattlesnake while perched on a cactus. On the other side there is a likeness of Jose Maria Morelos y Pavon, a founding father of modern Mexico and hero of the struggle for independence from Spain a century ago.	The word peso comes from a Spanish term for the word piece. The name was given to Spanish coins used throughout her New World colonies during the 16th century. Pesos from Mexico—home of some of the world's greatest gold mines— were particularly valued. The Mexican peso was used as a medium of exchange through- out this hemisphere and in all lands bordering the Pacific Ocean.	The U.S. dollar sign is inherited from the peso. The original abbreviation for peso was PS. During handwritten correspondence to the famous American explorer George Rogers Clark, the finance minister of the Louisiana Territory listed payments in pesos, overlapping the P's and S's to look much like today's $ sign. Today, the peso and dollar share this same sign.

The Three-Scent Response Inducement

A survey of spa and hot tub owners included, as inducement to respond, three "spa kisses"—small, pillow-shaped, plastic packets containing pink, yellow, and green scented oil to give the spa a pleasant aroma. The company that sold the product provided them free of charge, together with a promotional flyer. Although it required tremendous persuasion before postal authorities would accept the plastic liquid packs for shipment, recipients were delighted with the inducement and the response rate was superb.

Let Me Buy You a Cup of Coffee

One national mail survey arrived with a cover letter that began with the words, "Let us buy you a hot cup of coffee . . ." and below it a shiny, new half-dollar was attached to the paper. Below the coin, the letter continued, ". . . and perhaps while you're sipping it, you'll take just a few minutes to answer some brief questions." Many respondents did just that.

Discovering a Page from the Past

A large, metropolitan daily paper was conducting a survey of small business owners in the city. The researchers found that the owners' birthdates were on the business license file from which the sample was selected. They also learned that the newspaper had electronic archives of every edition of the paper for the past 87 years. Each survey recipient opened the letter to find a small copy of the front page of the paper—*dated the day he or she was born!*

GUIDELIST 7–6

For Including an Inducement to Respond

1. Send the inducement with the original mailing rather than promising to send it later if the recipient responds.
2. Don't make the gift contingent on respondents completing and returning their questionnaires.
3. Be sure respondents will see the gift as a token of appreciation rather than meager pay for helping.
4. Avoid any form of inducement that might influence the way people answer questions, introducing a bias.
5. Evaluate potential inducements using the six criteria as flexible standards for judgment, not rigid rules.
6. Don't use money as an inducement unless it's perfectly clear that it will be effective.

---

effective for individuals from the general public, but such reports are particularly attractive to business, organizational, or professional respondents when the survey is to measure work-related issues. The respondents are often eager to learn how others in their position or profession will answer the questions—how their own experiences and opinions compare with those of their counterparts elsewhere.

This kind of inducement requires respondents to reveal their identity in order to get the report. If that appears to be a problem, there is a means to alleviate it to some degree. The researcher can provide an entirely separate, preaddressed, postage-paid postcard on which respondents indicate they want the report of results and record their name and address. While many people would ordinarily enter a drawing for a prize that way, *without completing and returning the questionnaire,* very few will seek the results without participating in the survey themselves. It should also be noted that while this protects respondent anonymity and the negative effects of revealing identity, it also costs more for the separate card and postage. In addition, if respondents' identities are attached to the completed questionnaire, that would facilitate redropping only to those who haven't responded. It would also allow the researcher to combine the survey information with other information about the respondents that may be on file.

Guidelines for using an inducement to respond are listed in Guidelist 7–6. When an inducement to respond is to be used with a mail survey, the search for a suitable gift should begin several weeks before the mailing date. There are several specialized companies that deal exclusively with premiums, sales promotional items, and the like. They often carry a very large selection of inexpensive items and they can provide many hundreds or thousands of units. These goods are ordinarily not available in retail stores, but delivery may take a few weeks or more.

MAILING AND RECEIPT

There are still a few tasks and decisions concerning the mailing that remain, even after all components have been prepared and the mailing piece is complete and ready. These factors deserve no less attention than the earlier preparation.

Timing the mailing

The timing of the mailing will make a significant difference in the response rate in some cases. Obviously, a lower response rate will result from mailing during a holiday period or some other time of year when respondents are likely to receive large quantities of mail or be very busy and pressed for time. Such periods may also induce bias and decrease the validity of the survey. When the survey is addressed to businesses or organizations, a higher response rate can be expected if recipients receive the questionnaire during the middle of the month than if it arrives at the very beginning or end of the month. When choosing a time to mail, the researcher should also be aware of any external event that might influence either the response rate or the response itself. For example, a survey of political opinions would obtain different results immediately after a domestic or international crisis than it would before it or a few weeks later.

The cutoff date

Ordinarily, over 95 percent of all returns that will eventually be received will arrive within a period of three or four weeks. Rather than waiting a long time to begin analysis, the researcher is advised to monitor the number of returns received per day and to decide on a cutoff date. Usually, a large number of surveys will be returned within a few days after mailing. Then, fewer and fewer returns arrive each day until the point where the "yield" of additional surveys each day isn't worth the wait. A few more returns will be received, and sometimes an occasional questionnaire will be returned many months later. It's usually best to ignore this additional data.

Recording nondeliverables

Some mailing pieces will be returned to the sender because they can't be delivered to the addressee. The number of nondeliverable pieces should be recorded. The percent of non-deliverable mail is an indicator of the quality of the mailing list. If the list is very current, few addressees will have moved without a forwarding address or be deceased. If the list is accurate, there will be very few mistakes in the addresses. Poor quality namelists will result in a significant number of nondeliverable mailing pieces.

Response rate computation

The raw response rate can be computed by dividing the number of returns by the number of pieces mailed, less the number of nondeliverables. This is the gross response rate, because some of those returned will prove to be incomplete or unusable. The net rate can be computed in the same way, after editing and data transfer, based on only the number of usable responses.

Remailing and redropping

When the response rate is difficult or impossible to forecast, it may be necessary to follow the initial mailing with another, after computing the initial rate. This is called "remailing" because the same mailing piece is used, although it's sent to different individuals. An example may clarify this procedure. Suppose 300 completed responses are required. If an initial mailing of 2,000 questionnaires provided 200, the response rate would be 10 percent. An additional mailing of 1,000 questionnaires would probably provide the extra 100 returns that are required.

There may be some special situations where it would be useful to remind survey recipients to respond. This is called "redropping," and it can be done in two ways. One method is to send a postcard or note, identifying the questionnaire sent earlier and urging those who haven't done so to complete and return it. The other procedure is used when it seems likely that many respondents no longer have the questionnaire. If so, they're merely sent a duplicate mailing. This shouldn't be done, however, unless the researcher can identify *duplicate* responses from the *same individuals*. If the respondents aren't anonymous, then another copy of the questionnaire can safely be sent only to those who did not respond to the first mailing. Only a very few will then return both copies, and duplicates can be identified by a key number in the file. If response is anonymous, however, then redropping another question- naire is inadvisable. Many who have already completed and returned the first one may also fill in and send back the second questionnaire. Yet there wouldn't be any way to tell which or how many duplicates were received.

Sight-editing

As the returns are received, the research staff should open and discard the return envelopes, sorting the completed questionnaires and preparing them for data transfer and processing. When doing so, the questionnaires should be sight-edited, or examined to eliminate those that aren't usable. Additional editing and postcoding may be required, but the initial, cursory sight-edit permits computation of the net response rate and indicates the overall effectiveness of the measurement and quality of response. Additional guidelines for receiving, editing, and postcoding completed questionnaires and preparing the data for analysis are provided in Chapter 9.

Self-Administered Surveys

The discussion in this chapter has focused on *mail* surveys because that's a very common method of survey data collection. With mail surveys, respondents have to read the questions themselves and record their own answers. So all mail surveys are *self-administered,* but *not* all self-administered surveys are delivered by mail! Several other types of self-administered ques- tionnaires are identified in Example 7–3.

Self-administered survey instruments other than those sent by mail usually include only the questionnaire itself, but not such other things as delivery and return envelopes or induce- ments to respond. So the focus is ordinarily almost exclusively on the questionnaire itself, unless a return envelope is required. These questionnaires are often smaller and more brief than mail surveys, but not necessarily so. Example 6–1 depicts a very long, comprehensive, self-administered questionnaire, mainly to illustrate how various scales and sections are orga- nized. Nonetheless, an extensive self-administered questionnaire such as that could be used if a very substantial inducement was provided. In fact, for very long questionnaires, self- administration may be preferable to interviewing because the respondents can complete the instrument when and where it's most convenient for them.

Some questionnaires are partially or entirely self-administered because the information is

---

EXAMPLE 7–3

Typical Self-Administered Questionnaires

- **Application supplements.** Additional questions or sections on applications for credit, membership, or some other privilege, included to gain additional information about applicants.
- **Discount rebate coupons.** Questions about the purchase and buyer included on labels or package inserts offering manufacturer or store rebates to buyers. In effect, the rebate is not only an incentive to purchase, but an inducement to provide information about customers.
- **Order form supplements.** Supplementary questions included on order forms to gain information about buyers beyond that required for billing and delivery of the goods.
- **Patron questionnaires.** Often small questionnaires on card or paper stock asking hotel or restaurant patrons a few questions about their reactions to the service the establishment provided during their visit.
- **Periodical questionnaires.** Questionnaires printed in newspapers, magazines, or other periodicals seeking information from readers or subscribers. Results are often published in subsequent issues.

- **Premium request forms.** Questions included on forms for requesting premiums or to enter drawings or sweepstakes. The survey isn't the main purpose of the offer, but most entrants willingly supply additional information.
- **Statement insert forms.** Ordinarily brief questionnaires included with billing statements or invoices used to obtain additional information about customers or clients. They're often economical and effective because they cost almost nothing extra to send and almost everyone must respond with payment.
- **Warranty cards.** Brief questionnaires included with consumer appliances or equipment, asking the new owners to "register" their purchase. The implication (though false) is that the warranty won't be valid unless the information about the purchase and buyer is provided.

---

highly confidential. People may be more willing and open to respond honestly and candidly if they can sit down in complete privacy to record their answers and be absolutely assured of complete anonymity. Yet, if the survey was done by mail, most people would probably discard it. For such cases, the prospective respondents may be contacted and solicited by fieldworkers who gain the respondents' agreement to participate. They may then return for the sealed questionnaire when it's completed, and as with secret balloting, have respondents deposit it with others in a returns container. That assures both adequate response rates and respondent anonymity.

While the dimensions and ancillary materials for nonmail, self-administered questionnaires differ from those for mail surveys, virtually all the same principles of composition and construction still apply. Whether the survey instrument is mailed individually to prospective respondents or delivered in some other way, the self-administered questionnaire is an excellent way to interrogate respondents and obtain information, provided that the instrument is expertly and carefully crafted.

SUMMARY

Mail Data Collection Procedures

   A. Coordinate the production. Make the decisions about any one component in the light of their effects on the others and on the mailing piece as a whole.

   B. Make production consistent. Select paper, print, page layout, and assembly that are consistent among the components of the mailing piece.

   C. Use external services. Contact namelist sources, the post office, stationers, word processing shops, graphic artists, printers, and mailing houses.

   D. Evaluate vendors carefully. Obtain referrals or samples of work or products, and compare cost and time requirements among several outside sources.

   E. Use appropriate envelopes. Follow the principles and recommendations for addressing, return address, and selection and affixing of postage.

   F. Create an effective cover letter. Use the example and be sure that all 12 questions recipients might ask are clearly answered in the letter.

   G. Select an effective inducement. Examine many alternatives and evaluate them using the six major criteria for selection.

   H. Practice timing and follow-up. Select an appropriate mailing date, allow sufficient time for response, and monitor returns as recommended.

Chapter 8

Gathering Interview Data

ROLE OF THE INTERVIEWER

When a mail survey will be conducted, the mailing piece, in general, and the questionnaire, in particular, are the media through which the researcher holds a "conversation" with respondents. With an interview survey, the questionnaire plays an important role, but it isn't the key element. Instead, the *interviewers* are the communication media between the researcher and the respondent.

Once a mail survey questionnaire has been finalized and produced, it's an inert and invariable medium. Every mail questionnaire is identical to all of the others, and, in effect, exactly the same message reaches every respondent in exactly the same way. Interviewers, on the other hand, are neither inert nor invariable—quite the contrary! Thus, the messages that reach respondents through interviews always vary to some degree, both from one interviewer to another and from one interview to the next. This creates several major problems for those conducting interview surveys.

The reliability and validity of a study depend, in a large measure, on consistency. The more variation there is among interviewers and interviews, the greater the introduction of random error and systematic bias, and the lower the reliability and validity of the data. Consequently, the researcher must strive for consistency and control of the interview process in order to obtain reliable, valid results.

Mode of Interviewing

When conducting an interview survey, there's a choice between two basic modes of data collection: contract the interviewing to an external data collection agency, or manage an in-house data collection crew. Each has its own capabilities and limitations.

Agency capabilities and limitations

Perhaps the most important advantage of using a data collection agency is that these agencies are spread across the country. Every major metropolitan area is likely to have several data collection agencies. When an interview survey requires collecting data over a wide geographic area, it may be almost impossible to field an in-house interviewer crew to conduct personal interviews. Even when the interviews are done by telephone, toll charges may be prohibitive. When data collection agencies conduct telephone interviews from widely dispersed areas, several calling locations can be used, so each is closer to area respondents and toll charges are reduced.

When external data collection agencies are used to collect the survey data, the task can often be accomplished more quickly than through an in-house crew of interviewers. This is because the data collection agencies are already "in place" and have trained interviewers on call. When it's essential to collect the data quickly, the data collection agency can often assign more interviewers to the project than would be available for an in-house crew, so the collection process can be done more rapidly.

There may be substantial economy in using data collection agencies. It would be costly to recruit, select, and train a large, in-house crew of interviewers to conduct a single project that may take only a few days to complete. In effect, only one project must bear the entire development cost for an in-house crew. By contrast, data collection agencies use their interviewers for many data collection projects. Thus, the recruitment, selection, and training costs for both fieldworkers and supervisors can be spread over many such projects. To the degree these savings are passed on to the client, there may be significant savings.

The two major disadvantages to using data collection agencies are lack of quality assurance and lack of control. While some data collection agencies are well managed and maintain high standards of service quality, many others don't. To make matters worse, it's difficult to distinguish between the more capable and the less capable agencies before contracting the data collection project to them. In fact, it may be difficult to detect poor quality work, even *after* the data have been collected and analyzed. It's also difficult for the agency's client to maintain control of the data collection process, especially from afar. There are often communications problems between agency and client. Even when directions and specifications are clearly stipulated by the client and thoroughly understood by the agency, there's no guarantee the agency or its interviewers will follow them closely. Thus, contracting with an agency to collect the survey data certainly doesn't offer an easy, automatic solution to the data collection problem. Using a data collection agency only *changes* the nature of the decisions, tasks, and responsibilities of the researcher. It doesn't eliminate them.

Using in-house interviewers

When a crew of interviewers are hired and trained by those conducting a research survey, the researcher has much greater control over the data collection process. Because the interviewers are recruited, selected, trained, supervised, and compensated by the individual or organization conducting the survey, they're directly responsible to the researcher. Those conducting the research have a much wider range of choice, authority, and control over every aspect of the data collection process. There's more direct focus and concentration of effort on the project at hand. Thus, quality control and assurance may be much greater.

There are some significant disadvantages to using in-house interviewers that accompany the advantages. With an in-house field crew, the researcher has a much bigger burden of responsibility. It requires more expertise and effort by the researcher to recruit, select, train, supervise, and compensate interviewers. There may also be diseconomies of scale for data collection projects that take only a short time. The entire cost of obtaining and training the interviewers must be borne by a single, short-term project. If the project offers employment for only a few days, it may also be difficult to recruit qualified people as interviewers.

For most interview surveys, there's no single, clear-cut choice as to which mode of data collection would be best. Rather, the researcher must weigh the pro's and con's of the two modes. Before making a choice between an independent data collection agency and an in-house interviewer crew, the researcher has to be thoroughly familiar with the responsibilities and tasks associated with each mode. While the more seasoned researchers may have gained considerable insight from experience, those with less experience are well advised to study the process for *both* modes, before making a final choice.

DATA COLLECTION AGENCIES

It may be useful at this point to describe the typical agency before looking more closely at the process of data collection by an agency. Data collection agencies are usually local firms. They're often owned and operated by women who began by running their small businesses right from their homes—so-called kitchen table operations. Even the larger, older firms are typically entrepreneurships that remain under the direction of the person who began the business. These entrepreneurs have typically gained their knowledge and expertise through experience. Most have little or no formal training in survey research. Their skills are ordinarily specialized in data collection rather than in the survey process as a whole.

Data collection agencies usually have a small, permanent staff of supervisors and office workers who are full-time employees. The typical agency has a large number of interviewers who are temporary, part-time workers—usually middle-age women whose predominant role is that of a homemaker, but who supplement their family income by interviewing. These data collection agencies form a loose network that covers the metropolitan areas of the country. They can easily reach many nearby towns and rural areas as well. There are, however, many remote and sparsely populated areas that are difficult to reach through data collection agencies. Coverage is far from complete. In smaller cities, there may be only one or a very few data collection agencies, while the largest metropolitan areas may have over 100 such firms. Guidelist 8–1 suggests some ways to locate data collection agencies.

Nearly all these agencies belong to an industry association called The Market Research Association, or MRA. Their association allows them to work together, and it allows client firms to hire several agencies in order to cover a wide geographic area when conducting a regional or national survey.

The quality of data collection service varies dramatically from one agency to the next, and often from one time to the next for any given agency. For example, if an agency is very busy at the time, it may use interviewers that are marginal or inexperienced. They may also take less time and effort to train and instruct them. During busy periods they may be more lax or careless about field supervision and verification than they would otherwise be.

Facilities and services offered by data collection agencies also vary greatly. Some are very small, operating from the owner's home, with very limited physical facilities. Others may

---

GUIDELIST 8–1

For Locating Data Collection Agencies

1. Obtain an MRA directory or membership roster.
2. Visit an MRA national and regional conference.
3. Check other conferences or directories, such as the American Marketing Association (AMA) or the Academy of Marketing Science (AMS).
4. Look for advertisements in trade publications, such as the AMA *Marketing News*.
5. Refer to the yellow pages and local business directories.

---

have several locations, including shopping center storefronts for intercept and central location data collection. Facilities might also include test kitchens and dining areas for food preparation and taste testing, focus group facilities for observation during conferences with respondents, mobile field units, audio and video equipment for both recording and presentation to interviewees, and a host of other facilities. Despite the variation, virtually all of them will routinely *claim* to be able to provide almost *any* service to the potential client. Consequently, it's the researcher's job to check very carefully to be sure the claims are, in fact, reasonably accurate.

Agency Data Collection Process

When a data collection agency is used, the process can be divided into six steps or phases: (1) Initial contact and cost estimation. (2) Agency selection, notification, and alert. (3) Delivery of materials and acknowledgment of receipt. (4) Training, instruction, and initiation. (5) Monitoring, control, and supervision. (6) Receipt, verification, and payment. Each of the six phases will be discussed briefly below.

Initial contact and cost estimation

The initial contact with a prospective agency might be by mail or personal visit to the facility, but most often it's done by telephone. The project and sample requirements, the nature and length of the questionnaire, the anticipated initiation date and expected duration of data collection, and any other relevant details or requirements are described to the agency. They would inquire about any additional information they might need. It might take a day or two for the agency to assess availability and compute a cost *estimate*. Data collection agencies almost never provide a fixed bid or firm contract. In most cases, the only contract between the sponsor and the agency is a telephone conversation, occasionally followed by a letter of agreement.

Agency selection, notification, and alert

After obtaining the information on availability, timing, and costs from potential data collection agencies, the researcher can compare and contrast them, eliminating those that aren't acceptable. It's best to obtain references from the agencies, including the names and telephone numbers of former clients, rather than merely a client list. Before making the final selection, it's advisable to contact these former clients to get their recommendations and comments. The agency selected should be notified of the decision when it's final. The researcher should also alert the agency a week or so before sending the materials for a small project, and perhaps a month or more beforehand for a very large project. That allows the agency to obtain the required interviewers, schedule the project, and make any other preparations needed.

Delivery and acknowledgment

At the time of the agency alert or shortly thereafter, the agency should be sent a *precise* list of what materials will be sent, how they're being shipped, and when they can expect to receive them. A name should be assigned to the project so both the client and the agency can refer to it by name. All materials should be clearly labeled with this name. The project name and description of contents should be listed on the outside of each parcel of materials shipped to the data collection agency, together with instructions on when and how the contents should be handled, stored, and opened. That's necessary because data collection agencies often have many containers of materials from various clients. Not infrequently, materials or supplies for a data collection project are lost or misplaced, either during shipping or after receipt by the agency. Guidelist 8–2 lists the main tasks associated with shipping materials to agencies.

It's usually advisable to instruct the agency to inspect the outside of any parcels for damage, and then to acknowledge their receipt intact. If the acknowledgment isn't received shortly after the expected date of receipt, the researcher must call the agency to be sure the materials have arrived in good order. The agency should be instructed *not* to open containers of materials until just prior to the beginning of data collection. If such containers are opened and inventoried in advance, there's a good chance that some of the contents will be misplaced, destroyed, or used for another project. An itemized packing list should be included in each container, so when it's opened, the contents can be inventoried, checked off on a copy of the list, and the acknowledgment of contents returned to the client.

Training and initiation

It's ordinarily advisable for a member of the research staff to visit the data collection agency and help instruct and train the agency staff when the data collection is to start. This may not be practical if several data collection agencies are used, if the agency is very distant from the researchers' project headquarters, or if the data collection task is very simple and straightforward. In such cases, written instructions must be included. When no agency visits are planned, telephone conversations or telephone conferences among all agencies may be very helpful.

When a member of the research staff visits an agency at the start of the project, all materials and supplies for the project should be inspected and inventoried to be sure everything needed is there and in good order. The researcher can then instruct and train either the agency supervisors or both supervisors and fieldworkers. The researcher should start with a general introduction to the project and its purposes. This is followed by a listing of any special, verbal instructions. The trainees should then be given a copy of the materials that will be

---

GUIDELIST 8–2

For Shipping Materials to Agencies

1. Indicate on the outside of each container:
   A. The project name.
   B. The number of the container.
   C. The number of containers in the lot.
   D. The nature of the contents.
   E. Special instructions for storage.
   F. When the container is to be opened.
   G. How the container is to be opened.
2. Notify agency in advance of:
   A. The project name use.
   B. The number of parcels shipped.
   C. How the materials were sent.
   D. Where they were sent.
   E. When they were shipped.
   F. When they'll be received.

3. Include in each parcel or container:
   A. A detailed packing list of contents.
   B. Complete inventory instructions.
   C. A check-off list for acknowledgment.
4. Instruct the data collection agency not to open packages when they arrive, but wait until instructed to open them.
5. Telephone the data collection agency if the proper acknowledgments aren't received within a day or so of when they're expected.
6. Retain copies of all materials sent, so replacements can be produced if required in an emergency.

---

used, including the questionnaire, written instructions, rating cards, and the like. (Such equipment as pens and clipboards are ordinarily provided by the interviewers or the agency rather than by the client.) When interviewers are being trained, it's usually advisable to "walk through" the complete questionnaire first, noting each question, instruction, branch, and recording detail. This is usually followed by a "trial run," with the trainer conducting a mock interview of an interviewer. If any questions or problems arise, they're discussed and solved. Each interviewer can then conduct one or two interviews with the others, working among themselves to become completely familiar with every aspect of the instrument.

When interviewer training is done entirely by a data collection agency supervisor, he or she should be instructed to proceed with the process *exactly* as it has been described here. Data collection agencies will often try to abbreviate the training process, because they can cut their own costs and make their work easier by doing so. Guidelines for training interviewers are contained in Guidelist 8–3.

Monitoring and control

It's always advisable to monitor the process during the actual data collection. Waiting until the data collection project completion date when the completed records and materials should have been returned may result in serious, unexpected problems or delays. The data collection agency should be given the name and telephone number of a research staff member and be encouraged to call for information or direction *whenever* a problem or question arises. Typically, researchers who often use data collection agencies find it necessary to take the initiative to telephone the agency daily or a few times a week to be sure the process is going smoothly

---

GUIDELIST 8-3

For Training Interviewers

1. Train both supervisors and interviewers if possible.
2. Provide an overview of the project and its purposes.
3. Distribute a copy of all the materials for interviewing.
4. "Walk through" the instrument and other materials, describing each element and its use.
5. Do a "trial run" by conducting a mock interview of one of the supervisors or interviewers.
6. Answer any questions or solve any problems that arise.
7. Question supervisors and interviewers to be sure they understand each aspect of the interview task.
8. Have each interviewer conduct one or two interviews with one another, while monitoring the interviews and the recording of the data.
9. Distribute the necessary materials and supplies for the actual field or telephone work.

---

and the agency is on schedule with the data collection. The researcher should maintain a log of the number and proportion of interviews completed at each point in time.

When personal interviews are to be conducted at a certain place, when only certain respondents are to be selected, or when quota requirements are based on qualifying questions, it's usually necessary to monitor the respondent selection process as well as the mere degree of completion. These special selection options and specifications are discussed in more detail later in this chapter. It should be noted, however, that data collection agencies are much less likely to cut corners or deviate from the selection instructions if they clearly understand they'll be monitored and *won't be paid* if they don't adhere to instructions.

When interviewees are selected from a specific list of respondents, provided by the researcher, it may also be advisable to "salt" the list with auditors. These may be members of the research staff or sponsoring organization, or others solicited to secretly play the role of regular respondents. Interviewers who telephone or visit such auditors think they're naive respondents. Thus, they're likely to conduct the interview and record the responses as they would others. Any cheating, skipping, false recording, or other anomaly will be revealed easily and quickly.

Receipt, verification, and payment

When the completed survey instruments are received from the data collection agency, they should be sight-edited for completion and proper recording. Any questionnaires that aren't usable should be separated, and the reason for their removal should be noted clearly. They shouldn't be discarded until later, because it may be necessary to refer to them when renegotiating final payment with the agency. The complete, usable questionnaires should then be numbered, counted, and prepared for final editing, postcoding, and data entry.

A sample of some proportion of the completed questionnaires should be used for verification of response. A questionnaire may appear complete, accurate, and quite satisfactory, but it may prove to be invalid on verification. The interviewer may have merely filled out the form him- or herself, rather than actually conducting an interview. This is sometimes called "arm-chairing" in the industry, and the term is an apt metaphor. Other, less blatant forms of cheating or misconduct on the part of the interviewers or agency include skipping parts of the interview, cutting it short or terminating the interview early, or completing sections to which the interviewee refused to respond. The interview may also have been conducted at the wrong time or place, or with the wrong respondents or those unqualified to respond may have been included. Incidents of blatant cheating are much more rare than are honest mistakes or errors from carelessness. Nevertheless, the effect of either source of trouble is to introduce substantial bias and jeopardize the validity of results.

Verification requires the identification of respondents by first name and telephone number. A sample is then called and asked a few brief questions to reveal any of the forms of cheating described above. When such discrepancies are discovered, the individual questionnaire, all those from that interviewer, or all of them from the agency may be disqualified. Of course, the agency isn't paid for such inadequacy.

An itemized statement, in considerable detail, should always be required of the agency. When the invoice for payment is received, the amount will nearly always be greater than the original estimate. Each item can be examined closely for accuracy, and each cost can be compared to the estimate. Each deviation should be noted. It's the agency's responsibility to justify each exception or cost overrun. Renegotiation of the final amount is very common. To save time and effort, such discussions should always be held, from the very beginning, with an officer of the agency who has the authority to make and approve billing adjustments.

INTERVIEWER MANAGEMENT FUNCTIONS

An in-house interviewing crew is the alternative to using a data collection agency. A relatively small data collection project may require only one interviewer. Ordinarily, several interviewers will be needed, unless the data collection process can be extended over a long time. The data collection and interviewing often make it necessary to hire temporary, part-time employees as interviewers. Even the organizations that continuously do interviewing usually use part-time rather than full-time interviewers. Thus, it's often necessary to *recruit* applicants for the interviewing, *select* those that meet the requirements, *train* them to do the job, *supervise* their work, and *compensate* them on the basis of their productivity or time, plus any expenses they incur in their work. Guidelines for hiring interviewers are listed in Guidelist 8–4.

Interviewer recruitment

In most communities, there are two basic "pools" of temporary, part-time employment prospects: students and homemakers. Their composition obviously differs markedly by both age and sex, and these characteristics also affect the type and degree of interviewer bias that's likely to be introduced. The decision to recruit applicants from the student or homemaker populations, or both, should be governed in part by the "match" between the age and sex of interviewers and prospective respondents.

Ideally, a much larger number of applicants should be recruited than the project will actually require. This permits the selection of only the most qualified, and it provides a list of qualified applicants from which to hire any replacements or additional interviewers, if

---

GUIDELIST 8–4

For Hiring In-House Interviewers

1. Recruit from among those of the same sex, age group, and socioeconomic status as most respondents.
2. Recruit a much larger number of applicants than will actually be needed, to provide sufficient choice.
3. Request applicants to visit the office, complete an application, and be interviewed.
4. Check former employment and references very carefully.

5. Seek indications of personal responsibility, honesty, and integrity above all else.
6. Expect those who are relatively outgoing and gregarious to be most effective at the interviewing task.
7. Give preference to those with interviewing experience only if they're flexible and have been well trained.

---

needed. Usually only an advertisement or so in the "help wanted" section of the classified ads in the newspapers will produce enough applications. The advertisement can be brief, but it should indicate temporary, part-time employees are being sought. It should state the qualifications to be met, and indicate when, where, and how the prospects should apply. It saves time to have prospects apply in person and to interview them immediately when they first apply.

Selection of interviewers
The interviewers should be selected from the group of applicants based in part on the correspondence between their demographic characteristics and those of the intended respondents. In other words, it's usually advisable to use interviewers of the same sex, age range, and socioeconomic status as those of the majority of people they'll be interviewing.

Aside from correspondence with respondent characteristics, the principal consideration when selecting interviewers is their reliability. Their effectiveness depends on two factors: the degree to which they're *able* to follow instructions and adhere to directions and the degree to which they're *willing* to do so. In other words, both *skill* and *motivation* are prime factors, and both are absolutely necessary.

The task of interviewing respondents consists almost entirely of communication. Thus, capable interviewers are those who can both interrogate people effectively and also listen carefully to responses, perceive and interpret them correctly, and record them accurately. While it's usually desirable for interviewers to be gregarious, extroverted, or outgoing personalities who welcome and enjoy contact with others, they should not be too animated. If they're extremely verbose and talkative, they won't be able to pause, listen, and perceive the respondents' answers and comments accurately. In other words, they may not give the interviewee much opportunity to respond completely and thoroughly, nor grasp the more subtle verbal or nonverbal cues that constitute a part of the response.

Typically, interviewers are paid only minimum wage or slightly more than minimum, plus their direct expenses. The job is usually temporary and only part-time, so the pay doesn't represent a substantial proportion of their family income. Thus, strictly monetary considerations aren't at all sufficient to prevent them from cheating, cutting corners, or taking the route of least resistance, at the expense of the validity of the data. That depends mostly on the interviewers' own sense of honesty and integrity. Yet they may misbehave badly if they're paid so little they feel they're being cheated.

Interviewers almost always come to believe the risk of getting caught if they cheat is extremely small. In fact, it's difficult to detect it. So, the temptation to cheat can be very strong. The honesty and personal ethics of the interviewers are the strongest and most potent prohibitions against cheating. That means only those applicants who show every indication of complete honesty and diligence should be hired. Checking with previous employers about their experience with the applicant, including the applicant's record of absenteeism, is certainly recommended. It's also advisable to get personal references and to ask about affiliations, community involvement, and other indicators of personal and social responsibility. It's far better to hire an interviewer who is completely honest and trustworthy, even though he or she may not be highly skilled or experienced, than to choose a highly skilled, experienced person of uncertain character.

Whether or not it's advisable to select experienced versus inexperienced interviewers is an open question. There are both pro's and con's to using experienced interviewers. Obviously, if the researcher has used the interviewers for previous projects and they performed well, they should be hired again. On the other hand, experienced interviewers who worked for some other researcher or data collection agency in the past may not have been well trained, and they may have acquired many bad habits or practices that will be difficult to correct. Inexperienced interviewers require more training, but sometimes it's often easier to "begin from scratch" than to dispel inaccurate or inappropriate beliefs and habits. Experienced applicants must be evaluated just as thoroughly as the inexperienced, and perhaps even more so.

Interviewer training

The interviewers who are working more or less continuously for a data collection agency receive some initial training when they begin and get additional training in the field through actual experience with many surveys. Thus, they ordinarily need only to be introduced to the project at hand and to become familiar with the particular questionnaire and materials being used. Interviewers who are hired by the researcher must be trained in both the general nature of interviewing and the particulars of the task for the project at hand.

There are two broad classes of information new recruits must have to be effective interviewers: the "how" and the "why." First, they must know *how* to (1) locate, (2) identify, (3) contact, (4) greet, (5) qualify, (6) interrogate, (7) record, and (8) terminate. Second, they must know *why* it's important to follow the instructions and procedures for interviewing. Most interviewer training programs are much more effective at conveying how to do it than why it must be done that way. Yet, it's essential to teach new interviewers both things, because there are usually many ways to do each of the eight interviewer tasks listed above. Often the way the interviewers are instructed to do each of the tasks is more difficult for them than other ways they, themselves, could find for doing the job. The reasons for doing each task in the prescribed manner won't be obvious to new interviewers. So, the reasons for the procedures have to be stated and the consequences of deviating from them should be made clear to the interviewers.

When the new interviewers have received their instruction and training on survey interviewing procedures in general, they can be given additional instruction in using the particular questionnaire for the survey they're to conduct. The same procedure should be used at this point as that described earlier for training interviewers from a data collection agency.

Supervising the interviews

There are two aspects to interview supervision: monitoring the process and checking the results. The interview process can be monitored and supervised overtly or covertly. For example, supervisors should accompany personal interviewers during their first few trials and periodically throughout the process, to be sure they get off to a good start with the project and stay on track. It's also necessary to return to the field to be sure interviewers haven't become lax, picked up bad habits, or devised improper shortcuts.

When the interviewing is done by telephone, the first few calls should be done in the presence of a supervisor who might help or direct the placement of the calls and listen to the conversations on an extension beside the interviewer. Interviewing can also be monitored covertly, although that may not be necessary if the interviewers are both well trained and well motivated and there are no signs of cheating or other misconduct. If there's any possibility covert monitoring might be used during a project, it's absolutely necessary to inform the interviewers in advance this might be done. Good business and personal ethics demand this notification, and interviewers can be expected to be justly resentful if they weren't informed and discovered it later.

The basic reason for covert rather than overt monitoring is because interviewers are likely to behave differently when they know they're being monitored. This difference isn't necessarily intentional or deliberate. Covert monitoring of interviews can be done in two ways: One way is to include accomplices unknown to the interviewers on the list or at the location where interviews take place, and have them record the interview or report back to the supervisor. The other way is to have a supervisor listen to or record telephone or personal interview conversations without the interviewers' knowledge.

While some deviations or discrepancies from required procedure or good practice can be detected only by observing the process of interviewing, others may be revealed in the results. Thus, effective supervision also requires checking the results as early and as often as possible. Daily checking is advisable in most cases if it's feasible to do it that often. Each interviewer can be required to report to a supervisor at the end of the day and submit his or her finished work. The completed questionnaires are then counted and recorded in the day-log of finished work. That way, there's a "running record" of progress, and the researcher can tell if the interviewing is on schedule or if additional interviewers will be required. It's also desirable for the supervisor to sight-edit the questionnaires to be sure they're complete and that the data have been recorded correctly while the interviewer is present. This permits the supervisor to check with the interviewer about any unusual cases and to make any necessary corrections while the interview is still fresh in the interviewer's memory.

There's a very strong tendency for supervision to focus on any aspect of the interviewing that's wrongly or poorly done. This is equivalent to counting the number wrong, rather

---

GUIDELIST 8–5

For Supervising Interviewers

1. Monitor the process and also check the finished results.
2. Have a supervisor present during the first few interviews by each person to get them off to a good start.
3. Supervisors should return to the field or the phone room periodically to detect problems that might creep in.
4. Use covert monitoring only when necessary and always tell interviewers in advance it might be used.
5. Require completed work to be submitted in person to the supervisor daily when it's feasible to do so.
6. Finished work should be checked for completion, then counted and recorded in the day-log at the time it's submitted.

7. Check the day-log of finished work against the schedule to determine if more interviewers will be required.
8. Have supervisors sight-edit the questionnaires submitted while the interviewer is still present.
9. Provide coaching and make changes on work submitted while the case is fresh in the interviewer's mind.
10. Treat errors or problems in a matter-of-fact manner and never blame, deride, or insult the interviewers.
11. Compliment and praise the interviewers lavishly to enhance their confidence and motivation.

---

than the number right when testing, and it's a drastic mistake. In the first place, it's much easier for those teaching or coaching others to instill knowledge than it is to stamp out ignorance. Secondly, concentrating on the negative rather than the positive only discourages and demotivates those being supervised. Supervisors should express praise lavishly and compliment interviewers sincerely and often for what they do correctly. Interviewers should never be blamed or insulted, and it's only necessary to identify errors and show how they can be corrected. Interviewing can be difficult, but confident, well-motivated interviewers always do superior work. Guidelist 8–5 provides recommendations for supervising interviewers.

Compensating the interviewers

Interviewers are ordinarily paid either by interview or by hour. Rarely, if ever, are they paid a monthly salary or a fee for the entire job. Each of the two most common forms of compensation have their pro's and con's. Whichever method is chosen, interviewers must also be compensated for any direct expenses they incur.

Paying interviewers a set amount for each interview they complete has several advantages. One of the main ones is the fact that those who are most productive receive the most pay. The interviewers who work very quickly, who are more effective in getting the cooperation of respondents, or who work longer hours will receive more for their efforts, so all the others are encouraged to do so. That benefits both the interviewers and the researcher. At the same time, this formula also discourages sloppy work, because the interviewers are paid

---

GUIDELIST 8–6

For Compensating Interviewers

1. Interviewers should be paid for their direct expenses, such as travel and other such costs.
2. Interviewers might be paid either by hour or per interview completed.
3. Payment per interview requires the task to be roughly equal per interview or among interviewers.
4. Payment per interview may encourage cheating, hurrying respondents, or avoiding people who should be included.
5. Payment per interview is more equitable if circumstances permit and it makes cost estimation more accurate.
6. An hourly wage requires more supervision because such workers may be prone to waste time.
7. Hourly wages are usually more equitable when different interviewers work at different times or places.

---

only for completed questionnaires that are complete and usable. This method of payment permits the researcher to compute the cost of the data collection quite precisely, based on the number of responses that are required. Also, the interviewers know exactly what they must accomplish to earn a certain amount and they can easily compute how much they have earned at any given point during data collection.

There are also some notable disadvantages to paying a set amount per interview to field or telephone workers. Doing so may encourage cheating. It may also cause the interviewers to hurry respondents or record responses too hastily, or to avoid qualified respondents who should be included—to shy away from them because they appear to be too risky or too slow. When interviewers are paid per interview, the researcher must also assess the length and difficulty of the task quite accurately in advance, in order to arrive at an amount that's equitable to both the interviewers and the sponsor. There may be some cases when the interviewing task differs from one interview or interviewer to another. For example, quota requirements may differ, or some respondents may have to complete several sections of the questionnaire that others don't. Paying interviewers a set amount per interview would be appropriate only when the interviewing task is roughly equivalent or when any differences would almost certainly average out.

The advantages of paying interviewers per hour are the same as the disadvantages of paying per interview. Paying an hourly rate is appropriate when interviewers might otherwise be tempted to avoid certain types of respondents that ought to be included or to cut corners to make it easier to get interviews. With hourly pay, there's little or no incentive to misbehave in such ways. This method of compensation is also recommended when the task differs appreciably from one interview or interviewer to the next. Thus, if fieldworkers are stationed at different locations or telephone workers are assigned different calling times, some may be much more productive than others, more so because of the time and place than because of ability and effort.

When interviewers receive an hourly wage, it's ordinarily much more difficult for the researcher to arrive at an accurate estimate of total cost. An advanced estimate of the *average* cost per interview must still be made, in order to forecast data collection costs and make financial plans. Paying an hourly wage will also require much more rigorous supervision than when interviewers are paid per completed interview. As with hourly workers, interviewers paid in this way are more prone to be idle on the job, to chatter with one another, take long lunch and coffee breaks, and generally waste time, because they're still being paid for it. Recommendations for compensating interviewers are summarized in Guidelist 8–6.

INTERVIEWING ERROR

Random error reduces the reliability of the survey data, while systematic bias diminishes the validity of the results. These concepts were described and discussed in Chapter 3. The sources of error and bias resulting from sampling were also noted there. The error and the bias that might arise as the result of interviewing and the methods of controlling them are also major concerns. Guidelist 8–7 lists the principal methods for controlling interviewer error.

Instruction error
If interviewers don't present the instructions in precisely the way they're listed on the questionnaire, the deviations will introduce error. Deviating from the written instructions is very common. After reading them a few dozen times, the interviewers may automatically memorize them. Interviewers are likely to repeat the instructions from memory without reading them directly. After doing so several times, without reference to the written instructions, they're likely to repeat them differently. After many such small changes in wording, the memorized instructions may be entirely different from the written form.

Interrogation error
If questions are expressed differently from one respondent to the next, this will cause error. Even when asking for strictly factual information, people respond differently to different wording. For example, asking "What's your age?" will result in an older age, on the average, than asking, "How old are you?" Merely using the word "old" tends to cause some people to report a younger age. Interviewers don't realize how much even subtle differences in the wording affect respondents' answers.

Response option error
Interviewers may be instructed either to read or not to read the response options to the respondents. If interviewers read the alternative answers to respondents when they shouldn't do so, or fail to read them when they should, this will introduce error into the results.

Scale interpretation error
When scale cards are used, errors may result. Suppose a Likert scale card listed the option "Strongly agree" as number one, "Agree" as number two, and so on. Some respondents may reply with the numbers and others with the words. If both the numbers and the options aren't listed together on the questionnaire, errors are likely. In this example, some interviewers might record the number five for a response of "Strongly agree," rather than number one, as they should.

Recording error

The more the interviewers are required to write, the greater the recording errors will be. The likelihood of error is higher when verbatim responses are recorded than when interviewers just jot down a number or letter. Interviewers tend to abbreviate verbal responses, often by necessity. The average respondent speaks at a rate of 150 words a minute. Thus, even a 10-second response may require the interviewer to write a 25-word, verbatim answer.

Interpretation error

When interviewers are asked to interpret responses during the interview, errors are very likely. For example, interviewers may be instructed not to read the response options listed on the questionnaire to respondents. Instead, they may be asked to listen to the answers, then choose an option and circle it. Rarely will respondents use exactly the same words as those listed as response options. So the interviewers have to make judgments about the meaning of the response, and then record them. Such judgments are very prone to error when they're made in the field or while on the telephone.

Controlling interviewer error

The interview process must be monitored carefully, both at the beginning and periodically during the data collection process, to detect errors by interviewers. The supervisor should follow the conversation while reading a copy of the questionnaire. Any differences between the questionnaire and the interviewers' presentations of instructions, questions, or response options should be noted carefully. Simple observation of the interviewers at work in the field or at the telephone may also reveal whether they're reading the material precisely, or just speaking from memory. To reduce response option errors, a note in parentheses on the questionnaire should indicate if the options are or aren't supposed to be read to respondents, unless it's very obvious. If scale cards are used, the numbers and words should also be listed on the questionnaire just as they appear on the scale card, to reduce errors in scale interpretation.

Merely monitoring the interviewing won't detect recording error. The supervisor must monitor the conversation and also record some of the answers, and then compare the record with that recorded on the actual questionnaire by the interviewer. The objective is to *prevent* such errors in advance by composing questions and constructing a questionnaire to make recording quick, simple, and easy. It's usually not advisable to ask unstructured questions, where options aren't read to respondents, and then require the interviewers to interpret the answers and check an option. If such items are unavoidable, the interviewers should be trained and instructed very thoroughly on the criteria for choosing the response option. They should also be monitored carefully at the beginning and throughout the data collection to be sure they interpret answers consistently and correctly.

Interviewing Bias

The sources of interviewing *error,* discussed in the preceding section, affect survey results randomly. The effect of those sources of error is just as likely to "push" the results in one direction as another. Random error reduces the reliability of the data, and it also reduces the validity of the data indirectly, by reducing the reliability. There are also several sources of *systematic bias* associated with interviewing. Bias reduces the validity of the data directly, by consistently "pushing" the results in one particular direction. Because of this, bias is the more serious problem.

When the validity of the survey results is reduced by bias, it's very difficult to detect after the fact. There's a danger the researcher and sponsor will base decisions on the data, assuming it's quite valid when, in fact, it isn't. Consequently, it's essential to control interviewing bias as much as possible, before and during data collection. In other words, it's always advisable to exert more effort on the *prevention* of interviewing bias than on trying to detect it or correct it after the data have been collected.

Amplification of response bias

Twelve major sources of bias are identified in Chapter 4, Figure 4–1 on page 100. These sources apply both to self-administered questionnaires and to interviewing. However, the very presence of interviewers is likely to create or increase additional response bias. With a self-administered questionnaire, respondents feel greater anonymity. When they're interacting with an interviewer by telephone, and especially in person, any tendencies toward response bias are likely to be amplified rather than reduced. Thus, it's vital to guard against such response bias with even more effort when interviews are used to collect the data.

Creation of response bias

Aside from the effect of the mere presence of an interviewer, the telephone or fieldworkers' *performance* can create or increase response bias. For example, if the verbal or nonverbal actions of an interviewer are seen as intimidating by the respondents, this would create *threat* bias. If the interviewers were rude or overly pushy, *hostility* bias could be expected to affect the answers to questions, and so forth. To the degree interviewers are well trained, well motivated, and closely monitored, they're less likely to become a source of response bias in and of themselves. When training and monitoring interviewers, the trainer or supervisor should be especially aware of each source of response bias and must look for signs that the interviewers' actions are creating or amplifying one or more types of bias.

THE INTERVIEW QUESTIONNAIRE

Most of the principles for composing the survey questions and constructing the questionnaire apply equally, whether the data are collected by mail, by telephone interviewing, or through personal interviews. Nonetheless, there are some elements of the questionnaire and the other survey materials that differ, depending on whether the questionnaire is self-administered or administered by an interviewer. The principles and elements that apply only to questionnaires administered by interviewers but not to those that are self-administered deserve special attention here.

The interview greeting

The introduction for an interview survey differs markedly from a cover letter used in a mail survey. The most effective interview greeting is very short. This is because the interviewer can interact with the respondent, whether the interviews are conducted by telephone or in person. Guidelines for composing interview greetings are listed in Guidelist 8–8.

Four typical greetings are shown in Example 8–1. The two in the top section ask a question to determine if the individual is "qualified" to respond. A greeting with qualification questions would be used when only certain types of people are interviewed and they can't be identified in advance. The two greetings in the bottom section of the example don't ask qualifying questions. They merely introduce the survey and move quickly and directly to the actual survey questions. Such greetings as these would be used when those who qualify to respond can be identified in advance.

Notice that mail survey cover letters are much longer than interview survey greetings. Cover letters contain a substantial amount of information, but greetings by interviewers say practically nothing about the survey. At first glance, this may seem inconsistent. Those with little or no survey research experience may be tempted to compose a greeting that's much longer and contains more information. Avoid that temptation. The general rule is to keep the greeting and introduction by interviewers as short as possible. The objective here is to get the respondent to begin answering questions immediately. As long as the person's mind is engaged in answering the survey questions, the respondents' thoughts won't turn to consideration of whether or not they should participate.

There's a cardinal rule about interview greetings: NEVER, EVER ASK PERMISSION! Beginning with such questions as, "Do you have a few minutes to answer some questions?" or "Will you take a little while to participate in this survey?" provides potential respondents with an open invitation to decline. The refusal rate will be much, much greater than it would be when using a more correct and effective greeting—one that doesn't ask for permission. Remember, the sooner respondents start answering, the better.

Qualification criteria

The sample frame for an interview survey identifies the population from which the sample is selected. In some cases, the survey research staff may be able to select individual names and addresses or telephone numbers from the sample frame, according to the sampling design, prior to data collection. In such cases, the namelists provided to the interviewers would constitute the sample. It would, of course, be necessary to include a substantially larger number of names than the actual sample size needed, because the interviewers may not be able to contact or obtain responses from all of those listed. When all individuals identified on such a sample list are qualified to respond, the interviewers need not "qualify" respondents with preliminary questions. In that case, a greeting such as those in the lower portion of Example 8–1 would be used.

GUIDELIST 8–8

For Composing Interview Greetings

1. Keep the greeting as short and simple as possible, rather than including a lot of information about the survey.
2. Ask a question very quickly, to engage the respondents' attention and get them started right away.
3. Never ask the potential respondents if they have the time to answer questions or for permission to ask questions.
4. Ask questions to determine if respondents are qualified to respond if that can't be determined in advance.
5. Remember, anyone has the right to refuse, but the vast majority are friendly and cooperative and won't decline.
6. Be confident that once respondents begin the response task, they'll only rarely stop before completion.

For most interview surveys, it's impractical or impossible to select individual names and addresses or telephone numbers in advance. Consequently, interviewers are provided with a set of general directions concerning who and when to call on the telephone or when and where to go to conduct personal interviews. They're then instructed to interview only those who are qualified to respond and to ignore those who aren't qualified. To do so, they must be given a set of criteria by which to judge whether or not those they contact are qualified.

In some cases, qualification criteria for selecting respondents may be based on factors the

---

EXAMPLE 8–1

The Interview Survey Greeting

With Qualification

1. Good morning [afternoon—evening]. My name is _____ [first name only] and we are conducting a brief survey of registered voters here in the county. Are you registered to vote? [If YES, continue. If NO, ask for others and continue or terminate if none available.]
2. Good morning [afternoon—evening]. My name is _____ [first name only] and I'm with Expert Research Company. I have a few quick survey questions for those who own certain kinds of automobiles. Is your car an American make or an import? [If at least one American, continue. If foreign or none, terminate.]

Without Qualification

3. Good morning [afternoon—evening]. My name is _____ [first name only] and I'm calling for Field Research, Inc. I'd like to ask you some quick survey questions about your favorite candidate for mayor. [Ask first question immediately.]
4. Good morning [afternoon—evening]. My name is _____ [first name only]. I have some survey questions to ask about your preferences and opinions concerning supermarkets. [Ask first question immediately.]

interviewers can judge just by seeing or hearing potential respondents. For example, if only women were qualified, there wouldn't be a need to ask potential respondents any questions to ascertain their qualification. Simply seeing them or hearing their voice on the telephone would be sufficient to determine if they should be interviewed. In most cases, however, it will be necessary for interviewers to greet potential respondents and ask them one or more preliminary, qualifying questions. In that case, a greeting such as those listed in the upper portion of Example 8–1 would be used. When the qualification of respondents must be judged by interviewers before they're actually interviewed, it's important to provide clear, concise criteria concerning who should and shouldn't be included. When qualification is based on such factors as sex, age, or employment status, there's very little ambiguity about who qualifies to respond. When the criteria are based on less concrete or quantifiable factors, such as occupation, mode of dress, or respondent experience or history, the interviewers must be given a complete set of rules for determining who are qualified and who aren't.

In order for the respondent qualification process to yield reliable, valid results, two requirements must be met: consistency and accuracy. The actual selection of respondents will be consistent if precisely the same individuals are included or excluded, from one time to the next and from one interviewer to the next. The selection process will be accurate if: (1) *all* those who are, in fact, qualified are included and (2) *only* those who are qualified are included. Thus, the consistency and accuracy of the selection process depends very heavily on providing interviewers with clear-cut, unambiguous criteria.

Quota specification

When a quota sampling design is used, quota specification is a special case of stating qualification criteria. Without a quota, each interviewer uses the same qualification criteria for every respondent interviewed. When a quota sample is required, the qualification criteria differ from one interviewer to the next or from one potential respondent to the next. Aside from this difference, the same principles concerning the specification of qualification criteria apply to quota specification. There are, however, some other factors that must be considered when a quota is used. An example of a typical quota may clarify the discussion.

Suppose an interview survey sampling design specified a quota based on the age, sex, and marital status of respondents, with a total sample size of 240. The quotas for all interviewers might be specified in two different ways, as shown in Example 8–2. Each variable might be considered independently of the others, as in the upper section of the example. If so, it will be relatively easy for interviewers to fulfill the quota, but there's a "catch" to specifying the quota in this way. Because the three variables are considered independently of one another, it would be permissible for interviewers to fulfill this quota with all married men and all unmarried women, providing there were 80 from each age group. This is, of course, an extreme case, but if the quota variables are treated independently, interviewers aren't likely to provide closely proportional numbers of one category for each category of the other variables. Quota sampling is usually used to be sure the sample *proportionally* represents the various groups in the population. Thus, if the quota is based on more than one variable, the quota variables are ordinarily treated as interdependent, and the quotas would be specified as they are in the lower section of Example 8–2.

The quota specifications shown in the example above are for the total sample or all interviewers. If more than one interviewer is required, it's also necessary to specify individual quotas for each interviewer. Suppose four interviewers were required to collect the data for

EXAMPLE 8–2

The Quota Specification Sheet

Independent Quotas

	Variable	Groups	Number
1.	Marital	Married Not married	120 120
2.	Sex	Men Women	120 120
3.	Age	20–34 35–49 50–99	80 80 80

Interdependent Quotas

	Marital	Sex	Age	Number
1.	Married	Men	20–34	20
2.	Married	Men	35–49	20
3.	Married	Men	50–99	20
4.	Married	Women	20–34	20
5.	Married	Women	35–49	20
6.	Married	Women	50–99	20
7.	Not married	Men	20–34	20
8.	Not married	Men	35–49	20
9.	Not married	Men	50–99	20
10.	Not married	Women	20–34	20
11.	Not married	Women	35–49	20
12.	Not married	Women	50–99	20

the quotas listed in Example 8–2, and they're treated as interdependent quotas, as shown in the lower section of the example. There are three basic ways the quotas for individual interviewers might be specified. Each one is identified below, and the advantages and disadvantages of each are noted in turn.

The first method might be called "progressive exclusion." With this method, all interviewers would first be instructed only that those 20 years of age and over are qualified. During the early phase of the interviewing, no additional quotas would be needed, and the interviewers would accept those of different sex, age, and marital status, as they occurred in the population. The supervisor would keep a constant record of the number of respondents in each category that had been obtained on a tally sheet. When a sufficient number had been obtained from any one quota category, all interviewers would be instructed to qualify respondents and to reject any who fell into that group, because no more would be required. As each quota category was progressively fulfilled, additional respondents fitting that category would be excluded.

The disadvantage to this method is that it requires close supervision and a constant record of the number of respondents of each type. That may be practical for telephone interviewing from a central location. It may not be feasible for widely dispersed personal interviewing in the field, because it would require each interviewer to call the supervisor after each interview. When practical, this method is the most efficient, because the fewest number of people would need to be contacted and then disqualified and rejected.

The second method of quota specification for individual interviewers is to assign each one an equal portion of each quota. In the lower portion of Example 8–2, each of the four interviewers would be assigned a quota of five interviews for each from each group. This technique does not require a running record of the number of interviews completed in each group, but it's likely to require more interviewer time than the first method. This method is less efficient because one interviewer may be seeking a respondent for a particular group while another has fulfilled the quota for that category. Thus, some interviewers would reject potential respondents after contact while others are still seeking such respondents.

The third method of specifying individual interviewer quotas would be to assign the first three categories to the first interviewer, the next three to the second, and so forth. This technique is temptingly simple, but it's not ordinarily acceptable. The reason for avoiding it is complex but compelling. No matter how well-trained and motivated the interviewers are, they're likely to introduce *some* systematic bias. In other words, some of the differences in the answers will be attributable to the individual interviewers, themselves. Chances are, when the data are analyzed, the groups resulting from the quotas will be compared with one another. Suppose all married men are interviewed by one interviewer, all married women by another, and the analysis showed significant differences in the answers between these two groups. Such differences might be attributed to either the sex of the respondents or to differences between the interviewers, or both. In other words, the analyst would not be able to tell if the sex of the respondent affected the answers or not. In technical terms, this is called a "confound" between individual interviewers and different groups. Thus, the other methods of individual quota specification are much superior.

Interview questionnaire format

The appearance and cosmetic aspects of a self-administered mail questionnaire are extremely important because they affect both response quality and response rate. Ordinarily, interview questionnaires are read and handled only by the interviewers, and so they need not be especially attractive to the eye. On the other hand, they have to be constructed in a format that makes them easy to use. If the interviewer must take time to study the questionnaire or hunt for the next item while conducting the interview, this may jeopardize the success of the interview. Thus, the interview questionnaire writer has to anticipate and appreciate the conditions under which the interviewing will be done. Any format or compositional device that will assist the telephone or field workers to conduct the interview quickly and smoothly, with a minimum of hesitation or pause, should be employed when writing the questionnaire.

The Personal Interviewing Process

There are several aspects of personal interviewing that don't apply to telephone interviews, and vice versa. Those things of particular concern when personal interviewing is used to collect the data are discussed in this section, and those related to telephone interviewing are considered in the following section.

Timing

The time of day and day of the week when the interviews are conducted are likely to affect both the refusal or response rate and the nature of the answers to the questions. For example, it's advisable to conduct in-home interviews between the hours of nine o'clock in the morning and nine at night. It may also be advisable to avoid meal times when possible. When interviews are conducted during daytime hours on weekdays, homemakers and those who are retired are likely to be overrepresented, while those employed outside the home will be represented in smaller proportions than in the population as a whole. Thus, it's often desirable to conduct a substantial proportion of the interviews during evenings and weekends. Fieldworkers must be instructed and monitored carefully to be sure they conduct the interviews at the times specified. They ordinarily have a strong tendency to work when it's convenient for them rather than for the respondents or as directed by the supervisor.

The interview location

The locations at which the interviews are conducted must be carefully specified by the researcher, and the fieldworkers must be monitored to be sure they adhere to the location requirements. The interviewers aren't likely to realize that the location of the interview will affect the responses. In Figure 8–1, the most frequently used locations are identified and described. When the interviews require more than a few minutes and are conducted at the home of respondents, it's advisable for the fieldworkers to seek permission to enter the home and perhaps to sit at a table with the respondent. Most people will extend that courtesy, and doing so will facilitate accurate interrogation and recording.

Even when certain areas appear to be "public," in the sense that anyone is welcome to enter, they may, in fact, be proprietary to some company or organization. For example, most shopping malls, stadiums, and the like won't permit interviewing without prior written permission. If it has not been obtained in advance from someone authorized to approve it, the fieldworkers may be detected and ejected from the site. When such permission has been obtained, each interviewer should be given a copy of the written authorization, so no misunderstandings or delays result if they're accosted by authorities at the location.

Figure 8–1 *Common Personal Interview Locations*

1. **In-Home**
   The interviews are conducted at the residence of the respondents. They may be inside the home, at the door, or outside, on the property.
2. **Job Site**
   The interviews are conducted at the shop or office of the respondents. This location is ordinarily used only when the employer is the survey sponsor.
3. **Traffic Intercepts**
   One or more areas of pedestrian traffic are identified for fieldworkers. They then intercept all qualified respondents as they move through the area. Shopper intercepts are the most common. (It's ordinarily necessary to obtain permission to interview at proprietary locations, such as within a store or mall, or at a shopping center.)
4. **Mall Intercepts**
   These are similar to traffic intercepts, except the data collection agency may have an interviewing facility permanently located within the mall. Interviews may be conducted outside or inside the facility.
5. **Stationary Concentrations**
   Those attending or waiting at meetings, sports or entertainment events, and the like may be interviewed where they have congregated.

Distractions and interruptions

Fieldworkers should be instructed about how to handle the most common types of distractions or interruptions that are likely to occur during the interviews. For example, they should be told whether or not the interviewing may be done if one or more other people are present during the interview, so they could listen to the questions and answers (and/or contribute to the response). The directions given to fieldworkers should also indicate whether the interview should be continued if it's interrupted, and if so, how long an interval is acceptable. Ordinarily, interruptions of more than a few minutes require termination and rejection of the incomplete response. Whether respondents can or should refer to other people or to records or other materials in order to respond to the questions should be clearly indicated.

Rating cards and visual aids

When personal interview surveys make use of rating cards or other visual or physical materials to be examined by respondents, the fieldworker instructions clearly indicate how they're to be handled. For example, interviewers must know if they may hand the item to the respondent or merely show them the material, and they must also be told when such visual aids are to be withdrawn or removed. The appearance of such visual materials is very important, because they're viewed by respondents and their perceptions may affect the response. Thus, ordinarily the same such items are used again and again with each interview. It's vital to provide two or more "sets" of such material, because some are almost certain to be lost, destroyed, or defaced. It's also advisable to include a very prominent instruction at the end of the questionnaire to remind fieldworkers to reclaim any such visual materials from the respondent before leaving. They need the reminder because they're very likely to forget such things, fail to retrieve them, and then be unable to continue with the interviewing.

Recording observations and responses

When fieldworkers must record data they observe, they must be given firm criteria by which to classify or categorize the observational data. The same requirements for consistency and accuracy apply to these observations as to the qualification criteria noted earlier. When recording responses from the interviewees, it's advisable to compose the questionnaire in such a way that items need only be checked or circled or a number recorded, whenever possible. When unstructured or open-ended questions are included, fieldworkers should be instructed on what to record, such as whether they should record the complete, verbatim response word for word or only key words and phrases. Usually, fieldworkers must also record the time and location of the interview and provide an indication to identify themselves as the interviewer. The instructions for recording such data should be listed clearly and prominently at the end of the questionnaire.

The Telephone Interview Process

Telephone interviewing can be done either from a central location, such as the research headquarters, or from the interviewers' homes. It's always advisable to require interviewing from a central location when doing so doesn't add significantly to toll charges or data collection costs.

Calling location

A central calling location greatly facilitates the supervision and monitoring of the data collection. When the telephone workers do call from their own homes or other locations, they must be selected and trained very carefully, and their work supervised as closely as possible. One of the main advantages of a central calling location is the fact that supervisors can watch and listen into calls to be sure the interviewers interview at the right times and in the prescribed manner.

The central calling facilities of data collection agencies usually provide the most efficient and effective setting for telephone interviewing. Interviewers are typically seated comfortably at desks or tables in partially enclosed cubicles lined with sound-absorbing material. They usually use headsets so both hands are free to handle the questionnaire and record the responses. With facilities such as these, one supervisor can easily monitor, assist, and supervise many interviewers simultaneously.

The best-equipped and most sophisticated data collection agencies may offer computer-equipped calling facilities. These systems may permit the researcher or supervisor to input the text of the questionnaire and the branching instructions, so individual questions are displayed to the interviewer in the prescribed sequence. The list of numbers to be called may also be entered in advance, so the numbers are dialed by the computer rather than manually. Usually the responses are keyed directly to a data file rather than recorded with paper and pencil. Such systems make the interviewers, work much faster, easier, and more accurate. They also enhance the ability to monitor and control the entire telephone interviewing process for the project.

The namelist or directory

Telephone interviewing is often done directly from a telephone directory. Ordinarily, telephone workers are provided with directions concerning which names and numbers to select.

Figure 8–2   *Telephone Collection Results and Options*

Possible Call Results

1. Call answered by a qualified respondent.
2. Call answered by an unqualified person.
3. Number proves to be wrong location or subscriber.
4. Call isn't answered after 6 to 10 rings.
5. Busy signal is received for the number called.
6. Call answered by an answering service or device.
7. Number has been changed and new number is listed.
8. Number not in service and no new number is listed.

Telephone Interviewer Options

1. Interview respondent and place next call.
2. Ask if a qualified respondent is present.
3. Terminate and place call to next number.
4. Terminate and call back in a few minutes.

Such instructions must be very clearly written and provided to each interviewer for reference when a question arises. It's never sufficient merely to require interviewers to call every *n*th number. Rather, they must be instructed concerning where to start in the volume, where to begin the count on the page and column, and so on. They must also be told how to handle listings that are clearly not qualified, such as business listings when only residential listings are to be included.

Timing

With telephone interviewing, just as with personal interviewing, the time of day and days of the week during which calls are placed will affect the type of respondents that are interviewed. It's especially important to supervise and monitor the timing of calls, because telephone workers are much more likely to deviate from the prescribed timing than are fieldworkers conducting personal interviews. Respondents who are called after nine in the evening or before nine in the morning may agree to respond, but if the task is an unwelcome interruption or intrusion, this would certainly affect their answers to the questions.

The duration of the interview constitutes another important timing factor. Fieldworkers conducting personal interviews are ordinarily able to hold the attention and interest of respondents for substantially longer periods than are telephone interviewers. There's ordinarily little or no resistance or premature termination when telephone interviews are less than five minutes, and telephone workers experienced at building and maintaining rapport with the respondents may conduct interviews of 10 minutes or so in duration with few refusals or terminations. Telephone interviews of more than 15 minutes are likely to result in a very substantial number of refusals or premature terminations by the respondents.

Call results and options

The telephone workers must be provided with directions stating how to respond to the various outcomes that might result when a number from the list has been called. The eight possible outcomes and the four common options open to the interviewer are identified in Figure 8–2. Based on the sampling design and requirements, the researcher must compose instructions that indicate which of the four options should be pursued in case of each of the possible call results. Telephone workers should also be instructed to record the telephone number of the respondent, the date, time of the call, and their own identity. These instructions should be clearly listed at the end of the questionnaire.

SUMMARY

Interview Data Collection Procedures

    A. Understand the interviewer's role. The telephone interviewers or fieldworkers should be perceived as part of the measurement instrument, with the potential to create error and bias.

    B. Consider the data collection agency. Study the agency data collection process and check on agency cost, availability, and quality carefully.

    C. Appreciate the interviewer management task. Study the interviewer management functions and weigh the advantages and disadvantages of an in-house crew.

    D. Choose the mode of interviewing. Evaluate the capabilities and limitations of data collection agencies compared to an in-house interviewing crew.

    E. Reduce potential interviewing error. Consider instruction, interrogation, response, scaling, recording, and interpretation as possible sources of error.

    F. Control interviewing and response bias. Check each element of the questionnaire and process for each of the major sources of bias.

    G. Handle instrumentation carefully. Compose the greeting, qualification and quota criteria, interviewer instructions, and questionnaire format to avoid error and bias.

    H. Identify the unique aspects of each process. Recognize the distinctions between personal and telephone interviewing, making required adjustments for the mode selected.

Chapter 9

Processing the Data

RECEIPT OF QUESTIONNAIRES

Data processing should be thoroughly planned at a much earlier stage in the survey process, but the work actually begins with the receipt of the first completed questionnaires from the field. The final preparation and testing of the computer programs to be used for data analysis can be done while the survey is still in the field and the data are being collected. With mail surveys and with interviewing done by a data collection agency or a separate interviewer team, the researcher will often have a few weeks during data collection when there's little else to do with the survey except prepare the processing system. This extra time gives the data analyst an opportunity to get a head start on the processing phase. By completing a few blank questionnaires with fictitious data, the research analyst can begin constructing files, preparing the analysis programs, and specifying the tasks that will be needed for data analysis.

Data Receipt

It's usually necessary to monitor the collection of the data very carefully. With interview surveys, reports may be obtained from the field on a *daily* basis, or at least two or three times per week, from *each* interviewer or agency working on the survey. That way, adjustments can be made and extra effort exerted when it's required to avoid delays or procrastination by the fieldworkers and supervisors. Mail survey returns should be collected daily or with each delivery. Any "nondeliverable" pieces should be checked to determine why they couldn't be delivered to the intended recipient. That way the researcher can assess the quality of the mailing list and its source. When there are many nondeliverable pieces marked with a notation such as "no such address," that indicates the list is inaccurate. If many of the questionnaires couldn't be delivered because many of the addressees have moved and there's no forwarding address, that usually shows the list is "dated." The namelist was probably from many months or years earlier and wasn't kept current. This information is useful to assess the namelist quality. It's also valuable to judge the potential quality and accuracy of the survey results and the degree to which the sample validly represents the population as a whole.

Mail questionnaire returns should be opened immediately, and the date the questionnaire was received should be recorded on the back, at the end of the questionnaire. Similarly, interview questionnaires coming in from the field should be checked to be sure the interviewer has recorded the date of the interview, and perhaps also to record when it was received in the office. It may be necessary later to compare results from the earlier data collection period with that from the later period. With mail data collection, this comparison indicates differences between those who were most motivated and willing to complete the task and those who delayed it for some time. When the data are collected by interviewers, the comparison can show what affect interviewer inexperience versus experience may have had on the answers obtained.

During this period when the completed returns are received, it's always wise to keep a complete record of how many surveys were sent into the field, how many are still out at any given point, and how many have been completed and returned. This running record of data collection allows the researcher to anticipate the "cut-off" point, when collection can be terminated and additional responses ignored. It also shows whether the data collection process is on schedule and going according to plan. If there are serious delays, it may be necessary to take some action, such as assigning additional interviewers or extending the data collection schedule.

Handling Completed Questionnaires

The completed questionnaires are the documents from which computer files of survey data will be created. This period, during receipt of data, is usually the first time the researcher will actually experience the volume of data and documents created by the survey. With surveys of very limited scope there will be few surprises and little confusion. Larger survey projects are likely to produce more documentation than inexperienced researchers anticipate or for which they're prepared. The physical volume can be considerable. It's absolutely necessary to devise a system for handling the completed questionnaires and then stick by it throughout the receipt period.

The first step is to open mail returns or materials received from interviewers and record the date of receipt. After that, the extra materials that are returned, such as copies of the cover letter, envelopes, rating cards, interviewer instructions, and the like, can be discarded or filed for later use on another project. It may also be necessary to record the location of some mail survey respondents on the questionnaire by checking the postmark on the return envelope before it's separated from the completed questionnaire it contains.

Experienced researchers find it very useful to record consecutive numbers at the end of the questionnaires as they're received. Later this number can be recorded in the data file, together with the data, so the researcher can refer to a particular completed questionnaire at any time to make corrections in the data file, if necessary. These document identification numbers can be handwritten or printed with a consecutive number stamp. It's important always to note the *last* number used, to avoid duplication.

When more than one person will be sight-editing documents and transferring data to computer files, a systematic record of who has which documents will be needed. That's especially necessary when those working on the completed questionnaires will be taking them away from the survey office or headquarters to some other place. These completed questionnaires are quite valuable and they aren't replaceable. Those working on them are much more likely to handle them with care and avoid misplacing or losing them if they have to "check them out" before taking them. They'll know they're being held accountable for the documents they have. Another advantage of such records is that they show which individuals performed the various tasks required. If problems or mistakes are discovered later, they can be attributed to those responsible. If necessary, the individuals who worked on the documents and files can be questioned for clarification, and all the documents or cases they processed can be checked for similar discrepancies or problems. The degree of control that's achieved by recording who has each completed questionnaire at any given time is well worth the little extra time and effort required to keep such records. Guidelines for initiating data processing are listed in Guidelist 9–1.

Sight-Editing Documents

Once the completed questionnaires have been received, recorded, and sorted, the actual processing begins with a sight-edit of each document. Each one should be examined to see if it's acceptable for processing and to make any corrections or notations required. The initial sight-edit of early interview questionnaire returns also indicates whether the interviewers were instructed. Additional instruction or supervision can then be arranged if it's needed.

Judging completeness

Some questionnaires returned from the field, especially with mail data collection, will be obviously incomplete. Some may contain a comment or note of explanation by the recipient or interviewer. If so, a brief record of them should be kept as an indication of the reasons for failure to complete the instrument. These incomplete documents can then be eliminated from the pile of forms to be processed. (Save several blank questionnaires, if none were retained earlier, to use as scratch working forms during coding and processing.)

Each document that appears at a glance to be completed must be checked thoroughly. The editor should examine each page and section of the questionnaire to be sure the respondent followed instructions and recorded answers in the proper place. The researcher should establish fixed criteria concerning how much of the questionnaire must be completed to make the case acceptable. This is especially important when others will be assisting with the sight-editing. The editors probably won't be able to make judgments on their own, so they should be given guidelines concerning what to accept and what to eliminate. Have editors form three groups of documents: (1) those that are obviously acceptable, (2) those that are obviously rejects, and (3) those that are questionable. The researcher can then examine the questionable documents and make a more informed decision about them.

There will inevitably be individual items respondents fail to complete. Some missing data can be tolerated. If the questionnaire is substantially complete, with only an occasional missing answer, it can be used. On the other hand, if entire sections are incomplete or the

---

GUIDELIST 9–1

For Initiating Data Processing

1. Plan and obtain data processing facilities, files, records, and programs while the survey is in the field.
2. When a large number of questionnaires are involved, prepare the physical setting so there's a separate place to shelve each group or set.
3. Monitor collection and receipt of data carefully, obtaining daily reports of completion and receipt.
4. Record nondeliverable mail surveys by reason for failure to gauge the quality of the namelist and representativeness of the sample.
5. Record the date of collection and/or receipt at the end of the completed questionnaires, so early and later returns can be compared during analysis.
6. Maintain a record of the number of surveys sent into the field, the number remaining, and the number returned.
7. Record a unique, consecutive identification number on each completed questionnaire returned from the field.
8. Keep a record of who has which completed questionnaires, by number, when others are to sight-edit and postcode documents and transfer data to files.
9. Be sure those who assist or perform the processing tasks know they'll be held accountable for both the loss of any documents and the quality of their work.

---

respondent has completed only the beginning and then terminated prematurely, the case should be rejected.

Multiple questionnaire forms

Occasionally, one survey will require different forms of the questionnaire for different respondent groups. For example, some interviews may be conducted in person and others, to obtain only the most essential data, may be done by telephone. Two forms would then be needed. In such cases, the instruments of each type should be separated into two groups and treated individually in the initial phase of data processing. The more standard the task, the more efficient the editors and data transfer clerks will be. If multiple questionnaire forms are used, the researcher must also establish separate criteria for editing and accepting each form of the instrument.

Editing, branching, and exclusions

Some survey questionnaires may require a considerable amount of branching or contain many items with exclusionary conditions. For example, the respondent or interviewer may be instructed to skip an entire section or go to a later point in the questionnaire, based on response to a key item. There may be several items conditioned on the previous questions, such as a question beginning with "If so, then . . ." If there are many such branches or exclusions in the instrument, the sight-editing becomes more laborious and demanding. The editors should mark out answers respondents have inserted for items they should have ignored. Inappropriate or superfluous responses shouldn't be keyed to the data file. They might not be detected and eliminated later.

The most effective way to edit such questionnaires is to give each editor a "key" questionnaire. Items or sections that should sometimes be excluded should be boldly marked, as shown in Example 9–1. The "criterion" question or item—the one indicating whether the following item or section should be completed—can also be marked clearly on the key, together with an indication of the answers that include or exclude the following item or section. The editor should compare each page of the completed document with this key to be sure there are no inappropriate answers recorded. This is especially important for each editor to do for the first dozen or so questionnaires, until each one is thoroughly familiar with the sections or items that might be excluded and with the criteria for completing or excluding them.

When a respondent *failed* to complete an item or section of the questionnaire that *should* have been completed but wasn't because of a branching mistake, the editors should use the same criteria to judge acceptability or rejection of the case as they would for other items or sections. On the other hand, when a respondent has *completed* an item or section where they *shouldn't* have, it usually doesn't require rejecting the case. Often those answers can be safely ignored. The remainder of the data is usually acceptable. Guidelist 9–2 summarizes the procedure for sight-editing documents.

EXAMPLE 9–1

Key Questionnaire Branching Notation

D

Is *THIS* hotel your *favorite* hotel?

Branch on yes → _____ YES – If so, please skip to **E** below.

_____ NO– If not, please continue below.

Please check *one* space on *each line* to show how *this hotel* compares to *YOUR FAVORITE HOTEL.*
Compared to my favorite hotel, THIS ONE IS . . .

	Much Less	The Same	Much More	
Expensive	1		7	11
Convenient	1 2 3	4 5 6	7	12
Comfortable	1		7	13
Neat, Clean	1		7	14
Spacious, Roomy	1 2 3	4 5 6	7	15
Attractive	1 2 3	4 5 6	7	16

If this is their favorite, this section should be blank. Postcode all zeros.

GUIDELIST 9–2

For Sight-Editing Documents

1. Early returns should be sight-edited promptly to detect data collection problems that might be remedied.
2. The objective of editing is to determine the data and cases to be accepted and those to be rejected.
3. Establish firm criteria for editors concerning the degree of completeness required to accept a case.
4. Instruct editors to set aside questionable documents to be examined by the researcher for an informed judgment.
5. Ordinarily some missing data from a few items can be tolerated and the remaining data will still be of value.
6. Usually cases where entire sections are incomplete or only the first part has been completed must be rejected.
7. When multiple forms of a questionnaire are used, they should be segregated and treated individually.
8. With many branches or exclusions in the questionnaire, editors should be given a key showing their location and the conditions when items shouldn't be answered.
9. When respondents or interviewers have mistakenly recorded answers to questions where they shouldn't have, the superfluous data should be marked out.
10. Inappropriate or superfluous data don't usually require that the case be rejected.

POSTCODING THE DATA

If the questionnaire was written properly, most questions will be "structured." Almost all responses will fall into predetermined categories or they'll be scale values recorded by the interviewer or respondent. The questionnaire also should have been precoded with numeric values for each answer printed on the questionnaire. The record format for the data file should be listed at the far right margin. Even if the questionnaire was written that way, substantial *postcoding* of responses will usually be necessary. Postcoding consists of assigning code values to all responses that don't already have a precode. For example, an item may list several response categories followed by an "other" category and a note to specify what other response. Obviously, such responses couldn't be anticipated, so they have no precoded value associated with them. Consequently, the editors have to postcode such responses before the code values can be transferred to the data file for processing.

The postcoding can either be done simultaneously with the sight-editing or as a separate task. If there isn't much postcoding required and it can be done quickly, it's best to do both the sight-editing and the postcoding at the same time for each document. Doing so won't delay the sight-editing very much and the editors will handle each document only once. When the postcoding is more demanding and time-consuming, it should probably be done *after* the sight-editing is finished. Those postcoding the questionnaires can devote all of their attention to this one, complex task and it won't delay the sight-editing and recording of documents.

Those postcoding the questionnaires should have a blank, "key" questionnaire similar to that used for the sight-editing. It should highlight the items to be examined and postcoded, as shown in Example 9–2. If the same key is used to sight-edit and postcode the questionnaires, the two types of indications on the key must be *distinct* from one another, such as using different colors. Both must be easy to recognize.

The postcoding editors record two things: New codes for answers that have no precode values are inserted on the questionnaire so they can be transferred to the data file later. In addition and at the same time, the code value, *together with the answers themselves,* must be recorded in the codebook or on the codelist.

Example 9–3 may clarify this process. In the example, respondents were asked how many times they had stayed in some other kind of hotel. They were also asked to write in *what kind* of other hotel. On this particular completed questionnaire, the postcoder noted that someone had recorded the number 1 for "Some other kind of hotel" and written in "Health spa resort"—a response category not printed on the original questionnaire and therefore one for which there was no precoded value.

To postcode this item properly, the editor first referred to the codebook for the survey, turning to page two, which had the codelist for this section and item. Noting that two previous items were listed and assigned the code values of 1 and 2, the postcoder recorded the number 3 in the column for codes and wrote in the type of *other* hotel in the "label" column. Then the postcoder recorded a big, bold number 3 in the margin of the original questionnaire, just to the right of the record format column number 21, where that value will later be keyed.

Later, when the data are transferred to computer file, the data entry clerk will key the value of 1 in column 20 to show how many times that respondent had stayed in an "other" hotel. Then the code value of 3 will be entered in column 21 to show *what* other kind of hotel. Meanwhile, the analyst preparing the analysis program will label the categories for a variable called "What other hotel" according to the codelist for that item: 1 = *cruise ship,* 2 = *conference center,* 3 = *health spa resort,* and so on.

As the example indicates, there must be a codelist for each item that may require postcoding. The codebook should be set up in advance to contain one or more *separate pages* for

---

EXAMPLE 9–2

Key Questionnaire Postcoding Notation

O

Of the **last ten times** you stayed at a hotel,
how many times did you stay at. . . .

This particular hotel?	____ times	11-12
Another hotel in *this* chain?	____ times	13-14
A hotel that's part of *some other national chain?*	____ times	15-16
An individ~~Postcode this~~ →.................................	____ times	17-18
Some other kind of hotel? (What kind? ▓▓▓▓▓▓▓) ..	____ times	19-20
(Please make the TOTAL = 10) **Total = 10** times		

EXAMPLE 9–3

Postcoded Items

O

Of the **last ten times** you stayed at a hotel,
how many times did you stay at. . . .

This particular hotel?	*1*	times	11-12
Another hotel in *this* chain?	*3*	times	13-14
A hotel that's part of *some other national chain?*	*5*	times	15-16
An individual, *independent* hotel?	*0*	times	17-18
Some other kind of hotel? (What kind? ___Health spa resort___) ..	*1*	times	19-20

(Please make the TOTAL = 10)   **Total = 10** times   21   *3*

Hotel survey codebook, pg. 2
Section 0 – column 21   What other?

code	label
1	Cruise ship
2	Conference center
3	Health spa resort

each such item, with the item number or questionnaire location clearly indicated at the top of the page. That's because the researcher can't tell how many new codes and answers will result from any one item. There has to be room to enter new ones until all completed questionnaires have been postcoded.

Postcoding is a fairly simple, easy process when only one editor does the coding on any given day or at any one time. It's best to do it that way, either by assigning only one person to the task or by "staggering" the times and/or days when different editors will code the completed questionnaires. If that's not feasible, the editors must all work at the *same place* when they're coding at the same time. If two or more editors are postcoding at the same time and in *different* locations, they won't know what *new* codes the *others* have listed in *their* codebooks. A single code value will inevitably be assigned to two or more *different* answers.

The objective of the coding process is to provide a *unique* code for each acceptable answer.

Inexperienced researchers may minimize the importance of this potential problem and ignore the recommendation in order to "save time." Experience clearly indicates it's very dangerous to permit editors to work independently from different codebooks in separate locations. Serious errors and data problems will almost certainly result. Ultimately, it will take a lot more time to put things right than it would to do the postcoding as recommended here.

Criteria for postcoding

The researcher should specify the criteria for identifying and categorizing answers and assigning codes to them. The editors need guidelines about how "fine-grained" the categories should be and how to group individual answers into categories. For instance, in Example 9–3, if someone indicated "Some other kind of hotel" and listed a "*convention* center," how should that be handled? Should it be assigned a postcode value of 2—the same as a *conference* center, or should it be listed separately and assigned its own code value.

Without specific guidelines and criteria for coding, editors who aren't familiar with the survey process are likely to err in one of two directions: Some will assign a new code to virtually every new alternative, based on the precise, verbatim word or phrase noted on the questionnaire. This will create far too many codes and categories. Probably there will be only one or two cases for each such code. Other editors may simplify their task by "lumping" all responses that are even vaguely similar to one another into the same, large category. That would discard distinctions and data that might be regarded as useful by the researcher. Thus, postcoding editors need specific guidelines. They should also be monitored closely during the initial phase of the work.

When deciding on the level of detail—on how "fine-grained" the new categories should be—it's much better to specify categories that might be too narrow rather than too broad. If too much detail is recorded, this will result in more code values than are really needed. That isn't serious because the data easily can be regrouped into larger categories during computer processing. By contrast, if the data are grouped into categories that are too broad, there's no way to separate out smaller categories, short of returning to the completed questionnaires, postcoding them again, and transferring the data to file a second time. Once distinctions have been lost by grouping into broad categories, they can't be regained without reference to the completed questionnaires. Thus, experienced researchers normally prefer that postcoding editors create a new category and code if they're in doubt about its fitting neatly into an existing category.

Maintaining the codebook

It's very important to be sure the entries in the codebook are very neatly and legibly made. This point seems trivial until it's time to use the information during the analysis phase. It's far better to avoid a potential catastrophe than to spend hours trying to remedy one. Often the editors will be "clerical help" who aren't particularly interested in the survey results or familiar with the process. When there are several people postcoding, each will be making entries on the codelists. So there's likely to be many mistakes. The chance of errors increases markedly if the codelists aren't kept in a neat, orderly fashion. For example, editors may make "margin notes" when a sheet is full, rather than labeling and starting a new page. If they do, they or others probably won't notice the last entry. They may assign the *same* code

---

GUIDELIST 9–3

For Postcoding the Questionnaires

1. Postcoding is almost always required because any answer that doesn't have a code value must be assigned one.
2. New codes should be listed on the questionnaire so they can easily be recognized when transferring data to file.
3. A separate codelist page for the codebook should be created for each questionnaire item that might require postcoding.
4. It's vital that editors record every new code category they create on the codelist so others don't use the same code value for a *different* answer.
5. If more than one editor does postcoding, they must all work from the same codebook, either at different times or simultaneously, at the same place.

6. Simple coding can be done together with sight-editing, but substantial postcoding jobs should be done afterward.
7. Coding editors should have a "key" questionnaire with the items to be postcoded clearly marked.
8. The researcher should provide the guidelines for when and how to create new codes and group answers.
9. It's better for editors to create too many small categories than too few overly broad ones.
10. The codebook must be maintained neatly and clearly and should be recopied if it becomes disorderly.

---

to a *different* response. The necessity for neatness in the codebook is more than cosmetic—far more!

If the codelists become disordered or confusing, it's well worth the time and effort to rewrite them from the originals, creating a more orderly codebook. Note that the entries must *not* be changed in any way, and the same codes must apply to the same answers and categories. When categories are to be combined, that should be done only after the codes have been transferred to the data file, and not during the coding process.

The most common and detrimental error when coding completed questionnaires and making entries in the codebook is to fail to list a new code and category in the book. If that happens, the same code will be assigned to two different answers. That must be avoided at all cost. By contrast, if editors fail to notice that a particular response has already been coded and entered on a codelist, they will create a new code for the same answer. That's not serious because the two can be recoded to a single value during processing. Little, if anything, will be lost. A sketch of the main considerations for postcoding questionnaires is provided in Guidelist 9–3.

Transferring the Data

When all of the completed questionnaires to be included in the data have been sorted, sight-edited, and postcoded, it's time to transfer the data to computer files. If the precoding and postcoding have been done properly, data transfer should consist only of reading the codes for each item and recording them in the file according to the record format printed on the questionnaires. The type of file to which the data will be transferred depends on the type of processing that's selected. If the mode of processing was anticipated and the data record format printed on the questionnaire, as suggested earlier, then the data need only be keyed to file in precisely that format.[1]

If the data are keyed to computer files by data entry clerks who are unfamiliar with questionnaire data entry, they must be instructed thoroughly on *precisely* how to enter the data. The research analyst should be present or readily available while the first few cases are being keyed to file, so the operators can ask questions and get additional direction if they need it. Inexperienced researchers often make the mistake of assuming too much of the operators. Even though they may specialize in data entry, they're not likely to understand the research process or be familiar with *survey* data entry. Data entry clerks can be compared to typists. They may be very fast and accurate at data entry but know very little about the content of the data itself or its ultimate purpose.

Data Entry Documents

Survey data may be entered into one of five different types of documents: Spreadsheets, graphics program tables, word processor tables, word processor documents, or special data entry program files. Regardless of the type of document, the objective is the same: The data entry operators must know *exactly* where they are in the record and file at *every* point. In other words, the same item on every questionnaire (or variable for analysis) must be keyed to the same record and location in every case in the file. Analysis programs "recognize" a given item only by its location (or its sequence) in the data file being read.

Spreadsheet documents

The most common document for data entry, and probably the easiest to use, is a spreadsheet table. Spreadsheet programs for desktop computers are readily available and relatively easy to use. Figure 9–1 shows a blank portion of a typical spreadsheet. Only ten columns and twenty rows are depicted, but most extend to well over a hundred columns and perhaps thousands of rows. The user can "scroll" horizontally and vertically across the columns and up and down rows that are in use, displaying as many cells as the screen will hold. There are also commands allowing the operator to "go to" any designated column, row, or cell of the spreadsheet.

Each row in the spreadsheet should correspond to a single questionnaire or "case" for analysis. So the data are entered horizontally, and there will be as many rows as there are completed questionnaires. Typically, the rows of a spreadsheet are numbered and the columns are designated with letters. To use such a spreadsheet for data entry, the record format

---

[1] If the record format was not printed on the questionnaires in advance, a key questionnaire showing the record format must be created. For guidance, see Chapter 6—Precoding Record Formats, p. 170. The key questionnaire can be printed on transparencies and overlaid on each questionnaire page during data entry or set beneath and to the right of each questionnaire page so the margin is visible and indicates the record position for each variable to be keyed to file.

Figure 9–1   *Blank Spreadsheet*

A1		

≡≡≡≡≡≡≡≡≡≡≡≡≡≡≡≡≡ Untitled1 (SS) ≡≡≡≡≡≡≡≡≡≡≡≡≡≡≡

	A	B	C	D	E	F	G	H	I	J	⇧
1											
2											
3											
4											
5											
6											
7											
8											
9											
10											
11											
12											
13											
14											
15											
16											
17											
18											
19											
20											⇩

printed on the questionnaire should indicate *letters* of the column in which each item is to be entered.[2]

When the spreadsheet document has been initialized and dimensioned, data entry is accomplished merely by entering the code values for each item of the first questionnaire, followed by pressing the tab key. (As the values are keyed, they first appear in a section at the top of the screen or window, above the spreadsheet itself. The program inserts them into the next cell in sequence when the tab key is pressed.) The operator can move back and forth or up and down to make corrections by using the tab and back-tab keys, cursor

---

[2]If the column locations are *numbered,* rather than lettered on the questionnaire, these numbers can be entered in the first row of the spreadsheet to guide the data entry operator. They should be formatted in **bold** type to make them easily recognizable and distinct from the actual data. As the entry extends downward with the entry of each new case entered, these column number designations may scroll off the top of the screen, disappearing from sight. The first row can then be copied and transferred or *pasted* below the last case entered. Later, when all the data have been entered, these column numbers can easily be deleted from the file.

keys, or a "mouse" if the system is equipped with one. At the end of each questionnaire or case, the operator simply scrolls to the first column and begins entering data for the next case.

The questionnaire number or case number is entered into the first column or the last column of the spreadsheet, depending on the way the record format is specified on the questionnaires. There is no necessity to enter the questionnaires consecutively or in any particular order, since the data can easily be sorted by those or any other values later, if desired.

Two very important points deserve mention here: First, it's absolutely critical that the operator refer **very often** to the column designations to be sure the data are being entered into the correct column. That should be done at **many** points when entering data for **each** questionnaire. Second, the operator should **save the file** frequently during the process—perhaps after entering each case. Data entry is a laborious process. If there is a power interruption or system malfunction during entry, everything entered after the last saving of the file will be lost.

Graphics program documents

Programs designed especially to produce graphs and charts routinely allow the user to initialize and format tables to contain the data to be charted. They can often be used for data

Figure 9–2   *Blank Graphics Program Table*

entry in place of a spreadsheet, if necessary, whether or not graphs or charts are to be created from the data. If other analysis programs are to be used on the data, the analyst must be sure the data file can be saved in a format that can be "read" by the analysis programs or that it can be read and transformed into a format acceptable to the analysis programs.

Graphics program tables such as the one shown in Figure 9–2 operate in much the same way as spreadsheets. In fact, they are actually miniature spreadsheets with more limited capabilities. When each item is keyed, it appears directly in the active cell rather than above the table as with spreadsheets. Aside from that difference, many of the same operations—scrolling, formatting, sorting, and simple data manipulation—are almost identical to the corresponding operations of a spreadsheet.

Word processor tables

The more sophisticated word processing programs allow the user to create *tables,* such as the one shown in Figure 9–3, that consist of a grid or matrix similar to the body of a spreadsheet. The number of columns and rows can usually be specified when the table is initiated or created. They can then be labeled and the data typed directly into the table, moving from cell to cell with the tab key.

This mode of data entry document may be appropriate only for surveys with a very limited number of questionnaire items or variables. That's because they may not allow the user to create more than 20 or 30 columns and they may have limited scrolling ability. In other words, they're restricted in their *horizontal* operations, although they may not be *vertically* limited. They will usually handle hundreds of *rows,* so they may be usable for surveys with hundreds of respondents or cases, providing there are only a few items or variables for each.

Figure 9–3   *Blank Word Processor Table*

Case	v1	v2	v3	v4	v5	v6	v7	v8	v9	v10

Word processor text files

Some word processor programs display an indication of the cursor location directly on the computer screen. In Figure 9–4, the print at the bottom right of the screen isn't actually in the document. Rather, it's information the program displays only on the screen to show the user where the cursor is in the document at the time. If the word processor has such a position indicator, it may list the location on the line in inches and fractions of an inch or in some other unit of measure, such as picas or centimeters. That's of no value for data entry, but the indicator can usually be changed to "units" or digits by referring to the setup menu of the program. In that mode, each number, character, or space is one unit. Similarly, the program ordinarily will allow the user to specify whether or not the lines should "wrap" around when the right margin of the screen is reached, or whether the screen should automatically "scroll." The latter should be specified.

This type of data entry document is uniquely suited to handle a *fixed format* data file, described in Chapter 6. As the data are entered, the operator need only be sure the position indicator value corresponds to the record format numbers printed on the questionnaire beside the *next* item to be keyed. (It is also helpful to specify a *fixed space* type font, rather than proportionally spaced type. That way, the columns of type "line up" vertically, regardless of the character width.)

Figure 9–4   *Display with Position Indicator*

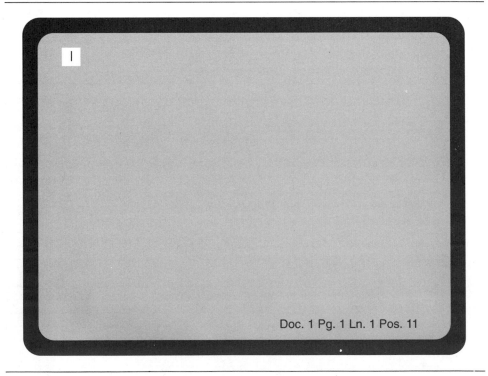

Doc. 1 Pg. 1 Ln. 1 Pos. 11

Word processors allow the user to save a "text" file, sometimes referred to as "ASCII text," which is free of special formatting codes used by the word processor program, itself. Most analysis programs will accept *fixed format* data if so instructed. While they can usually read *text* files, they *can't* read files in the word processing program's own format. As the data are entered, the operator should save the file in the usual fashion for that program. When all data are entered, however, the file should be saved as a text file only.

Special data entry documents

Many statistical analysis programs include a special feature to facilitate data entry. Some have formats similar to a spreadsheet. Others provide a position indicator similar to that just described. Either version is quite acceptable for data entry, providing that it corresponds to the type of record format printed on the questionnaires.

The least desirable data entry program or feature provides neither spreadsheet-type columns nor a position indicator. Instead, it merely lists a ruler or scale at the top of the screen. The operators have to scan downward vertically to be sure they're at the proper position in the file. That process is error-prone, and the analyst would be well advised to select another type of data entry program and document if at all possible.

The most sophisticated and elegant data entry programs are designed especially for firms and research agencies that do many surveys and a high volume of data entry. The screen may display a blank replica of the actual questionnaire. As the numbers (letters or words) are keyed, they appear in place on the replica shown on the screen. With such physical mapping, data entry operators can see exactly where they are at any point and there's far less chance of error.

Such data entry programs and similar ones with less elaborate display screens often have *data screening* capability. As the program and data file are being initialized and formatted, the analyst indicates what type of data—numeric, alphameric, special characters, and so on— are acceptable for each variable. In addition, the *range* of numeric values may be specified. Thus, if response to a given item is based on a 5-point scale and the operator attempted to enter a 6, a letter, punctuation mark, special character, or anything other than the numbers 1 through 5 or a zero or blank, the program wouldn't accept it. Instead, it would "beep" or give an audible indication of the error and perhaps display an error message until the correct value is entered. This kind of data entry is, of course, the best, but unfortunately beyond the reach of most.

Computer Data Editing

Once the data have been keyed to computer file, they must be edited thoroughly to be sure they're acceptable for analysis. This is *far more important* than it might seem. If the data aren't perfectly clean and in the proper condition for analysis, two serious problems can result: First, the analysis routines may fail to run, and, even if they do, they may generate reports with obviously invalid values. Second, and far worse, the programs may run and generate erroneous results that appear to be okay.

Computer data editing should seek to identify and correct three kinds of errors:

1. Records that are missing, superfluous, or out of order when there are multiple records per case.

2. Records that deviate from their prescribed format—where variables have been keyed to the wrong columns or fields.

3. Variables that contain the wrong kind of data or whose values exceed the acceptable range for the item.

There are several methods for checking each kind of error, but it's always advisable to investigate each type in the sequence listed here.

As soon as the data have been completely entered and before any processing has begun, at *least* one copy of the original file should be created and stored on a separate medium, preferably at another location. In other words, the file should be copied to a "backup" diskette, and that should be kept at another location. In addition, it's also advisable to make *backup* copies of each "generation" of the data file—each time major modifications are made or substantial effort has been exerted on the file. That way, if a working file is destroyed or damaged in some way, the backup file is available and only the most recent changes and efforts are lost.

Checking record sequence

Even when there's only one record or line of data per case, it's important to check the file to be sure every line contains legitimate data and that no questionnaires were inadvertently keyed to file twice or more. All spreadsheets and charting programs, some word processors with data in tabular format, and most other data entry programs allow the user to sort the *entire file* on one column. (It's essential that the user specify sorting *all* the columns based on the values in just one. Otherwise, the program may sort *only* a single column, and that copy of the file would be virtually destroyed unless the sorting can be "undone.") If the program is capable of sorting the records, the file should be sorted on the questionnaire numbers or *case numbers,* as they'll be called henceforth. After that, the analyst may scroll down the file and visually examine the records, checking the conditions listed in Checklist 9–1. If there are missing or erroneous data, the data can be rekeyed from the completed questionnaire whose number corresponds with the case number of the deviant record.

Checking fixed format data files

Data in a fixed format that was entered with a word processor or data entry program providing a position indicator won't be in tabular columns that can readily be sorted. Instead, the "columns" are defined only by position on the line or record—one column or position for each character or space. The data for each record will begin and end in a given column, specified by the record format. If there's more than one record or line of data for each questionnaire or case, they may not all end at the same point on the line, but the same record in each case should begin and end at the same place.

It's usually advisable to have operators key a zero in the record if no data are present, rather than leave columns blank in the data file, so the data will extend to exactly the same place for each similar record. To check the record format, the data can be printed in a fixed-space type font as shown in Figure 9–5. Drawing lines with ruler at the endpoint of each record makes errors more obvious to the eye. Lines that extend beyond their format limit can be identified by case number and checked against the completed questionnaire. Similarly, those that are too short should also be checked. This usually indicates the operator has one

> **CHECKLIST 9–1**
>
> ### To Detect Data Record Errors
>
> 1. Are there any duplicate case numbers, indicating the same questionnaire has been keyed to file two or more times? If so, duplicates should be deleted.
> 2. Are there any totally blank rows or rows that contain only a ruler or positional scale used during data entry? If so, they should be deleted.
> 3. Are there rows with data only in the beginning columns but not in the later ones? If so, the questionnaire may not have been completely keyed.
> 4. Are there any blank cells in the last column that should contain data? If so, one or more items or variables for that case may have been skipped.
> 5. Is the column just beyond the last one to be used completely blank? If *not,* a variable for the deviant case may have been keyed twice.

or more items or has failed to enter the correct number of digits or spaces for a variable on the record.

Errors of this nature are particularly troublesome and often create serious problems. If the data deviates from the format and the error was "early" in the record, toward the beginning or left side, this will not only result in the wrong value for the particular variable that was miskeyed, but probably in erroneous values for all of the data on the remaining part of the record. Thus, all such records should be corrected in the file before beginning the check of the field range.

Checking deviations from variable range

Each variable in the data file has an acceptable range of data. For example, if the item used a six-point scale, the range would be from one to six, and if missing data were tolerable for the item, zero (or perhaps blank) would also be acceptable. Similarly, if only adults were to be accepted as respondents, then no age keyed as a continuous numeric item should be below 18, 21, or whatever age was used to qualify young respondents. Each and every variable must be checked to be sure the data are within the permissible range.

When the data file is in *tabular* format, such as that in a spreadsheet, charting program,

Figure 9–5   *Fixed Format Data File*

```
001 1 3345343342|254|3243|
001 2 3444543265|455|
001 3 7182544322
002 1 4544311222|423|4544|
002 2 3334445413|443|
002 3 2573538900|    |    |
```

or word processor table, each variable to be checked is in a single column. The data can be sorted on each column, in turn. (Again, *the analyst must be warned!* The program may require specifying which columns are to be associated with the one being sorted. If so, *all* columns must be specified, so the program doesn't sort only one column, ruining the data file.) Then the highest and lowest value in that column, in the first and last rows, can be checked after each sort. If the extreme values are out of range, the data for any such case can be checked against the corresponding, completed questionnaire. The data entry operator may have merely entered the wrong value for one variable, but such errors may also result because *several* variables were entered into the *wrong columns*. Thus, it's important either to rekey the entire case or to check the values of the *other* variables for the case against the questionnaire.

Whether the data are in *tabular* or *fixed format,* the range for each variable can be checked by running a preliminary data description analysis. A *frequency table* or *bar chart* can be generated by a spreadsheet, charting, or statistical analysis program for variables with only a limited range, such as rating scale data. Obviously, there should be a category only for the *legitimate* values. If the variable has continuous numeric data that can legitimately include a wide but bounded range of values, such as the age of *adult* respondents, the spreadsheet, charting, or statistical analysis program usually include data description routines that will indicate the maximum and nonzero minimum values of a variable.

The disadvantage to this process is the fact that when invalid values are found, there's no indication of the case numbers from which they were derived. The researcher may have to examine all of the cases in the file to identify the errant values. Other alternatives may also be available. One is to instruct the statistical analysis program to select only those cases with the *illegitimate* values and print the cases or case numbers. Another is to *cross-tabulate* the variable in question with the case numbers. Erroneous values can then be identified with their respective case numbers. Complete guidelines for editing data by computer are outlined in Guidelist 9–4.

DATA PROCESSING

The data processing and statistical analysis requirements are often a bit intimidating to inexperienced survey researchers. Computer operations and statistical manipulations may appear to be highly technical, if not mystical. Fortunately, modern computer technology makes survey data processing and analysis vastly simpler and easier than it's ever been, rather than more complex and demanding. The burden of data handling and computation that once rested on the analyst's shoulders has been taken on by the computer software and hardware. In addition, analysis systems are increasingly user-friendly, freeing research analysts to turn their attention and effort to the content and meaning of the information. The discussion that follows assumes only a basic understanding of computers, and it does not demand a sophisticated understanding of mathematics or statistics.

Purpose of Data Processing

Surveys generate a very large volume of "raw" data, but these are of little or no use to those who seek survey information. It would be extremely impractical for researchers to examine each such datum for each item on each completed questionnaire. Even if they did, it would

---

GUIDELIST 9–4

For Computer Data Editing

1. Computer data editing is required to be certain the data analysis won't produce erroneous results—especially errors which aren't apparent in the reports.
2. The editing should seek out three types of errors: missing, superfluous, or disordered records; deviations from record format; and deviations from the acceptable range of variables.
3. Record format deviations often result from one or more pieces of data being skipped over or keyed twice.
4. Editing should examine the ends of each record or line of fixed format data to be sure it's neither too short nor too long.
5. Format errors are more serious than field range errors because they may cause all the following variables on the record or in the case to be incorrect.
6. Establish the "permissible range" of data for each item on the questionnaire, to establish acceptable variable ranges.
7. Each variable in each record of each case should then be checked to be sure it's within legitimate range.
8. The variable range of data in *tabular* file format can be checked by sorting each column in turn (together with all the others) and checking the extreme values at the top and bottom of the table after each sort.
9. The variable range of both *tabular* and *fixed format* data can be checked by running simple, preliminary data description analysis producing frequency tables, bar charts, or reports of the maximum and minimum numeric values.
10. When errors are detected during process editing, refer to the completed questionnaire by case number to make the required corrections in the data file.

---

be virtually impossible to glean any meaning from them as a whole. Thus, the difference between *data* and *information* is that data are meaningless on inspection, while those who examine information can understand it and obtain meaning from it. The primary purpose of data processing is to *summarize* the data into information. The objective of data processing and analysis is to *suppress* the detail and reveal the important and meaningful patterns and relationships contained in the data.

SCALE AND DATA TYPES

The various statistical tools and procedures described in the following chapter require the data to meet certain conditions or be in a particular form. The type of scale and data dictate, in part, which statistical techniques are appropriate and which are inappropriate. Thus, before actually beginning the statistical analysis, the analyst should identify the scale and data types for *each* questionnaire item *in advance*. Then the appropriate method of analysis and statistical tool will be more easily and more accurately selected.

Four different types of scales are identified below and diagrammed in Figure 9–6: nominal, ordinal, interval, and ratio. Study the description of the scale types, identify each item on the questionnaire as one of the four scale types, and note it on the *key* questionnaire

Figure 9–6 *Scale Data Type Diagram*

beside each item or in each section of similar items. This key can then be used to identify the scale and data type for any given item when selecting statistical tools, without the necessity to reassess each item several times.

Nominal scale data

Computers handle numbers more readily than letters or words, so the different verbal meaning of answers to a survey questionnaire are typically assigned a numeric code value, even if it doesn't actually designate a quantitative value. For example, respondents might check the word "male" or "female" to indicate their sex. Male may then be assigned the numeric code of 1 and female the value of 2 when the survey instrument is coded. In this case, the numbers don't designate a quantity. They're only *names* for the categories "male" and "female." Data values that don't stand for any quantity are called *nominal* data.

Other examples of nominal data might be the ZIP code of respondents or a person's telephone number or social security number. The assignment of the numbers is completely arbitrary, so long as every category is assigned a *unique* number. For convenience, the response category of questionnaire items are usually numbered in consecutive sequence, but they need not necessarily be so. No mathematical or arithmetic operations—addition, subtraction, multiplication, or division—can be legitimately applied to nominal data. For instance, it would make no more sense to calculate the average response to a multiple-choice question than it would to compute the average *ZIP code* for the sample.

Notice that in Figure 9–6 the *nominal* scale values are attached to different shaped objects and they don't appear in any orderly sequence—they aren't arrayed on a spectrum or dimension. The numbers only identify categories—in this case, shapes. Most analysis programs allow the analyst to attach verbal "labels" to each code to make the categories more easily identifiable on the reports. So, in the example, 3 might be labeled *circle,* 5 labeled *triangle,* and so forth.

Ordinal scale data

If respondents *ranked* several brands of a product, these rankings could constitute an *ordinal* scale. Similarly, if they were asked to indicate the order in which they did a series of tasks, that question would produce ordinal data. Ordinal values show the *sequence* or *order* in which things occur within the range of the scale. On a 5-point ordinal scale, a value of 4 indicates 3 things come before and 1 comes after, or that 3 is *lesser* and 1 is *greater*—nothing more. The ordinal scale shown in Figure 9–6 shows 1 on top, 6 on the bottom, and the other values in order between them, but the spaces are *unequal.* Ordinal scales do *not* have equal intervals between the integers.

An ordinal scale is somewhat more powerful—it provides more information, in a sense—than a nominal scale. The numeric values have more meaning. With a nominal scale, the numbers are only names that make one category *distinct* from another, but they don't indicate any *relationship* whatsoever. Ordinal scale values do show relationship in terms of *sequence* or *order,* so the numbers have more meaning than nominal values. On the other hand, the values of ordinal data have less meaning than do those of the two other types of scale data described below.

Ordinal data can't legitimately be used in mathematical *equations.* They can only be manipulated in what are called *systems of inequalities*— systems whose terms consist of "greater than" and "less than." Statistical analysis of ordinal data requires what are termed *nonparametric* statistics, rather than more common and powerful statistical tools. Because of these limitations, survey researchers are well advised to avoid scales yielding ordinal values in favor of those providing *interval* or *ratio* data.

Interval scale data

A scale with numeric values equidistant from one another is an interval scale. Interval scales are sometimes called *"equal interval"* scales because the interval between each integer on the scale is the same. Interval scales need not include the value of zero. If they do, as in the scale shown in Figure 9–6, the zero value doesn't really indicate the complete absence of whatever is measured—it doesn't represent *nothing.*

A typical example of an interval scale is the Fahrenheit scale of temperature. The interval between one integer value and the next is exactly the same, no matter where the value is on the scale. Yet the zero doesn't represent the *absence* of heat—it's not *absolute* zero.

Because the zero may be absent from an interval scale (or, if it is present, it doesn't stand for the absence of the thing measured), the arithmetic operation of *division* isn't permissible for interval data. For example, if the low temperature last night was 40°F and the high temperature today is 80°F, this doesn't imply that last night was half as warm as today. Such a statement would have no meaning or validity. In short, the ratio of one value to another has no meaning for interval scale data. On the other hand, interval scales used in survey questionnaires, such as a *linear, numeric scale,* permit the analyst to use the most common statistical tools. Little is lost by the fact that zero isn't absolute.

The ratio scale

There's only one difference between an interval scale and a ratio scale: zero is absolute on the ratio scale. For example, distance in miles or age in years would be ratio scales. In this society, at the instant of birth the infant's age would be zero, and, if an object stays in the same place, it would have traveled zero distance. In both cases, the zero is absolute; it stands for no age or no distance. On the ratio scale shown in Figure 9–6, zero represents *none—no* part of the whole of 100%.

Because zero actually means nothing of what's being measured and the distance between any two points on a ratio scale is always equal to that between any other two, ratio scales impose the least amount of restrictions on the mathematics or statistics that can be used to manipulate these values. They're called ratio scales because ratios of one value to another have meaning. For example, if one person travels 20 miles and another travels 40, the first has traveled half as far (1:2 or 1/2) as the second, or the second has traveled twice as far

Figure 9–7   *Data Type Descriptions*

Nominal Scale

1. The numeric values are merely the names of categories.
2. The numbers are used only to make categories distinct.
3. The values don't indicate any magnitudes.
4. The values don't indicate any relationships.
5. No arithmetic operations can be used on the numbers.
6. Statistical manipulation is extremely limited.

Ordinal Scale

1. The numeric values show the order or sequence.
2. The values are not a measure of magnitude.
3. The interval between values doesn't indicate magnitude.
4. The values do show relationships by order or sequence.
5. The values can't be used in mathematical equations.
6. Statistical manipulation is somewhat limited.

Interval Scale

1. The numeric values show both order and magnitude.
2. The interval between integer values is equal.
3. A zero value doesn't indicate absolute zero.
4. The values show relationships by order and magnitude.
5. The values can't be used to form ratios.
6. Statistical manipulation isn't very limited.

Ratio Scale

1. The numeric values show both order and magnitude.
2. The interval between integer values is equal.
3. A zero value does indicate absence of the thing measured.
4. The values show relationships by order and magnitude.
5. The values can be used to form ratios.
6. Statistical manipulation isn't limited.

┌───┐

CHECKLIST 9–2

To Identify the Scale Data Type

1. Are the values only names to designate independent categories? If so, and the categories don't represent some order of magnitude, the scale data are *nominal*.

2. Do the values indicate only sequence or order of magnitude? If so, and they don't indicate the actual magnitude or interval between values, the scale data are *ordinal*.

3. Do the values indicate actual magnitudes with equal intervals between the scale points? If so, and zero *doesn't* represent *absolute* zero or complete absence of the thing measured, the scale is *interval*.

4. Do the values indicate actual magnitudes with equal intervals between the scale points? If so, and a value of zero *does* represent *absolute* zero or complete absence of the thing measured, the scale is *ratio*.

└───┘

---

as the first (2:1 or 2/1). Thus, arithmetic operations of division and multiplication are permissible with ratio scale data and the "quotient" or "product" that result from them, respectively, are meaningful values.

Ratio scale data are least restrictive regarding the types of statistics that can be used. Yet, it's important to note that many things measured on a survey questionnaire don't lend themselves to the use of a ratio scale. Thus, interval scales are much more commonly used. There are ordinarily very few differences between interval and ratio scales, in terms of the ability to manipulate the data with statistical tools, so little if anything is lost by using an interval scale rather than a ratio scale. On the other hand, a substantial amount of information or meaning *is* lost or unmeasured by using an ordinal scale in place of an interval scale. A nominal scale even more strictly limits the use of statistical manipulation. These characteristics of scale data are summarized in Figure 9–7. Checklist 9–2 identifies the principal areas to examine to ascertain the type of data each scale yields.

RECODING THE DATA

There are some situations where the analyst may want to change the form of the data from that in which it was collected. Spreadsheets, charting programs, and statistical analysis programs all allow their users to regroup or *recode* the data to a more suitable form. Either the original variable can be altered or a *new* variable based on the same data can be created and modified. Usually this work should be done as part of data preparation rather than waiting until the statistical analysis phase is underway.

Recoding for fewer values

Sometimes recoding is done to reduce the number or range of different values in the distribution of response to a survey item. For example, respondents may have been asked to record their age. That kind of question yields continuous ratio data. For a large sample of adults, there would be many different values, perhaps ranging from the late teens to the nineties. That wouldn't be a problem if the distribution could be adequately described by several statistical coefficients to be discussed in Chapter 10, such as the mean, standard deviation, skewness, kurtosis, and so forth. Those experienced with statistics may be comfortable with those descriptive values because they may be able to *visualize* what they represent. In fact, however, most survey information seekers wouldn't get much information from them.

In this situation, the analyst can present the data in a more meaningful form by *recoding* the many different age values into only a few categories, such as by decades. The analysis program would be instructed to code all those under 20 into group 1, those from 20 to 29 into group 2, and so on. Then these new code values can be *labeled* as "teens," "twenties," and so on. Since there would now be less than ten values, rather than several dozen, the data can readily be shown in a table showing the number and percentage of respondents in each category—a *frequency* table. Reporting the data that way is far more understandable to those seeking the information. For even more clarity, the number or percentage in each age category could be graphically portrayed in a bar chart. But neither tabular nor graphic display of the data is feasible until the continuous array was recoded into a few categories.

Recoding to meaningful categories

In the sample questionnaire shown in Example 6–1–G in Chapter 6 (page 145), respondents were asked to record their *formal education* in years. Notice this original scale was a *ratio* scale. If the respondents' educations ranged from lower elementary school to postgraduate degrees, there might be well over 20 different values for this variable. That's too many to show readily in a frequency table or bar chart. More importantly, the individual number of years isn't as meaningful as the *categories* associated with completion of certain levels. In other words, there's probably far less distinction between those who have 10 years of education and those who have 11 than there is between those with 11 and those with 12 years. The latter pair are distinguished by the fact that some have *graduated* from high school and some have not.

In this example, education was gathered as continuous ratio data simply because it's a better and easier way to *collect* the data. During data preparation, those with 8 years of education or less can be recoded into category 1—*Elementary Only;* those with 9, 10, or 11 years into category 2—*Some High School;* those with 12 years into category 3—*High School Graduate;* and so on. The objective here isn't merely to *reduce* the number of values. Rather, it's mainly to group the data into more *meaningful* categories.

There are three rules to follow when recoding a variable into new categories: (1) The categories must be all-inclusive. (2) The categories must be mutually exclusive. (3) There must be more variation in the thing being measured *between* categories than within them. All-inclusive categories mean there must be a new category for *every* data point. Often when data are recoded, the upper and/or lower category will be an "open-ended" category. In the example, all those with more than 16 years of education were classified as postgraduates. In the example where age was to be converted from years to ten-year groups, there will probably be only a few people in their eighties or nineties. The upper category might be "70 and over" so all ages—even the most advanced—are included and the rule concerning all-inclusive categories is respected.

To ensure *mutually exclusive* categories, there must be no "overlap" between categories. In other words, there should be no response that would fit into more than one category. Errors in this regard are more common when the researcher is writing multiple-choice questions and composing the questionnaire than they are when recoding. Nonetheless, it's important to be careful about specifying boundaries between numerical categories, lest confusion result. For instance, if a variable is recoded so that zero to 10 equals 1, 10 to 20 equals 2, 20 to 30 equals 3, and so on, in which categories will the values 10, 20, 30, and so on be classified? It's an ambiguous issue because the rule of mutual exclusivity was violated by the "overlap." Most programs will capture a value in the first category in which it's included—*most,* but perhaps not all!

When listing values to recode data, it's *never* advisable to allow overlap. Instead, the specification should be in either of two forms: zero to *9* equals 1, 10 to *19* equals 2, 20 to *29* equals 3, and so on, or, alternatively, zero to 10 equals 1, *11* to 20 equals 2, *21* to 30 equals 3, and so on, depending on which is more meaningful for the information seeker.

When new categories are formed and the data recoded into them, it's very important that the categories are *meaningful* ones. Thus, the thing being measured and the underlying conditions should show more variation *between* categories than within them. For instance, the behavior and opportunities resulting from education wouldn't be expected to differ as much between those who left high school in their sophomore year and those who left in their junior year. On the other hand, there's likely to be a substantial difference between those who quit and those who graduated. Consequently, in the example, those with 9, 10, and 11 years are grouped together. Similarly, those with 13, 14, and 15 years could all be grouped into the category—*Some College.* Those with 12 years and those with 16 years of education had presumably graduated from high school or college, respectively, and so they would be grouped into a separate category from those who had attended but not finished.

Recoding and category *n*-sizes

The shorthand term used to designate the number of respondents or cases in a sample, subsample, or category of a variable is *n-size.* In their other words, it just means the *number* of respondents or cases. Normally, the *broader* the categories and the *fewer* the categories into which the data for a variable are recoded, the *larger* their *n*-size will be. Inversely, the *narrower* the cateogries and the *more* the categories into which data are recoded, the *smaller* their *n*-size will be. The goal is to produce categories whose *n*-sizes are neither too large nor too small.

During the recoding process, the analyst should run some preliminary data description routines, such as frequency and percentage tables or bar charts, to determine how many respondents are in each newly created category. If the *n*-size of a newly formed category is too large—for instance, over half the entire sample—it may contain cases or respondents who are actually quite dissimilar to one another in some important respects. Yet, the distinctions among them would be lost, since they occupy the same category on this variable. Newly combined categories with an overly large proportion of the sample should be again recoded from the *original* values into more, *smaller* categories for analysis.

At the other extreme, it's rarely advisable to have a category containing only a very small number or percentage of responses. The categories that contain only a few cases or respondents are seldom useful or meaningful to those seeking the information. They represent too small a proportion of the population. What's more, *percentage* information based on very small *n*-sizes can be misleading if the variable is cross-tabulated or compared with other variables.

Suppose a sample contains about 50 respondents in each of four categories and only 5 respondents in the fifth category. Subsequent analysis might reveal that only about 20 percent of the respondents in each of the first four categories were members of a particular organization while *80 percent* of the fifth category were members. It would *appear* that there's a strong association between being in the fifth category and being a member. Yet, that association is based on the membership status of only *five* respondents, four of whom belong and one of whom does not.

Statistical comparisons between variables, such as cross-tabulation (to be discussed in the next chapter), would probably reveal that the relationship described in the preceding paragraph was *not* statistically significant—that it was probably just due to chance. Yet many such comparative statistics *require* a sufficient number of respondents within each category if they're to yield reliable results. Thus, the statistical tools themselves may demand that each category of nominal data have a satisfactory number of cases or respondents. When the *n*-size of either an original category or one newly created by recoding is too small, the category should be *combined* with an adjacent or similar one.

When a survey variable has been transformed, recoded, or used to create a new variable in a different form, the analyst should note these changes on the blank key questionnaire that's used as a working document or index of the actual data file. While it may appear to be fairly easy to keep these changes and modifications in mind, that seldom proves to be the case. If the work extends over several days or working sessions, as it normally does, there's a tendency to forget modifications or changes in the data file or programs. There's less danger that confusion will result if a brief record of these changes is diligently maintained. The main data recoding considerations are outlined in Checklist 9–3.

Subsample Selection

Some analysis programs allow the researcher to select only certain cases from the entire data file for particular tasks or analyses. Thus, the cases selected form a "subsample" of data from which the reports are generated. When the analysis routine doesn't contain such a provision and there's a need to select only certain groups or categories of respondents, such as only males, or only those in a certain occupation, these cases may also be singled out and segregated into a separate data file for analysis. When such subsample selections are used to generate reports, it's important that the subsamples are recorded and the details noted on the report, so information seekers can clearly tell the results are based on only a certain portion of the entire sample or represent only a specific group within the population.

Report Labeling

Virtually all spreadsheet and charting programs and most statistical analysis programs allow the user to enter names or labels for the variables and categories to be analyzed. These names or labels are usually limited to a specific number of letters or characters, so it may not be possible to list the entire item from the questionnaire. Instead, the analyst should create brief names or abbreviated labels to stand for each item or variable and each category of nominal

---

CHECKLIST 9–3

To Recode Survey Data

1. Would different categories be more meaningful for analysis and interpretation than those in which the data were gathered? If so, create new categories by recoding the variable.

2. Is there a need to portray continuous numeric data with a large number of values in frequency tables or bar charts? If so, recode the data into a dozen or fewer larger categories.

3. Might there be a need to maintain continuous numeric distributions for statistical analysis? If so, form a new variable identical to the original and recode the new one into categories.

4. Are the new categories *all-inclusive,* so every original value can be recoded into a new category? If *not,* change the classifications or include a miscellaneous category for "other" responses.

5. Are the new categories *mutually exclusive,* so each original value can be recoded into only *one* new category? If not, change the recoding specification to eliminate the overlap.

6. Is there more variation in the underlying meaning of the variable *between* the new categories than within them? If not, select new categories that have greater meaning.

7. Do any of the new categories have very large proportions of the cases or respondents within them? If so, divide the large categories into meaningful ones with smaller proportions of the sample in each.

8. Do any of the original or new categories have very small numbers of the cases or respondents within them? If so, combine them with adjacent or similar categories to form categories containing larger numbers of cases.

---

data, including those created by recoding. The names and labels should be listed on the key questionnaire or working index document. Doing so will avoid mistakes or confusion at later stages of analysis.

Some inexperienced survey research analysts may be inclined to skip the rather tedious, time-consuming job of entering a long list of variable names and category labels into the spreadsheet, charting program table, or analysis program. The longer the list, the greater is the temptation to avoid the task. And the longer the list, the *more important* it is to do it! There's a very compelling reason: These names and labels ordinarily need to be entered only *once* at the data preparation stage. If it isn't done now, it might be necessary to do the naming and labeling *many, many times* on output and reports generated by analysis programs.

Some analysis programs may lack provisions for labeling the variables, categories, and tasks performed on their reports. They may merely list or report the variables in the sequence of the data format used for a particular task, such as "Variable 1." If that's the case, the variable listed by the routine as number one may or may not be the first variable on the questionnaire or in the entire data file. For example, if a task used only the 13th and the 65th variable of the questionnaire, only those may be specified in the format statement for the program. The routine would see them only as *first* and *second.* In short, the analysis program may not "know" about all of the variables, and may number or label only those it has been instructed to recognize or analyze. With such routines, it's *vitally important* to clearly label the print output after *each* report is generated—while it's still perfectly clear which survey variables were processed and what was run. Otherwise, the researcher may be faced with the totally unpleasant task of trying to figure out which of dozens of pages contain the report on which variables or what procedures.

SUMMARY

Survey Data Preparation

A. Get a head start. Prepare for processing while the questionnaires are still in the field.

B. Expect a large volume of paperwork. Surveys generate more material than many researchers anticipate.

C. Keep it neat and orderly. Have a place for everything and keep everything in its place.

D. Maintain adequate records. Record things promptly and make notes rather than depending on recollection.

E. Sight-edit documents thoroughly. Establish criteria for acceptance or rejection of completed questionnaires and use them consistently.

F. Postcode questionnaires carefully. Every item that isn't precoded must be assigned a code value and be recorded in the codebook.

G. Monitor data transfer. Be sure the data are keyed or recorded in files promptly and accurately.

H. Edit the computer data files. Check to be sure the records conform to the format and the variable values are within range.

I. Identify scale data types. Record the designations on a "key" questionnaire to use as a working guide.

J. Reclassify data with care. Select categories that are more meaningful, and recode continuous items with many values into fewer but larger categories.

K. Enter names and labels. List variable names and category labels on the key questionnaire and enter them into the analysis routines.

PART IV

Interpreting and Reporting Results

Chapter 10

Analyzing the Results

STATISTICAL TOOL SELECTION

Data analysis requires the use of a set of statistical tools that reduce the amount of detail in the data, summarizing it and making the most important facts and relationships apparent. The researcher need not know a great deal about the internal workings of the statistical tools in order to use them effectively. On the other hand, the analyst must be able to select the correct statistical tool to generate the information required, based on the type of data. As with any tool, there are two types of things that dictate what statistical tool should be used or would work best: the nature of the data—the "material" to which the tool is applied, and the nature of the report—the "product" that's to be created. In other words, the researcher has to know what tool would work best for a particular type of data and a particular type of report. Ironically, those who learn a great deal about the tools themselves are often still in a quandary about which to use in a given situation. That's because they lack information about the types of data such statistical tools require and the type of information that can be obtained from each of the statistical procedures.

The types of scales and data were discussed in the previous chapter. This chapter describes two general categories of statistical tools used to analyze survey data: those used to describe individual survey items, and those used to measure associations or relationships between two variables. There are several statistical tools in each category. It isn't as important for the research analyst to know how these statistical tools work as it is to know *how to use them correctly!* Since the choice of an appropriate statistical tool depends so heavily on the type of data to be analyzed, this discussion will focus more on the characteristics of the data distributions than on the workings of the statistics themselves.

It's almost never appropriate to use the same statistical tool for every survey item. Some scales are different from others, and they require different tools for their analysis. *Nominal, ordinal, interval,* and *ratio* scales were described in the previous chapter. The analyst has to be completely familiar with these scale types to select the proper statistical tools described in the chapter.

The data from each, individual survey question or item is known as a "variable" because it can vary from one respondent to the next. Some statistical tools, called "univariate" statistics, are used to describe just *one* variable at a time. Others, known as "bivariate" statistics, may include *two* variables and show the relationship *between* them. Still others, called "multivariate" statistics, may include *several* variables and show the *pattern* of relationships among them.

Virtually all survey analyses use univariate statistics. Almost all surveys also use bivariate statistical tools. Only more elaborate survey analyses use multivariate statistical analysis. This chapter will include univariate and bivariate analyses, but it will exclude multivariate statistics. If and when multivariate statistical analysis is required, the researcher should get assistance from a specialist or refer to one of the many textbooks or computer program manuals for guidance and instruction.

Category Data Description

Survey questionnaire items or variables form "distributions." The choices or values respondents provide for any item are *distributed* across some spectrum of *values* or response *categories.* Usually, the analyst's first analysis task is to run data descriptions for each variable.

Frequency and percentage tables

Frequency and percentage distributions of response, or just *frequency* tables for short, are the most common form of data description for a limited number of values or categories. All nominal scales yield *categorical* data, but numeric data distributions from ordinal, interval, and ratio scales can also be treated as categorical and be described in frequency tables if there are a limited number of different scale values—about a dozen or less. Frequency tables provide a very complete picture of the distribution of data for the variable. Their use is limited mainly by the number of scale points or categories that can be shown. When there are a dozen or fewer categories or scale points, frequency tables are ordinarily practical and meaningful to researchers.

Example 10–1 shows the frequency and percentage of respondents at five levels of education. The tables in this example are very typical of those generated by several different computer programs for analyzing survey data. Starting from the left, the first column of the frequency tables in Example 10–1 shows the labels for the various categories. When only numbers with a limited range are being reported, such as "trips to the bank in the past week" or "number of coffee breaks taken yesterday," no labels may be required and the column would be blank.

The second column of the frequency tables in Example 10–1 shows the code value. This is merely the precode or postcode that was assigned to the alternative or answer and keyed to the computer file. The third column, labeled "Freq.," is the *number* of respondents that indicated that particular response. This value is sometimes of interest, but in most situations the percentages are more meaningful.

The fourth column of the frequency tables, Pct., in Example 10–1 is the percentage of all respondents to the survey or to that section of the questionnaire who indicated each of

EXAMPLE 10–1

Frequency Table Print Output

No Missing Values Specified

Category	Code	Freq.	Pct.	Adj.	Cum.
Some high school	1.	28	4.2	4.2	4.2
High school graduate	2.	191	28.5	28.5	32.7
Some college	3.	141	21.0	21.0	53.7
College graduate	4.	136	20.3	20.3	74.0
Postgraduate	5.	118	17.6	17.6	91.5
Refused	6.	57	8.5	8.5	100.0
Total		671	100.0	100.0	100.0

Zero Specified as a Missing Value

Category	Code	Freq.	Pct.	Adj.	Cum.
Some high school	1.	28	4.2	4.6	4.6
High school graduate	2.	191	28.5	31.1	35.7
Some college	3.	141	21.0	23.0	58.6
College graduate	4.	136	20.3	22.1	80.8
Postgraduate	5.	118	17.6	19.2	100.0
Refused	0.	57	8.5	---	---
Total		671	100.0	100.0	100.0

the various alternatives. In other words, this is the percentage distribution rather than the frequency distribution. These percentages are computed by dividing the frequency for each category by the total number of respondents to the survey or section. The decimal point is moved two places to the right to express the fraction as a percentage.

The next to the last column in Example 10–1 is labeled "Adj." for "adjusted percentages." The "adjustment" is based on the missing values for the variable being reported. This *isn't* the same as those who failed to respond to the survey. There will ordinarily be some respondents who participate in the survey and provide completed questionnaires but fail to respond to some individual items. For example, they may refuse to list their education or income, they may simply skip the item by mistake, or they might not complete it for some other reason. It's usually not practical to discard all questionnaires that aren't *perfectly* complete. To do so would often eliminate a large part of the responding sample. So the adjusted percentages are computed in the same way as the previous ones, except they're based on only those who responded to *that particular item*.

Notice that in the upper portion of Example 10–1 the percentages and the adjusted percentages are identical. That's because those who refused to indicate their educational level were assigned a code value of six and weren't specified as "missing values." They're included in the adjusted percentage column. By contrast, in the lower section of Example 10–1, those who refused were assigned a code of zero and that value was listed in the program that generated the table as a missing value for that item. Thus, the 8.5 percent of respondents who failed or refused to answer the item are listed in the percentage column, but nothing is listed in the adjusted percentage column. The dashed line indicates the percentage isn't zero, but rather that the percentage for this alternative isn't applicable. In this table, the adjusted percentages differ from the unadjusted, and of course they're slightly larger because they're based on a smaller total.

The last column at the far right of the frequency table in Example 10–1 is labeled "Cum." to designate "cumulative percentages." The percentage for the first row of the table will always be the same as the adjusted percentage for that row. The cumulative percentage for the second row is the sum of the adjusted percentages for the first and second rows, and so forth. Each cumulative percentage is the total of the *adjusted* percentages for that row and those above it.

Cumulative percentages have little meaning or value for nominal data, where the categories aren't related to one another in any fashion. They're meaningful and they can be quite useful when ordinal, interval, or ratio data are shown in a frequency table. In the lower section of Example 10–1, the reader of the table can easily see that nearly 59 percent of those responding have less than a college education. When the rows are ordered from "lowest" to "highest," the value of the column for any row shows the percentage of respondents who are in that category or "less," and 100 minus the value shows what percentage were "greater." The cumulative percentages also indicate the approximate point or value on the scale at which those in the 50th or some other percentile reside. Percentile merely means those who rank at some place out of 100 typical cases.

Often several columns on frequency tables such as those shown in Example 10–1 are of little or no interest to the analyst or information seekers. The listing of the code values themselves is useful for checking and editing data to be sure it's correct, but once that's been done, they have no real meaning. So they're not usually listed in final reports. The frequency distributions are more difficult to interpret than the *percentage* distributions, so they may or may not be included in the report table.

Percentage distribution tables

The percentage distributions are often more easily interpreted and of more interest than are the frequency distributions. This is because percentages can be compared from one item or survey to the next, even though they may be based on different total frequencies. More importantly, the sample percentages can be used directly as an estimate of the percentages of the total population that might indicate each alternative response. Thus, the percentage distribution is often the most important column on the frequency table for those interpreting the survey results.

Example 10–2 shows two percentage distribution table formats. Usually the *adjusted* percentage distribution is more meaningful than the unadjusted percentages. If only the adjusted percentages are shown, the *n*-size listed should be a number for *that variable or item,* rather than the number of respondents for the entire sample. The *cumulative* percentage distribution is useful only in special cases.

Graphic data description

Some statistical analysis routines, most spreadsheets, and all charting programs have the ability to describe category data in graphic form rather than frequency tables. Figure 10–1 contains

EXAMPLE 10–2

Percentage Distribution Tables

Frequency and Percentage Reported

Educational Level	Number	Percent
Some high school	28	4.2
High school graduate	191	28.5
Some college	141	21.0
College graduate	136	20.3
Postgraduate	118	17.6
Refused	57	8.5
Total	671	100.0

Percentage Only Reported

Educational Level (*N* for Item = 614)	Percent
Some high school	4.6
High school graduate	31.1
Some college	23.0
College graduate	22.1
Postgraduate	19.2

two bar charts portraying the same data as that shown in Examples 10–1 and 10–2. Spreadsheets and charting programs may offer vertical plots, pie charts that show proportions, or other graphic displays of the categories in the distribution. These graphic formats will be discussed in more detail in Chapter 12.

Continuous Distribution Description

Frequency tables cannot be used to describe continuous numeric distributions with a large number of values, but there are a variety of ways they can be described by statistics. Different types of scales require different types of statistics. There are three different characteristics of

Figure 10–1   *Frequency and Percentage Bar Charts*

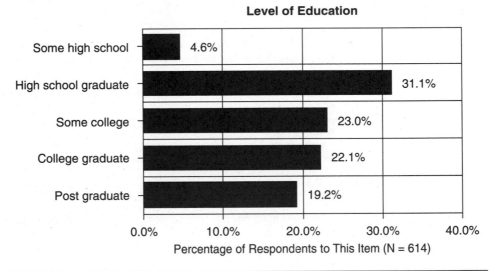

the distribution that researchers ordinarily measure and describe: (1) *average*—the most typical value; (2) *spread*—the amount of deviation from the average; and (3) *shape*—the form of the distribution. The technical term for a coefficient that indicates the most typical value is a "measure of central tendency." Measures of central tendency will be referred to here simply as "averages." The technical name for the amount of deviation from the average is *dispersion* or *variance*. The term *spread* will be used here to indicate the amount of deviation from the central point or average. The form of the distribution will be called its *shape* in the discussion

Figure 10–2   *Tool Selection for Descriptive Statistics*

Scale Type	Average	Spread	Shape
Nominal	Mode		
Ordinal	Median Mode	Range Maximum and minimum	
Interval	Mean Median Mode	Standard deviation Range Maximum and minimum	Skewness Kurtosis
Ratio	Mean Median Mode	Standard deviation Range Maximum and minimum	Skewness Kurtosis

that follows. The statistics to describe distributions of the four different types of data are shown in Figure 10–2.

In order to select the most appropriate statistical tool, the analyst has to identify which of the four types of scale data the variable represents. When more than one coefficient could be used, the most common and most often appropriate is listed first, followed by the next most likely. In general, any tool that's appropriate for a "lower level" of scale data (one listed above in the table) would be acceptable for the scales of a higher level (listed below it in the table), although it may not be the most preferable. If no statistic is listed in the table, as in the case of spread or shape for nominal or ordinal data, this means no common statistical coefficient is appropriate to describe them, and the distributions may have to be described in tabular or graphic form.

Central Tendency and Averages

In most cases, the use of the term *average* refers to the *arithmetic* mean, but this is only one of several averages that can be used. The three averages described each has different characteristics that make it more appropriate for some distributions and less for others. The average of a distribution is almost always reported because it represents the most typical response, or the researchers' "best guess" of how someone picked at random from the population sampled would respond. The choice is often based on the type of scale data that forms the distribution.

The mean

The arithmetic mean, usually called simply the *mean,* is the most common average used to indicate the most typical response. While the median and mode can also be used to describe central tendency for interval or ratio data, the mean is usually the most meaningful statistic. It's computed simply by dividing the sum of the values by the number of values or cases.

While the mean is the most commonly used average, it has some restrictions and limitations that make other averages more appropriate in some situations. First, it isn't valid to use the mean for *nominal* data because the values are merely names. If unmarried respondents were assigned a code value of one and married respondents a value of two, it wouldn't make sense to compute the *mean* marital status. If half the respondents were married, the mean would have the fractional value of 1.5, but that would be meaningless because respondents are either married or they aren't. Consequently, it would be completely invalid to say the most typical respondent was "half single and half married," since that's impossible.

The mean shouldn't be used for ordinal data, such as that obtained from an ordinal scale or a set of rankings. That's because with ordinal data, the code values indicate only that each sequential value is *greater than* those with a lower value and *less than* those with a higher value. Consequently, the intervals between code values on the ordinal scale aren't necessarily equal. A fractional value would have little meaning. Thus, the median or mode is a more appropriate average for ordinal data.

Even with distributions of interval or ratio data, there are some situations where the mean has limitations that may make another average a more appropriate and meaningful representation of the most typical case. The mean tends to be overly sensitive to influence by only one or a few *extreme* values in the distribution, known as *outliers,* because they lie outside the normal range. An example may clarify this. Example 10–3 shows two distributions of ratio data—contributions to a charitable fund drive. The maximum contribution

EXAMPLE 10–3

Outlier Effects on Averages

No Outlier					One Outlier			
Amount	**Number**	**Percent**	**Cum.**		**Amount**	**Number**	**Percent**	**Cum.**
$1.00	25	6.3	6.3		$1.00	25	6.3	6.3
$2.00	150	37.5	43.8		$2.00	150	37.5	43.8
$3.00	125	31.3	75.0		$3.00	125	31.3	75.0
$4.00	75	18.8	93.8		$4.00	75	18.8	93.8
$5.00	25	6.3	100.0		$5.00	20	5.0	98.8
					$50.00	**5**	**1.3**	100.0
Total	400	100.0			Total	400	100.0	

Mean	**Median**	**Mode**	**Mean**	**Median**	**Mode**
$2.80	$3.00	$2.00	**$3.38**	$3.00	$2.00

on the frequency table at the left was $5. The distribution shown on the right is exactly the same, except that five people gave $50 instead of $5—there are five *outliers*.

Although these five cases constitute only about 1 percent of the sample, their presence changed the mean from $2.80 to $3.38. To be meaningful and useful, an *average* should be an indication of the most typical respondent. Yet, with outliers, the mean isn't very typical of either the vast majority of cases or of the outliers. Notice, however, that the median and mode are exactly the same for both distributions. Both are completely insensitive to changes in extreme values.

The median

The median value for a distribution is another form of average or indication of the "most typical" case. The value of the median is readily computed by the analysis routine, but it's easily understood logically. Suppose all of the cases in the sample are arrayed in order from the lowest to the highest value for the variable. The median would be the value for the "middle" case in the array. In both frequencies in Example 10–3, inspection of the *cumulative* frequencies shows the *50th percentile*, or the middle value, is $3.00 for both distributions. Since it's merely the middle value, the median isn't affected by changes in extreme values or the existence of outliers. To put it another way, the middle value or median will be the same, no matter how much greater or lesser the values on the extremes turn out to be. Consequently, the median is likely to be more typical of the *majority* of cases in the distribution and a better average to use than the mean with asymmetrical distributions where there are outliers. The *shape* of the distribution will be discussed more fully later in this chapter. It's important to note that the median is also preferable for distribution of *ordinal* data.

The mode

The mode is simply the category or value with the greatest frequency of cases. It's the only acceptable indicator of the most typical case for distributions of nominal data. In Figure 10–3, based on Example 10–3, the mode is $2.00 for both distributions because that

Figure 10–3 *Distributions With and Without Outliers*

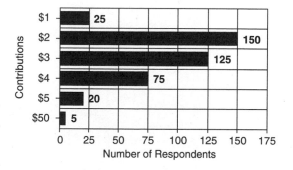

category has the highest frequency and percentage of cases in both. This category would be the "best guess" for predicting how much any one member of the population sampled would contribute. In other words, it's the *most likely* value an individual has contributed or would contribute.

Continuous numeric distributions of ordinal, interval, and ratio data also have one *primary* modal value. In the distributions shown in Figure 10–4 and Figure 10–5, the mode is the "peak" of the distribution—the high point, where the line tapers off toward a lower frequency in either direction. Often there will be just one such point—a *primary* mode only—

Figure 10–4   *Normal and Skewed Distributions*

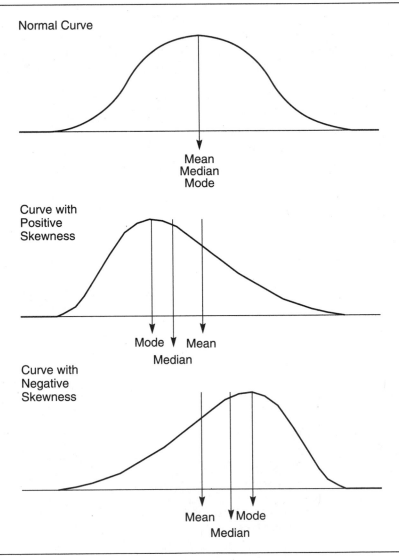

Figure 10–5   *Normality and Kurtosis of Distributions*

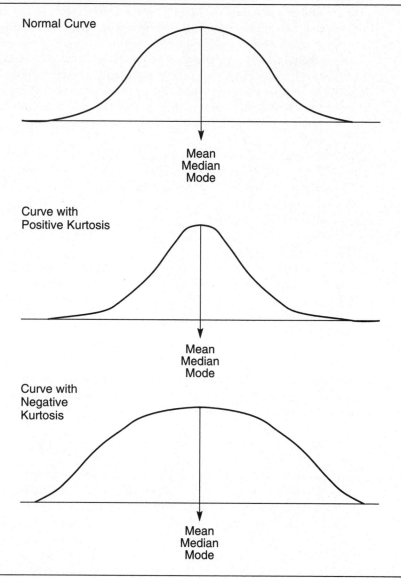

but those cases where there are more than one will be discussed more fully later in this chapter.

Measures of Dispersion or Spread

Continuous numeric distributions of ordinal, interval, or ratio data have a value that's regarded as "most typical." They also tend to be spread out around that value, usually in both directions. The amount of spread or *dispersion* around the average is often as meaningful to the analyst and information seekers as the value of the average itself. One way to gauge the spread of a distribution is to portray it graphically in a plot or chart. While graphic displays of distributions are often useful, they have some shortcomings that limit their value during analysis: They take considerable time and effort to create, they require a lot of space, and, most importantly, they can't be manipulated mathematically or statistically. Consequently, the analyst will often have to depend on numeric coefficients or values that describe the amount of dispersion or spread of the distributions of variables to be analyzed.

Maximum and minimum

The minimum value indicates how far the spread extends toward the lower direction, and the maximum value shows the extent of spread toward the upper direction from the average. These values are often of interest simply because they define the *extremes* of the distribution. They describe the respondents or cases that represent the least and the most on whatever dimension is being measured.

Range of the distribution

The range is simply the maximum minus the minimum, showing the total spread between extremes. While the maximum, minimum, and range may certainly be of interest for many distributions, they're often lacking in one important respect: They're defined only in terms of the extreme values. Unfortunately, they say nothing about the spread of the cases within those boundaries.

Standard deviation

Fortunately, there's a measure of spread or dispersion that permits the researcher to estimate and report the *proportion* of respondents or cases within certain ranges in the center part of the distribution, as well as toward the extremes, *providing that the distribution doesn't deviate very markedly from the normal, bell-shaped curve.* The *standard deviation* is a measure of the deviation or spread away from the mean. It's a single value that indicates the amount of spread in a distribution. It's routinely computed by statistical analysis programs and often by spreadsheets and charting programs as well. It can be computed quite easily by the more sophisticated hand calculators, provided there are only a limited number of cases and variables to be entered. (Mathematically, the standard deviation is the root mean squared [R.M.S.] deviations from the mean—the square root of the mean of the squared deviations.)

The standard deviation can be computed for any distribution, regardless of its shape, but when the distribution conforms closely to the standard normal distribution shown in the top section of Figure 10–4, a given proportion of the survey cases will always fall within certain ranges that are determined by the standard deviation (S.D.) of the distribution. Thus, the standard deviation is an excellent indicator of spread, and its interpretation will be discussed more fully in the following chapter.

Shape of the Distribution

The shape of a distribution can be inspected by displaying it graphically. That's often useful, but the same limitations to graphic portrayal cited earlier still apply: It takes substantial time, effort, and space, and graphs can't be manipulated statistically. Thus, the analyst often depends on two coefficients that indicate the degree and direction for distributions of interval and ratio data with large numbers of values that deviate from a normal distribution. They're the coefficients of skewness and kurtosis.

Skewness of distributions

The *skewness* of a distribution is a measure of the degree and direction of its *asymmetry*. If a distribution is symmetrical, such as the normal curve shown in Figure 10–4, one side of the distribution is precisely the "mirror-image" of the other and the coefficient of skewness will be zero. Often distributions of data for survey variables are somewhat asymmetrical; they "lean" toward one direction or the other.

In the middle section of Figure 10–4, the bulk of the distribution is skewed to the left, toward the lower values of the distribution. The extreme values tail out from the mode further to the right or higher side than toward the left or lower side. The coefficient of skewness for a distribution with such a configuration will have a *positive* value. In the reverse case, shown in the lower section of Figure 10–4, the coefficient of skewness will be negative. So the *sign* of the coefficient of skewness indicates which *direction* the distribution is skewed. The *absolute magnitude* of the coefficient of skewness indicates just how much the distribution deviates from symmetry—how much different one side is from the other.

It's often important to measure the degree of skewness in a continuous numeric distribution with many values when the data are analyzed to provide data description. That's because the standard deviation, as a description of spread, provides a close estimate of the proportion of cases within a given range around the mean *only* if the distribution is *symmetrical,* as with the normal curve. Thus, the sign and the value of skewness indicate the degree of *accuracy* with which the standard deviation can be used to estimate the amount of spread in the distribution. In addition, several statistical measures of the *association* between pairs of variables, to be discussed in the next chapter, are inaccurate and illegitimate if one or both distributions deviate significantly from symmetry.

Kurtosis of distributions

The *kurtosis* of a distribution is an indication of how peaked or flat it is, compared to the normal curve. The value of the coefficient of kurtosis for a normal curve is zero. In the middle section of Figure 10–5, the distribution has a higher, more narrow peak, with the tails extending out in each direction at a low level. The coefficient of kurtosis will be positive. By contrast, a negative value of kurtosis indicates a curve such as that shown in the lower section of Figure 10–5. It has a broad, low peak and "wings" that extend out at a rather high level before falling off. The distributions shown in Figure 10–5 are all symmetrical (with zero skewness), but either the coefficient of skewness or of kurtosis can be computed for any distribution, regardless of the value of the other.

Example 10–4 contains the data description coefficients for the two distributions of data shown in Example 10–3 and Figure 10–3. For both distributions, the median contribution is $3, the modal contribution is $2, and the minimum is $1. The mean increased over 50 percent, from $2.18 to $3.38. All the other coefficients changed dramatically with the inclusion of the outliers. While the standard deviation and coefficient of skewness were extended

EXAMPLE 10–4

Data Distribution Statistics

No Outliers		Some Outliers	
Mean	2.183	Mean	3.375
Median	3.000	Median	3.000
Mode	2.000	Mode	2.000
Standard Deviation	1.015	Standard Deviation	5.344
Skewness	0.383	Skewness	8.355
Kurtosis	−0.488	Kurtosis	70.707
Maximum	5.000	Maximum	50.000
Minimum	1.000	Minimum	1.000
Range	4.000	Range	49.000

substantially by the inclusion of outliers, the coefficient of *kurtosis* increased almost 150 times in absolute value.

At first glance, the bar charts for the two distributions shown in Figure 10–3 appear to be quite similar. That's because bar charts are designed mainly to display *nominal* data where the categories don't take on a magnitude or stand in any sequential relationship to one another. So the $5 contributions and the $50 contributions are merely treated as two different *categories* on a bar chart. There's no indication that one is ten times the other. By contrast, examination of the descriptive coefficients in Example 10–4 clearly indicate that one distribution is markedly different from the other.

While bar charts don't display the *shape* of a data distribution, area plots such as those shown in Figure 10–6 do. They portray the shape of the distribution, taking into regard the *numeric value* of each data point rather than treating each as an independent category. Examination of these plots makes it easy to see why the coefficients of skewness, and especially kurtosis, are so different for these distributions.

When no outliers are present, as in the upper plot of Figure 10–6, the shape is a rough approximation of a normal distribution. The coefficient of skewness is near zero because the curve is fairly symmetrical. The coefficient of kurtosis is only very slightly negative, indicating there's a little less data in the tails of the distribution than there would be in a normal curve.

By contrast, the distribution containing outliers plotted in the lower section of Figure 10–6 is obviously very asymmetrical—skewed sharply to the left with a tail extending far out to the right. Thus, the value of the coefficient of skewness for that curve exceeds +8.

Figure 10–6   *Data Plots With and Without Outliers*

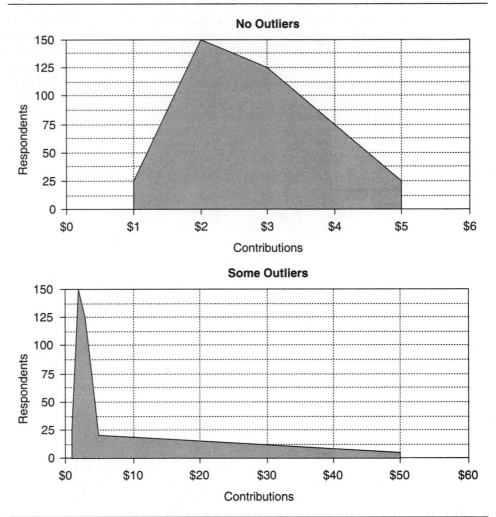

Similarly, since there is much more data in the right tail of the distribution, because of the outliers, the coefficient of kurtosis exceeds +70, indicating radical departure from normal.

If the coefficient of kurtosis departs substantially from zero, that also excludes using the standard deviation as a meaningful measure of spread. The standard deviation will accurately indicate how much data is within given ranges of the mean only when the data distribution approximates a normal curve. The interpretation of skewness, kurtosis, and standard deviation is discussed more fully in the following chapter. It's only necessary to note here that these coefficients should usually be obtained for continuous numeric distributions with a large number of values during the data description phase of analysis.

RELATIONSHIPS BETWEEN VARIABLES

The statistical tools and analyses discussed earlier allow the researcher to describe or portray individual variables. Analysis of individual variables may satisfy many of the information requirements, but typically the analyst will also want to learn about the *relationships* between pairs of variables. There may be substantial meaning in the description of each of two survey items viewed *individually*, but there may be even more interest in how they're related to one another. In other situations, there may be very little value in the results of two variables viewed *independently*, but, when studied in conjunction with one another, there may prove to be substantial value to the information.

This latter situation is demonstrated in Example 10–5. The percentage distribution shown in the upper left section indicates half of the respondents were of each sex. The percentage distribution displayed in the upper right section of Example 10–5 shows that half of all respondents agreed with the issue and half did not. If only these percentage distributions were presented, the analyst and information seekers would remain ignorant of the relationship between these two variables—sex of respondent and agreement with the issue. They would probably *assume* that about half of all men and half of all women in the population were in agreement. Unfortunately, that would be a serious error.

In the lower section of Example 10–5, these same two variables are *cross-tabulated* with

EXAMPLE 10–5

Interaction Between Variables

Percentage Distributions of Response			
Sex of Respondent		**Agreement with Issue**	
Men	50%	Agree	50%
Women	50%	Disagree	50%
Total	100%	Total	100%

Cross-tabulation of Variables			
	Men	**Women**	**Both**
Agree	25%	75%	50%
Disagree	75%	25%	50%
Total	50%	50%	100%

one another. The row and column totals at the right and on the bottom agree with the percentage distributions shown above. But the really *pertinent* information lies in the cells of the *body* of the table. It turns out that *three times* as many women as men are in agreement with the issue in question. Equipped with this information, the survey sponsor or information seekers may address the men and women in their audience very differently or otherwise adjust their actions toward their public, depending on their sex. If so, the principal value of the information doesn't lie in knowing about individual variables, but in knowing about their *relationship* to one another!

When the responses to a pair of survey items or variables are compared to one another, over the individual respondents, there are two possible results: either the answers to the two items may vary or "move" together, indicating they're significantly related to one another, or they may be completely independent of one another, indicating there's no relationship between the two. The statistical tools to measure associations (relationships) between variables are designed to indicate precisely that: whether they are systematically related or completely independent.

Dependent and Independent Variables

When two variables are associated with one another, they may have one of two types of relationships: one can be regarded as partially *causing* or determining the value of the other, or they may be viewed simply as varying or changing together, *without* any causal implications. It's important to note that the statistics used to measure associations don't indicate whether or not one is causing another. That must be determined by the researcher, based on knowledge about the meaning of the items or variables, themselves. The statistics only measure the presence and degree of relationship between items. The existence and direction of causality must be inferred by the researcher, in advance, because the choice of an appropriate statistical tool often depends on whether or not a *causal* relationship is implied.

The selection of the proper statistical tool for the task at hand is just as important for measurement of association between variables as it is for portraying or describing individual items. When individual items are analyzed, the choice of the proper statistical tools depends on the type of variable described or portrayed. Similarly, the choice of an appropriate statistical tool to measure association does depend on the types of variables being analyzed, but it also depends on whether *causality* is implied. If it is, it also matters which item is being affected by the other. Thus, to choose the proper statistical tool to measure a relationship between two items, the researcher must determine two things: What type of variable each item is, and which item will be viewed as "dependent" and which as "independent" if causality is implied. The dependent variable is the one being caused or affected, and the independent variable is the one causing or affecting the other.

The analyst should first determine the variable types and direction of causality, and then refer to the simple matrix shown in Figure 10–7 to select the proper statistical measure of association. Nominal and ordinal data in categories and continuous numeric distributions of interval and ratio data were identified and described in the previous chapter. The analyst should be thoroughly familiar with these different types of data in order to select the proper statistical tool to measure association.

With some statistical measures of association, it doesn't make any difference whether one

Figure 10–7   *Statistical Measures of Association*

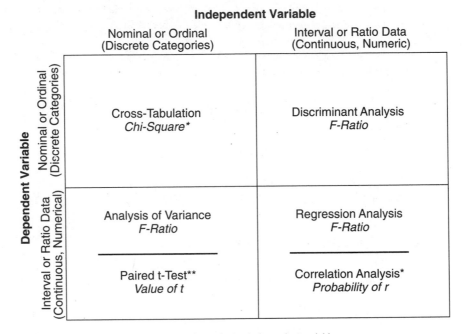

Independent Variable

	Nominal or Ordinal (Discrete Categories)	Interval or Ratio Data (Continuous, Numeric)
Nominal or Ordinal (Discrete Categories)	Cross-Tabulation *Chi-Square**	Discriminant Analysis *F-Ratio*
Interval or Ratio Data (Continuous, Numerical)	Analysis of Variance *F-Ratio* ——— Paired t-Test** *Value of t*	Regression Analysis *F-Ratio* ——— Correlation Analysis* *Probability of r*

Dependent Variable

* Either variable may be regarded as the dependent or independent variable.
** The *independent* variable defines the pairs. Both are *continuous, dependent.*

item is causing or affecting the other and, if so, which is affecting the other. Other statistical tools for measuring the association between variables do require the analyst to decide which one can be regarded as affecting the other. The variable that's causing the other to vary or affecting the other is called the *independent* variable. The variable that's being affected or that's presumed to vary because of the value of independent variables is called the *dependent* variable. The direction of causality is from *independent* variable to *dependent* variable.

Merely knowing the name of a variable or what it represents doesn't necessarily indicate whether it will be a dependent or an independent variable for a particular measure of association. The analyst has to know more than that about the meaning of the variables and the possible relationships or dynamics between them. The dependent and independent variables are *operationally defined*—they're identified by how they *operate,* not what they are. The analyst must study the nature of the two items and determine which, if either, is likely to cause or affect the other. At first glance, it might seem that such survey items as demographic characteristics will always be independent variables, while opinions or attitudes are nearly always dependent variables. While that's usually the case, it's certainly not always so in every conceivable situation.

Some survey items may be treated as independent variables for some measure of association or in relation to one set of other variables, and then be treated as dependent variables for another measure of relationships with another set of items. The analyst should identify a variable as dependent or independent for *each analysis* or "pairing," rather than merely identifying each survey item as dependent or independent for all measures.

STATISTICAL MEASURES OF ASSOCIATION

The most common statistical tools to measure the relationship between two survey variables are listed in Figure 10–7. To identify the proper statistical tool, the analyst should identify each variable by type—*categorical* or *continuous*—and by operation—independent, dependent, or with no causality implied. Where no causality is implied and the focus is merely on the degree of association between the two variables, it doesn't matter which is regarded as independent and which dependent. Note, however, that only cross-tabulation and correlation analysis don't require specification of causality. All others listed in Figure 10–7 do require identification of dependence and independence. Once the variable types have been identified and the direction of causality determined, the analyst can refer to the appropriate row and column of the matrix to find the proper statistical tool to measure association. It's important to note, however, that there are *other conditions* regarding the data distributions that have to be met before some of these tools can be used legitimately. They will be discussed below.

An example of the use of the matrix for selecting a statistical tool may prove helpful. Suppose one survey item to be analyzed is the marital status of the respondents and it's a categorical variable, *married* or *not married*. Another survey item might be a simple, *yes/no* answer to some question. If the sponsor wanted to know if the sex of the respondent affects the answer to the yes/no item, sex would be the independent variable. It's a nominal, categorical variable, so the appropriate tool will be in the *first column* of the matrix. The yes/no item is the dependent variable, defining the rows of the matrix, and it's also a nominal, categorical variable, indicating the *top row*. To measure this relationship, the analyst would use cross-tabulation of the two items, because it's listed in the first column, top row. (The technical name for cross-tabulation is *contingency table analysis,* but it's often simply called *cross-tabs*.) The significance of the relationship would be indicated by the chi-square (pronounced *kie*-square) statistic. Thus, selection of the proper statistical tool is mostly a matter of finding the correct cell of the matrix by row and column.

Each of the statistical measures of association between variables listed in Figure 10–7 will be discussed in the remainder of this chapter. The focus here will be on the selection criteria and data requirements for each statistical tool. The interpretation of the coefficients and values each statistic yields will be discussed and exemplified in the following chapter. Readers who wish to focus specifically on only one particular statistical tool or method of analysis are encouraged to refer to the corresponding section on that method in Chapter 11 after examining the brief description of the tool and the selection criteria for using it provided in this chapter.

Cross-Tabulation

Cross-tabulation is by far the most common measure of association between survey variables. It's used much more frequently than all of the other techniques combined. Cross-tabulation is so common and popular in part because the method is effective, it can easily be understood and interpreted, and it can be tabulated very readily by spreadsheet, charting, and analysis programs. It's also very flexible and robust! In other words, it will readily accept any data that can be put into a limited number of categories. It may lack the power and sensitivity of other measures of association between variables, but cross-tabulation makes up for it by placing very few demands on the type of data it can legitimately analyze. So cross-tabulation is to the statistician's toolbox what a monkey wrench is to the mechanic's toolbox.

Very often, survey items that are continuous are obtained from scales that have only a few scale points or values, so these variables can be treated as categorical and used in cross-tabulation. Even when continuous survey variables have a wide-ranging scale with many values, the data can often be recoded into meaningful categories to provide categorical data for cross-tabulation with other items. This technique will be discussed in more detail below.

Cross-tabulation tables, or "cross-tabs," indicate the relationship between two categorical variables. The procedure doesn't require one variable to be identified as dependent and the other independent, although that's often the case, as it was for the cross-tab table shown in Example 10–5. If it is, either variable can be listed to define the rows or the columns of the table. The analyst is free to set up the table the way it's most readily interpreted and understood. The selection of row, column, and table frequencies will be discussed in more detail later.

There are only three, fairly basic requirements for using cross-tabs: (1) The data can be nominal, ordinal, interval, or ratio, but they must be in *categories*. (2) There should be a *limited number of categories* for each variable. (3) The total *n*-size or *number of cases* must be large enough to provide a sufficient minimum cell frequency.

Categorical data. Nominal data are always categorical, but ordinal, interval, and ratio data can often be treated as categorical, even though such data are numeric and hypothetically define a continuous spectrum of values. For example, values from a 5-point linear, numeric scale are equal-interval data, but the range of values is limited. There are no fractions or decimals in such data, and the integer values can be used to define five or seven categories for analysis of the relationship with another categorical variable using cross-tabs.

Number of categories. If an ordinal, interval, or ratio variable has a very large number of values—if it's truly continuous—it can usually be recoded rather easily into a small number of categories by the analysis program. This recoding process was discussed in the previous chapter. Thus, if the questionnaire asked the respondents to record their age or education in years or their income in dollars or thousands of dollars, there may be many different values for such variables. By recoding age into decades (20s, 30s, 40s, and so on), education into stages (some high school, high school graduate, some college, and so on), and income into broad categories of several thousands of dollars, these variables can be "reduced" into fewer than ten or twelve categories for cross-tabulation with other variables.

It's important to note that with such recoding of continuous variables into categories, some information is lost. Namely, the information about the *differences* between values that are cast into the same category are obliterated. All the cases within a given category are "seen" and treated as identical to one another. Thus, it may not always be advisable to recode such data and use cross-tabs if another statistical measure of association could be used to assess relationships with other survey variables. When it is necessary or desirable to recode continuous data into categories, the analyst should take precautions not to *destroy* the original continuous variable in the process. If the recoding is temporary and does not permanently modify the data file, the analyst can return to the continuous values at a latter stage of processing if necessary. When recoding *will* permanently change the variable, the recommended procedure is to first create a *new* variable identical to the original continuous one. Then one can be recoded into categories, leaving the continuity of the other intact.

Number of cases. Neither the frequency or percentage values in the cells of a cross-tab table nor the chi-square statistic used to judge the statistical significance of the relationship between variables is informative unless there are sufficient numbers of cases in the analysis. Specifically, there must be a sufficient number *in each column* and *on each row* of the table. Checking on the minimum *expected* cell frequency required by the chi-square statistic will be discussed in detail below. At this point it is important only to recognize that column and row totals are a function of three things: the total number of cases for analysis, the number of rows and the number of columns, and the way the data are distributed over the rows and columns.

If the sample size is large and the analyst is working with thousands of cases, it might be quite acceptable to have a 10-by-10 table; that is, a table formed by two variables with 10 values each. By contrast, if there are only 100 or fewer cases in the sample, there may be very few, if any, cases on some rows or in some columns of a large cross-tab table. The rule-of-thumb is simply this: If the *n*-size is relatively small, recode the variables so each has only a few categories, values, or "levels." The analyst should begin by looking at the frequency and percentage distributions for each variable to be submitted to cross-tab analysis. If there appear to be an adequate number on each level of each variable, they can be submitted to cross-tabulation. Fortunately, cross-tabulation is usually fairly quick and easy. If there are too few cases on some rows or columns, it's ordinarily a simple process to recode the variables and again run the cross-tab analysis. The more sophisticated the analysis programs are and the more adroit the analyst is, the easier it is to use simple trial-and-error to arrive at an acceptable number of rows and columns for cross-tabulation.

Cross-tabulation formats

There are a wide variety of formats for cross-tab tables, depending on the analysis routine used and the analyst's preferences. The tables range from the most clean, simple formats, such as that shown in the lower portion of Example 10–5. to more copious computer print outputs, such as the tables shown in Example 10–6. Both of the tables shown in Example 10–6 contain actual survey data, and the tables, together with the chi-square statistic associated with them, were generated by a computer program for analysis of survey data. The components of the tables will be discussed here. Interpretation of chi-square and statistical significance is described in the next chapter.

The data for both tables in the example are for the same survey and respondents. Scores on a brief test were recoded into three categories: larks, wrens, and owls, indicating if the person was most active and energetic in the morning, at midday, or in the evening. The "wrens" were excluded in the first table, and only the "larks" and "owls" were cross-tabulated against marital status. In the second table, the age variable was recoded into three categories and cross-tabulated against all three groups.

There are three values in each "cell" of the first table. The top one is the frequency or number, as the key at the upper left of the matrix indicates. For example, 47 married respondents were larks and 101 were owls. The second value in each cell is the row per-

EXAMPLE 10–6

Cross-Tabulation Print Output

Number Row Pct. Col Pct.		Married 1.	Not Married 2.	Row Total
Larks	1.	47 39.2 31.8	73 60.8 54.1	120 42.4
Owls	3.	101 62.0 68.2	62 38.0 45 9	163 57.6
Column Total		148 52.3	135 47.7	283 100.0

Chi-square = 14.40   d.f. = 1   Prob. = 0.0002

Number Col Pct.		Under 35 1.	35 to 49 2.	Over 49 3.	Row Total
Larks	1.	69 44.5	17 20.0	34 21.2	120 30.0
Wrens	2.	42 27.1	26 30.6	49 30.6	117 29.2
Owls	3.	44 28.4	42 49.4	77 48.1	163 42.4
Column Total		155 38.7	85 21.2	160 40.0	400 100.0

Chi-square = 27.72   d.f. = 4   Prob. = 0.0000

centage. This is merely the number in the cell divided by the total number for that row. In the upper table of the example, 39.2 percent was obtained by dividing the 47 in the upper left cell by 120, the number in the top row, and moving the decimal two places to the left to convert to percentage. The third number in each cell is the column percentage—the number divided by the total for the column. Thus, row percentages will total to 100 percent across the rows and column percentages total to 100 down the columns. The totals and percentages for each row and each column are shown at the right and lower margins.

The object of cross-tabulation is to show whether the distributions for one variable differ significantly for each value or level of the other variable. If the two variables aren't related to one another, then the row percentages in each row will be nearly the same as the percentages at the bottom of the table and the column percentages in each cell will be nearly equal to the percentages at the far right. In the example, if marital status did not affect the tendency to be a lark or an owl, or vice versa, then about the same proportion of married people would be larks as would those who aren't married. In the lower table of Example 10–6, only the column percentages were requested and listed on the table. Age can be considered the independent variable and time of day preferences the dependent. Thus, if age did not affect preference for time of day, about 30 percent of those in *each* column would be larks, about 29 percent would be wrens, and about 42 percent would be owls.

The interpretation of cross-tabs will be discussed in the following chapter, but it's interesting to note that both marital status and age are significantly related to preference for morning, midday, or evening. For example, the lower table indicated younger respondents are significantly more often larks and significantly less often owls than are middle-age or older respondents. Age doesn't seem to have much effect on the frequency of preference for midday. These conclusions were reached by noting that 44-1/2 percent of those under 35 were larks, while only 30 percent of all age groups were so. Only about 28 percent of that age group were owls, while about 42 percent of the entire sample were owls. Similarly, all of the percentages in the wren category were approximately the same as one another and the total for all groups. Notice that the same sort of analysis can be done by row, rather than by column, if the row percentages had been listed on the table.

Row, column, and table percentages

Many computer analysis routines permit the researcher to obtain row, column, and table percentages within the cell, as well as the frequencies. Row percentages total to 100 percent across the rows; column percentages total to 100 percent down the columns. Table percentages are just the percentage of all the cases in the table that fall within a given cell. Row or column percentages are usually required because it's very difficult to interpret the distributions in the cross-tabulation table based on the frequency or number of respondents in each cell. Ordinarily there will be different numbers of cases in each row and in each column, as there are in the example. So the proportions and relationships are difficult to gauge. Table percentages are only rarely useful for some special situations where the researcher would like to infer the percentage in the population who answer each of two survey questions in a certain way. In the majority of cases, the researcher will use either the row or the column percentages for the bulk of the analysis and interpretation.

Minimum cell frequencies

The chi-square statistic can be computed from the cross-tabulation table to indicate the statistical significance of the relationship between the two variables. The meaning and interpretation of chi-square for cross-tabulations will be discussed more fully in the following chapter. There's one important point that must be noted here, however. The chi-square statistic won't be valid or accurate if one or more of the *expected* cell frequencies is too small. In other words, there must be a sufficient number of cases in the rows and columns in order for the statistic to work correctly and accurately.

GUIDELIST 10–1

For Computing Expected Cell Frequencies

1. Find the smallest row total in the table, usually listed to the right of the row.
2. Divide it by the total number of cases in the table, usually listed at the lower right.
3. Find the smallest column total in the table, usually listed below the columns.
4. Multiply it by the fraction obtained above to determine the minimum expected cell frequency.
5. If less than five, recode one of the variables to obtain a larger row or column total.
6. Generate another table and follow the same procedure to check the minimum expected cell frequency.
7. Remember, the smallest *actual* cell frequency is irrelevant, and it's the *expected* cell frequency that must still be checked.

Most computer programs that compute chi-square for cross-tabulation produce a table and a statistic, regardless of whether or not the expected cell frequencies are adequate. The routines do what they're told. They don't require a minimum cell frequency for their computations. Yet, the statistic they generate and the significance value based on it won't be valid. Thus, it's imperative the analyst checks the minimum cell frequency for each cross-tab table. Some analysis programs routinely report the smallest expected cell frequency for each table. If the program doesn't do so, the analyst can quickly and easily calculate it with a minimum amount of effort.

The smallest expected cell frequency for the chi-square statistic to be valid is generally regarded to be five cases. If the smallest *expected* cell frequency is less than five, the analyst should recode a row or column variable, combining rows or columns until an adequate expected cell frequency is achieved. Notice that this requirement refers to *expected* cell frequency, not to the actual or observed cell frequency or number of cases actually in the cell. Untrained researchers commonly err by inspecting the table to see if the smallest actual cell frequency is five or greater. It doesn't matter if the actual cell frequency is *zero,* so long as the *expected* cell frequency is five or more.

The cell of a cross-tab table with the smallest *expected* cell frequency is the one on the *row* with the smallest total and the *column* with the smallest total. Thus, it isn't necessary to calculate the expected values for all the cells. The three-step process is very simple: (1) Find the smallest *row* total, usually listed on the right margin of each row. (2) Divide it by the *table* total, often listed at the bottom right. (3) Multiply this value by the smallest *column* total, usually listed at the bottom of each column. The result is the smallest expected cell frequency. If it's less than five, the analyst should recode either the row variable or the column variable to obtain a larger total. Either one will generate a larger expected cell frequency. This calculation must be repeated after generating a new table to ensure that the values for other cells aren't too small.

The lower table of Example 10–6 can be used to demonstrate the computation of lowest expected cell frequency. The smallest row total is 117. The total number of cases included in the table is 400, so 117 divided by 400 equals 0.2925. The smallest column total is 85,

---

GUIDELIST 10–2

For Using Cross-Tabulation

1. The objective is to determine if the distributions of one variable differ for each category of the other.
2. The variables to be cross-tabulated must *both* be derived from nominal scales or have few enough values to be treated as categories.
3. One variable may be identified as independent and the other dependent, but they need not be.
4. The chi-square statistic and its probability are used to measure the statistical significance of the relationship.

5. The minimum expected cell frequency must be computed to be sure it's five or greater for chi-square to be valid.
6. If the minimum expected cell frequency is less than five, either rows, columns, or both should be combined to increase the minimum expected cell frequency.
7. Either column or row percentages are most useful for interpretation, but table percentages are usually much more difficult to interpret.

---

and 0.2925 times 85 equals 24.8625. Thus, the smallest expected cell frequency for that cross-tabulation table is well-above the required value of five. This procedure is outlined in brief in Guidelist 10–1. The main requirements for using cross-tabulation are summarized in Guidelist 10–2.

Analysis of Variance

When the independent variable is categorical and the dependent variable is continuous, the data can be described in a *breakdown* table or on a bar chart or graph. The appropriate technique to measure the statistical significance of the differences between two or more means is analysis of variance, often referred to by its acronym, ANOVA. When the difference between only two mean values is to be assessed, a statistical *t-test* can also be used. It's merely a "special case" of ANOVA for only two distributions. Analysis of variance can be used to measure differences between means for two *or more* distributions.

An example may illustrate the use of analysis of variance. The upper section of Figure 10–8 shows the plots of two groups of 170 men and 170 women from the same sample of 510 respondents. These distributions of ratio data are almost identical, but, on average, the men's scores are lower than the women's. The descriptive statistics for the two groups individually and for both combined are shown in the breakdown table in the middle section of Figure 10–8. The lower section contains a vertical bar chart portraying the difference in mean scores on the dependent variable in graphic form.

Breakdown tables and bar charts are very adequate ways to present data description, but they leave a very critical question unanswered: "What's the chance this much difference in mean scores between groups would result merely from *sampling error?*" In other words, how safe is it to make the *assumption* that men's and women's scores actually do differ this much or more in the population as a whole? How *significant* are the differences in mean values? That question can be answered by submitting the data to analysis of variance.

Figure 10–8 *Association Between Sex and Scores*

Plot of Group Distributions

Breakdown Table of Group Means

Group	Count	Mean	Standard Deviation
Men	170	16.5	4.6
Women	170	18.5	4.6
Total	340	17.5	4.7

Bar Chart of Group Means

The assumption is that the reason one group has higher scores than the other is because they are of different sexes. So the sex of the respondent is *causing* a difference in scores. Thus, the continuous, numeric, interval scale *scores* constitute the *dependent variable*—the one being caused or affected. The *nominal categories* for the sex of the respondents is the *independent* variable—the one that is affecting the other.

Obviously, the greater the difference between group means, the *less* likely it resulted merely from sampling error. The *smaller* the difference between group means, the greater probability there is that the sample just happened, by chance, to include one group with higher values and another with lower. These relationships are depicted in Figure 10–9. If these four sets of data were submitted to ANOVA, the differences in the lower section probably wouldn't prove to be significant. Those in the other sections certainly or probably would.

Requirements for using ANOVA

It's important to note that analysis of variance *requires* the data distributions to have certain characteristics: First, the *dependent* variable must be from interval or ratio scales. The second requirement is that each case must be independent of the others—each value of the dependent variable must be from a different person, responding independently of the others. When

Figure 10–9 *Differences Between Group Means*

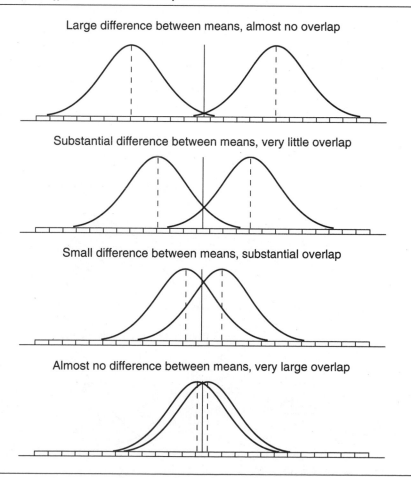

two interval or ratio values are obtained from the *same* respondents, a *paired t-test* can be used to assess the significance of the difference in means. When *more than two* interval or ratio values are obtained from the *same* respondents, testing the significance of the differences among the means requires a special, *repeated measures* design that's beyond the scope of this discussion of ANOVA.

Analysis of variance also requires that the distributions of data for each group have nearly

Figure 10–10   *Distributions Unacceptable to ANOVA*

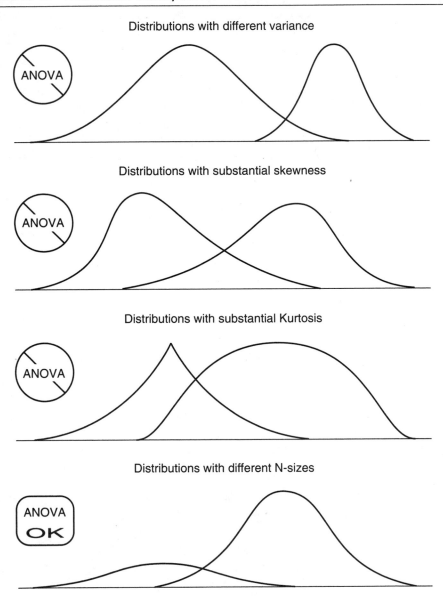

GUIDELIST 10-3

For Using Analysis of Variance

1. The objective is to determine if the mean values of the dependent variable for each category of the independent variable are significantly different from one another.
2. The independent variable must be categorical and the dependent variable must be continuous.
3. The dependent variable must be derived from either an interval or a ratio scale, but not an ordinal scale.
4. The values of the dependent variable must be obtained from different respondents, so they're completely independent of one another.
5. The variance in the dependent variable must be about the same within each category of the independent variable.
6. The distributions should be normally distributed or nearly so, with neither substantial skewness nor kurtosis.
7. The independent variable may have two or *more* categories for analysis of variance, but only two for a t-*test,* which is a special case of ANOVA.
8. The groups need not be of the same size, providing the smallest is of adequate size and is no less than about 4 or 5 percent of the largest group.
9. When two values of a continuous, dependent measure are obtained from the *same* respondents and their means are to be compared for significant differences, a *paired* t-*test* should be used in place of analysis of variance.

---

the same variance or spread and that they don't depart significantly from a *normal* distribution. These conditions are depicted in Figure 10–10. Most statistical analysis programs allow the user to request the routine to analyze the distributions and report their *homogeneity of variance, skewness,* and *kurtosis.* The more the distributions deviate from these requirements, the more likely the significance level the routine reports will be erroneous.

ANOVA does *not* require the groups be of the same size. If some groups are very small, with only a few respondents in them, the independent variable should be recoded in the same way as that for cross-tabulation. The only other restriction on group size is that the ratio of the smallest to the largest group should not be extremely small. The results tend to be unreliable if the smallest group is less than about 4 or 5 percent of the largest.

Occasionally, a survey will obtain ratings or other continuous interval or ratio data for two or more variables from the *same* respondents. The analyst may want to determine if the mean value for one is significantly greater or lesser than the other. If so, the values wouldn't be "independent" of one another, as noted in the fourth requirement for ANOVA listed in Guidelist 10–3. Analysis of variance shouldn't be used in such cases. Instead, the analyst should use a *paired t-test.* With this procedure, only one pair—two variables—can be compared with each analysis. The *independent* variable becomes, in effect, whether the value is that of the first variable or the value of the second.

Discriminant Analysis

When the independent variable is continuous and the dependent variable is categorical, Figure 10–7 indicates that *discriminant analysis* is the appropriate statistical tool to test the significance of the relationship between variables. The technical term for the procedure is

---

GUIDELIST 10–4

For Using Discriminant Analysis

1. The objective is to measure the degree and significance of influence of a continuous independent variable on the category membership of a dependent variable.
2. The procedure requires a continuous independent variable derived from an interval or ratio scale and a categorical dependent variable.

3. The statistical procedure and results are complex and difficult to interpret, so analysis of variance is usually preferable.
4. If analysis of variance is used in place of discriminant analysis, the level and interpretation of statistical significance are usually identical or nearly so.

---

analysis of the linear, discriminant function, or *discriminatory analysis,* and it's sometimes called simply *discrimination.*

With both analysis of variance and discriminant analysis, one variable is a continuous, numeric distribution from an interval or ratio scale and the other is a categorical variable. Discriminant analysis is the converse of ANOVA in the sense that the dependent and independent variables are reversed. If the analyst wants to measure the relationship between a continuous, numeric variable and a categorical variable when *no causality* is implied—when it isn't necessary to assume one is affecting the other—ANOVA should be used. Analysis of variance is highly preferable because it's far more common and understandable. In addition, statistical programs to do ANOVA are much more readily available and easier to use.

Discriminant analysis is a complex statistical tool that's most applicable and useful only under rather stringent conditions. For example, if there are only two groups—two categories or levels of the dependent variable—and *multiple* interval or ratio scale variables, discriminant analysis can be valuable. Such multivariate analysis is beyond the scope of discussion here, but discriminant analysis and a host of other powerful, multivariate statistical tools can be studied in many texts devoted to statistical analysis.

Experienced researchers commonly prefer analysis of variance if there's no compelling reason to use discriminant analysis. The analyst who needs only to establish the significance of the relationship between a continuous numeric variable and a categorical variable would be well advised to use analysis of variance, even though technically the causality is "reversed," so to speak. Guidelines for using discriminant analysis are contained in Guidelist 10–4.

Regression and Correlation Analysis

When the objective is to test the degree and significance of the relationship between two continuous variables from interval or ratio scales, the appropriate technique is either correlation or regression analysis. Regression requires that one variable be identified as independent and the other dependent. Correlation analysis measures only the degree to which the two are related, or tend to move together, but there's no assumption that one is causing or affecting the other. If one or both variables are from *ordinal,* rather than interval or ratio, scales, a special form of correlation analysis, called *rank* correlation, can be used. Its interpretation is similar to that for the more common *product-moment* correlation method.

Correlation analysis

A correlation between two continuous variables is just what the word implies, "co-relation," and it's based on covariance, or movement together. Correlation analysis generates a single value, the correlation coefficient, that shows how much the two variables move together. The correlation coefficient is usually symbolized by the letter r. It ranges from a value of zero, indicating there's no relationship between the variables, to a plus or a minus one, indicating a perfect linear relationship. Figure 10–11 depicts six scatterplots together with the correlation coefficient for each. An r value of 1.000 indicates a "lockstep" relationship

Figure 10–11 *Scatterplots and Correlation Coefficients*

between the two variables. In other words, if the value of one of the items increased by one unit from one case to the next, the value of the other item would always move by a given amount, although it need not be the same number of units as the other variable moved.

The plus or minus sign on the correlation coefficient indicates the *direction* of the correlation. If the correlation is positive, the two move in the same direction. If it's negative, they move in the opposite direction. In other words, the plus or minus indicates a *direct* or an *inverse* relationship between the two variables. The absolute value (ignoring the plus or minus signs) shows how much the two items are correlated or moving together. The closer to zero, the less the relationship, and the closer to one, the greater the relationship. Thus, both the sign and the value of the correlation coefficient provide information about the relationship between the variables.

Interpreting the "degree" or strength of the relationship between two variables using the correlation coefficient can be a little misleading, because this coefficient doesn't show what proportion of a "perfect" relationship the two variables have. The proportion of "shared variance" is actually indicated by the *square* of the correlation coefficient, and that's called the coefficient of *determination,* symbolized by r^2 or abbreviated as RSQ.

To clarify this interpretation, suppose two survey items are submitted to correlation analysis and the coefficient of correlation is 0.50. This doesn't mean that they're "half" as closely related as they might be if they were perfectly associated with one another. If $r = 0.50$, then r^2, the coefficient of determination, is 0.25 and only 25 percent of the variance in the two items would be "shared" between them. Similarly, if the correlation coefficient was .90, they would share 81 percent of the variance, not 90 percent.

The research analyst will also want to know whether or not r^2 indicates a statistically significant relationship between the variables. The significance level is the probability such a relationship would result purely by chance from sampling error if the two items were uncorrelated in the population. Virtually all statistical analysis routines will report that probability. If the significance level isn't reported, it can be checked by reference to standard statistical tables ordinarily appended to statistics and research texts. The analyst need only know the value of the correlation coefficient and number of cases or "degrees of freedom" reported by the routine.[1] The probability can then be determined by referring to Table B–4 and following the procedure outlined in Example B–4 in Appendix B on page 418.

There are two kinds of correlation analysis and statistical routines often used by survey research analysts. The most common requires the data be from either *interval* or *ratio* scales. It's called *Pearson product-moment correlation,* or just *product-moment* or *PM* correlation. When the term *correlation* is used without specifying what kind, it refers to product-moment correlation. When one or both variables to be correlated are *ordinal,* rather than interval or ratio data, *Spearman rank correlation,* or just *rank correlation,* must be used in place of PM correlation. Rank correlations can also be used for interval or ratio data, but that's not advisable because this method is less sensitive and powerful. Product-moment correlation must not be used with one or both *ordinal* distributions because the results are likely to be erroneous. Guidelist 10–5 summarizes the requirements for using correlation analysis.

---

[1] $t = \dfrac{r\sqrt{n-2}}{\sqrt{1-r^2}}$ and d.f. $= n - 2$ where $r =$ correlation coefficient and $n =$ number of cases.

GUIDELIST 10–5

For Using Correlation Analysis

1. The objective is to determine the degree to which two variables move or vary together from one case to the next, and to test the significance of the relationship.

2. Both variables must be continuous, but they need not be identified as dependent and independent.

3. Product-moment correlation requires that both variables are interval or ratio data, but rank correlation can be used when one or both are derived from ordinal scales.

4. The correlation coefficient ranges from zero— no relationship—to plus or minus one—a perfect relationship.

5. When the coefficient is positive, the variables move together in the same direction, and when it's negative, they move together in opposite directions.

6. The percentage of all possible shared variance or movement together is indicated by the *square* of the correlation coefficient, the *coefficient of determination.*

Regression analysis

When one continuous interval or ratio variable can be identified as an independent variable and a similar variable as the dependent variable, *regression analysis* is the appropriate technique to measure the relationship between them and assess its significance. When the analysis includes just one independent variable, the more precise term is *simple, linear regression.* This is the technique described here, but there are extensions of the method, called *multiple regression,* which include a single dependent variable and multiple independent variables.

There are two possible objectives of regression analysis: One is to measure the degree and direction of the influence of the independent on the dependent variable and, of course, to assess the statistical significance of the relationship. Another is to obtain a formula to *predict* the value of the dependent variable for a new case based on knowledge of the independent variable. A brief example may demonstrate these two objectives.

Suppose a clothing shop sponsors a survey to determine the age of their customers and the dollar value of their purchases during the recent past. Both age in years and purchases in dollars are continuous, ratio scale variables. Since the customer's age might affect the volume of purchases, but not vice versa, age is the independent variable and purchase value is the dependent variable. Figure 10–7 indicates that regression analysis is the appropriate statistical tool to assess the relationship between these two variables.

The first objective would be to determine if age had a *statistically significant* influence on purchase behavior. If it did, the analyst would want to know how much and in what direction. (If the analyst wanted only to measure the significance of a relationship, correlation analysis, rather than regression, would accomplish only that.) If a significant relationship exists, the analyst may also want to know how to predict the purchase level of customers of different ages and how accurate these predictions are likely to be. If purchases could be predicted with reasonable accuracy, the shop sponsoring the survey could adjust their merchandising and promotional policies to obtain the age group with greatest potential sales volume. It might also use the information to forecast sales based on the ages of those visiting the store or shopping center.

Regression analysis produces a coefficient that's practically the same as the coefficient of determination for correlation analysis. It's ordinarily called r^2 (r-square) or abbreviated rsq. Some statistical programs also compute and report the significance of r-square, but if not, the analyst can refer to statistical tables to determine the significance level. With correlation analysis, the square of the coefficient indicates the proportion of variance in the two variables that's "shared" between them. With regression analysis, the r-square value indicates the percentage of variance in the dependent variable that's "explained" by the values of the independent variable, as depicted in Figure 10–12. Thus, r-square is an indication of how much influence the independent variable has on the dependent variable. Some statistical programs also compute the signficance of r-square. If the value isn't reported, the significance can be determined by using the procedure described in the previous section for determining the signficance of a correlation coefficient.

While the correlation coefficient is either positive or negative, indicating the direction of the relationship, the r-square value is always positive (because it's a squared value). The value of r-square ranges from zero to one. A value of zero indicates the independent variable has no influence whatsoever on the dependent variable, as in the lower sections of Figure 10–11. A value of one indicates that the value of the dependent variable could be predicted exactly if the value of the independent variable is known, as in the upper sections of Figure 10–11. In other words, just as with correlation, the variables are in a perfect, linear, "lock-step" relationship with one another from one case or respondent to the next.

Figure 10–12   *Variance Explained by Regression Line*

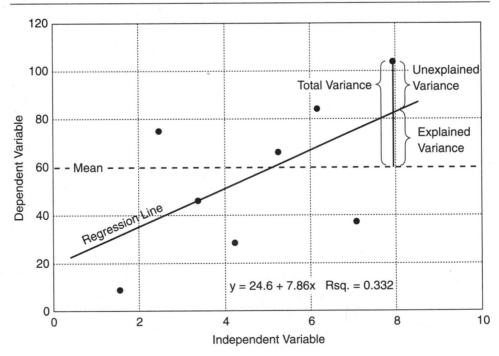

Regression analysis generates a "regression equation," as well as the r-square value. The regression equation is the formula for computing a predicted value for the dependent variable, based on the value of the independent variable. There are only two values required in the equation for simple, linear regression: a constant and a regression coefficient. (This is merely the equation for a straight line: $y = a + bX$, where a is the constant y intercept and b is the slope of the line.) Using the equation shown in Figure 10–12 to predict the value of the dependent variable for a new case when only the value of the independent variable is known, the analyst would multiply that value by the value of the regression coefficient, 7.86, and add the constant, 24.6.

In Figure 10–13, the points are very close to the regression line, indicating that the r-square value will be very high and that one could make very accurate predictions of unknown values for the dependent variable based on known values of the independent variable. An r-square value of 0.96 means 96 percent of the variance around the mean is "explained" by the regression line. On the other hand, when the data points on a scatterplot "splay" widely from the regression line, the r-square value and the ability to predict will be low.

Requirements for regression

Regression analysis requires that both the independent and dependent variables are from interval or ratio scales. Each pair of values must come from an independent case or respondent. The relationship between the variables must be *linear*. That means if the cases were plotted, the points on the plot must be arrayed approximately in a straight line. Figure 10–14 shows a case where the corridor of data points are sharply curved rather than linear. If these data were used for regression, the r-square value would be deflated and predictions for the dependent variable would be too high for low and high values of the independent variable and too low for medium levels.

Figure 10–13   *A Linear Regression Scatterplot*

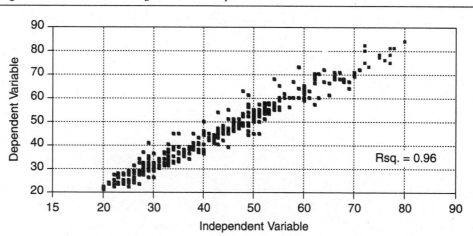

Figure 10–14 *A Curvilinear Scatterplot Pattern*

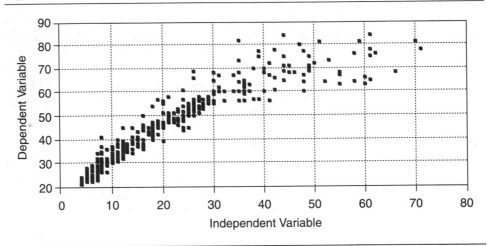

Most statistical analysis programs include optional routines that indicate whether the scatterplot departs significantly from linearity. Such tests should routinely be run during analysis. It may also be advisable to plot the data points and visually examine the plot. Analysis routines will compute the statistics regardless of whether or not the plot is linear, but the results are very likely to be grossly misleading or completely erroneous if the requirements aren't met properly.

Figure 10–15 *A Funnel-Shaped Scatterplot*

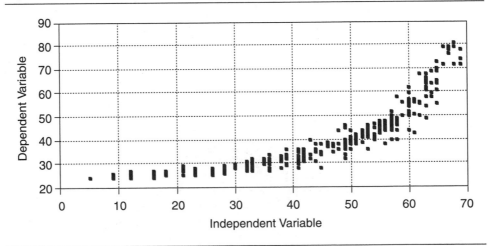

GUIDELIST 10–6

For Using Regression Analysis

1. One objective is to measure the degree and direction of influence the independent variable has on the dependent variable.
2. Another objective is to obtain an equation to predict an unknown value of the dependent variable, based on the known value of the independent variable.
3. One variable must be identified as independent and one dependent, and both must be derived from interval or ratio scales.
4. The strength of the influence of the independent on the dependent variable is indicated by r-square, ranging from zero (no influence) to one (perfect determination).
5. The regression equation consists of a constant and a regression coefficient, indicating the direction and amount of influence, or slope of the regression line.

6. When the regression coefficient is positive, the relationship is direct and the slope is upward to the right. When it's negative, the relationship is inverse and the slope is downward to the right.
7. Regression analysis requires that the relationship be linear rather than curved or kinked.
8. Regression also requires the variance of the dependent variable around the regression line to be approximately equal from one end of the line to the other.
9. Both *linearity* and *homogeneity* of variance around the regression line can be checked by visual inspection of a scatterplot or by statistical tests during analysis.

Another requirement of regression analysis is that the spread or variance around the regression line be approximately equal. If not, erroneous results will be generated. Figure 10–15 shows a pattern that's very common for survey data. Notice the data points are closely clustered around the regression line for the lower values of the variables, but they splay outward quite widely for the higher values. Again, the statistical analysis programs for regression usually allow the user to specify a test to determine if the variance of the dependent variable around the regression line is the same across the range of independent variable values or differs significantly from homogeneity. Guidelines for using regression analysis are provided in Guidelist 10–6.

ANALYSIS VERSUS INTERPRETATION

This discussion of statistical analysis may assist in selection of the appropriate statistical tool, but many questions concerning interpretation are likely to remain. The interpretation of the results and the response to information requirements are the topics of the next chapter.

The statistical tools described here and in the next chapter are the most *fundamental*. They're designed for basic data description and measurement of bivariate relationships. They're probably adequate for analysis and interpretation of the data from the vast majority of survey research projects. It's important to note, however, that there are a host of more complex, multivariate statistical tools readily available to those who know how to use them properly and effectively. If the survey project, information needs, and resources warrant more sophisticated analyses than those discussed here, the analyst may seek either guidance from advanced statistical texts or the advice and assistance of an expert statistician.

SUMMARY

Statistical Analysis of Data

    A. Remember the objectives. Statistics are designed to suppress detail and reveal *important* findings.

    B. Provide data description first. Treat individual variables for the entire sample before examining relationships.

    C. Always identify the scale types. The nature of the scale determines, in part, the proper descriptive measures.

    D. Treat variables both ways. Continuous items with only a few scale values can be treated as categorical.

    E. Portray information when feasible. Showing the entire distribution is more effective than describing it.

    F. Describe data with care. The shape of the distribution affects the choice and interpretation of descriptions.

    G. Determine the data type. Continuous and categorical data require different statistical measures of association.

    H. Show relationships with cross-tabs. The cross-tabulation tables are more easily understood than other measures of association.

    I. Assess causality carefully. Choice of independent and dependent variables depends on their underlying meaning.

    J. Select the simplest tool. The simplest method used well is far more effective than a complex method that's used incorrectly or misunderstood.

Chapter 11

Interpreting Statistics

DESCRIPTIVE STATISTICS

The statistics used to analyze survey data fall into two broad categories: those that describe individual variables and distributions and those that measure the relationships between variables. Complete data descriptions, for both continuous and categorical data, are ordinarily generated and studied by the research analyst before turning to measures of association between variables. The first part of this chapter will discuss the interpretation of statistical descriptions of categorical and continuous data. The second part is devoted to statistics for measuring relationships between pairs of survey items.

Interpreting Category Data

Frequency and percentage distributions are the most common methods for describing categorical survey variables. Bar charts and pie charts can also be used to display categorical distributions graphically. The format and content of such tables and charts were discussed in the previous chapter. When the variable being analyzed can only be considered as categorical, so there's really no continuum or relationship between categories, the only statistic that's appropriate to describe the distribution is the mode—the category with the largest frequency and percentage of cases.

When data from an ordinal scale are displayed in a frequency table, the *cumulative* percentages may be meaningfully interpreted. In Example 11–1, the cumulative percentage column indicates over 40 percent of respondents had at least a college education and over 95 percent graduated from high school. These proportions could have been calculated mentally if only the percentage column was shown, but the interpretation is quicker and easier with inclusion of the cumulative percentages.

EXAMPLE 11–1

Interpreting Cumulative Percentages

Level of Education	Frequency	Percentage	Cumulative Percentage
Post graduate	118	19.2	19.2
College graduate	136	22.1	41.3
Some college	141	23.0	64.3
High school graduate	191	31.1	95.4
Some high school	28	4.6	100.0
Total	614	100.0	

Graphic plots of cumulative percentages are sometimes more readily interpreted than just the adjusted percentage values. Figure 11–1 shows two plots of data from a survey item that sought to learn what percentage of people were still awake and what percentage were asleep at various points throughout the first hour after "lights out." The bar chart in the upper section isn't very informative because it shows when during the hour various percentages fell asleep. By contrast, the plot of *cumulative* percentages in the lower section of Figure 11–1 provides precisely the information sought. The area in the upper left shows the proportion still awake and the area in the lower right depicts the proportion who have fallen asleep at each point.

When continuous ordinal, interval, or ratio data are obtained from scales with a limited number of scale points or values, this type of variable can be treated *both* as continuous and as categorical data. Each scale point can be treated as a separate category, even though they're on a continuum. Doing so isn't only permissible, it's advisable. Of course, the conventional descriptive statistics, such as averages, measures of the spread, and shape of the distribution, can also be computed for such items.

When continuous variables have too many values to be listed in a frequency table, it's often advisable either to recode the variable into fewer, larger categories or to generate a "duplicate" variable and recode it into categories, as suggested in the previous chapter. The range of the interval for each category should be identical, and there should be no more than a dozen categories, and preferably only six or eight. When a continuous variable has been recoded into categories in this fashion, it can be treated as *either* continuous or categorical, providing certain conditions are met. For example, if age in years resulted in 40 or 50 different values, the variable might be recoded into five or six 10-year categories. There are then two options: One is to create a duplicate variable, recode it into categories with equal intervals, and list the categories in frequency tables and perhaps use them for cross-

Figure 11–1   *Plot of Cumulative Percentages*

tabulation later, when relationships between variables are analyzed. The duplicate age variable that was retained in continuous form might also be described with the statistics appropriate for continuous distributions.

Another option is to recode the *original* variable into categories with equal intervals. If no duplicate continuous variable is retained, then each category should be coded with the value of the *midpoint* of the interval. For example, if age was reclassified into 10-year categories: 20s, 30s, 40s, and so on, then each category should be recoded with the values: 25, 35, 45, and so on. That way, the descriptive statistics for continuous distributions can be used together with the frequency tables. These statistics would be interpreted in the same way as they would when a strictly continuous variable was analyzed, except that all of the values and coefficients will be slightly different because all those in one group or category will be treated as identical during the computations.

While it takes time and effort to recode continuous survey variables this way, it's often worthwhile. The statistics for describing the data and measuring relationships between items are more complex and difficult to interpret for continuous variables than for categorical ones. For the vast majority of all survey data, frequency tables are used to describe the distributions, and cross-tabs are used to measure the associations between items. These methods are usually more understandable to information seekers than the techniques for describing continuous numeric data and measuring the associations between such items. Some information is lost when recoding continuous data into categories, but the loss is usually negligible.

Interpreting averages of distributions

The three most commonly used averages, the mean, median, and mode, were described in the previous chapter. All three are often computed, leaving the researcher to decide which would be the best indicator of the most typical case. If the data were obtained from an ordinal scale, the mode is acceptable but the median is preferable. If the data were derived from an interval or ratio scale, the choice depends on the *shape* of the distribution. If the coefficient of skewness is very near zero, indicating the distribution is symmetrical, the mean, median, and mode will all be the same value or nearly identical to one another. If the distribution is skewed to the left or the right, as in the upper section of Figure 11–2, the mean, median, and mode depart from one another in the directions shown. The lower section of Figure 11–2 depicts distributions with positive and negative kurtosis. But since they are *symmetrical,* the mean, median, and mode don't depart from one another. Thus, the choice of the most appropriate *average* is affected only by skewness or deviation from symmetry, but not by kurtosis.

Figure 11–2 indicates the mean is sensitive to extreme values on the high side, off to the right, for positive skewness and to the low or left side for negative skewness. This characteristic of the mean was discussed in the previous chapter. The greater the amount of skewness in a distribution, the *less* appropriate the mean will be as a measure of the most typical case. In other words, the greater the skewness, the more likely the *median* will best represent the most typical case.

The mode was described earlier as the only proper measure of the most typical case for categorical data, where the modal category is merely the one with the largest percentage of responses. For continuous data, the mode is the "high point" in the distribution. In Figure

Figure 11–2   *Averages of Nonnormal Distributions*

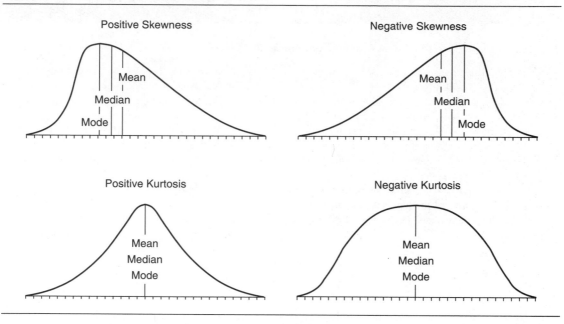

11–2, the mode would be the scale value where the distribution has reached its peak. It's often used as the best indicator of the most typical case when a distribution is *extremely* skewed to one side or the other. The mode is an especially appropriate average to use if the distribution both is skewed to one side and also has a high peak, indicated by a positive value for the coefficient of kurtosis. This is because a large portion of the cases will be very close to the mode. This kind of distribution will be discussed in the next section.

The median is the approximate value of the case that would be in the middle, if all cases were arrayed from low to high value on the variable. It isn't the center point on the horizontal axis of the plot shown in Figure 11–2, because that's merely the midpoint of the scale. In the figure, the number of cases is represented by the *area* under the curve, rather than the horizontal distance on the scale. When the distribution is slightly skewed, when it's relatively flat so that the value of kurtosis is negative, or when it's near normal with only a few very extreme values far to one side, the *median* is the most appropriate average to indicate the most typical case. Note that the median is only influenced by the *number* of cases with higher values and with lower values, but it isn't sensitive to *how much* the values are higher or lower. Guidelines for selecting the most appropriate average are contained in Guidelist 11–1.

Interpreting spread of distributions

When a distribution conforms closely to the standard normal curve, a given proportion of the cases will always fall within certain ranges that are determined by the standard deviation (S.D.) of the distribution. As the top section of Figure 11–3 shows, about 68 percent of the cases will be within ±1 S.D. of the mean, 95 percent within ±2 S.D. On the extremes of

---

GUIDELIST 11–1

For Choosing the Best Average

1. If the data are from an ordinal scale, the median should be used.
2. If the skewness is zero or very nearly so, the distribution is symmetrical and the mean, median, and mode will all be the same or nearly identical.
3. If the skewness is positive, the mode or peak will be to the left of center, the median greater, and the mean the highest.
4. If the skewness is negative, the mode will be to the right, toward the high side, the median will be a lower value, and the mean, the lowest value.

5. If the distribution is nearly normal but there are a few very small or very large values, they are called "outliers" and the median is the best indicator of the most typical case.
6. If the distribution is skewed and the kurtosis is zero or negative, indicating a normal or flat curve, the median is the best average to show the most typical case.
7. If the distribution is skewed and the kurtosis has a high, positive value, the distribution has a high peak with many cases around the mode, and the mode is the best average to represent the most typical case or value.

---

a normal distribution, only 1 percent of the data lie beyond 3 S.D. above or below the mean, so 99 percent fall within ± 3 S.D.

Suppose the survey data for a certain variable is normally distributed and there are 200 cases. If the mean value was computed to be 30 and the standard deviation was five, this would mean that 68 cases would have values between 25 and 30 and another 68 cases would have a value between 30 and 35. In total, 132 cases, or 68 percent, would be between 25 and 35. This is within one standard deviation above and below the mean. Similarly, 190 cases or 95 percent would be within two standard deviations of the mean, with values between 20 and 40. Only about one case would have a value of less than 15 and one a value of more than 45, because about 198 cases or 99 percent would be within three standard deviations of the mean. In this way, the research analyst can see the range and describe the spread of the distribution for the variable simply by knowing the mean and standard deviation, *providing the "shape" of the distribution is approximately NORMAL.*

The standard deviation provides a close estimate of the proportion of cases within a given range around the mean *only* if the distribution is symmetrical. The distributions shown in the middle and lower sections of Figure 11–3 are positively and negatively skewed, respectively. The mean and the approximate percentages of data within one, two, and three S.D. are listed. The *proportion* of cases is represented by the area under the curve for each section. So about 74 percent of cases fall within ± 1 S.D. rather than the 68 percent that would be in that range for a normal distribution.

The absolute value of the coefficient indicates the degree of accuracy with which the standard deviation can estimate the amount of spread in the distribution. When the coefficient of skewness is positive, there will be many more cases within 1 S.D. to the left of the mean than to the right of it. The opposite is true for negative skewness. Thus, the *sign* of the coefficient tells only in what *direction* the distribution is skewed.

Figure 11–3   *Zero, Positive, and Negative Skewness*

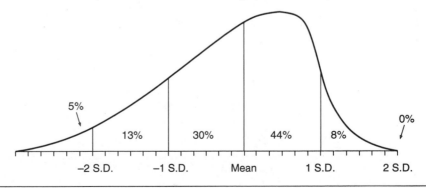

Figure 11–4 *Kurtosis Zero, Positive, and Negative*

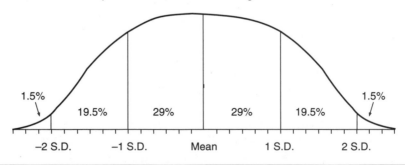

GUIDELIST 11–2

For Spread of Nonnormal Distributions

1. If either skewness or kurtosis depart significantly from zero, the distribution isn't normal and S.D. won't indicate the proportion of data in a given range.

2. If the scale has only a few values, obtain a frequency table and use the percentages and cumulative percentages to show proportions within ranges and above and below points on the scale.

3. If the variable has a large number of values, it or a duplicate may be recoded into fewer, larger categories of equal intervals displayed in a frequency table.

4. The distributions of continuous, numeric variables with many values can also be plotted to allow visual examination of the shape and spread of the distribution.

Nor can the standard deviation be used to show the range within which a given percentage of cases will fall if the coefficient of kurtosis departs markedly from zero in either a positive or negative direction, as in the middle and lower sections of Figure 11–4. If the value of kurtosis is positive, indicating a more peaked distribution than normal, *more* than 68 percent of cases will fall within ±1 S.D. of the mean. On the other hand, if the distribution is flatter than normal, indicated by a *negative* kurtosis value, then fewer than 68 percent of cases will be within ±1 S.D. of the mean.

In summary, the standard deviation can be computed despite how much the distribution departs from normal. But if skewness, kurtosis, or both deviate significantly from zero, the standard deviation does *not* indicate the *proportion* of data within a given range of standard deviations from the mean. If the distribution is skewed, there will be more or less cases above the mean than below it, depending on the direction of skewness. If the distribution has substantial kurtosis, *more* or *less* than two-thirds of the cases will be within 1 S.D. of the mean, depending on the sign of the coefficient. Thus, when using the standard deviation to gauge the proportion of cases within some range around the mean, it's important to check the skewness and kurtosis. Guidelist 11–2 summarizes the recommendations for assessing the spread on nonnormal distributions. Guidelines for the spread of normal distributions are listed in Guidelist 11–3.

Interpreting shapes of distributions

The coefficients of skewness and kurtosis do suggest the shape of a distribution of data, but it requires substantial experience to visualize a distribution based only on those values. A variety of readily available desktop computer programs, including most statistical analysis programs, spreadsheets, and charting or graphing programs, are capable of creating plots of survey data distributions. Such data plots are very helpful to both research analysts and information seekers to visualize and comprehend the shape of the entire distribution of data for a survey item.

Figure 11–5 contains the data plots and descriptive coefficients for six actual survey variables. The values are combined favorability ratings for phone or mail-order shopping

---

GUIDELIST 11–3

For Using Standard Deviation with Normal Curve

1. About 34 percent of cases are between the mean and +1 S.D.
2. About 34 percent of cases are between the mean and −1 S.D.
3. About 68 percent of cases are within ±1 S.D. of the mean.
4. About 95 percent of cases are within ±2 S.D. of the mean.
5. About 99 percent of cases are within ±3 S.D. of the mean.

6. About 50 percent of cases will be above the mean.
7. About 50 percent of cases will be below the mean.
8. The percentage of cases above and below other points on the scale, defined by the standard deviation, can be determined by adding and subtracting these percentages.

---

via six modes: magazines, catalogs, newspapers, television, direct mail, and retail stores. The minimum possible score was 8 and the maximum was 40.

The descriptive statistics for each variable shown in Figure 11–5 are listed below the plot of each distribution. Careful comparisons between the coefficients and the plots will clarify many of the conditions discussed earlier. The averages indicate that *stores* were rated most highly, followed by *catalogs*. These two distributions are further to the right than those for the other four shopping modes. Each distribution is slightly skewed to the right, with a few cases of very low scores tailing off to the left. Thus, all the coefficients of skewness have slightly negative values. The distribution of ratings for *stores* is rather flat and the coefficient of kurtosis is slightly negative. All the others are more peaked than normal and the corresponding kurtosis values are slightly positive.

Floor and Ceiling Effects

Survey data distributions are sometimes asymmetrical or skewed to the left or right because of what are called "ceiling" or "floor" effects. Figure 11–6 displays two distributions of data from a seven-point rating scale. On the left, nearly 17 percent of respondents indicated the *minimum* scale value. It seems reasonable to assume their ratings would have been even lower if they were not limited by the *floor* of the scale. By contrast, more than one out of five respondents chose the *maximum* value for the variable described at the right of Figure 11–6. This suggests their reactions were bound by the upper limit or *ceiling* of the seven-point scale.

With strong *floor* effects, a large proportion of cases will be grouped at the *lower* boundary of the scale. The coefficient of skewness will have a *positive* sign because the distribution is skewed to the *left*. On the other hand, if there are strong *ceiling* effects, with a substantial proportion of respondents clustered at the *upper* limit of the scale, the distribution will be

Figure 11–5 *Six Distributions of Survey Data*

Magazines

Mean	23.8	Std. Dev.	5.09
Median	24.0	Kurtosis	0.84
Mode	24.0	Skewness	-0.13

Catalogs

Mean	27.5	Std. Dev.	5.23
Median	27.0	Kurtosis	0.58
Mode	27.0	Skewness	-0.11

Newspapers

Mean	22.7	Std. Dev.	4.70
Median	23.0	Kurtosis	1.20
Mode	24.0	Skewness	-0.23

Television

Mean	22.8	Std. Dev.	5.28
Median	23.0	Kurtosis	1.10
Mode	24.0	Skewness	-0.14

Direct Mail

Mean	22.5	Std. Dev.	4.92
Median	23.0	Kurtosis	1.36
Mode	24.0	Skewness	-0.37

Stores

Mean	30.9	Std. Dev.	4.78
Median	31.0	Kurtosis	-0.19
Mode	32.0	Skewness	-0.09

skewed to the *right* and the coefficient of skewness will be *negative,* as indicated in Figure 11–6.

Floor and ceiling effects on survey data distributions are highly disruptive. The departures from symmetry they create inhibit the use of the standard deviation as a meaningful measure of the spread of the data distribution. More importantly, such asymmetry prohibits the

Figure 11–6   *Scale Floor and Ceiling Effects*

Floor Effect				Ceiling Effect		

Floor Effect

Value	Frequency	Percent
1	121	16.6
2	203	27.8
3	184	25.2
4	120	16.5
5	60	8.2
6	35	4.8
7	6	.8
Total	729	100.0

Ceiling Effect

Value	Frequency	Percent
1	11	1.5
2	23	3.1
3	68	9.1
4	105	14.1
5	166	22.3
6	202	27.1
7	170	22.8
Total	745	100.0

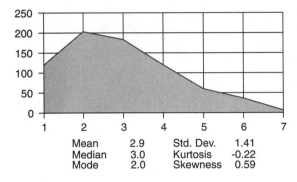

Mean	2.9	Std. Dev.	1.41
Median	3.0	Kurtosis	-0.22
Mode	2.0	Skewness	0.59

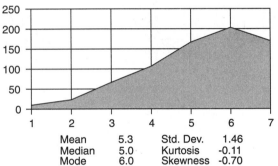

Mean	5.3	Std. Dev.	1.46
Median	5.0	Kurtosis	-0.11
Mode	6.0	Skewness	-0.70

legitimate use of some measures of association to be described later in this chapter, such as analysis of variance or regression analysis. Thus, survey researchers strive to prevent floor or ceiling effects. Yet they aren't as easy to avoid as it might seem.

It may appear, at first glance, that floor and ceiling effects could be avoided by using a "wider" scale—a scale with more values. In fact, that's rarely the answer. For instance, in the example shown in Figure 11–6, if a nine-point or even a 100-point scale had been used, about the same proportion of respondents would probably have clustered at the lower and upper extremes, producing almost identical effects.

The answer to the avoidance of floor or ceiling effects lies not so much in the breadth of the scale as in the manner in which the question or item is expressed or the way in which the extremes of a scale are labeled. It's not always possible, but sometimes the researcher can *anticipate* the possibility of strong positive or negative reactions to an item. If that's the case, the wording of the question and/or the labeling of the scale's extremes can be expressed to capture the full range of potential response. For example, a scale labeled "Good—Bad" may produce floor or ceiling effects, while such effects would be mitigated by the labels, "Terrible—Superb."

There are other situations where floor and ceiling effects are virtually impossible to prevent because it's the nature of the underlying distribution in the population—for example, with such items as personal income, because nobody reports negative income. Almost everyone has a few thousand dollars per year of income, while most report many thousands. On the high side, a few respondents may report income in the hundreds of thousands of dollars or more, so there's virtually *no ceiling*. This causes the distribution to be skewed positively, toward the left or low side of the distribution. In effect, the "floor" of zero cuts off the distribution on the left, but it can extend far toward the right extreme.

The opposite tendency occurs when there are ceiling effects on the scale for the variable or item. For example, suppose respondents were asked to indicate how many days per month, on the average, they drive their automobile for any purpose at all. Some may report only a few days, but many are likely to report they use the car every day. Since there's a maximum of 31 days per month, nobody could report more than that ceiling value. The distribution would be negatively skewed toward the right or high side of the distribution. When asymmetry due to floor or ceiling effects can't be avoided, the analyst has little choice but to recode the variable into categories and use the statistical tools appropriate to ordinal, categorical data.

The Meaning of Bimodality

Most of the distributions shown in this and the previous chapter were "unimodal" (single-mode) distributions. This isn't always the case. Sometimes a distribution of continuous numeric data will have two or more modes or peaks, such as that shown in the upper section of Figure 11–7. For such distributions, the coefficient of kurtosis will be quite negative, indicating a very flat curve, because that's the way the computational routine would "see" the distribution. In fact, the distribution dips sharply downward in the middle and then rises to a second mode on the right.

The distribution of categorical data shown in the lower left section of Figure 11–7 is also bimodal. The *primary* mode has a value of 6, while the *secondary* modal value is 3. Such bimodal distributions usually indicate there are two, fairly distinct "populations" or groups of respondents concealed in the responding sample. If so, each group might provide a fairly normal distribution of response for the item. Yet, when they're combined into one sample, the curves are, in effect, overlaid on one another. A bimodal distribution results.

This is precisely the case exemplified in Figure 11–7. In the upper section, the plots of the two, distinct distributions have been overlaid on the "combined" distribution for the variable. In the lower left section of Figure 11–7, the "combined" distribution is shown in a *stacked* bar chart. If the two distinct subsample distributions hadn't been identified and the data were displayed in an ordinary bar chart, it would appear just as it does but without the two segments for each bar. The two distinct distributions are plotted separately in a *split* bar chart in the lower right section of the figure to reveal that each is approximately normal in form. When the research analyst discovers a bimodal distribution, it's often a clue that some factor or characteristic serves to distinguish one group from the other within the responding sample. The important question is, *what* characteristic?

The content of the survey question or item may suggest what may separate the two groups, causing each to range around a different point on the scale. The analyst should note any bimodal distributions that are detected, examine the item or question generating the

Figure 11–7   *Continuous, Bimodal Distributions*

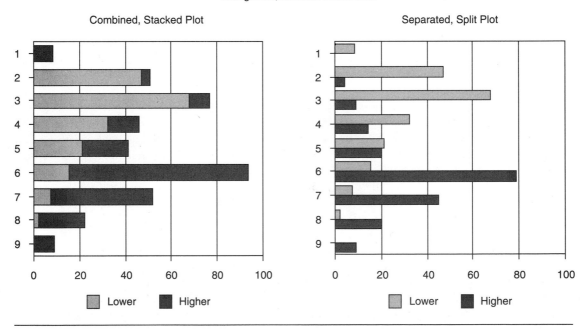

distribution, and perhaps analyze the relationship between the variable and others in the survey, such as the demographic items. Often, such demographic characteristics will prove to be strongly related to items with bimodality.

For example, a bimodal distribution of frequency of air travel may be strongly related to occupational groups, indicating higher frequencies for business travelers and lower frequency of travel by those in occupations that don't require it. This may be of major importance to those seeking the information because the average amount of travel for the whole sample *wouldn't be typical of either group,* but the average for each separate population might be highly accurate and informative. Similarly, men and women often respond in systematically different ways, as do married and unmarried respondents, those with children in the family and those without, those who are and those who aren't employed outside the home, those with college degrees and those with less education, or those in blue-collar and those in white-collar jobs. There may be no way to explain bimodality based on the survey results, but often an explanation can be found. If so, it might provide highly valuable information to the sponsor.

STATISTICAL INFERENCE

Ordinarily, researchers and sponsors aren't really interested merely in the results obtained from a sample. For nearly all surveys, they want to "estimate" the *parameters* of the population, based on the *statistics* obtained from a sample. This process of making inferences about the population from sample statistics is called *statistical inference.* It must be based on a random sample, or at least a close approximation to random selection. With a random sample, the respondents to be included in the sample are randomly selected, and each individual's probability of being picked is exactly equal to that for any other person. This discussion of statistical inference and reliability is based on random sampling.

Suppose a researcher wants to learn the average age of those in a particular population, such as those living in a well-defined geographical area. A sample of some portion of the people within the area might be surveyed to learn the age of each, and the average age of the people in the sample could be computed. If the sample were selected at random from among all those in the population, the average age for the sample would be an unbiased estimate of the average age of all the people in the area. The average age of the population would be *inferred* from the sample. If, on the other hand, the sample were picked only from among those living in the part of the area closest to the survey headquarters, that wouldn't be a random sample and the sample statistics wouldn't be representative of the entire population. It would be a biased estimate of the population, and no legitimate inferences could be made about the population as a whole. Thus, statistical inference is based on random sampling. The more the sampling design deviates from random selection, the less legitimate any such inferences about the whole population would be.

Standard Error of the Estimate

The fact that no sample is likely to be perfectly representative of the entire population was noted earlier. In other words, no sample survey data are perfectly *reliable*. In the example above, the average age of the people in the sample is likely to be slightly different from the actual average age of everybody in the population. Those who seek survey data would often like to know just how "good" the estimate really is. In other words, they want to know about the *reliability* of the estimate. The term *reliability* is used here in exactly the same way as it was explained in Chapter 3. Reliability is determined by the ability of a procedure—in this case, sampling—to produce the same results with multiple replications.

To illustrate the reliability of estimates from samples, suppose a sample of 100 adult respondents were selected *at random* from a very large population and the ages of each were recorded. The mean age of the sample could then be computed. If this procedure were done hundreds or thousands of times, it would result in hundreds or thousands of sample means. Of course, they wouldn't all be identical. They would vary a little from one another, since the sampling isn't perfectly reliable.

In effect, this procedure would result in a data distribution—a *distribution of sample means*. It would be a *sampling* of all possible samples of this type. So, statisticians refer to this hypothetical distribution as the *sampling distribution of sample means*. This distribution could be treated like any other data distribution. In other words, one could compute the *mean* of the *sampling distribution of sample means,* and this would be an unbiased estimate of the *population mean.* The *standard deviation, skewness,* and *kurtosis* could be computed, as well. One of the nice properties of this sampling distribution is that it tends to be normal or very nearly so, regardless of the shape of the population distribution from which the samples were randomly selected.

It was noted in Chapter 3 and earlier in this chapter that if the distribution is normal, about 68 percent of the data falls within ±1 S.D., 95 percent within ±2 S.D., and 99 percent within ±3 S.D. of the mean. So, if the mean of this hypothetical distribution were 40 years and its S.D. were equal to 2 years, that means that 95 percent of random samples of 100 respondents would yield a sample mean between 36 and 44 years (i.e., ±2 S.D.).

Now, suppose a research analyst selected one random sample of 100 adults from this same population and the mean age of the respondents was 45 years. *If* the analyst knew (without going through the entire process of selecting hundreds of samples) that the S.D. of the *sampling distribution of sample means* was equal to 2 years, that would be extremely helpful. Since 95 percent of the means of such samples as this will fall within ±2 S.D. of the population mean, there's a 95 percent chance *this* sample mean is within 4 years of the population mean. Similarly, there's a 99 percent probability it's within 6 years of the mean for the entire population.

In fact, research analysts *can* learn the value of the standard deviation of the *sampling distribution of sample means* without going through the laborious process of multiple sampling. Virtually all statistical analysis routines and some spreadsheet and charting programs can compute and report the *standard error of the estimate of the mean,* usually called simply the *standard error* or abbreviated as S.E. The standard error is actually the standard deviation of this would-be *sampling distribution of sample means* computed from many different samples of exactly the same size from precisely the same population.

The standard error of the estimate is *directly* related to the *variance* in the population. In other words, the more the respondents tend to differ from one another or vary in their response to the item, the higher the standard error will be. The standard error is *inversely* related to sample size. The larger the sample, the more representative of the entire population it's likely to be. Thus, the mean from a large sample is less likely to be different from that for the whole population than the mean from a small sample.

Confidence Interval

The confidence interval is a range around the sample mean based on the standard error. Thus, the 68 percent confidence interval is the range from −1 S.E. below the mean to +1 S.E. above the mean. Similarly, the 95 percent confidence interval is the range within ±2 S.E., and the 99 percent confidence interval is the range within ±3 S.E. The range of the standard error is shown graphically in Figure 11–8. Since the mean is 10 and the S.E. is 1, there's a 99 percent chance the actual population mean is between 7 and 13 (±3 S.E.). Similarly, there's a 95 percent chance the population mean is between 8 and 12, and a 68 percent chance it's between 9 and 11.

Many statistical analysis programs routinely compute the 95 percent confidence interval by subtracting twice the value of S.E. from the mean for the lower value and by adding twice the value of S.E. to the mean for the higher value. When only the standard error is computed and reported, the analyst can easily compute the confidence interval in the same way. Guidelines for interpreting confidence intervals are provided in Guidelist 11–4.

To interpret the confidence interval to sponsors, the researcher need only indicate there's a 68 percent chance, a 95 percent chance, or a 99 percent chance the mean for the whole population is within a given range, depending on whether ±1, ±2, or ±3 S.E. is used for the calculation. All three confidence intervals might be reported for key variables. Reporting the confidence interval around a mean provides those seeking the survey information with a sense of the reliability of the estimate and the confidence they may have when making inferences about the whole population.

It's important to note here that the standard error of the estimate and the confidence intervals computed from it can be used for *both* normal distributions and those that depart from normality, no matter how much they depart. In other words, the distribution need not have a skewness and kurtosis value near zero for the standard error to be valid. There's no equivalent to S.E. for categorical data. That's why it may be desirable to retain the continuous form of a numeric variable, creating a new, identical one to be recoded into categories when it's desirable to treat it as categorical for some analysis.

Figure 11–8   *Confidence Interval Diagram*

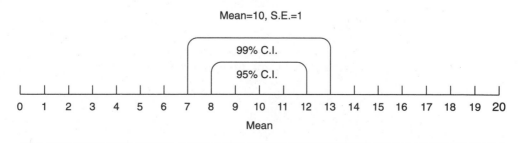

GUIDELIST 11–4

For Interpreting Confidence Intervals

1. Confidence intervals are based on the *standard error of* the estimate, often called S.E.

2. Confidence intervals apply only to continuous numerical variables.

3. A confidence interval is always based on a given level or probability, usually 95 percent or 99 percent.

4. The 68 percent confidence interval is the range from −1 S.E. below the mean to +1 S.E. above the mean.

5. The 95 percent confidence interval is the range from −2 S.E. below the mean to +2 S.E. above the mean.

6. The 99 percent confidence interval is the range from −3 S.E. below the mean to +3 S.E. above the mean.

7. Confidence intervals are used to indicate the probability the actual *population* mean is within a given range around the sample mean.

8. The standard error and the range of the confidence intervals are measures of reliability.

9. The more *variance* there is in the distribution, the lower the reliability, the larger the standard error, and the wider the confidence intervals will be.

10. The larger the *sample size,* the greater the reliability, the smaller the standard error, and the more narrow the confidence intervals will be.

MEASURES OF ASSOCIATION

The statistics discussed so far in this chapter are used to analyze *individual* variables and make inferences about the population based on their sample values. When the research analyst studies the *relationships* between pairs of variables, other statistical tools are required. The previous chapter provided guidance for selecting the appropriate statistical tools to measure such relationships. In the remainder of this chapter, the statistical values and coefficients produced by those procedures will be explained and interpreted.

Statistical significance

Virtually all of the measures of relationships between variables are designed not only to show the degree of association between the items, but also to report the *statistical significance* of the relationship.[1] The word *significance* has a very special and consistent meaning when used in this context. It does *not* mean importance! If a relationship between two variables is statistically *significant,* this simply means it *signifies* or *signals* there's a good chance the two items are actually related to one another in the population, just as they are in the sample. By contrast, if the relationship is *not* significant, this means there's too high a chance this much of a relationship could result only from sampling error, even if it didn't exist in the population

---

[1]If the probability or significance value isn't reported by the analysis routine, the researcher must refer to the appropriate example and statistical reference tables in Appendix B to determine if the probability is above or below such critical values as .05, .01, or .001. These are the values most often listed in statistical tables.

at large. Consequently, *significance* is required to make a *statistical inference* about the population, based on the sample. An example may clarify the meaning and interpretation of statistical significance.

Suppose the respondents to a survey are asked to record their age and sex in the demographic section. The sponsor may want to know if the men in the *population* tend to be older, the same age, or younger than the women surveyed. To answer that question, the analyst will need to assess the *relationship* between two variables: *age* and *sex* of respondents. Age is a continuous ratio variable and sex is a nominal, categorical item. The age of the men and women can be compared by computing the average age of each group. Suppose the average age of everyone was 40 and half of the respondents were of each sex. The men in the sample may have an average age of 41 and the women an average age of 39. This *suggests* the men in the *population* are about two years older than the women. That may or may *not* be true.

There's always some chance the sample "happened," purely by chance, to include a group of men who were somewhat older than the actual average age for all men in the population. There's also some chance that the sample contained a disproportionate number of younger women from the population, also purely by chance. Because of this possibility, there's a chance the average age of men and of women in the population as a whole is exactly the same—40 years. Yet the sample seems to indicate men were older. The research analyst needs a way to determine the *probability* the sample would produce such differences between men and women even if the average age of all men and women in the population were the same. If the sample has been selected *randomly,* there is a way to determine that probability. In this example, the analyst would use *analysis of variance* to assess the significance of the difference between the average age of men and women.

The question regarding statistical significance is simply this: WHAT'S THE CHANCE OF THIS MUCH RELATIONSHIP BETWEEN THE VARIABLES RESULTING ONLY FROM SAMPLING ERROR IF THERE WERE NO RELATIONSHIP WHATSOEVER IN THE POPULATION? The *significance probability* is the answer to that question! Example 11–2 lists five ways to phrase the interpretation of statistical significance for each of the five measures of association to be discussed here. The same basic wording could be used interchangeably for any of the statistics. The only difference is the type of relationship being analyzed—differences in proportions for cross-tabs, differences in means for ANOVA and paired *t*-tests, or covariation for correlation and regression analysis.

The most important point is that the *smaller* the significance probability is, the *less likely* the association between the variables resulted *only* from sampling error. So the *smaller* it is, the *more* it *signifies* a similar relationship between the variables in the entire population from which the random sample was selected.

How sure does the sponsor or information seeker want to be? That depends on the *costs* of making either of two kinds of errors, described in Checklist 11–1. Statisticians call them *Type* I *errors*—rejecting the *null* (no relationship) hypothesis when it's actually true—and *type* II *errors*—accepting the *null* hypotheses when it's actually false. This same dichotomy of potential error is common to other fields as well. Medical researchers refer to *false positives*—finding an indication of a condition when it does *not* really exist—and *false negatives*—finding no indication when a condition *does* actually exist. In most areas of predictive decision making, there are corresponding errors. There are *go errors* and *no-go errors*—doing something

EXAMPLE 11–2

Interpretations of Significance Probability

Example A — Cross Tabulation

| Chi-square = 11.5 | d.f. = 4 | Prob. = 0.050 |

There is a *five percent* chance this much of a relationship would result purely from sampling error if the two items were *not* related in the population.

Example B — Analysis of Variance

| F = 8.2 | d.f. = 1 | Prob. = 0.002 |

Two times out of 1,000 this much difference in means between the two groups would result from sampling error if the means in the population were the same.

Example C — Paired T-Test

| T = 1.9 | d.f. = 932 | Prob. = 0.049 |

This much difference between means for the two variables would result only from sampling error less than *one time out of twenty* if the means were identical in the population.

Example D — Correlation Analysis

| r = 0.03 | n = 933 | Prob. = 0.333 |

About *one third* of the time, a sample of this size would show this much correlation between the variables due only to sampling error, if the items had zero correlation in the population.

Example E — Regression Analysis

| Rsq. = −0.09 | d.f. = 931 | Prob. = 0.004 |

The independent variable would explain this much variance in the dependent variable due exclusively to sampling error *less than one half of one percent* of the time if the two items were completely unrelated in the population.

when it turns out one should *not* have done it and deciding against doing something that ultimately would have been beneficial, respectively. Anyone who has gone ahead with a picnic only to have it rain or canceled an outing for what turns out to be a beautiful day has an intuitive understanding of such errors. A major advantage of statistical analysis is computation of the *probability* of making the first kind of error—of assuming a relationship

---

CHECKLIST 11–1

For Determining Significance Levels

1. Would it be very costly to *mistakenly assume* the relationship actually exists in the population when, in fact, the two variables are unrelated in the population? If so, the results *shouldn't* be regarded as *significant* unless the probability is extremely low.

2. Is there much to lose by *mistakenly assuming* the relationship resulted only from sampling error and not because it exists in the population when, in fact, it does? If so, the results *should* be regarded as *significant* unless the probability is quite high.

3. Would it be extremely costly to make an error in *either way?* If so, the sampling reliability can be increased by subsequently sampling a larger proportion of the population on a random basis and combining the results to obtain a larger sample size.

---

exists in the population when, in fact, it shows up in the sample only because of sampling error. Guidelines for assessing statistical significance are presented in Guidelist 11–5.

It's important to note here that significance is related to the importance of a relationship between variables, but the two aren't the same thing. In technical terms, significance is *necessary,* but not *sufficient* for importance. That simply means that if a relationship or difference isn't statistically significant, it can't be regarded as important. On the other hand, simply because it's significant doesn't imply that it will necessarily prove important. In the example used earlier, suppose the difference between the average ages of men and of women was rather large but it was *not* significant. The difference would then be attributed to sampling error, despite its size. It wouldn't make good sense to treat the two groups in the population as though they were different in that respect.

Now suppose the difference proves to be slight but it was statistically significant. That means one can be very sure the ages of the two groups in the population are indeed different from one another; yet that slight difference may not be of much *importance* to the sponsor. Statistical significance is a function of several things—the sample size, the amount of variance in the variable within the population, and the actual relationship between the variables in the population. These determine the value of the significance probability. The importance of a relationship depends on the meaning of the variables and relationships to the sponsor. It depends on the actions that are implied or the consequences that result.

Interpreting Cross-Tabulation

Cross-tabulation is used to assess the relationship between two categorical variables. (The technical name for cross-tabulation is *contingency table analysis.)* It doesn't matter whether causality is assumed. If it is, it doesn't matter which variable is regarded as dependent or independent. Nor does it matter whether the data are nominal, ordinal, interval, or ratio

---

GUIDELIST 11–5

For Assessing Statistical Significance

1. Significance is determined by the probability that a sample would show such a relationship if it did *not* exist in the population as a whole.

2. If a relationship between variables is regarded as significant, it's taken by *inference* to *exist* in the population as a whole.

3. A relationship can't be viewed as important if it isn't significant, because there's too great a chance it resulted only from sampling error.

4. A relationship that's statistically significant may or may not be important, because importance depends on the strength and meaning of the relationship.

5. The researcher or sponsor must determine the critical value of probability below which the relationship will be viewed as significant and above which it will be attributed only to sampling error.

6. If the probability or significance value generated by an analysis routine is .05, this means there's only a 5 percent chance of such a relationship in the sample if it did not actually exist in the population.

---

variables. The only statistical requirement is that the minimum *expected* cell frequency for the table must be 5 or more. Guidelines for checking the minimum *expected* cell frequency were provided in the previous chapter. From a *practical* point of view, the only limitation on the use of cross-tabulation is that there should be a limited number of categories for each variable—preferably only 5 or 6, and certainly no more than 10 or 12. Very large tables are too bulky and complex to interpret effectively.

The cross-tab table

The cross-tab table in Example 11–3 will be used to illustrate how cross-tabulation works. The top value in each cell is the *count* or *frequency*. The bottom number in the cells is the *total percentage*—the percentage of *all* cases that are in the cell. The row and column totals are self-explanatory. The row and column percentages printed below those values are the percentages of all data contained in each row and column. The middle values in each cell, the *expected* values, are the number of cases one would *expect* if the proportions in each cell were the same as the proportions for the row totals or column totals. In other words, the *expected* values are the frequencies that would yield the same *percentage* distributions for each row or each column as the *percentage* distribution for the row or column totals.

Cross-tabulation is a way to show how much the frequency or percentage distributions of one variable differ according to various levels of another variable. In the left section of Example 11–3, the *expected* and *actual* frequencies or counts are exactly the same in each cell. The column totals are 50:50 and so are the values in the cells of each row. There's *perfect* proportionality. In the right section of the example, proportion of Group 1 respondents who are also Type A is *disproportionately* low. Instead of 60 cases in that cell, there are only 40. The counts in the other cells are also disproportionate to the row and column totals. So, the chances of an individual being Type A or Type B depends on whether the

EXAMPLE 11–3

Significance of Cross-Tabulation Tables

Proportionate, No Relationship			Disproportionate, Strong Relationship		
Count Exp. Val. Tot Pct.	Group 1	Group 2	Row Total		Group 1	Group 2	Row Total
Type A	60 60 30%	60 60 30%	120 60%	Type A	40 60 20%	80 60 40%	120 60%
Type B	40 40 20%	40 40 20%	80 40%	Type B	60 40 30%	20 40 10%	80 40%
Column Total	100 50%	100 50%	200 100%	Column Total	100 50%	100 50%	200 100%
Chi-Sq. = 0.0 d.f. = 1 Sig. = 1.00000			Chi-Sq. = 33.33 d.f. = 1 Sig. = 0.00000		

person is in Group 1 or Group 2. In other words, the two variables—*Group* and *Type*—appear to be related to one another.

Statistical significance of cross-tabs

Visual examination of a cross-tab table (or a graphic picture such as a split bar chart) will reveal the amount of disproportionality to the analyst or information seeker. But the question of *statistical significance* still remains: *What's the chance of this much disproportionality among the rows or columns resulting only from sampling error if there were no disproportionality whatsoever in the population?* The chi-square statistic answers that question.

The chi-square statistic and the significance probability associated with it are based on the amount of difference between the *expected* values for each cell and the actual *count*.[2] The *more* proportional the rows and columns are to the totals, the smaller the chi-square value will be. In the left section of Example 11–3, the differences between the *expected* and *actual* frequencies is zero and so is the chi-square value. In the table in the right section of the example, the differences are large and the chi-square value is also relatively large. The significance probability indicates there's virtually no chance this much disproportionality would result only from sampling error if the two variables—*Group* and *Type*—were unrelated in the population. The probability of the chi-square value is listed as zero, but there's always

---

[2]Chi-square is *not* merely the sum of the differences. Rather, it's the sum over all the cells of the *expected* minus the *actual* count, squared, and divided by the *expected* value.

GUIDELIST 11–6

For Computing Cross-Tab Chi-Squares

1. Cross-tabulate the variables by row and column to list the *count* or *frequency* in each cell.
2. Record the row totals and column totals in the right and lower margins respectively.
3. Record the grand total, or number of cases, at the lower right margin.
4. For each *row,* divide the *row total* by the *grand total* and record the decimal *row-to-total ratio* just below each row total, for reference at the next step.
5. For each *cell,* multiply each *row-to-total ratio* times the *column total* and record these *expected frequencies* in each cell for reference at the next step.
6. For each *cell,* subtract the *cell count* from the *expected frequency,* square the product, and record the *squared value* in each cell for reference at the next step.
7. For each *cell,* divide the *squared values* by the *expected frequency* and record this *cell chi-square value* in each cell for reference at the next step.
8. *Sum* the *cell chi-square values* for all cells and record the *table chi-square value* at the bottom of the table.
9. Compute the *degrees of freedom* for the table by multiplying (*number of rows* minus 1) times (*number of columns* minus 1).
10. Refer to Appendix B, Example B–2 and Table B–2, to determine the statistical significance of the relationship based on the value of *chi-square* and the number of *degrees of freedom.*

some probability the relationship is due merely to sampling error. The analysis routine printed only five significant digits beyond the decimal point, and the probability is so small it registers as zero—and for practical purposes, it can be treated as zero.

The calculation of the chi-square statistic is fairly simple but rather time-consuming to do manually. Yet it can be done with relative ease with a spreadsheet or charting data table where rows and columns of numbers can be manipulated. Guidelist 11–6 contains the computational steps for hand tabulation. Analysts using a spreadsheet or charting table must perform the same calculation, but they would, of course, record the intermediate values in appropriate columns and rows of the program's table.

Most statistical analysis routines calculate and print not only the chi-square value, but also the significance probability associated with it. But if the analyst is using a spreadsheet or some other routine to create the cross-tabulation tables, it may be necessary to compute the chi-square value and refer to Appendix B, Example B–2 and Table B–2, to determine the probability. Table B–2 requires both the chi-square value and the *degrees of freedom* (d.f.). The value of d.f. for cross-tabulation is simply the number of rows minus 1 times the number of columns minus 1, as Guidelist 11–6 indicates.

In Example 11–4, the column percentages are listed in the table in the upper section and the row percentages are used in the lower section. If the research analyst wanted to see how people in different age groups differ in their time of day preferences, the column percentages would be compared across rows in a table such as the one in the upper section. Thus, over twice the percentage of young people are "Larks" than those of other ages, and so forth.

EXAMPLE 11–4

Cross-Tab Row and Column Percentages

Time of Day Type by Age Group

Column Percentages	Under 35	35 to 49	Over 49	Total
Larks	44.5%	20.0%	21.2%	30.0%
Wrens	27.1%	30.6%	30.6%	29.2%
Owls	28.4%	49.4%	48.1%	42.4%
Total	38.7%	21.2%	40.0%	100.0%

Chi-square = 27.72   d.f. = 4   Prob. = 0.0000

Row Percentages	Under 35	35 to 49	Over 49	Total
Larks	57.5%	14.2%	28.3%	30.0%
Wrens	35.9%	22.2%	41.9%	29.2%
Owls	27.0%	25.8%	47.2%	42.4%
Total	38.7%	21.2%	40.0%	100.0%

Chi-square = 27.72   d.f. = 4   Prob. = 0.0000

If, on the other hand, the analyst wanted to see how people with each time of day pattern differ in age, the row percentages could be compared down the columns. For example, only about 28 percent of "Larks" were 50 or older, while nearly 42 percent of "Wrens" and about 47 percent of "Owls" were in the elder group. It would also be possible to reverse the bottom table so the time of day patterns defined the rows and the age groups defined the columns. Column percentages could then be listed and used to make the second type of assessment described above. Guidelist 11–7 summarizes the guidelines for interpreting cross-tabulation.

Interpreting Analysis of Variance

Analysis of variance (ANOVA) is used to measure the degree and significance of a relationship between a categorical independent variable and a continuous numeric dependent variable. The independent variable can be from a nominal, ordinal, interval, or ratio scale. The only limitation is on the number of values or categories formed by the variable. If there are too many categories—more than about eight or ten—the results will be legitimate but the interpretation can become rather difficult. The dependent variable for analysis of variance must be from an interval or ratio scale and must meet other requirements as well. The

GUIDELIST 11–7

For Interpreting Cross-Tabs

1. Check the minimum expected cell frequency as described in the previous chapter to be sure it's five or greater.

2. If degrees of freedom and probability aren't listed, compute d.f. by multiplying (number of rows minus one) times (number of columns minus one).

3. Refer to Appendix B, Example B–2 and Table B–2, to determine the statistical significance of the relationship based on the value of *chi-square* and the number of *degrees of freedom*.

4. Table B–2 lists *chi-square* values for the 0.20, 0.10, 0.05, 0.025, 0.01, and 0.001 levels of probability.

5. If the chi-square value from the cross-tab is *larger* than the value in the table, the probability is *smaller* than the probability level listed, and the relationship is significant.

6. If the relationship isn't significant, explain to information seekers that the variables are probably not related in the population.

7. If the relationship *is* significant, inform sponsors that in the population as a whole, distributions across the rows are likely to differ systematically from column to column, or vice versa.

8. It doesn't matter which variable is listed on the rows and which on the columns when doing the computations, so the table should be arranged the way it can be most easily read and interpreted.

---

requirements for the appropriate use of ANOVA are discussed in the previous chapter and outlined in Guidelist 10–3, page 295.

Figure 11–9 contains the description of job satisfaction score distributions by three employment types: government, corporate, and self-employed respondents. Based on inspection of either the plot of distributions, breakdown table, or bar chart, it would appear that job satisfaction is strongly related to the type of respondents' employment. But the question of *statistical significance* still remains: *What's the chance of this much difference among mean group scores resulting only from sampling error if there were no such differences whatsoever in the population?* ANOVA can answer that question.

The ANOVA table

The ANOVA table for the variables described in Figure 11–9 is shown in Example 11–5. This is a very conventional format for an ANOVA table. Statistical analysis routines almost always produce a table like this or something very similar, although they may also, either optionally or by default, include additional coefficients such as *range* tests and tests of *homogeneity of variance*.

The terms and values contained in an ANOVA table are explained briefly in Guidelist 11–8. The steps for computing the ANOVA table values, shown in Guidelist 11–9, are very simple and easy. Although they require only addition, subtraction, and multiplication, it's a rather tedious process if done manually. On the other hand, the ANOVA table values can very readily be calculated with the use of a spreadsheet or charting program that performs operations for entire columns of data instantly.

Figure 11–9   *Distributions for Three Respondent Groups*

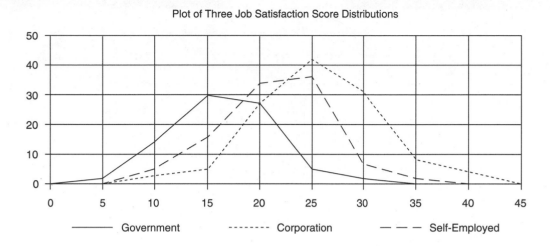

Plot of Three Job Satisfaction Score Distributions

———— Government   ········ Corporation   — — — Self-Employed

Breakdown of Mean Job Satisfaction Scores by Employment Type

Employment	Count	Mean	Std. Dev.	Std. Error
Government	80	18.6	5.1	0.57
Corporation	120	27.4	5.7	0.52
Self-Employed	100	23.3	5.0	0.50
Total	300	23.7	6.4	0.37

Bar Chart of Mean Job Satisfaction Scores by Employment Type

EXAMPLE 11–5

Analysis of Variance Print Output

	Analysis of Variance				
Source	Sum of Squares	D.F.	Mean Squares	F-Ratio	F Prob.
Between Groups	3713.42	2	1856.71	65.95	.0000
Within Groups	8361.57	297	28.15		
Total	12074.99	299			

Statistical significance of ANOVA

The F probability of .0000 means there's virtually no chance this much difference in mean scores between groups would result purely from sampling error if the group means in the population were identical. Thus, in this case, the analyst would conclude that the two variables are significantly related—that employment type, the *independent* variable, has a significant effect on job satisfaction scores, the *dependent* variable. If the analysis routine reports only the F value and doesn't list the actual probability, the analyst must refer to Appendix B, Example B-3 and Table B-3, for the *F*-distribution, at the appropriate level of probability, such as .05 or .01, and for the correct numerator and denominator degrees of freedom. If the F-ratio from the ANOVA is *larger* than the value listed in the table, the differences in means are significant. In other words, the *larger* the F-ratio, the *more* likely the differences in means between groups will be statistically significant. Guidelist 11–10, on page 335 provides the guidelines for interpreting analysis of variance.

Interpreting Paired t-Tests

At times it may be necessary to check the significance of differences between two continuous variables that were both provided by the same respondents. If so, a *paired t-test* provides a better measure of statistical significance than ANOVA does. Figure 11–10 provides a comparison of results from the two statistical tools. The data represent the *initial* and *final* reaction scores of 220 respondents regarding a political issue, taken before and after they received a mailing about the issue. The results of the *paired t-test* are shown below the breakdown table in the upper section of Figure 11–10. The middle section contains an ANOVA table. Analysis of variance treats the *initial* and *final* as individual cases, as though they were obtained from different respondents, rather than two ratings by the same individuals.

The ANOVA results indicate the significance of the difference between mean values is .05—one chance in twenty that such results would be obtained purely because of sampling

---

GUIDELIST 11–8

For Understanding ANOVA Table Terms

Analysis of Variance	Comparison of all the variance around the grand mean with the amount of variance around the mean for each group.
Source (of Variance)	The "source" of the variance on each row, depending on what means were used to compute the variance.
Total [Source]	The total variance values obtained when the variance is computed around the grand mean without regard for the groups in which each case resides.
Within Groups [Source]	The variance values obtained by computing variance of each data point from around the mean of the group in which the data point resides, combined for all groups.
Between Groups [Source]	The differences between the *total sums of squares* and *mean squares* and the corresponding values from *within groups*.
Sums of Squares (S.S.)	The sums of the squared deviations of each data point from around a mean value—either the grand mean or the mean for the group within which the data point resides.
D.F. (Degrees of Freedom)	The "adjusted" value of the number of cases and/or groups in the analysis, as a divisor to convert total variance values to average variances.
Mean Squares (M.S.)	The sums of the squares for each source of variance divided by the degrees of freedom for that source to constitute an "average" variance for the source.
F-Ratio	The ratio of the *between groups mean squares* to the *within groups mean squares,* expressed as a decimal value.
F Probability	The probability of obtaining an F-ratio of a given value or greater, based on the F probability distribution for numerator and denominator degrees of freedom.

---

error if there were no difference in means in the entire population. By comparison, the t-test results proved to be a much more sensitive test. The significance of the t-value was .01, or one chance out of a hundred in obtaining such a difference due only to sampling error. Thus, the t-test provides greater assurance of significance than ANOVA for the same data distributions.

The plot of the two distributions is displayed in the lower left section of Figure 11–10 on page 336. The picture clearly shows there's only a slight difference between initial and final reactions. In the lower right section of Figure 11–10, the data are portrayed in a scatterplot with the initial reaction scores on the vertical axis and the final reactions on the horizontal. The two reactions appear to be correlated with one another. (The actual value of the correlation coefficient is 0.41.) The reason a *paired* t-test provides a better measure of significance than ANOVA for two measures from the *same* respondents can be understood intuitively. ANOVA ignores the fact that some people tend to rate *both* measures relatively

GUIDELIST 11–9

Steps for Computing Analysis of Variance

1. Calculate the mean for each group and the *grand* mean for all cases.
2. Subtract each data point from the *grand* mean and square the difference.
3. Sum these squared values over all cases for the *Total Sums of Squares*.
4. For each group, subtract each data point from the *group* mean and square the difference.
5. Sum these squared values over all groups for the *Within Groups Sums of Squares*.
6. Subtract the *Within Groups Sums of Squares* from the *Total Sums of Squares* for the *Between Groups Sums of Squares*.
7. Subtract 1 from the number of *groups* for the *Between Groups Degrees of Freedom*.
8. Subtract 1 from the total number of *cases* for the *Total Groups Degrees of Freedom*.
9. Subtract the *Between Groups Degrees of Freedom* from the *Total Groups Degrees of Freedom* for the *Within Groups Degrees of Freedom*.
10. Divide the *Between Groups Sums of Squares* by the *Between Groups Degrees of Freedom* for the *Between Groups Mean Squares*.
11. Divide the *Within Groups Sums of Squares* by the *Within Groups Degrees of Freedom* for the *Within Groups Mean Squares*.
12. Divide the *Between Groups Mean Squares* by the *Within Groups Mean Squares* for the *F-Ratio*.
13. Refer to Appendix B, Example B–3 and Table B–3, for the F-distribution to determine if the F-Ratio is larger than listed for the critical significance, indicating the actual probability is less likely.

high or relatively low. By contrast, paired t-tests focus on the *difference* between each *pair* of scores. In effect, this controls for the variance in *both* measures from one respondent to the next. Guidelines for interpreting paired t-tests are listed in Guidelist 11–11 on page 337.

Interpreting Correlation

Correlation measures the degree, direction, and significance of relationships between two continuous numeric variables *without* assuming causality—without identifying one as independent and the other as dependent. The method known as Pearson product-moment correlation or just PM correlation can be used for interval or ratio scale data. Spearman rank correlation is the most common nonparametric correlation method for ordinal scale data. Both are interpreted in the same way. Most statistical analysis routines will perform either PM or rank correlations. Many spreadsheet and charting programs can also produce scatterplots of the data with correlation coefficients as well as the linear regression equation, which will be discussed in the next section of the chapter.

Figure 11–11 on page 338 shows the tables and plots of two *pairs* of variables. In a sample of 300 men and 300 women, both sexes responded to a series of items that were totaled to produce a score indicating their degree of trust in the news media. Later in the questionnaire, they were asked to indicate the percentage of time they felt television news reports were totally accurate. Both variables were interval data, but neither was ordinarily identified as causing the other.

GUIDELIST 11–10

For Interpreting Analysis of Variance

1. The object is to compute the mean value of the dependent variable for each category of the independent variable and determine if the means for the groups in the analysis are significantly different.

2. If the probability is computed by the analysis routine, it's the probability that as much difference in means would be due merely to sampling error if, in fact, the groups had the same means in the population.

3. The larger the F-ratio value, the smaller the probability and the greater the likelihood of significance. The smaller the F-ratio, the less likely the relationship will be significant at a given probability.

4. If the probability isn't reported by the analysis routine, the analyst must refer to Appendix B, Example B–3 and Table B–3, for the F-Distribution.

5. If the value listed for the appropriate numerator and denominator *degrees of freedom* and the .05 or .01 level of significance is *smaller* than the F-ratio value from the analysis of variance, this indicates the relationship is significant at that level.

The scatterplots in the lower section of Figure 11–11 list the accuracy scores on the vertical (y) axis and the trust scores on the horizontal (x) axis. The coefficient of *correlation* (r) and the coefficient of *determination* (r-square) are listed below each plot. The significance probability for women indicate there's virtually no chance of obtaining a relationship of this magnitude purely by sampling error if it didn't exist in the population. By contrast, there's a near-perfect probability of obtaining the minuscule relationship between these variables for the men in the sample strictly by sampling error if it didn't exist in the population.

Example 11–6 shows a *correlation matrix* for each pair of five variables. This is a common print output format when all the two-way relationships among a group of variables are analyzed. In this example, the probability for assessing significance appears below the correlation coefficient in each cell. Often only the upper right half of the matrix is printed because both sides of the diagonal are identical.

Chapter 10 noted that the range of r is from zero, no relationship, to ±1, a perfect "lock-step" relationship. The absolute value indicates the strength of the relationship. The sign of the coefficient indicates if the two variables are moving in the same or the opposite direction—if they're *directly* or *inversely* related. It's also important to note that the value of the correlation coefficient can easily be misinterpreted. In Example 11–6, variables 2 and 4 have a correlation coefficient of 0.479. This *appears* to be a fairly strong relationship, since it's *half* the maximum value of r. In fact, however, the more informative number is r-square, the coefficient of determination, since it identifies the percentage of *shared* variance. In this case, r-square equals only 0.229. Thus, less than a quarter of the variance in the two variables is "shared" between them. Most experienced analysts depend more on r-square than r to interpret correlations.

Figure 11–10   *t-Test versus ANOVA Results*

T-Test Breakdown Table

Reaction	Count	Mean	Std. Dev.	Std. Error
Initial	220	23.80	4.87	0.33
Final	220	22.89	4.66	0.31
Total	440	23.34	4.78	0.23
Difference	220	0.09	5.19	0.35

t-Value=2.58   d.f.=219   2-tail Probability=.01

Analysis of Variance Table

Source	Sum of Squares	D.F.	Mean Squares	F-Ratio	F-Prob.
Between Groups	90.00	1	90.00	3.96	.05
Within Groups	9945.18	438	22.71		
Total	10035.18	439			

Plot of Distributions

– –   Initial Reaction   ——   Final Reaction

Scatterplot of Relationship

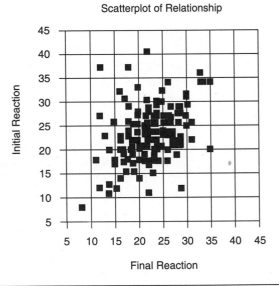

GUIDELIST 11–11

For Interpreting Paired t-Tests

1. The objective is to measure the statistical significance of the difference between two means when the variables are "paired" because the same respondents provided both.

2. The probability of as much difference (in either direction) purely by sampling error if there were no differences in the population is based on the t-value.

3. If the probability isn't listed, analysts can refer to Appendix B, Example B–4 and Table B–4, for the t-distribution, using the value of d.f., the number of cases minus one.

4. If the absolute value of t, ignoring the plus or minus sign, is larger than that listed in the table, the difference is significant at the given level of probability.

It's important to note that a significant correlation between variables does *not* imply causality, in and of itself. This is a *very* common interpretive mistake, sometimes perpetrated by researchers, but more often so by the news media. In fact, if A and B are correlated, there are *four* potential causal relationships, aside from sheer chance: A may be causing B, B may be causing A, A and B may be *interacting* (dynamically causing one another in turn), or C may be causing both A and B. Guidelines for interpreting correlations are listed in Guidelist 11–12.

Interpreting Regression Analysis

Linear regression analysis is used to measure the effect of one continuous variable on another. So, one must be specified as the *independent* variable and the other the *dependent* variable. Both must be from either interval or ratio scales. The other requirements for the legitimate use of regression analysis were discussed in Chapter 10 and outlined in Guidelist 10-6, page 303.

The regression table

Example 11–7 contains a typical regression table report from a statistical analysis routine. The values and coefficients in the table are described in Guidelist 11–13 on page 341. A *scatterplot* of the same data from a charting program is shown in the upper section of Figure 11–12. These data provide an example of the interpretation of regression.

In this example, a group of resident *homeowners* in a planned development community were surveyed to measure their *expected* spending at one of the recreational facilities—the *independent* variable for analysis. During the following period, their *actual* spending was recorded—the *dependent* measure. The scatterplot, regression equation, and r-square value are shown in the upper section of Figure 11–12 on page 342. The lower section shows the corresponding information for another group of 300 *renting* residents who were surveyed in the same way. Both pairs of dependent and independent variables are significantly related to one another, but comparison indicates that expectations of *homeowners* are much better *predictors* of spending than those of *renters*.

Figure 11–11   *High and Low Correlation Plots*

Female Trust Scores

Mean	23.2	Std. Dev.	4.9
Median	24.0	Kurtosis	1.058
Mode	24.0	Skewness	-0.408

Male Trust Scores

Mean	22.7	Std. Dev.	5.2
Median	23.0	Kurtosis	1.131
Mode	19.0	Skewness	-0.232

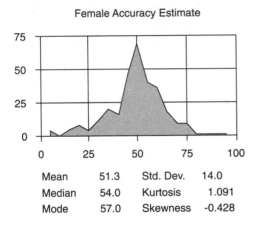

Female Accuracy Estimate

Mean	51.3	Std. Dev.	14.0
Median	54.0	Kurtosis	1.091
Mode	57.0	Skewness	-0.428

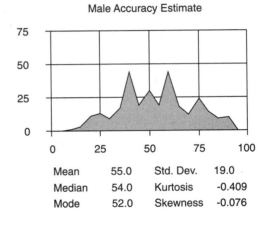

Male Accuracy Estimate

Mean	55.0	Std. Dev.	19.0
Median	54.0	Kurtosis	-0.409
Mode	52.0	Skewness	-0.076

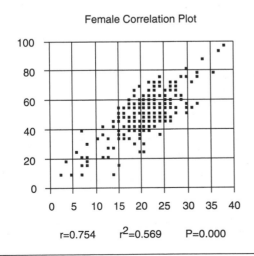

Female Correlation Plot

r=0.754 r^2=0.569   P=0.000

Male Correlation Plot

r=-0.002 r^2=0.000   P=0.975

GUIDELIST 11–12

For Interpreting Correlations

1. The object is to measure the direction, degree, and statistical significance of relationships between two continuous variables when no causality is implied.
2. Product-moment correlation analysis is used for interval and ratio scale data, and rank correlation analysis is used for ordinal data.
3. The correlation coefficient ranges from zero, indicating no relationship, to plus or minus one, indicating a perfect, linear (lockstep) relationship.
4. The sign of the correlation coefficient shows whether the variables are directly or inversely related (moving in the same or opposite directions).

5. The probability for assessing significance is the chance that such a relationship would result purely by sampling error if the variables weren't related in the population.
6. If the probability for assessing significance isn't listed, the analyst must compute the values of the t-statistic and degrees of freedom.[3]
7. The significance probability can then be determined by referring to Table B–4 and following the procedure outlined in Example B–4 in Appendix B.
8. Correlation doesn't imply that one variable is causing the other, because A may cause B, B may cause A, A and B may interact, or C may cause A and B.

EXAMPLE 11–6

Correlation Matrix Print Output

	Var 1	Var 2	Var 3	Var 4	Var 5
Var. 1	1.000 —	.303 .001	.011 .402	.164 .001	.094 .018
Var. 2		1.000 —	−.098 .014	.479 .001	.083 .032
Var. 3			1.000 —	−.193 .001	.425 .001
Var. 4				1.000 —	.010 .408
Var. 5					1.000 —

---

[3] $t = \dfrac{r\sqrt{n-2}}{\sqrt{1-r^2}}$ and d.f. = n − 2 where r = correlation coefficient and n = number of cases.

EXAMPLE 11–7

Regression Analysis Print Output

Descriptive Statistics					
Independent Variable					
Mean	22.450	Std. Dev.	4.700	S.E. Mean	0.271
N of Cases	300	Skewness	−0.371	Kurtosis	1.079
Dependent Variable					
Mean	22.663	Std. Dev.	4.660	S.E. Mean	0.269
N of Cases	300	Skewness	−0.425	Kurtosis	1.353
Regression Table					
Corr. (r)	.79538	N of cases	300	Missing	0
R-Squared	.63263	S.E. Est.	2.82923	Sig. R	.0000
Intercept (A)	4.958113	S.E. of A	.798464	Sig. A	.0000
Slope (B)	.788651	S.E. of B	.034814	Sig. B	.0000

Analysis of Variance					
	S.S.	D.F.	M.S.	F	Sig.
Regression	4107.65059	1	4107.65059	513.16657	.0000
Residual	2385.34608	298	8.00452		

Regression analysis predictions

The significance of r, the correlation coefficient, indicates the degree, direction, and significance of the relationship between two variables. Regression analysis and the resulting *regression equation* provide two additional kinds of information: It describes *how* the variables are related and it also provides a method for *predicting* the value of the *dependent* variable for new cases based on the value of the *independent* variable. Causality doesn't matter for *correlation* analysis. It *does* matter for *regression*. As the plots and regression equations in Figure 11–13 on page 343 show, regressing *actual* spending on *expected* spending isn't the same thing as regressing *expected* on *actual*. The correlation coefficient is the same, but the regression equation and scatterplots are different.

In regression scatterplots, the causal independent variable is conventionally shown on the

GUIDELIST 11–13

For Interpreting Regression Tables

Corr. Coef. (r)   The product-moment coefficient of correlation between the two variables, described earlier in this chapter.

N of Cases   The sample size or number of cases in the analysis that's the basis for computation of the *degrees of freedom* for the analysis.

Missing Values   The number of cases for which one or both variables had missing or unacceptable values (e.g., zeros, blanks, outlying values, etc.)

R–Square   The coefficient of *determination* is the square of the correlation coefficient (r). It indicates the percentage of *explained variance* as described in Chapter 10 and shown in Figure 10-12, page 300.

S.E. Est.   Standard error of the estimate around the *regression line,* depicted in Figure 11–15. It determines *confidence intervals* around the regression prediction just as its counterpart is used for estimates of the mean.

Sig. R   The probability of obtaining r of this value or greater because of sampling error if the variables were unrelated in the population.

Intercept (A)   This constant is the predicted value of Y when X is zero. In effect, it's the height of the regression line on the Y axis.

S.E. of A   Standard error of the estimate of the Y intercept value.

Sig. A   The probability of obtaining A of this value or greater because of sampling error if it were the mean of Y in the population.

Slope (B)   The slope of the line, defined as the *rise over the run* in terms of Y and X values, respectively.

S.E. of B   Standard error of the estimate of the slope of the regression line.

Sig. B   The probability of obtaining a slope of this inclination or greater because of sampling error if the slope was zero (horizontal) in the population.

ANOVA (for regression)   Analysis of the proportion of *total variance* around the mean of Y *explained* by knowing the values of X. The regression ANOVA is analogous to *analysis of variance* around the means for groups, described earlier in this chapter. The terms of the ANOVA table are similar to those described in Guidelist 11–8. The F-value and significance level are computed and interpreted in the same way.

---

horizontal X axis, and the effect dependent variable is plotted on the vertical Y axis. The regression equation refers to X and Y values, and the independent and dependent variables are often called the X and Y variables, respectively.

Another analytical factor that affects the values of the regression equation is the *range* of the independent (X) variable included in the analysis. Figure 11–14 on page 344 contains four scatterplots, regression equations, and r-square coefficients for the same variables—the expected and actual spending of homeowners. The plot in the upper left is merely a miniature of that in the upper section of Figure 11–12. It includes the full range of nonzero

Figure 11–12   *The Strength of Regression Relationships*

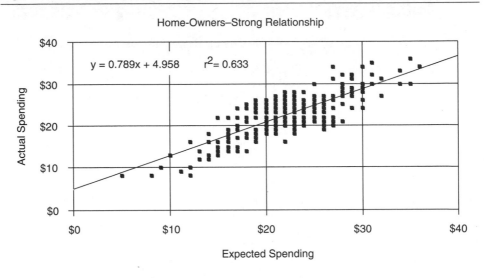

Home-Owners–Strong Relationship

$$y = 0.789x + 4.958 \qquad r^2 = 0.633$$

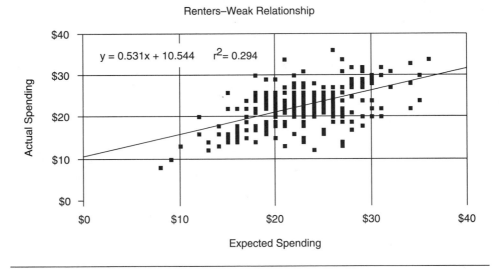

Renters–Weak Relationship

$$y = 0.531x + 10.544 \qquad r^2 = 0.294$$

expected spending. The remaining sections sequentially reduce the range of the X variable. As the range changes, so do the regression equation and r-square value. Thus, when predictions are to be made based on regression analysis, it's important to be sure the analysis includes the proper range of the *predictive independent* variable.

An example of the use of the regression equation from the upper section of Figure 11–12 may clarify the application of this kind of analysis. The facility that sponsored the survey

Figure 11–13   *Direction of Causality for Regression*

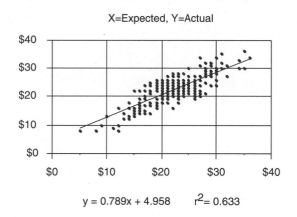

X=Expected, Y=Actual

y = 0.789x + 4.958 r^2= 0.633

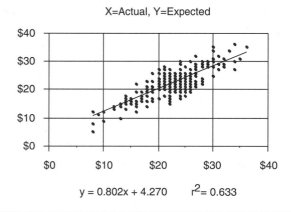

X=Actual, Y=Expected

y = 0.802x + 4.270 r^2= 0.633

wanted to predict the demand for equipment and services in subsequent periods by *new* homeowners coming into new sections of the closed community as additional phases of development were completed. To do so, they surveyed new owners to learn the amount of *expected* spending. In one case, the family *expected* to spend $33.00. This is the value of the X variable for prediction of Y, their actual spending. The regression equation is: Y = 0.789x + 4.958. Substituting the value of X, the prediction is Y = 0.789 (the slope) times 33.00 + 4.958 [the constant] = 30.995. So they can expect this new homeowner to spend about $31 per month at their facility. This example is shown graphically on the scatterplot in Figure 11–15 on page 345.

The relationship between expected and actual spending isn't perfect—the r-square value isn't 1. While a lot of the variance around the mean of Y has been "explained" by the regression line, there is obviously some error remaining. This raises the questions, "What

Figure 11–14   *Variable Ranges and Predictive Ability*

are the chances the estimate is incorrect, and by how much?" Those questions can be answered by computing the *confidence intervals* around the estimate in much the same way as the confidence intervals around a mean value from a sample are calculated. In other words, the standard error of the estimate around the *regression line* is akin to the standard error of the mean. Ninety-five percent of the actual values will be within 2 S.E. of the regression estimate and 99 percent will be within 3 S.E.

In the example the *predicted* value of spending was $31.00 and S.E. is $2.83. So, there's a 95 percent chance their actual spending will be between $31.00 ± $5.66, or between $25.34 and $36.66. Similarly, there's a 99 percent probability the actual spending will be between $22.51 and $39.49. These values could be verified visually by extending a vertical line and horizontal lines to the boundaries of the confidence interval corridors in much the same way as the estimate was plotted. Guidelines for interpreting regression analysis are contained in Guidelist 11–14 on page 346.

Figure 11–15   *Standard Error of the Regression Estimate*

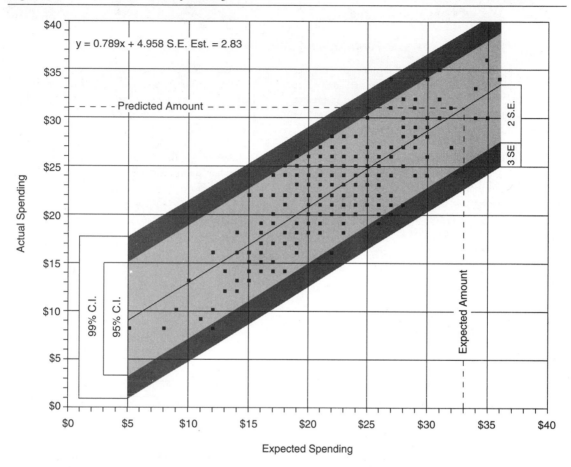

INTERPRETING VERSUS REPORTING

This chapter has focused on helping the survey research analyst to understand the various terms, values, coefficients, and relationships revealed by statistical analysis. While it may be necessary for the analyst to comprehend such information, it typically isn't required of the *sponsors* or *information seekers* to whom the information will be reported. In fact, without a statistical background, most sponsors and information seekers won't find the "raw" reports from analysis routines much more meaningful or informative than they would the "raw" data. Thus, there's an important distinction between *interpreting* statistical results and *reporting* the information to those who seek it. While some components of the final report are very similar to what was shown and discussed in this chapter, most of the formats and language differ sharply. The formats, guidelines, and recommendations for *reporting* the statistical findings are provided in Chapter 12.

GUIDELIST 11–14

For Interpreting Regression Analysis

1. Regression is used to determine the degree, direction, and significance of one variable's effect on another *and to* obtain an equation to predict values of the dependent variable based on the values of the independent variable.

2. The r-square value ranges from zero to one and indicates the proportion of variance in the dependent variable that's *explained by the values* of *the* independent variable.

3. *The assessment* of significance is determined by the value of r, the correlation coefficient, and significance is checked in the same way as for correlation analysis.

4. The regression equation consists of a coefficient to be multiplied by a known value for the independent variable, plus a constant to be added, to compute a predicted value of the dependent variable for a "new" case.

5. The constant, often designated with the letter A, is the intercept, the value of the dependent variable when the independent variable is zero.

6. The regression coefficient, often designated with the letter B, is the *slope* of the regression line, or the rise on the dependent variable scale for each unit of the independent variable.

7. A positive coefficient indicates a *direct* relationship and a regression line sloping upward toward the right, while a negative coefficient indicates an *inverse* relationship and a line sloping downward to the right.

SUMMARY

Interpreting the Survey Results

A. Begin with data description. Organize and interpret the descriptions of individual variables before turning to measures of association.

B. Choose the best average. Consider both the type of scale and the shape of the distribution when selecting the best average.

C. Recode data when necessary. Recode continuous variables into fewer, larger categories to use frequency tables and cross-tabs.

D. Treat data both ways. Treat continuous variables with only a few scale points as both continuous and categorical data for both description and measures of association.

E. Make inferences carefully. Choose an appropriate level of probability for making inferences about the population and assessing statistical significance.

F. Depend on cross-tabulation. Use cross-tabs to measure associations between variables when feasible, rather than more complex measures of relationships.

G. Use prediction cautiously. Be sure that equations for prediction from regression or discriminant analysis are valid and stay within the range of the database.

H. Check causality carefully. Remember that an association between variables doesn't automatically imply that one is causing the other.

Chapter 12

Reporting the Information

INFORMATION NEED SATISFACTION

Report generation is the task of making the survey results respond directly and meaningfully to the information needs. When the questions, scales, and questionnaire were composed, the items were arranged to make it easy and understandable for respondents. During the reporting phase, they're usually rearranged to make the information understandable and easy to grasp by those seeking the information. The main information requirements and the most important items or facts are ordinarily listed first, followed by those of lesser importance, regardless of the order in which they appeared in the questionnaire.

The last two chapters discussed two kinds of statistics—data description and measures of association between items. The information is usually presented in that order in written reports and presentations. That means showing the results for all of the *individual items* or sections first. After that, the main *relationships* between items are presented. The most common way to report survey results to sponsors is with a combined narrative and condensed tabular report. Charts and graphs may also be prepared and included in written reports or used in oral presentations. Computer print output may be organized, indexed, bound, and delivered to the sponsor for later reference. Such documents are only very rarely the major report vehicle.

In this chapter, the emphasis will be mainly on composition of an effective *written* report including *tabular* results and *narrative* explanations. Such reports are the "work horses" for reporting survey information. Yet the value of graphic reports shouldn't be underestimated. Most spreadsheet programs have the ability to produce several types of charts and graphs that are useful for reporting survey information. Some word or page processing or desktop publishing programs also include graphing features. Of course, there are also many charting and graphing programs designed specifically to create such visual material. Some will also do simple statistical data description.

Words and numbers usually have to be manipulated mentally by those reading or listening to the report. In other words, if the report says 40 percent of respondents answered in one way and 60 percent in another, the reader has to mentally *visualize* a 4 to 6 ratio. Such proportions would be clearly and instantaneously visible in a simple graphic such as a pie chart. Graphics of this kind don't rely on words or numbers. Instead, they use *space* and *position* to portray quantities and relationships.

This chapter begins with a discussion of the main features and organization of written reports and oral presentations. After that, guidelines and examples of *data description* reports for each type of question and scale discussed in Chapters 4, 5, and 6 are provided. The remainder of the chapter contains recommendations and examples for reporting each *measure of association* between variables discussed in Chapters 10 and 11. While narrative and tabular components get the bulk of the attention, examples of graphs and charts are included where space permits.

Report Introduction

Perhaps the most useful and practical form of organization for a survey report is one that might be called the "newspaper" format. With this approach, the results are presented two or three times, rather than just once, but the level of detail increases substantially each time and the sections are divided and identified.

Executive summary

The first section might contain an "executive summary" of the information. Often no more than a page or so, this first section includes only the *major highlights* of the results. It addresses only the most important information needs and presents a very brief sketch of only the most valuable findings. An executive summary such as this often uses *bulleted* paragraphs ranging in length from a single line to only a few lines.

Executive summaries may also be in *brief* form—paragraphs of no more than two or three sentences each, headed or titled with a key phrase to identify the type of information. The entire executive summary should take no more than a few minutes to read. It should only "hit the high points" of the information acquired in the survey and excite the interest and curiosity of readers, enticing them to look further to the next section.

Response summary questionnaire

Often the people seeking the information have participated in creating the questionnaire. If so, they're probably very familiar with the instrument. The questionnaire can be used effectively *in addition* to the executive summary. Many researchers find it both quite easy and useful to produce a facsimile of the questionnaire containing brief listings of the distributions of response. It's sometimes called a "Response Summary Questionnaire." It may be appended to the executive summary or included between that and the body of the report. It's *never* advisable merely to jot in the results on a blank questionnaire form. If it's to be used, it should be very neat and presentable.

The cosmetic aspects of the report may not seem to be very important compared to the contents and results. Wrong! The appearance of the report is *always* important. Every experienced researcher should be able to attest to that. The reason is simple: Sponsors are seldom

---

GUIDELIST 12–1

For Writing the Report Introduction

1. Begin with an executive summary of one or two pages.
2. Use bullets or brief paragraphs of two or three sentences each.
3. Cover only the major highlights and information needs.
4. Use headings or key phrases to identify sections.
5. The summary must stimulate interest and excite curiosity.
6. Use a *response summary questionnaire*, if appropriate.
7. Delete superfluous content from the response summary.
8. Type all entries and compose the summary very neatly.

---

experts at judging the technical performance of the survey designer or researcher. They ordinarily have some doubts concerning how accurate, reliable, and valid the results of the survey will be. They have very few ways to judge these things. Thus, they'll invariably place more confidence and value on any report that's neatly and carefully composed and presented than on one that's quickly or ineptly composed. Despite what those receiving reports may claim, and regardless of their impatience to receive the information, the researcher can be sure bad appearance or the discovery of even minor errors or omissions will *seriously* jeopardize the confidence of those who read the report.

When a response summary questionnaire is included, the superfluous record format indications and precoding values should be deleted. Any instructions or notations that aren't relevant to understanding either the results or the way in which questions were asked should also be removed. The distributions of response to categorical items and the appropriate averages for continuous items should be *typed* in the proper places, next to the questions or items. The advantage of including a response summary questionnaire is that sponsors can turn to it later to see how the actual questions were phrased, the order in which they were presented, and the nature of the surrounding material. This can be quite helpful because the items are usually abbreviated or presented in a different sequence and context in the narrative and tabular report. The disadvantage of a response summary is that it's organized in a way that's convenient for respondents, rather than according to the categories of information needs or by the importance of the issues. Nevertheless, if there's any doubt about whether or not to include a response summary questionnaire, it's advisable to do so because it's so quick and easy to prepare. Basic guidelines for composing report introductions are outlined in Guidelist 12–1.

Narrative Reporting

The executive summary and response summary questionnaire should serve only as a prelude to the body of the survey report. This part, containing well-formed and composed tables and graphs, also includes a complete narrative discussion of the survey results. The text should be divided into major sections, according to the various types of information requirements, topics, or issues that were the focus of the survey. The narrative should refer to the tables or figures by number or letter where appropriate. The tables or figures shouldn't appear *before* they're referenced in the text. It's also important to avoid technical terms or phrases because sponsors probably won't be familiar with the jargon associated with survey research, data processing, or statistical analysis. With care and effort, even the most complex results can be expressed in lay terms. The objective of the report is to convey information, and not merely to impress the reader. It's far better to violate every rule of grammar in order to say something clearly than to express it "correctly" but obscurely.

Use simple, direct sentences. They're more powerful and concise than long, flowing sentences. They make reading the report easier and more enjoyable for those seeking the information. Be *very* careful about identification of antecedents and object references. Don't use pronouns, such as *they, them, its, those,* and so on, unless their antecedents are perfectly clear. Always use the noun to identify the person or thing being referenced if there might be doubt, even if it must be repeated in the same sentence. Refer to tables, graphs, variables, or items by name or number, even though it might seem obvious. Simply saying "The table indicates . . ." too often leads the reader to ask, "*Which* table?" That's especially true if the table being referenced gets moved to another page.

The narrative text of the survey report should consist of a verbal description of the major results for each section or category of information needs. Even though those seeking the information may be well able to read and understand the tables or figures, the narrative is virtually always necessary and valuable for several, very good reasons: First, the narrative

---

GUIDELIST 12–2

For Composing Narrative Text

1. Divide the text into major sections according to the types of information needs, topics, or issues.
2. Include the tables after they have been referenced in the text, not before.
3. Avoid technical jargon used in statistics or processing in favor of the simpler, lay person's vocabulary.
4. Use short, simple, direct sentences rather than long, complex ones.
5. Use nouns repetitively to avoid any confusion about the antecedent of pronouns such as it, them, they, and so on.
6. In references to tables, figures, and other inclusions, identify them by their number or letter rather than by indefinite terms such as "*the* table."
7. Make the text interpretive rather than just descriptive of the results.
8. Introduce each major section by identifying its purpose or the reason for including it.
9. Discuss the major facts or relationships contained in each table or figure, but make the text fairly independent so it's meaningful without reference to tables.
10. Include additional ideas, conclusions, or suggestions, based on previous experience or intuition, but clearly note when they go beyond the actual results.

text is *interpretive* rather than merely descriptive. The text indicates the meaning of the values and relationships revealed by the survey.

Second, virtually everyone can communicate more effectively in words than in numbers or symbols. Those who seek the information constantly deal with concepts and images that are largely verbal and only rarely numeric or symbolic in nature. Consequently, they can often perceive the meaning of facts and relationships expressed verbally much more readily than those expressed numerically or with symbols.

Third, the researcher can often provide additional insight, ideas, and information quite aside from the purely tabular or graphic portrayal of results. By virtue of having worked so closely and intimately with the project, the researcher will inevitably acquire intuitive understanding or a "gut feeling" for certain facts or relationships. These insights can't be expressed in numeric form, but they can and should be stated verbally in the narrative text. Whenever the researcher offers opinions, suggestions, or recommendations based on judgment or intuition, rather than concrete survey results, that must be clearly noted in the text.

Lastly, researchers who are knowledgeable about survey research because of their past experience with such work can often provide very helpful and useful perspectives on the results. Researchers can draw freely from previous survey experience, provided they respect the proprietary nature of the actual results of other surveys conducted for other sponsors.

For each section of the survey report, the narrative text should provide a brief introduction to the information. This is usually done by citing the information need category or, more simply, by stating the questions in the mind of those seeking the information during the initiation of the survey. It's often advisable to say why the information was sought as well, if that can be expressed easily. For example, the narrative for a new section might begin:

> Survey respondents were asked six questions to learn their attitudes toward the issue of new work rules. Their reactions were sought to gauge their potential acceptance of the proposed new policy.

Following this type of introduction to a section, the text would cite the tables or figures where the information was presented, then continue to identify and highlight the most important results. This is usually done by directing the reader's attention to the specific facts or relationships, thus:

> Notice the attitudes of new employees were markedly more positive than the attitudes of those who have been with the company for several years. This is very consistent with employee ratings of several other topics as well.

The researcher must often provide explanation and interpretation of the values shown in tabular or graphic form, but this is usually only part of the report writer's responsibility. At the very least, the researcher should be willing and able to identify the most relevant facts and relationships in the narrative text. For those with a grasp of the material being measured by the survey, much more extensive comment may be appropriate.

There may be a question concerning whether concrete recommendations should be included, whether merely suggestions would be appropriate, or whether only the bare facts should be noted. It's always advisable to ask those seeking the information for their preference and then abide by their request. When researchers provide concrete recommendations, there are two possibilities for problems: Those reading the report may feel the researcher has infringed on their prerogatives as executives or decision makers, or they place too much reliance on such recommendations, in the face of other, *contradictory* information. To avoid either extreme, the researcher can simply provide *suggestions* and identify the data that serve as a basis for them. That allows those reading the report to contradict when appropriate and to weigh the suggestions against their own background, experience, and body of accumulated information.

Each narrative report section should conclude with a very brief summary of the results for that section. These conclusions are usually only a few sentences. They're quite similar to the individual entries in the executive summary that heads the report. Thus, the narrative report process can be outlined in three steps for each section: (1) say what results will be presented, (2) present the results, and (3) say what was presented.

It's important to note that the narrative text shouldn't be too "dependent" on the tables and figures. Just as the reader should be able to gather the gist of the results from the tables and figures alone, so, too, should they be able to comprehend the major results by reading only the narrative text. Guidelist 12–2 summarizes the main guidelines for composing narrative text.

Tabular Reporting

The tables in the report should be edited versions of those generated by the analysis programs. Only the relevant values and entries should be included. The tables can usually be condensed so the results for many similar survey items can be contained in a single table or shown graphically on just one figure. The composition of meaningful, easily understood tables and figures is an art that can be cultivated easily and accomplished readily. All it really requires is careful attention and effort. Guidelist 12–3 summarizes the guidelines for creating report tables and figures.

There are two basic things the researcher must decide when composing tables or figures: The first is the *format* and the second is the *labeling* to use. When choosing a format, use space as effectively as possible. Arrange rows, columns, and sections so they contain *similar* material or apply to the same concept or topic. Allow enough "white space" so the tables or figures don't appear to be glutted with numbers or words. Separating different types of content helps the reader to recognize what's being presented.

It's usually best to use vertical rather than horizontal pages for the entire written report. Horizontal formats allow much more information on a single line, but it's often cumbersome for the reader who must turn the document to the side to read the contents. Another practical policy for writing tables is to use a *very consistent* format. This helps the report reader because, once familiar with the format, no further study is required to comprehend those that follow in a similar format. Lastly, it's good to remember a table can contain too much information. The general rule is that no one table or figure should require more than a very few minutes of study to comprehend.

The second major factor to consider when composing tables or figures is the *labeling*. Each table or figure in the report should be *named* and *titled*. Consecutive numbers make better indicators than letters, Roman numerals, or other symbols. The title should *say what's in the body of the table or figure*. If the body of a table contains frequencies, the table might be labeled, "Number of Respondents Indicating Each Alternative." If percentages are listed,

---

GUIDELIST 12–3

For Composing Tables and Figures

1. Name each table and figure with a consecutive number, and preferably not with letters or Roman numerals.
2. Title each one with a brief description of exactly what's contained in the *body* of the table.
3. Label rows, columns, and sections with meaningful words, rather than codes labeled at the bottom of the table or graph.
4. Use a standard format whenever possible, so many tables are quickly recognized once the first is understood.
5. Use space and distance effectively to show relationships or provide identification.
6. Keep similar content in the same columns, rows, or sections, using space to separate distinct content.
7. Allow sufficient "white space" and don't contain too much information in one table or make it too dense.
8. Note statistical significance with an asterisk or letter superscript and note the probability level in a table footnote.
9. Use vertical rather than horizontal pages whenever possible, even if more tables or figures are needed.
10. Remember, each table or figure should virtually "stand alone," so it's meaningful without reference to text.
11. Always try to keep it *clean* and *simple*.

---

they should be identified in the title. If averages are contained in the body of the table, the title must indicate not only that they're averages, but also *what* averages—the means, medians, or modes. For example, the title might be "Average (Mean) Estimates for Four Series." It's essential the title of the table or figure tells the reader exactly *what the table contains*. The reader should be able to understand clearly what's in the table *without* reference to the text or knowledge of any other part of the report.

The columns and rows of tables and the sections or parts of figures should also be labeled clearly. In order to conserve space, some report writers attach codes, such as 1, 2, 3, and so on or A, B, C, and so on to the rows or columns. Then they list a key at the bottom of the table to show the items or categories to which these codes refer. This method is almost *never* advisable. It's virtually always better to include less information on each table and use as many as needed. The only possible exception is when it's necessary for the reader to *compare* items. That can be accomplished more easily within a single table than among multiple tables. Statistical significance can best be shown in tables with the use of asterisks beside the appropriate values, such as $25\star$, or with letter superscripts, such as 25^a. The significance is then noted in a footnote to the table.

Graphic Reporting

All types of graphic figures—graphs, charts, plots, and diagrams—have one thing in common, and it's their main advantage over tabular reports: They "map" quantities and relationships more directly than words or numbers. Graphics use size and shape to represent

Figure 12–1 *Graph and Chart Types*

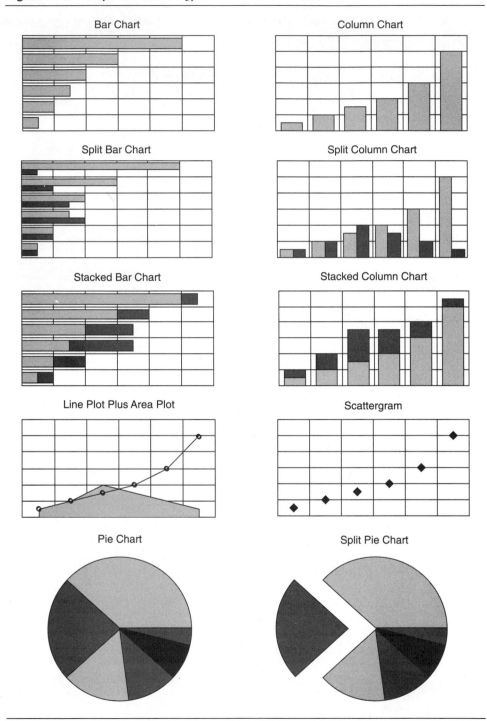

quantities. They use location and juxtaposition to display relationships visually. Cosmetic features are important for survey research reports, but graphics offer far more than just that. They can convey *configuration*—the *total* picture in an instant. They can make meaningful to viewers what words and numbers couldn't possibly convey and do it very simply and elegantly. But of course, they do it at a price. They not only take considerable time and effort to produce, they also consume very large amounts of space in a written report.

Figure 12–2   *The Anatomy of a Graph*

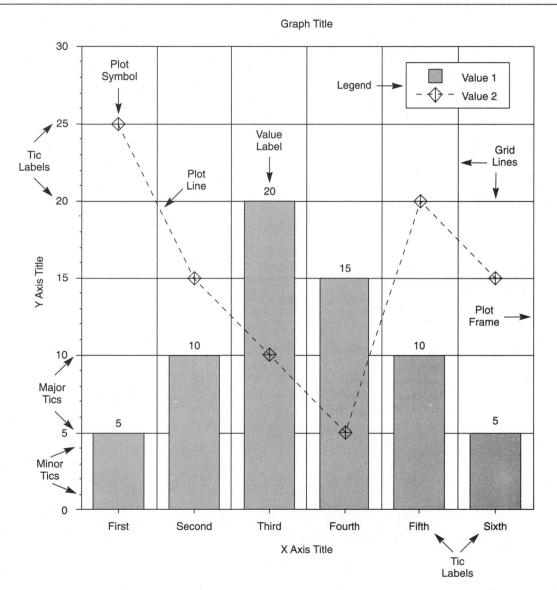

GUIDELIST 12–4

For Creating Graphic Figures

1. Name each graph or chart with a consecutive number, rather than with letters or Roman numerals.

2. Title each one with a brief description of exactly what *quantities* the *lines, bars,* or *areas* represent.

3. Use X axis and Y axis titles to indicate what spectrum or dimension each axis represents.

4. If multiple variables are plotted, label the plot elements or show a legend on or beneath the graph to indicate what each represents.

5. Include tic labels to show the levels, quantities, or proportions on the X axis and Y axis scale.

6. Use enough grid lines to allow the reader to estimate quantities but not so many as to make the graph dense or cluttered.

7. Including *value labels* on bars, plot points, or pie segments may allow the graph to *substitute* for a table rather than just supplement it.

8. Use the same graphic format consistently whenever possible so the elements are quickly recognizable once the reader is familiar with the first.

9. Use the same *proportions* and *scales* when results are to be compared from one graph to the next.

10. Allow sufficient "white space," and don't contain so much information on one graph as to make it overly complex.

11. Note statistical significance with an asterisk or letter superscript and note the probability level in a footnote below the figure.

12. Always try to keep it *clean* and *simple!* When there's a choice between a simple and a complex format, always select the more elementary one.

There are a wide variety of special-purpose charting and graphing programs for desktop computers of all kinds. They range from very basic, simple "utility" routines to highly complex and sophisticated programs. But regardless of their simplicity or complexity, learning to use them initially takes some time, effort, and patience. Once familiar with the program, however, most users find them fairly quick and easy to operate. Most spreadsheets, integrated "works" program packages, and statistical programs also include the ability to produce basic charts and graphs such as those shown in Figure 12–1 on page 354. These rather rudimentary models are very satisfactory for almost all survey research reports. About the only thing that more sophisticated graphics have to offer over these simple ones are the ability to show depth, plot in three dimensions, overlay one set of data on another, display bars and areas in pictures, and display the information more colorfully, in both the figurative and literal sense of the word.

The same recommendations that apply to naming, titling, and labeling tables apply as well to graphic figures, except that they are referred to as "Figure #" or "Exhibit #" rather than "Table #." Graphic figures should have their own, independent sequence of consecutive numbers. Rarely will there be a corresponding graph for every table, so there's no need for the numbers of tables and figures to correspond.

Graphics can play one of two roles in a report, relative to the tables: They may *replace* tables or they may *supplement* them. Using them as supplements is more common for written reports. For oral presentations using slides or transparencies, it's more common for graphic figures to replace tables. In the examples that follow, both tables and graphs or charts are provided. But this isn't to imply that they must always both be present.

The choice of the best type of graph to use in a given situation or to portray a specific set of information is a difficult one. There are no fixed rules or even firm guidelines about what kind of graph to use for data from a particular type of scale or item. At times it may be obvious that only one type is suitable and nothing else would do. At other times there may be a choice between two·or more kinds of graphs. There are rare situations where *no* type of graph is really able to show the information effectively.

The following examples suggest the kinds of graphs or charts best suited to displaying the types of information contained in the corresponding tables. Once the type of graph has been chosen, the report writer must also decide what individual elements should be included on the graph. The basic anatomy of a graph is shown in Figure 12–2. Some of the individual elements shown there are optional. Others are almost always advisable to use. The guidelines for creating effective graphic figures are provided in Guidelist 12–4.

REPORTING DATA DESCRIPTION

The next section of this chapter contains a series of examples to serve as models for reporting the results of *practical* survey research. Sample results from each of the scale types shown in Chapter 5 are presented in a series of data description tables. An *alternative* or *supplementary* graph or chart is also provided. Examples of narrative text that might accompany the tables and graphs are also included. There's no one, *correct* way to report results, but these examples are designed to provide report writers with suggestions for table, graph, and narrative format and content.

Reporting Multiple-Choice Items

Multiple choice items such as those shown in Example 5–1 on page 116 are categorical data. They're usually described by listing the percentage of respondents choosing each category. Example 12–1 shows a variant of the frequency table discussed earlier. Only percentages are shown because ordinarily these proportions are generalized to the population by statistical inference. The number of respondents for the item is shown, so readers could calculate the number for each response if they wished to do so.

In Example 12–1, there were 7 percent who indicated some other, miscellaneous newspaper. Because there were so few and the frequency of any one publication was usually only one person, the *others* are grouped into this miscellaneous category. Usually the others identified are recorded on a codelist and entered into the data file for processing, but they're not ordinarily listed in a report *unless* a substantial number of respondents select one particular "other" alternative or the sponsors express an interest in having these so-called *write-ins* reported. If they're needed, they could either be included in the table or listed in a separate table with the percentages based only on those who selected and entered some additional, miscellaneous alternative.

Notice the alternatives were listed in Example 12–1 with the modal category first, followed in descending order of percentages, with the "other" category always presented last. Alternatively, the sequence used in the questionnaire could have been maintained in the table if there were a logical order to the alternatives.

EXAMPLE 12–1

Single Response Item Table

The kind of newspaper they *most often* read for business news	
Newspaper	Percent
National, daily paper	43%
Local, morning paper	22%
Local, evening paper	14%
Local, weekly paper	9%
National, weekly paper	5%
Other, miscellaneous papers	7%
Total	100%
Number = 160	

Figure 12–3 presents the tabular information of Example 12–1 in two graphic forms—a bar chart and a pie chart. Both provide good indications of the relative proportions of respondents in each category. The pie chart emphasizes the nature of a *single response* question—the percentages total to 100 with no overlap among categories. The choice between the two graphs depends on what the report writer wants to emphasize.

The narrative discussion of this information is likely to be brief. The table and/or graphs are largely self-explanatory. It's usually important only to identify the most popular categories, and perhaps to comment on the results if they're not intuitive, thus:

> The national daily newspaper proved to be the single, most often used source of business news for the respondents in this population. The survey questions about subscription, to be shown later, suggest *The Wall Street Journal* is by far the most popular, and probably four out of five who indicated a national daily paper here were referring to that newspaper. Nearly all the others are likely to be referring to *Barrons,* because there were few other national dailies to which respondents subscribed at home or at work. It's also interesting to note the local *evening* paper was less popular than was the morning paper, since the morning paper is generally more often read by business people than the evening paper.

Example 12–1 is a single response item, so it constitutes a single survey variable. The statistical analysis generates only one frequency table from which the percentages were drawn. In Example 12–2, the respondents could select more than one alternative. Conse-

Figure 12–3   *Single Response Item Graphics*

Simple Bar Graph

Simple Pie Chart

quently, this single survey question generates *six* variables, to which the respondents actually indicate "yes" or "no." Consequently, the analysis generates six frequency tables, one for each alternative that's a variable. Example 12–2 lists all six sets of percentages in a single table to save space and facilitate comparison. It wouldn't even be necessary to list the percentages in the "No" column, because this is easily recognized, given the percentage who did check the category. It would be presented as it is here and in Figure 12–4 only if there was as much interest in the proportion who did *not* read each paper as there was in who did. The narrative text to accompany this table or graph would be very similar to that for the previous ones, citing major categories and knitting the survey results together.

EXAMPLE 12–2

Multiple Response Item Table

Any and all types of newspapers they regularly read for business news		
Newspaper	Yes	No
National, daily paper	41%	59%
Local, morning paper	38%	68%
Local, evening paper	22%	78%
Local, weekly paper	7%	93%
Other, miscellaneous papers	3%	97%
National, weekly paper	2%	98%
Number = 160		

Figure 12–4 *Multiple Response Item Bar Chart*

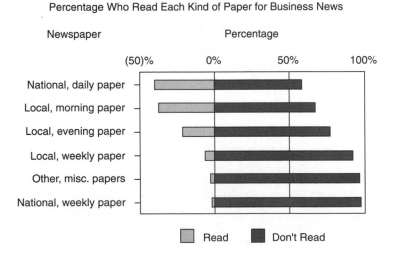

Percentage Who Read Each Kind of Paper for Business News

Likert Scale Item Reports

Multiple Likert scale items such as those shown in Example 5–2 on page 118 can also be shown in a single table. In Example 12–3, the scale categories are listed vertically to save space. It may be tempting to list the code values above the columns and print the scale below the table. That's never advisable in a final report if it can be avoided. It puts too much burden on the reader, and that's contrary to the basic objectives of survey reporting.

In Example 12–3, six items are shown in a single table, but many more could easily have been listed. This saves space and saves time for those reading the reports, but there's a more important reason for condensed tables like this: They allow the reader to make direct comparisons quickly and easily among comparable items. Such formats provide more information and enhance the value of the results. They require more work by the report writer, but they're well worth the extra time and effort.

Showing the entire distributions of response to Likert scale items in the fashion used here has both advantages and disadvantages. Ordinarily, the entire distributions are of interest. They should be listed if it would be useful to compare each *category* with the others. It takes more space and makes the comparisons among *items* more difficult because there are so many values to study. An alternative would be to list only the *median* values for each item. Using the median as a single indicator of the level of agreement is recommended to facilitate comparison among *items* and to save space when there's no need to compare *individual categories*.

The distributions from Example 12–3 are shown in a stacked column chart in Figure 12–5. The scale is shown on the legend, while the items are slanted and listed above each

---

EXAMPLE 12–3

Tabular Likert Scale Report

How much do you agree or disagree with each statement?	Strongly Agree	Agree	Neutral	Disagree	Strongly Disagree
A man should never cry in public	8.4%	11.5%	27.7%	36.5%	15.9%
A woman's place is in the home	12.9%	16.2%	19.1%	31.5%	20.3%
A man should help a woman in public ...	6.5%	19.4%	24.9%	29.6%	19.6%
Women should always pay their share ...	10.4%	18.0%	16.5%	26.2%	28.9%
Men must take the lead in sex matters ...	16.6%	18.3%	19.0%	22.1%	24.0%
Women should put family before career ..	21.5%	26.4%	18.2%	13.5%	20.4%

325 Respondents

Figure 12–5   *Likert Scale Stacked Column Chart*

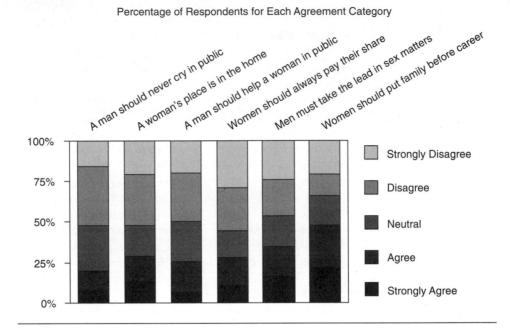

Percentage of Respondents for Each Agreement Category

column. The shading is graduated to correspond with the amount of agreement. This kind of chart sacrifices precise, numeric detail to facilitate comparisons among variables and make the distinctions more vivid.

Verbal Frequency Scale Reports

Example 12–4 shows a tabular report of some of the data from the *verbal frequency scales* shown in Example 5–3 on page 120. As with the Likert scale, this scale generates ordinal data. The format in Example 12–4 is very similar to the previous one, except the names of the categories are short enough to be listed horizontally.

Only five verbal frequency items are shown in the table contained in Example 12–4, but of course many more might have been listed in the table. Analysis routines often generate one page for each such item, containing the frequency and percentage table and perhaps the median value. With such reports, comparisons among items are difficult. A table such as that in Example 12–4 is an excellent way to condense the information and make items very comparable with one another.

Figure 12–6 presents the data distributions from Example 12–4 graphically. The items in the table and graph haven't been rearranged so their sequence represents the order of magnitude of the responses. Rather, the original order was retained here because it represented a rough "continuum" from minimal involvement in political issues to involvement. This is

EXAMPLE 12–4

Tabular Verbal Frequency Report

How often do you do each of the following things?	Always	Often	Some-times	Rarely	Never
Seek information about candidates . .	5.3%	13.9%	22.4%	28.5%	29.9%
Vote in local elections	3.1%	6.4%	39.5%	17.8%	33.2%
Vote along strict party lines	8.4%	17.7%	19.5%	13.2%	41.2%
Contribute money to candidates . . .	1.3%	3.9%	9.4%	6.3%	79.1%
Volunteer to work on campaigns . .	0.8%	1.6%	3.3%	16.6%	77.7%
220 Respondents					

quite common with well–composed survey items and well–constructed questionnaires. The format and sequence permit the report reader to examine the *change* in the distributions from one item to the next, moving downward in the table or upward in the graph to detect patterns as the level of some underlying dimension increases or decreases. Thus, showing the items together enhances the meaning of the information to those seeking it.

Figure 12–6   *Verbal Frequency Stacked Bar Chart*

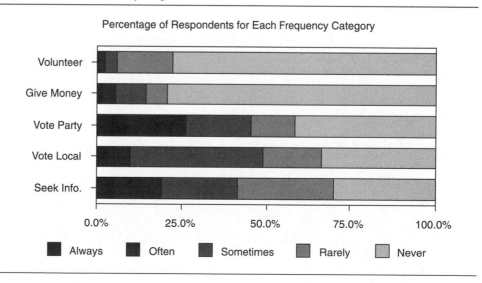

Percentage of Respondents for Each Frequency Category

Always   Often   Sometimes   Rarely   Never

Ordinal Scale Reports

Both the Likert scale and the verbal frequency scale generate ordinal data. The categories are listed in a sequence representing the increase or decrease in the order of magnitude, although intervals or "steps" between scale points aren't necessarily equal to one another. Other things besides the amount of agreement or the frequency of something can be arranged in a fairly large number of such sequential steps as well. When this is the case, the scale is called an *ordinal* scale because it shows *only* the order of things and generates ordinal data. Example 5–4 on page 122 shows a situation where the scale steps are times of day defined not by the hour and minute, but rather by daily activity patterns of respondents. It's not so important to sponsors to know the exact time of the occurrence according to the clock, because different families perform activities at different times of day. Rather the times, *relative to the families' daily activities,* are of greater importance.

Example 12–5 shows the tabular report of the data from the ordinal scale shown in the upper section of Example 5–4 on page 122. Notice that, as always, the number of respondents is listed clearly on the table so readers know the total on which the percentages are based. Rather than just listing the percentage distribution by category, the *cumulative* percentages are also shown. The cumulative percentages are often very revealing for ordinal scale items. The reader of the report can then obtain two types of information from the

EXAMPLE 12–5

Ordinal Scale Cumulative Table

When TV is turned on, weekdays	Percent	Cumulative
The first thing in the morning	6.3%	6.3%
A little while after awakening	4.5%	10.8%
Mid-morning	5.2%	16.0%
Just before lunch	2.1%	18.1%
Right after lunch	11.8%	29.9%
Mid-afternoon	7.6%	37.5%
Early evening, before dinner	18.1%	55.6%
Right after dinner	21.0%	76.6%
Late evening	17.7%	94.3%
Usually don't turn it on	5.7%	100.0%
165 Respondents	100.0%	100.0%

table simultaneously: The percentage of people who, in this case, turn on their TV set at a certain time of the day, and also the percentage who *have* turned on their TV set *up to that point* in the day. This latter piece of information is obviously very useful, especially given the assumption that some fixed proportion of television sets have remained on once they're originally turned on.

Figure 12–7 portrays *only the cumulative* percentages for the same variable reported in Example 12–5. Such a graph could easily be misperceived as showing "TV Sets On" at any given point. To avoid mistakes, a note was inserted directly on the chart, clearly indicating what's shown and how the values were derived.

In the narrative interpretation of such a table, it's important both to explain the cumulative percentage distribution, if that has not been done earlier in the report, and also to note the relevant results in terms of both category percentages and cumulative percentages. Notice how a typical narrative also makes suggestions and refers to cross-tabulation to check them:

> Respondents indicated the time during a typical weekday when they or someone in the family turned on the television set. They indicated they did so according to certain daily activities, rather than by the clock, because daily activity patterns differ widely from family to family. The results are shown in Table 5. The percentages are all based on 165 respondents who answered the question, and the largest percentage turned on their television sets *right after dinner,* but very nearly as many did so in the *early evening before dinner,* and in the *late evening.* The cumulative percentages indicate that less than one family in five had turned on the TV by *lunch time,* while over a third had done so by *mid-afternoon,* well over half by *early evening, before dinner,* and three quarters *right after dinner.* These results suggest very light morning viewership for this audience, and only moderate afternoon viewing for "soaps," the "game shows," and the "sit-com" reruns.

Figure 12–7   *Ordinal Scale Cumulative Bar Chart*

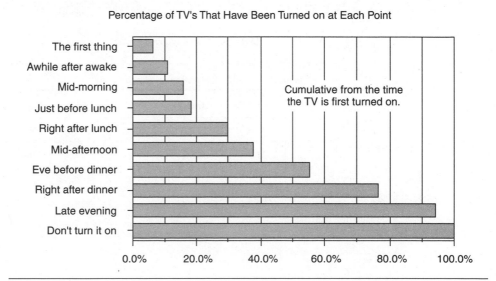

Percentage of TV's That Have Been Turned on at Each Point

On the other hand, the marked increase in the cumulative percentages just before dinner suggest a youthful audience coming in during late afternoon, perhaps after school, for the "cartoon" and "kid show" programming, as well as the early evening news for some stations and networks. These suggestions will be tested further when this item is broken down by *family life cycle* to measure differences in viewing patterns for those in different stages of the life cycle.

Forced Ranking Scale Reports

Ranking alternatives creates an ordinal variable for each item ranked. In Example 5–5 on page 123, four brands of cola were ranked according to the respondents' degree of preference. An analysis routine to generate frequency and percentage distributions might produce one table for each item ranked. These data can be condensed into a single table, such as in Example 12–6. The percentage distributions for each brand (variable) are shown by row, totaling to 100 percent at the far right. Each row of the table was derived from a frequency and percentage table for that particular brand or variable.

Aside from saving report space and reader time, there's another advantage to condensing tabular reports of rankings such as those shown in Example 12–6. Each respondent must rank each item, and no two items can be ranked the same. This is why the scale is called a *forced* ranking. If the data are edited properly, the rows should also total to 100 percent. Thus, either the columns or the rows can be compared with one another by those studying the relationships among the items.

The table provides those seeking the information with an entire "picture" of the *pattern* of preferences, rather than merely information about individual items. Thus, patterns are revealed merely by the choice and composition of the table format. This table *doesn't* show

EXAMPLE 12–6

Forced Ranking Scale Distributions

	1st	2nd	3rd	4th	Total
Percentage Ranking Each Brand at Each Rank					
Coca-Cola	46.5%	44.0%	6.7%	2.8%	100.0%
Pepsi-Cola	31.2%	51.6%	11.3%	5.9%	100.0%
Royal Crown Cola	19.1%	3.1%	67.5%	10.3%	100.0%
Like Cola	3.2%	1.3%	14.5%	81.0%	100.0%
Total (119 Respondents)	100.0%	100.0%	100.0%	100.0%	

Figure 12–8 *Forced Ranking Stacked Column Chart*

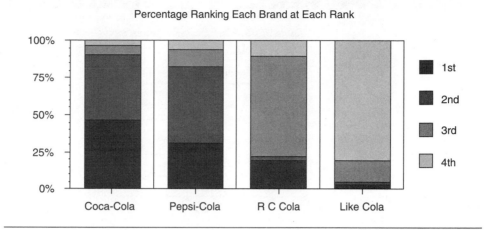

how those who ranked a particular item a certain way ranked the other items, but that can be determined by a set of cross-tabulations for each pair.

Figure 12–8 contains a stacked bar chart of the distributions shown in Example 12–6. The four brands are listed from the most to the least popular, and the legend identifies the rankings. The graph makes the distinctions more striking, but at the expense of the numeric precision found in the table. In such cases, where it's impractical to include value labels on the graph, *both* the table and graph might be used in the report.

Paired Comparison Scale Reports

Paired comparison scales are used only rarely in surveys because the data from them are difficult to analyze, as noted in Chapter 5. The items used in Example 5–6 on page 125 are the same cola brands used in Example 5–5. The object was to demonstrate the superiority of other scales to the paired comparison scale. However, there are some situations where it's appropriate to use paired comparisons because the scales actually mirror "real-world" choices the respondents must sometimes make. In Example 12–7, only three items and thus three pairs are listed. The items to be compared are three kinds of meat. There was an explicit reason for using the paired comparison scale. Both personal preference and dietary laws of some religions dictate certain choices. So, respondents are sometimes in a position of making a choice between such pairs.

In Example 12–7, there's a footnote indicating transitivity was forced by the elimination of intransitive cases. Since only three items and three pairs were used, there were very few such cases. *Intransitivity* results when a respondent indicates they prefer: A over B, B over C, and C over A. That's a logical impossibility, but it often happens with paired comparisons when many pairs are being rated. It's one of the main reasons paired comparisons are inferior to *rating* the items on an interval scale. When paired comparisons are used in surveys and

EXAMPLE 12–7

Table of Multiple Paired Comparisons

Percentage of Choice Between *Pairs*★				
Beef	82%	versus	18%	Pork
Beef	96%	versus	4%	Lamb
Pork	88%	versus	12%	Lamb
120 Respondents				
★Transitivity forced by deleting intransitive cases.				

reported in tables such as Example 12–7 or graphs such as Figure 12–9, either the *coefficient of transitivity* should be reported, or if the cases were eliminated, that should be noted.

The narrative should also briefly explain transitivity, at least the first time the term is referenced in the report, as well as explaining the meaning of the results, thus:

> Respondents rated their preference for beef, pork, and lamb when each was paired with one other variety of meat. There were two respondents who indicated they preferred beef to pork, lamb to beef, and pork to lamb, so their choices were intransitive and the data from these two

Figure 12–9   *Paired Comparison Stacked Bar Chart*

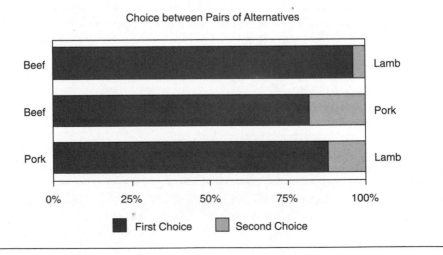

cases were disregarded here. The results indicate: (1) A strong general preference for beef, as might be expected. (2) A fairly pronounced dislike for lamb. (3) A preference for lamb over pork by more than one in 10 people. The results suggest that if only two varieties are offered, beef and pork or beef and lamb would be much more acceptable than would pork and lamb. The choices seem to be governed by both preferences and *prohibitions;* by both "likes" and "dislikes" of respondents. Comparisons of these results with religious preference and affiliation may provide more evidence for this conclusion.

Comparative Scale Reports

When an absolute reference is lacking or inadequate and comparisons or *relative* measures are required, there's no necessity to use *paired* comparisons. Example 5–7 on page 126 shows a method for obtaining interval scale data based on a relative frame of reference rather than on an absolute standard. This scale can also be used for *multiple* comparisons. Example 12–8 reports the results of comparisons between the sponsor's retail store and six other shops. As in Example 5–7, a five-point scale was used, but instead of scale values ranging from one to five, they were oriented around zero and ranged from a negative two to a positive two. The table in Example 12–8 lists both the entire percentage distributions of response and also, since the scale is interval level, the average (mean) values.

When the percentage distributions are listed as they are in Example 12–8, those who read the table can easily make comparisons of *categories* of response across the rows. For a quick comparison of the *items* among one another, the averages can be compared more readily

EXAMPLE 12–8

Multiple Comparative Scale Table

Competitor	Very Inferior	Inferior	Very Similar	Superior	Very Superior	Mean
Abbot's	11.5	16.4	35.3	20.1	16.7	+0.14
Baker's	44.0	16.7	14.5	14.2	10.6	−0.69
Clark's	20.0	22.9	35.4	14.5	7.2	−0.34
Drake's	58.8	31.3	7.5	1.7	0.7	−1.46
Evert's	9.5	16.8	19.9	37.4	16.4	+0.34
Frost's	6.6	14.4	40.9	23.1	15.0	+0.26

Rating of Each Competitor Compared to *This* Shop

175 Respondents

Figure 12–10 *Mean Comparative Score Bar Chart*

Mean Scores of Others Compared to This Shop

	Very Inferior	Inferior	Very Similar	Superior	Very Superior
Drake's	-1.46				
Baker's		-0.69			
Clark's		-0.34			
Abbot's			0.14		
Frost's			0.26		
Evert's			0.34		

than the entire distributions. Finally, the averages also provide a quick and fairly indicative measure of the relationship between each competing shop and the "standard," the sponsor's own shop. The plus or minus sign provides a very visible indication of whether the other shop is regarded more or less favorably than the standard for comparison when the scale pivots on zero. The magnitude of the average value shows how much more or less favorably the other shops were perceived by respondents. Thus, this form of table provides a wealth of information to those seeking it.

The mean scores from Example 12–8 are graphed in Figure 12–10. Rather than listing the competitors in alphabetical order, as on the questionnaire, they're shown here in order of inferiority or superiority. Orienting the bar chart around the zero point representing the sponsor's store—the standard of comparison—highlights the direction and magnitude of the differences.

Linear, Numeric Scale Reports

Perhaps the most common scale used in survey research for continuous interval data is the linear, numeric scale, such as that shown in Example 5–8 on page 128. A tabular report of the results from such a scale, used to rate 14 attributes of sports equipment, is shown in Example 12–9. Because this scale has equal intervals, the mean values were computed and listed rather than the entire distribution for each item. The table also notes the range of the scale and the number of respondents for the item.

The linear, numeric scale data from Example 12–9 is plotted graphically in Figure 12–11. As in the tabular report, the items have been ordered from the most to the least important attributes. This provides a visual profile of the things that are important to those shopping for sports equipment. Since the plot in Figure 12–11 has sufficient space, the value labels

---

EXAMPLE 12–9

Linear, Numeric Scale Table

Mean Importance Ratings When Choosing Sports Equipment*			
Factor Rated	**Mean**	**Factor Rated**	**Mean**
Quality of merchandise	4.8	Help and advice offered	3.5
Selection of brands	4.6	Speed of service	3.5
Variety of products	4.6	Store hours	3.4
Service after purchase	4.4	Location of store	3.2
Store guarantees	4.4	Size of the store	2.7
Price of the goods	4.2	Attractiveness of store	2.5
Courtesy of service	3.7	Availability of credit	2.2
Five-point scale.		325 Respondents	

---

have also been printed. There's no need to note the scale range, since it's shown on the graph. The number of respondents is noted. In effect, the plot would probably *substitute* for the table rather than supplementing it in a report.

Semantic Differential Scale Reports

Semantic differential scales are widely used in survey research for the measurement of image profiles. This method of scaling is shown in Example 5–9 on page 130. The same items are reported in tabular format in Example 12–10 and in graphic form in the upper and lower sections of Figure 12–12. The table in Example 12–10 isn't an effective way to report semantic differential scale results. It contains all the information and shows the values for each, individual item, but it's almost impossible to see the *image profile*.

In the upper section of Figure 12–12, the items are listed *exactly* as they appeared in the questionnaire. The comparison of that plot with the one in the lower section of Figure 12–12 demonstrates an important objective of survey reporting. When the questionnaire was constructed, the survey items were ordered in a sequence dictated by the *response* task. Thus, the items were randomly ordered and some were listed with the positive adjective first while others were reversed. Consequently, when the modal values are listed in a table or plotted as they are, they don't actually form a *profile* for interpretation and reporting. It's difficult

Figure 12–11   *Linear, Numeric Scale Plot*

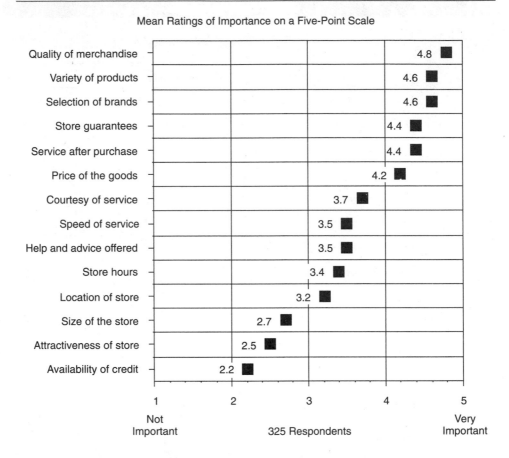

Mean Ratings of Importance on a Five-Point Scale

and time-consuming to understand the profile or form a mental picture of the results from either the table in Example 12–10 or the plot in the upper section of Figure 12–12.

In the lower section of Figure 12–12, the modal values are again shown, but there are two modifications in the plot: First, several of the items were "reflected" or reversed so all positive adjectives are shown on the left, with their negative counterparts listed on the right. Second, item pairs were reordered so those receiving the most positive responses were listed first and the less positive items followed in sequence down the page. In the data analysis for this example, the means were also computed. So, when two or more items had the same value for the mode, the one with the highest mean value was listed first to break the "tie."

A major goal when composing tables and graphs for reports is to enhance the information by facilitating the recognition of patterns and the comparisons among items. This often requires reordering and reflecting items. The plot in the lower section of Figure 12–12 much more readily portrays the image *profile,* by comparison with the table in Example 12–

EXAMPLE 12–10

Semantic Differential Table

Modal Ratings of the Pizza Served Here*			
Adjective Pair Rated	**Mode**	**Adjective Pair Rated**	**Mode**
Hot . . . . Cold	2	Good . . . . Bad	2
Bland . . . . Spicy	6	Unattractive . . . . Attractive	6
Expensive . . . . .Inexpensive	3	Fresh . . . . Stale	1
Moist . . . . Dry	1	Small . . . . .Large	5
Soggy . . . . Crisp	4	Natural . . . . .Artificial	3

* Seven-Point Semantic Differential Scale Labeled on Each Extreme.   168 Respondents

10 or the upper section of the figure. When the table or graph is composed properly, the reader easily gets a clear picture of the relationships shown.

Adjective Checklist Reports

The most simple and direct way to measure image attributes in a survey was shown in Example 5–10 on page 131, although it certainly isn't the best way in most cases. The price of the simplicity is that only categorical, dichotomous data are obtained for each item. Thus, the reports of such items consist only of the proportion of respondents who checked each item. Such a report is shown in tabular format in Example 12–11. If the data for the entire sample, combined, were to be shown in such a table, they would be obtained by generating an individual frequency table for each item, then listing only the percentage checking the item in the condensed, tabular report. In Example 12–11, the percentages are shown for each of two departments, using the same items as those shown in Example 5–10. Thus, the data shown are for two individual subsamples, and the proportions checking each item for the entire sample as a whole aren't shown because this would be "mixing apples and oranges" from the view of those seeking the information.

These percentages could have been obtained by first selecting only one subsample or department and obtaining frequency tables, then repeating the computations for the second subsample or department. This wasn't the procedure used here, however, because to do so requires doing the same analysis twice and doesn't provide a measure of the statistical significance of differences between the two departments. Rather than using frequency distributions, these data were cross-tabulated, so each table contained the percentages checking

Figure 12–12   *Modal Semantic Differential Plots*

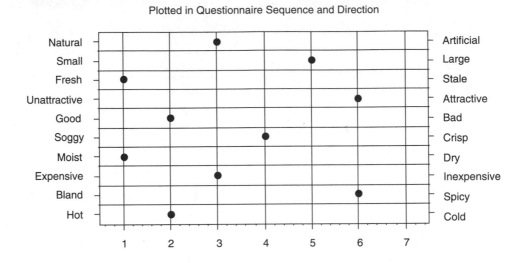

Plotted in Questionnaire Sequence and Direction

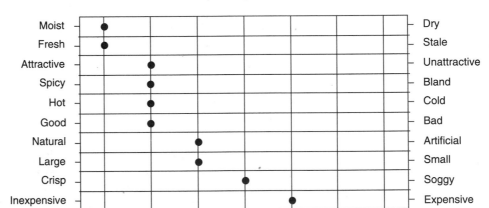

Plotted in Report Sequence and Direction

and not checking the item for each department. Consequently, Example 12–11 shows a data description report that was actually based on a measure of association—cross-tabulation. Notice the number in each department is listed at the bottom of the table and the statistical significance is shown in a footnote.

The original order of the items, used in the questionnaire and shown in Example 5–10, was retained in the tabular report in Example 12–11. For the graph in Figure 12–13, the items were sorted from those *most* often to *least* often checked by respondents in Dept. B,

EXAMPLE 12–11

Adjective Checklist Percentages

Percentage of Each Dept. Checking Each Characteristic*					
Dept. A	Dept. B	Factor Rated	Dept. A	Dept. B	Factor Rated
9%	31%	Easy	91%	65%	Safe
88%	7%	Technical	55%	39%	Exhausting
3%	77%	Boring	74%	40%	Difficult
71%	12%	Interesting	62%	8%	Rewarding
12%	55%	Low-paying	41%	70%	Secure
8%	41%	Strenuous	3%	29%	Slow-paced
2%	88%	Routine	62%	17%	Enjoyable
16%	48%	Dead-end	5%	44%	Rigid
91%	12%	Changing	38%	21%	Pleasant
55%	9%	Important	59%	25%	Satisfying
79%	16%	Demanding	1%	14%	Degrading
1%	18%	Temporary	2%	17%	Risky

72   315 Respondents
*Differences between departments are all statistically significant, $P < 0.01$.

the larger of the two departments. Examination of the split bar graph shows even more dramatically how much the two departments differ in their image of their job. The narrative description of these results would point out the differential patterns between the two departments, based on comparisons between items and between departments.

Semantic Distance Scale Reports

Yet another method for measuring image profiles is the semantic distance scale, described in Chapter 5 and shown in Example 5–11 on page 133. Each distribution for each item could be described by generating a frequency and percentage table for each. But these items are actually continuous, interval level variables, so the averages for each can be used appro-

Figure 12–13 *Adjective Checklist Split Bar Chart*

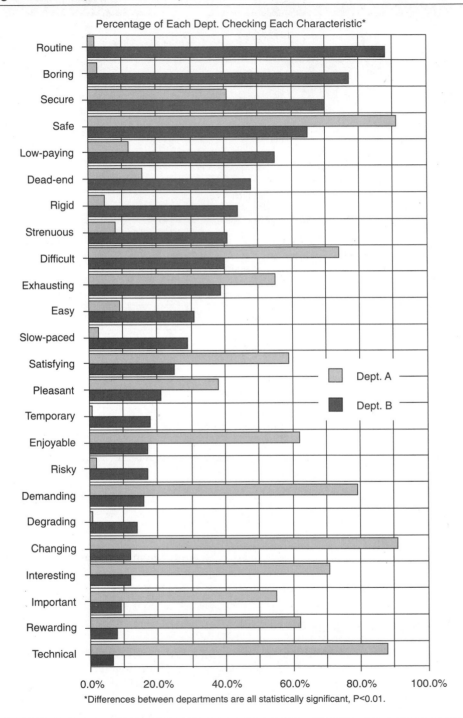

Percentage of Each Dept. Checking Each Characteristic*

*Differences between departments are all statistically significant, P<0.01.

EXAMPLE 12–12

Semantic Distance Tabular Report

Median Ratings of This Shop*			
Characteristic Rated	**Median**	**Characteristic Rated**	**Median**
High quality products	4.9	Fast counter service	3.9
Neat and clean	4.8	Expensive goods	3.4
Wide selection	4.8	Bad location	2.6
Helpful staff	4.6	Understaffed	2.1
Friendly	4.5	Hard to find	2.0
Large	4.4	Deliveries often late	1.9
Ample parking	4.3	Short on experience	1.7
Fun to shop	4.2	Hard to reach, phone	1.7
Convenient hours	4.2	Unattractive	1.6
Easy to visit	4.0	Intimidating	1.1

* Five-point semantic distance scale from not descriptive to very descriptive. 325 Respondents

priately. The table in Example 12–12 shows the results of a series of semantic distance scale items listing attributes of a retail outlet. The median value was chosen as the appropriate average to list, based on the skewness and kurtosis of the distributions. The median is more representative of the most typical rating when the distributions are highly skewed, as they obviously were for these data, given the "floor" and "ceiling" effects. The mean is overly sensitive to the small number of extreme cases in the "tail" of the distribution furthest from the mode.

In the table shown in Example 12–12 and the plot of the data in Figure 12–14, the items were reordered from the sequence used in the questionnaire. As in previous examples, the items in this example and figure are arranged by order of magnitude of the ratings. So, those most descriptive were listed first, followed in sequence by those regarded by respondents as less descriptive. This was also done in Example 12–11, but when a semantic distance scale is used to measure an image profile, there's no need to reverse the items. In fact, doing so would be inappropriate. The "negative" items shouldn't be converted to "positive" meaning by reflecting the scale. For example, the last item in the table in Example 12–12 is "Intim-

Figure 12–14   *Semantic Distance Profile Plot*

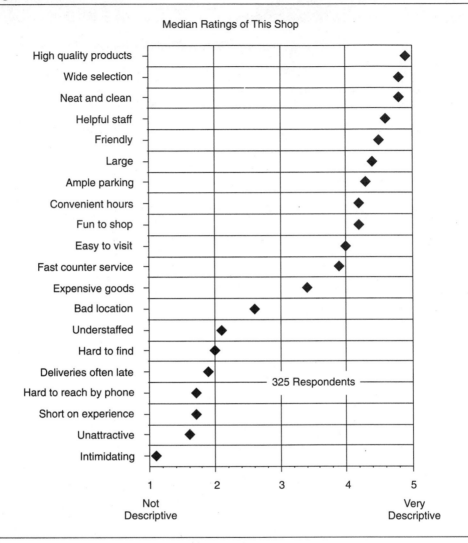

idating." It was least descriptive. If the item had been "Unintimidated," it may or may not have resulted in an average rating near five on the scale. To assume so wouldn't be at all permissible. One of the main reasons for using a semantic distance scale, rather than a semantic differential, is to avoid the need to identify *bipolar* adjectives. Thus, it would make no sense to do just that during the reporting phase.

Fixed Sum Scale Reports

The fixed sum scale was described in Chapter 5 and shown in Example 5–12 on page 134. Such scales yield as many variables as there are items, but the objective is to show the *proportions* of each item, based on a specific total of incidents. To convey the complete meaning of the data, all the variables from the scale must be reported in a single table or chart, as in Example 12–13 and Figure 12–15.

The items in the table were sorted according to the magnitude of the proportions because they are merely types of food and don't stand in any logical sequence or relationship to one another. If they had some inherent, orderly sequence, they should be presented in that sequence in the report.

Despite the fact that the items are individual variables, the data can be converted from whatever fixed sum or given total was used to a base of 100. So, the item *mean* values are actually percentages. The mean percentage is the appropriate average because the median or modal percentage values wouldn't necessarily total to 100 or any other fixed sum.

Pie charts such as that in Figure 12–15 lend themselves especially well to portraying results from fixed sum scales. In this split pie chart, the slice representing pizza has been "split" or separated from the rest of the pie to emphasize the sponsor's product relative to the others.

The narrative description of the table or graph reporting a summary of the fixed sum scale should indicate the *actual value* of the given total used in the questionnaire if the proportions have been converted to percentages. It may also have to explain the nature of the scale if it's the first time such data are presented in the report. By inserting such clarifications in the narrative text, the researcher can avoid confusion and the possibility that report readers might perceive the inconsistency in the table as an error, reducing the credibility of the survey. Thus, the narrative might begin:

Survey respondents indicated the number of times they ate each type of food, out of the *last 10 times* they ate fast food. The average values were then converted to percentages, as shown.

EXAMPLE 12–13

Fixed Sum Scale Table

Mean Percentage of Each Food Type Based on Last Ten Fast Food Meals	
Food Type (200 Respondents)	Mean Pct.
Hamburgers	41.8%
Pizza	28.4%
Sandwiches	15.0%
Chicken	8.3%
Some other	6.5%
Total	100.0%

Figure 12–15   *Fixed Sum Split Pie Chart*

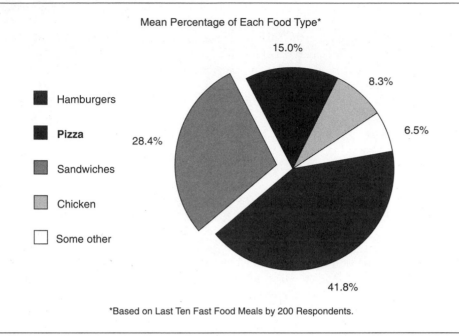

Mean Percentage of Each Food Type*

- Hamburgers
- **Pizza**
- Sandwiches
- Chicken
- Some other

15.0%
8.3%
6.5%
28.4%
41.8%

*Based on Last Ten Fast Food Meals by 200 Respondents.

MEASURES OF ASSOCIATION

The previous discussion of survey reporting focused on *data description,* mainly for *individual variables.* Although the condensed tables and graphs typically show the results for a "family" of items with the same type of scale, the emphasis is mainly on the set of individual values rather than on the *relationship* between the variables.

When the relationship between variables is to be shown, the data reported within one table, graph, or section are often derived from different types of scales. The focus isn't so much on the description of each variable as on the *relationship* between the variables. The remainder of this chapter concentrates on reports of the *measures of association* between variables described in Chapters 10 and 11, including cross-tabulation, analysis of variance, paired t-tests, correlation, and regression analysis.

Statistical analysis routines to measure the associations between variables almost always provide many more coefficients and values than needed in the final report. Some of that detail may be very important to the *research analyst,* but much of it wouldn't be understandable to report readers. So, the following discussion about reporting measures of association will emphasize not only what should be *included,* but also what can and should be *ignored* when writing the final survey report. It's important to note those conducting and reporting *academic* rather than *pragmatic* survey research may wish to provide their readers with more comprehensive and detailed reports of results than those for business, government, and organizational practitioners.

Cross-Tabulation Reports

When the relationship between two *categorical* variables is to be measured, cross–tabulation is the appropriate method. Typical analysis routine printouts from this type of procedure are shown in Examples 11–3, page 327, and 11–4, page 328. The information from four such cross-tabs are reported in Example 12–14. This format is called a vertical banner because the same categories are listed on the columns for all four sections. The data are condensed in the table, both to save space and to facilitate comparison of the measures among the four different demographic variables.

Notice the table in Example 12–14 clearly identifies what row item in each section is being cross-tabulated with the item defining the columns of the table. These lines containing only section headings and no numbers are called "slugs." They effectively divide the table into sections to avoid confusion among several variables contained in a table.

The number of respondents is listed so readers know the total on which the percentages are based. In each section of the table, the *combined* percentages in the last column at the right show the percentage of respondents in each category, totaling to 100 percent for the entire sample. The combined percentages in the bottom row are the percentages of the entire sample within each column. They're the same for each section because the columns represent the same categories, but they're listed in each section so the row percentages for each category of the variable can be compared with the combined total, as well as with one another. All rows total to 100 percent, and the "Total" column is listed so readers will quickly recognize the percentages total *across* the rows and *not down* the columns. The first two demographic variables are listed with an asterisk and a footnote indicates the differences in the distributions are statistically significant. The other two cross-tabulations aren't significant.

The narrative text to accompany a table such as in Example 12–14 should *briefly* explain the format if it's the first table of its kind or the first time this format appears in the report. It would then note the statistical significance and identify the major results:

There's less than a 5 percent chance that the distributions of Larks, Wrens, and Owls would differ as much as they do among age groups and among educational levels, for a sample such as this, if they actually did not differ in the whole population. Consequently, these differences are statistically significant and we can assume those in the population really do differ by age and education level in their time of day preferences. The differences between the sexes and occupational groups in this sample are *not* large enough to assume they exist in the population as well.

The proportion of Larks, Wrens, and Owls differs very little between those who are in the middle and those in the upper age groups. By contrast, a much higher proportion of the youngest group tends to be Larks, a somewhat smaller proportion than the other groups are Wrens, and a markedly lower percentage are Owls.

Educational level also seems to affect time of day preferences. It's interesting to note that those with *no college* and those who are *college graduates* have similar proportions of Larks, Wrens, and Owls, while those with *some college* are much more often Larks and less often Owls. But if education actually affects time of day preferences, and education certainly affects membership in occupational groups, then time of day preferences should also differ between blue and white collar occupations. They *don't*. To check further on this puzzling relationship, age groups were cross-tabulated with educational level. The results indicate that a large proportion of those with

EXAMPLE 12–14

Cross-Tabulation Vertical Banner Report

Time-of-Day Types by Demographic Characteristics					
400 Respondents	**Larks**	**Wrens**	**Owls**	**Total**	**Comb.**
Age Group★					
Under 35	44.5%	27.1%	28.4%	100.0%	38.7%
35 to 49	20.0%	30.6%	49.4%	100.0%	21.2%
50 and over	21.2%	30.6%	48.1%	100.0%	40.0%
Combined	30.0%	29.2%	40.7%	100.0%	100.0%
Education★					
No college	24.7%	32.5%	42.8%	100.0%	41.5%
Some college	40.0%	28.8%	31.2%	100.0%	31.3%
College graduate . .	26.6%	24.8%	48.6%	100.0%	27.2%
Combined	30.0%	29.2%	40.7%	100.0%	100.0%
Sex					
Males	31.4%	26.6%	42.0%	100.0%	51.7%
Females	28.5%	32.1%	39.4%	100.0%	48.3%
Combined	30.0%	29.2%	40.7%	100.0%	100.0%
Occupation					
White collar	43.9%	26.7%	29.4%	100.0%	63.8%
Blue collar	31.0%	33.8%	35.2%	100.0%	36.2%
Combined	30.0%	29.2%	40.7%	100.0%	100.0%

★Differences by *age* and *education* are statistically significant.

some college are young students, so the conclusion is that age is the most important determinant and education plays only a small role.

Another format for reporting several cross-tabs in the same table is shown in Example 12–15. In this format, the same four ratings define all *rows*. Each *pair* of columns shows the percentages for women and for men, for each variable or *brand*. Column percentages are listed in the body of the table, so they total downward to 100 percent. Since there were exactly as many women as men, there's no need to show the combined percentages for both sexes. The focus is directed exclusively to the comparison between the ratings of men and those of women for each brand. By presenting the distributions for all four brands in one banner, the comparison between brands is also facilitated, but it's important to note that measuring *significance* of differences *between brands* would require cross-tabulations between pairs of brands, for each sex, individually.

Analysis of Variance Reports

The statistical method for measuring the significance of differences among *mean* values of a continuous dependent variable for the categories of an independent variable is analysis of variance. A typical ANOVA table from an analysis program is shown in Example 11–5 on page 332. Reports of academic research ordinarily show the results very much as they're listed in Example 11–5. Pragmatic survey research reports usually contain only the tables of mean values. Typically, they omit the analysis of variance table itself as in Example 12–16.

In the example, the actual probability is listed, rather than merely noting statistical significance. This is quite acceptable, providing the narrative explains the meaning of the

---

EXAMPLE 12–15

Cross-Tabulation Horizontal Banner Report

	Brand A		Brand B		Brand C		Brand D	
	Women	Men	Women	Men	Women	Men	Women	Men
Excellent ..	31%	19%	8%	12%	17%	26%	36%	44%
Good	42%	36%	21%	33%	40%	38%	51%	38%
Fair	19%	26%	39%	41%	32%	21%	10%	22%
Poor	8%	19%	32%	14%	11%	15%	3%	4%
Total	100%	100%	100%	100%	100%	100%	100%	100%

Ratings of Four *Brands* by 100 Men and 100 Women★

★*Differences between sexes for all four brands are statistically significant.*

EXAMPLE 12–16

Analysis of Variance Table of Means

Breakdowns of: Lark-Owl Test Scores by Demographic Variables			
Group	**Probability**	**Mean**	**Number**
Age Group	.0000		
Under 20		2.09	11
20 to 29		5.14	97
30 to 39		6.18	73
40 to 49		7.00	59
50 to 59		6.72	78
60 to 69		6.90	51
70 and over		6.71	31
Combined		6.18	400
Marital Status	.002		
Married		6.67	215
Not married		5.60	185
Combined		6.18	400
Family Life Cycle	.0014		
Young single		5.19	113
Young couple		6.18	39
Child under 6		6.77	30
Child 6 to 15		6.18	44
Child over 15		6.72	54
Elder couple		6.97	74
Elder single		6.26	46
Combined		6.18	400
Scores not significantly different for other demographic items.			

probability, or the report readers are *all* very likely to know the meaning from an earlier explanation or previous training and experience. The footnote to the table in Example 12–16 indicates the other demographic variables in the survey did not prove to have significantly different test scores when they were analyzed. Thus, there was no purpose in showing the means for each category of those variables, because they're automatically assumed to be the same for all categories of each in the population.

The narrative text to accompany a tabular report such as that in Example 12–16 would typically identify the highest and lowest mean value for each category, for one variable at a time. Any trends or identifiable relationships among categories, in terms of the mean values, should be noted in the narrative, and the major differences by category should be discussed as well.

Paired t-Test Reports

When the significance of the difference between means is to be measured for a *pair* of continuous variables *both obtained from the same respondents*, a *paired* t-test can be used. The report of such an analysis from a statistical program is shown in the upper section of Figure 11–10 on page 335.

In Example 12–17, the analyses of the differences between the mean time respondents *actually* did four daily activities and the time they would *ideally* like to do them are reported in the same, condensed table. For academic survey research reports, the table would probably contain much more detail. For more pragmatic survey research, the reports usually show only the mean values, just as with analysis of variance. It's also advisable to show the direction

EXAMPLE 12–17

Paired t-Test Table of Means

Comparisons of Mean Actual versus Ideal Times for Activities				
Activity	**Actual**	**Ideal**	**Difference**	**Probability**
Get up	6:47 AM	7:12 AM	−25 Min.	.000
Start work . . .	8:16 AM	8:35 AM	−19 Min.	.000
Finish work . .	4:02 PM	4:21 PM	−19 Min.	.000
Have dinner . .	6:31 PM	6:30 PM	+1 Min.	.598
Go to bed . . .	11:00 PM	11:03 PM	−3 Min.	.126
400 Respondents				

and magnitude of *differences* in means in paired t-test reports. Of course, there must be some notation of the statistical significance as well. Example 12–17 lists the actual probability for gauging significance.

In many cases, there's no need to list relationships that don't prove to be statistically significant. For example, the table in Example 12–16 merely notes that the means for the other demographic variables weren't significantly different. The actual means weren't listed. The table shown in Example 12–17 does show the actual and ideal *dinner times* and *bed times,* even though the differences are clearly not statistically significant. This is a case where it's just as important to recognize the *similarity* in the mean values as it is to identify *differences.* Whenever such similarity in values is as notable or even more remarkable than are differences in values, the similar pairs of means should be listed, even though the differences aren't statistically significant.

The inclusion of five, comparable paired t-test analyses in one table, as in Example 12–17, allows the report to compare similarities and differences between pairs in the narrative text, thus:

> Survey respondents clearly indicated in their listings of actual and ideal times that they would prefer to arise in the morning about a half hour later than they do. The results shown in Table 17 also indicate they would like to start and finish their workday about 20 minutes later. By contrast, the results show they eat dinner in the evening at almost exactly the time they would like to do so, and also retire for the night at very nearly the ideal time.
>
> These relationships suggest two things: (1) The average individual in the population would like to start and finish work a little later than they're required to do so. (2) The fact they must start work earlier than they would ideally like causes them to *arise* earlier than they want to, but they *dine* and *retire* in the evening when they would like. Thus, they sacrifice *sleep* time to meet work requirements.

Correlation Analysis Reports

When the *means* of two continuous variables that are both responses from the same respondents are to be compared, the paired t-test is used. When the relationship between such variables is to be measured in terms of their change or variance from one respondent to the next, *correlation* is the appropriate measure. Correlation analysis doesn't assume one is causing or determining the other. When the data are from interval or ratio level scales, product-moment correlation is used. When the data are from ordinal level scales, rank correlation is appropriate. The results are shown in reports and interpreted in exactly the same way, but when rank correlations are shown, it should be noted in the report table. If the table simply lists correlation coefficients, the assumption would be that the coefficients are product-moment correlations.

In Example 11–6, page 339, each pairing of five variables was reported in tabular form by the analysis routine. The variables were only identified by number and weren't labeled to indicate their meaning. The same results are shown in Example 12–18, but the table is labeled with the variables' names and the redundant "halves" of the matrix are both shown. Thus, readers can locate a pair by approaching from the top or the side of the matrix. In Example 12–18, the probabilities for assessing statistical significance are listed. This assumes the readers are *all* completely capable of understanding and interpreting them. If that weren't the case, only the correlation coefficients would be listed. An asterisk would be attached to

EXAMPLE 12–18

Correlation Matrix Table

	Creative	Assertive	Patient	Outspoken	Cooperative
Creative		r = +.30 p = .001	r = +.01 p = .402	r = +.16 p = .001	r = +.09 p = .018
Assertive	r = +.30 p = .001		r = −.01 p = .014	r = +.48 p = .001	r = −.08 p = .032
Patient	r = +.01 p = .402	r = −.10 p = .014		r = −.19 p = .001	r = +.43 p = .001
Outspoken	r = +.16 p = .001	r = +.48 p = .001	r = −.19 p = .001		r = +.01 p = .408
Cooperative	r = +.09 p = .018	r = −.08 p = .032	r = +.43 p = .001	r = +.01 p = .408	

Correlations Among Ratings of Self-Image for Five Attributes

500 Respondents   r = Correlation Coefficient   p = Significance Probability

the significant coefficients and a footnote would indicate their significance. The narrative interpretations would merely identify the direction and intensity of each significant correlation.

Regression Analysis Reports

When the effect of one continuous variable on another is to be measured, regression analysis is the statistical method to do so. In Example 11–7, page 340, the relationship between *expected* and *actual* dollar expenditures is assessed and reported by the analysis routine. A less detailed tabular report of the same data is shown in Example 12–19.

It's always advisable to list the mean, minimum and maximum values for the variable in regression analysis reports. The prediction equation is usually valid and accurate only within or very close to that range. The table in Example 12–19 also lists the difference in means and the probability for assessing the significance of the difference. This measure is the same as a paired t-test, and it's interpreted in the same way. It merely indicates that in this case, actual expenditures weren't significantly different from the expected expenditures. The correlation coefficient is also listed in Example 12–19, along with the probability for assessing its significance. The meaning is precisely the same as for product-moment correlation described earlier.

The value of r-square is shown in the regression analysis report to indicate the degree to which the independent variable affects the dependent variable. It indicates the percentage of variance in the actual expenditures that's "explained" by knowing the expected value. It suggests how accurate a prediction based on the regression equation might be. The standard error of the estimate and the standard errors of the constant and the regression coefficient might also be included in the report, if the readers are sufficiently informed or familiar with regression analysis. In Example 12–19, the prediction equation is listed at the bottom of the table in verbal rather than symbolic form for those who aren't familiar with prediction equation symbols.

Regression analysis is a powerful tool, but it's also rather complex. Showing the data in a scatterplot such as that in Figure 12–16 sometimes makes it easier for information seekers to comprehend the more abstract numeric values. That way, they can actually see the relationship between the independent and dependent variables.

Regression analysis often requires a fairly complete and elaborate narrative explanation for report readers and sponsors who aren't completely familiar with statistical methods. If the focus of the information needs is on *measurement of the existing relationship,* the narrative would deal with that aspect. If *predictions of the dependent variable* are required, the narrative

---

EXAMPLE 12–19

Regression Analysis Report

Regression of *Actual* on *Estimated* Expenditure in Dollars				
Variable	**Mean**	**Minimum**	**Maximum**	**Number**
Estimated expenditure	22.45	5.00	31.00	300
Actual expenditure	22.66	8.00	28.00	300
Item	**Symbol**	**Value**	**Std. Err.**	**Probability**
Mean difference	D	0.213	0.173	0.2180
Correlation	R	0.795		0.0000
Determination	R^2	0.633	2.829	0.0000
Slope	B	0.789	0.035	0.0000
Intercept	A	4.958	0.798	0.0000

Prediction equation: *Predicted Expenditure* = 0.789 times *Estimate,* plus $4.96.

Figure 12–16 *Regression Scatterplot*

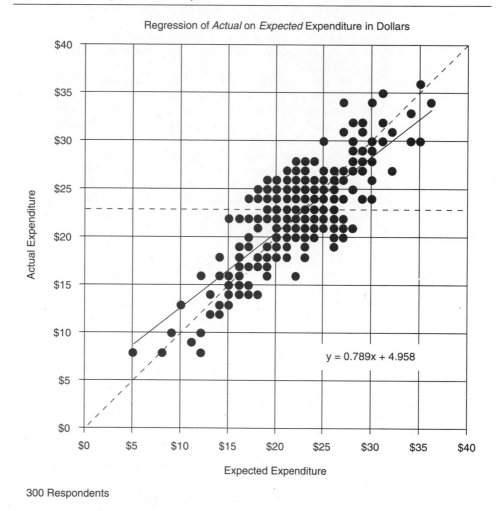

Regression of *Actual* on *Expected* Expenditure in Dollars

y = 0.789x + 4.958

300 Respondents

would place more emphasis on that. It would focus on accuracy and especially on meeting the requirements for valid application—such as staying within the range of values used to compute the equation. This narrative example focuses on both the relationship between the variables and on prediction:

Three hundred of the newest homeowners within the complex who anticipated using the new facility were asked how much they *expected* to spend there per month. These values were recorded for each lot number. The lot numbers for those making subsequent, *actual* expenditures were also recorded with the amount spent. The results are shown in Table 19 and plotted in Figure 16. The average values were both very close to $22.50 per month. They didn't significantly under- or overestimate how much they would spend *as a group.*

This might seem to suggest that we could estimate each *new* homeowner who moves in will spend about $22.66 per month at the facility, represented by the horizontal, dashed line in Figure 16. That would only be true *on the average, over all newcomers*. In fact, however, *individual* spending does vary substantially from one family to the next, as the plot shows. The regression equation indicates over 60 percent of that variation is "explained" by the differences in what they *expect* to spend. In other words, these people have a *fairly* good idea of what they'll actually spend at the facility.

To predict how much each new homeowner will spend, we could simply ask them their expectations and take *that* as the estimate. If they expected to spend $15, we would predict $15, and if they expected to spend $30, we would predict $30. That way to predict is represented by the diagonal, dashed line in Figure 16. It's a much better predictor than the average for the group, but it's not the *best* way.

The solid regression line plotted in Figure 16 shows that people who *expect* to spend *less* than the average actually *underestimate* their spending. They tend to spend a little more than they expected. By contrast, those who *expect* to spend more than the group average tend to *overestimate*. Their actual spending turns out to be less than they expected. So, the best predictor of how much a new family will spend is based on what they expect, but we would compute it with the regression equation.

If they expect to spend $10 per month, we would multiply that by the slope of the line, .789, to get $7.89, then add the adjustment of $4.96. So we would expect them to spend $12.85 a month, not $10. Similarly, if they estimated $30, the prediction based on the regression equation would be $30 times .789 + $4.96 = $28.63. It's important to note this applies only to *homeowners* and only for predictions under $40. *Renters'* spending can't be predicted in this way. Nor do we have the data to predict how someone who *expected* to spend over $40 would *actually* spend.

This portion of a narrative text discussing the regression relationships in Example 12–19 and Figure 12–16 first cited the insignificant differences in mean values. Then it indicated the strength of the relationship, based on the r-square value. It compared a prediction based on the mean versus one based directly on the individual's expectation, the independent variable, making reference to the scatterplot to clarify the methods visually. Finally, it cited the regression equation as the best predictor and gave two examples of prediction calculations. The narrative did *not* discuss the confidence intervals around the regression prediction because that was beyond the scope of detail for the report. If the report's audience were knowledgeable about statistics, the narrative might have explained the prediction would be within $5.66 over 95 percent of the time and $8.49 over 99 percent of the time, based on the standard error of the estimate. The narrative report was also careful to note the restrictions on application of the regression equation, such as similar subjects (homeowners) and within the proper range (under $40.).

CONCLUDING THE PROJECT

The final report of the results should be carefully edited and a clean copy typed using a dark print that can be copied clearly. Multiple copies are often required for sponsors and those seeking the information. The pragmatic survey research report should be headed with a title page that identifies the sponsor, project, and researcher or organization who conducted the survey. It's important to note on the title page the address and telephone number of the person or office responsible for the project, so they can be contacted at a later time for clarification, if that should be needed.

All of the pages within a survey report should be consecutively numbered, and the page numbers should appear in the same place on every page. When the report is of substantial size, an index should be included directly following the title page. The major sections of the report should be listed with the page number, and a list of tables or figures should follow the list of contents or index, if there are several.

If the final survey report consists only of a few pages, they should be stapled together in the upper left corner or attached in a small binder or folio to keep the document together and intact. When the report consists of many pages, it can be punched and contained in a ring binder or bound in some other form by a copy service. Larger reports stay more neat and readable when they're bound within durable covers. Ring binders are available with clear plastic "envelopes" on the covers so title pages can be inserted. The title is then visible from the outside. When the report is bound, it's advisable to use a clear plastic cover to make the report easily identifiable without opening it.

The researcher should retain data files and documentation for a *substantial* period after completing a project. Very often sponsors or those seeking the information will have additional questions after studying the report. These additional information needs can usually be met quickly and inexpensively if the data files, programs, and documents are retained in good order. All of the survey materials, including the source documents, data files, special programs, and other materials obtained specifically for the survey, are the property of the sponsor unless otherwise specified in the contract. Thus, when these materials are clearly no longer of use to the researcher for the project at hand, the sponsor should indicate which are to be delivered to the sponsor's office and which are to be destroyed. In most cases of commercial survey research, all of the materials are regarded by the sponsor as proprietary information. Consequently, extra copies of the reports or other documents must usually be delivered to the sponsor or destroyed, so they don't fall into the hands of those who aren't entitled to the information.

Whether the survey research project was conducted to meet academic requirements or professionally, as the result of employment or a contract, most experienced researchers find one source of "payment" to be very valuable. That's merely the sense of satisfaction and accomplishment that's inevitably achieved at the completion of a job *well done*. No matter how simple or mundane the content of a well-conceived and conducted survey might be, those who do the project can be assured of its value. This society both generates and consumes vast amounts of information. Our social, political, economic, and technical systems are heavily dependent on it. Consequently, those who use survey research to generate *information* that's both reliable and valid have contributed significantly to the progress and satisfaction of the society.

SUMMARY

Generating the Final Report

    A. Spend the time and effort. Avoid the temptation to rush through the report and do it carefully, even though sponsors may be overly anxious.

    B. Keep it very neat. The appearance and cosmetic aspects of the report often indicate to readers, rightly or wrongly, the credibility of the survey results.

C. Use an executive summary. Pragmatic survey research reports should begin with a quick summary of the main highlights and major results.

D. Include a response summary. Prepare a blank questionnaire listing the simplest form of data description and removing any superfluous codes or instructions.

E. Compose tables first. Condense the information with clean, simple formats in a single page, so patterns and relationships can readily be perceived.

F. Display the information. Create charts, graphs, and diagrams when values and relationships can be represented more clearly by size and shape than by words and numbers.

G. Write a simple narrative. Avoid jargon and use plain vocabulary to describe the major findings revealed in each table, with introductions and summaries of each section.

H. Keep components independent. Tables and graphs should be clearly labeled and the narrative written so report readers can obtain the major gist of the results from either mode.

I. Conclude the project. Edit, copy, and bind the reports, including a title page for identification, and maintain data and documents until directed to deliver or destroy them.

Conducting Focus Groups

FOCUS GROUP CHARACTERISTICS

Focus group discussions or conferences are usually called merely *focus groups*. A typical focus group consists of eight to twelve people seated around a conference table with a group moderator who *focuses* their discussion on a series of topics or issues of interest to the research sponsor, while the proceedings are being observed and recorded for analysis and interpretation later. Focus groups have a relatively short history, compared to survey research, but they have become an increasingly popular method of inquiry. Focus groups provide *qualitative* information rather than quantitative data. The results don't generalize reliably to the population as a whole. Consequently, focus group research definitely should be and typically is regarded as *exploratory* and *preliminary* rather than conclusive.

Surveys are expensive and time-consuming. So, it's vitally important to ask the right questions and to ask them in the right way! By conducting one or more focus groups before initiating a survey, both sponsors and researchers can sometimes get a better grasp of the problem and formulate the research questions more accurately. Well-conducted focus groups may also help the researcher to understand the prospective survey respondents' general perspective on the issues, frame of reference, way of thinking, and typical vocabulary when dealing with the topics at hand.

There are four key aspects of focus group inquiry that deserve attention: The agenda, the participants, the moderator, and the interpretations. The advantages and disadvantages of focus groups should be considered before turning to those issues.

Advantages and Disadvantages

There are both advantages and disadvantages to conducting focus groups before initiating a survey project. It's important for both sponsors and researchers to recognize the strong and weak points of this technique. Focus group research isn't always necessary or appropriate. When it is, the objective is to get the most from it while avoiding both the most common and the more obscure pitfalls.

Major capabilities

The main advantages of focus groups are briefly outlined in Figure A–1. Focus groups tend to be very dynamic and spontaneous, compared to a one-on-one interview. Rather than just responding to the moderator, group members interact, engaging one another in conversation about the topics and issues in focus at the moment. These groups are large enough so no one person feels he or she holds the exclusive attention of the moderator. Yet they're small enough to be "conversational," so even those who are rather shy about speaking before a group aren't threatened by the situation. Since there's an agenda, the discussion is loosely, but not rigidly, organized. The moderator can direct the discussion toward the topics of major interest to the research sponsor. However, this doesn't preclude pursuing fortuitous, unanticipated avenues that often arise in the course of the group discussion.

The focus group moderator can probe and delve into the assumptions and feelings that underlie the attitudes and opinions expressed, so the results are richly textured with detail. The sponsor's representatives can observe the focus group, either directly or via audio or video recordings. Nuances of voice, expression, and manner reveal more than just the verbal records of what group members said. The results often have a strong impact on interested survey sponsors and information seekers.

Focus group participants reveal far more than just their overt opinions and preferences—

Figure A–1   *Advantages of Focus Groups*

Spontaneity	Focus group participants typically respond very spontaneously, volunteering their opinions and reactions, sharing their experiences, and providing comments far beyond just responding to questions.
Subjectivity	Participants are encouraged to express their personal opinions and reactions freely in their own vocabulary, addressing what's most important to them rather than responding in someone else's terms.
Stimulation	Group participants usually feel free to reveal themselves, sharing personal experiences and disclosing personal reactions that stimulate others to describe their own views and reactions.
Speed	Moderators, facilities, and participants can be secured and focus groups can be conducted very quickly, so focus group inquiries may not seriously delay the start of a survey project.
Simplicity	Focus group results are expressed verbally and qualitatively, rather than in numeric, tabular reports, so both the process and the findings are readily understood by sponsors.
Structure	The inquiry is indeed *focused* and the conversation is centered on the specific topics and issues of greatest interest to the sponsor, covering each area in a meaningful, comprehensive way.
Specialization	Focus group inquiries can address very specific topics and issues in depth, dealing in great detail with the finer nuances and subtle ramifications of certain positions and special conditions.
Selectivity	The participation of people who represent special segments of the populations can often be obtained readily, allowing inquiries to be addressed to either opinion leaders or the common man or woman.
Secrecy	Since only a small number of people are involved, focus group inquiries can be conducted without revealing the existence, nature, and purpose of the anticipated survey to rivals or competitive firms.

they also reveal *themselves*. In the course of conversation, they show something of their own, individual personality. So researchers and sponsors learn *who it is* that thinks, feels, and acts that way. Rather than seeing only a demographic profile of the respondents, focus group participants have names and faces. Their opinions and reactions are revealed in the context of their daily lives. So when survey research analysts, sponsors, and information seekers are making choices and decisions that depend on respondent reactions, they have a vivid picture in their mind's eye of the "real people" whose reactions are represented in the more abstract survey findings.

Major limitations

Perhaps the primary disadvantage of focus group research is the limitation on the number of participants who can be included. Even if several focus group discussions are held, findings based on such a small sample can't be generalized to the population as a whole with any degree of confidence. Unfortunately, some sponsors and researchers do use focus groups as a substitute for survey research, rather than a preliminary, exploratory method. They do so at great peril of making false assumptions and serious errors based on *unreliable* information. Consequently, generalization of focus group data to a broad universe of people is virtually never advisable.

Focus groups require a great deal of skill and expertise on the moderator's part. By comparison with field interviewers, focus group moderators should be much more thoroughly trained in the art of asking questions and guiding the discussion. It may *look* easy, but the task of moderating a focus group is vastly more difficult than it appears. There are usually one or two people in a focus group who dominate the conversation and dictate the opinions of others, if they're allowed to do so. They have to be restrained without offending them. There are also likely to be a few who are rather shy and withdrawn—reluctant to give their own opinions and reactions. They must be drawn out and engaged, but without threatening them. Most important of all, the moderator must protect the *diversity* of opinion and reaction within the group, despite the strong tendency toward *group consensus* that inevitably emerges in any prolonged group interaction. These demands, among many others, make it difficult to find a competent focus group moderator. Yet, the validity and practicality of the information depend very heavily on the moderator's skill and expertise.

While focus groups are a relatively fast research method, they're also rather expensive. Each focus group among ordinary lay people from the general public might cost the sponsor anywhere from about $2,000 to $5,000 or more. Focus groups that include commercial, organizational, governmental, or professional executives or decision makers are even more expensive, ranging as high as many thousands of dollars each for special groups. Yet, one survey research project might call for several focus groups to be conducted, in order to cover the entire range of topics and the complete spectrum of potential participants from the population to be surveyed. In addition to the cost of this qualitative, exploratory information, the sponsor has to fund the survey itself to obtain more reliable and generalizable primary, quantitative data.

Focus Group Requirements

Informal or ad hoc focus group discussions are sometimes conducted at the sponsor's facilities or in public meeting rooms such as those provided by hotels and conference centers. So, focus groups don't really require special facilities and personnel, but they do benefit by them. The vast majority of focus groups for business and politics are conducted by specialized personnel in facilities specifically designed for such research. Many, if not most, data collection agencies have special facilities for focus groups, and the majority of commercial focus groups are held in and conducted by data collection agencies.

Facilities and equipment

Special-purpose focus group facilities usually include several components: A reception area and small waiting room, the conference room or rooms, adjoining observation rooms, administrative offices, bathrooms, and equipment storage rooms. The conference rooms themselves are more comfortably furnished than most meeting rooms. Usually there's conference table seating for a dozen or more people. To encourage a more intimate, relaxed atmosphere, some focus group rooms are furnished with couches, lounge chairs, and coffee tables rather than the conventional conference table and chairs. Microphones for recording the conversation are usually hidden from sight or at least rather obscure. That's not really to conceal the fact that the discussion will be recorded but to avoid making participants blatantly aware of the fact during the discussion. These rooms almost invariably have one or more large mirrors that are, in fact, one-way windows between the conference room and the observation and/or camera rooms.

The observation rooms adjacent to the conference rooms often house and conceal audio and video recording equipment and technicians as well as observers. Researchers and sponsor representatives usually sit comfortably in semidarkness, watching and noting the focus group discussion while it's being conducted and speaking quietly among themselves without the notice of the participants in the next room. Some researchers and sponsors prefer to attend and observe the group discussion rather than merely to listen to or view the recording. It affords them a more direct and comprehensive impression.

Focus group discussions are sometimes only an hour or less in duration. Others extend over a little longer period. If so, the group may take a break at midpoint. If the researchers or sponsors are present, the moderator can speak briefly with them to gain their impressions and get suggestions concerning the avenues to be explored during the remainder of the focus group discussion. But whether they're present or not, focus group discussions are routinely recorded for later study. They may only be recorded on an audiocassette, but usually they're videotaped for viewing later.

Special focus group facilities are desirable and widely available, but they aren't absolutely necessary. Focus groups can be conducted in a hotel, office, school, church, or public meeting room. If that's the case, the researchers, sponsors, and information seekers may still attend and observe, but they absolutely should *not* participate! Both their presence and that of the recording equipment and technicians should be as unobtrusive and inconspicuous as possible. The *more* the participants become or remain aware of their presence, the *less* validity and accuracy the results will have.

Personnel and participants

The moderator plays a key role in focus group inquiries, although others are certainly involved in the process. The sponsors and information seekers help to identify the main topics to be discussed. The lead research analyst has overall responsibility for the focus group inquiry. The data collection agency or focus group center staff usually takes care of the preparation, recruitment, reception, and compensation of participants. Of course, the focus group participants who actually provide the information during the group discussions are central to the success of the focus group inquiry.

Research surveys of broad scope may include hundreds or even thousands of participants: No one of them has a dominant effect on the outcome or the information obtained. But since focus groups by necessity include a few participants, the responses of each individual may represent a very large number of others who have similar views and reactions. Consequently, the recruitment, selection, and participation of each focus group participant should and usually do receive a great deal of consideration and attention.

FOCUS GROUP AGENDA

The focus group agenda is a list of topics on which the discussion is to center. But the agenda for a focus group differs dramatically from a survey questionnaire. First, the questions on the agenda are framed much more loosely and broadly. Second, the agenda is much more flexible, since the discussion may suggest additional topics of inquiry to be pursued. Third, the topics and issues on the focus group agenda need not be approached in the order in which they're listed. The dynamics of relatively free-wheeling discussions dictate in large measure which topics and issues will precede or follow which others.

Translating Information Needs

The information needs to be satisfied by focus groups aren't necessarily the same as the ultimate information needs of the survey research. Focus group inquiries may provide some directly applicable information to the research sponsor. However, their *main* objective is to provide information to guide the survey research analyst and staff.

Identifying key issues

It was noted earlier that focus groups are actually an exploratory research method. Sponsor information needs are specified in the terms of the information seekers who will apply it to decisions and actions. But the questions addressed to survey respondents have to be expressed in the terms and couched in the conditions that are familiar to the public from which the survey sample will be selected. Thus, focus group inquiries are often designed to bridge that gap, to facilitate that translation.

The typical focus group agenda is expressed in very broad terms. Those composing the agenda first identify the key issues, the principal concerns and uncertainties of the research sponsor. The initial draft might be in the form of statements or phrases identifying discussion topics rather than as actual questions to be asked of the focus group participants. At this point, the effort is directed toward including all the key factors of concern.

Once the analyst is confident that all the main issues have been listed as topics, some weight or priority should be assigned to each, according to their degree of importance. Usually a simple, three-level breakdown is sufficient: (1) *Essential* information that's absolutely necessary, (2) *important* information that has substantial value to the sponsor and/or researcher, and (3) *supportive* information that amplifies and extends the value of the findings.

After identifying all of the key topics for discussion and assigning a priority to each to indicate the amount of time and degree of emphasis each one deserves, this skeleton framework can be fleshed out by listing the subsidiary issues and topics associated with each main category. So a two-level, or perhaps a three-level, outline constitutes the agenda.

Framing the questions

The questions to be addressed to focus group discussants aren't designed to be answered with a single word or phrase, as they so often are on a survey questionnaire. Instead, the focus group agenda that the moderator brings to the discussion contains what might be called "trigger" questions, designed to draw out various opinions and stimulate a conversation about some issue. There are a couple of rather different approaches to writing such questions: One is to ask a question that will reveal participants' conclusions about the issue, then follow with a series of "probing" questions to learn what lies behind their opinions. The other approach takes just the opposite tack: first soliciting information about the background situation, then proceeding to inquire about the conclusive opinion that results under such conditions.

Some moderators are given strongly to one tactic or the other, but the best of them can approach a given issue either way, depending on what best fits the character of the group and the dynamics of the conversation during the discussion. Either way, the focus group questions should be rather loosely framed rather than tightly phrased and worded. The object is to tease out the *varying* perspectives and opinions on the topic. To do that, focus group questions often begin with a preamble that defines an entire spectrum of thought on the issue at hand, strongly implying that any and every position is as acceptable and respectable as any other. This helps to prevent the more dominant members of the group from leading or pulling others toward their own position, as though it were the only valid one.

Organizing the Schedule

The schedule of questions for a focus group discussion must be organized according to some principle, so that the conversation doesn't jump abruptly from one topic or issue to a completely different one without a smooth transition. Without a well-defined train of thought, the discussion will be rather chaotic and disjointed. That makes the results far more difficult to interpret and it also inhibits the response of the participants. The mind abhors chaos and disorder. It doesn't readily move from consideration of one topic to a completely different and unrelated one without a meaningful connection or some advance warning. So, the analyst and moderator should plan smooth transitions and create "bridges" from one set of ideas to the next.

Schedule flexibility

While some organization is necessary, it's a mistake to follow a rigid structure within a focus group discussion. Ordinarily, there are many incidents during the discussion where the participants themselves will take the conversation in an unexpected direction, following some train of thought the researcher or moderator didn't anticipate. By allowing that to happen, the inquiry benefits from the serendipitous information that comes forth. Were the moderator to adhere tightly to the schedule of questions, that opportunity would be lost.

When scheduling the questions, the objective is to provide organization when it's needed, yet not to impose a structure when it's not required. The moderator should willingly, even eagerly, let the conversation go where it will, providing it doesn't go too far afield of the main topics or issues. It also implies that the moderator must be able to find the way back to another topic on the agenda when the current conversation has exhausted the issue it spontaneously pursued. Thus, the adroit, well-practiced moderator has to be able to build such connections or bridges extemporaneously.

Generality to specificity

The most effective focus group schedule moves from the general to the specific. For instance, the discussion of a topic might begin by focusing first on a very broad set of issues or principles, then move smoothly to consideration of various aspects or details of each. The participants might be questioned first about their general attitudes and policies concerning some issue, practice, or experience, then asked about specific instances and tactics. When the focus group discussion moves from one main topic category to another, the new set of questions should begin with the general issues, then explore the more specific, detailed opinions and actions. If the pattern were reversed, moving from the specific to the general, isolated examples or atypical details might dictate response to more general questions. By approaching the broader issues first, then ferreting out the specific incidents, the moderator helps prevent the participants from verbally "painting themselves into a corner."

FOCUS GROUP PARTICIPANTS

Recruitment and selection of the focus group members are certainly key elements, if not the most crucial elements of this exploratory method of inquiry. After all, it's they who will ultimately provide the information. Since there are so few participants, the information provided by each is a major part of the whole.

Selection Criteria

The focus group participants should be homogeneous in one respect and heterogeneous in another—similar in some respects but different in others. If the participants differ greatly in every way, they'll have a hard time relating to one another. By contrast, if most or all members of the group are of an almost identical ilk—if they're practically clones of one another—then they're likely to react as one. There would be too little diversity and too much redundancy.

Socioeconomic composition

When all members of one focus group share a similar set of socioeconomic characteristics, that facilitates group interaction. For instance, a group consisting only of married women who are mothers of two or more children, none of which are working outside the home, are likely to share many experiences and perspectives—they have the same problems and troubles, they face similar needs, and they enjoy about the same set of opportunities and satisfactions. This is especially true if their educations and family incomes are similar and they share other such demographic characteristics. Such group participants are more easily able to identify with one another and they're likely to interact freely with one another: They'll quickly and easily find a common ground. If, on the other hand, the group contained some such women, while others were younger, single, better educated, and career-oriented women, the differences would be so large and so obvious they would inhibit a free, easy discussion of the topics at hand.

Obviously, there can be some diversity in the participants' backgrounds, but beyond some point, communication will be inhibited. If the population to be represented by the focus group participants consists only of one, fairly homogeneous socioeconomic segment, then a single focus group might represent the population quite well. If the population to be surveyed is very heterogeneous, consisting of many diverse socioeconomic segments, it may be necessary to conduct several focus groups. When time or budget requirements preclude conducting several such focus group conferences, it's usually better to single out only the most important socioeconomic segment for study than to include widely diverse participants within only one or two focus groups.

Position representation

While the similarity of the participants for any one focus group is desirable, the members should certainly not be identical to one another in their *reactions to the topics and issues* to be discussed. In other words, the group should provide varying views on the issues on which the discussion focuses. The objective, after all, isn't to obtain close consensus; far from it. Rather, the researcher should strive for a group composition that will represent various positions and views on the topics and issues to be discussed and to preserve that diversity in the information obtained.

With focus group inquiries, the goal isn't to measure and project the size or proportion of the population that takes each position or holds each view. That will be accomplished with the survey. Instead, the goal of each focus group is to discover and reveal the nature, range, and diversity of positions. Consequently, the criteria for selecting focus group participants might stipulate that a certain proportion of the people chosen must hold a certain view or have a certain kind of experience. It may even be necessary to prescreen candidates with a brief questionnaire to be sure various views or positions are represented.

Screening Candidates

Focus group participants are typically recruited by the data collection agency or focus group center where the inquiry will be conducted. The recruiters should be given the criteria for seeking and selecting the candidates. Whether or not the participants are to be screened before acceptance, it's incumbent on the sponsor or researcher conducting the inquiry to provide firm guidelines regarding who is and who isn't eligible. Lacking such guidance, those selecting participants are very likely to choose those who are the quickest and easiest to obtain. They probably won't represent the population to be sampled in the survey very well.

Conformity to criteria

The criteria for selection of focus group participants might include either specification of the *groups* from whom participants are to be obtained or of the actual *characteristics* of those who are chosen. For instance, the directions for a focus group dealing with children's home study materials might state that the participants are to be obtained only from the P.T.A. roster of mothers of third and fourth grade elementary school pupils from a certain school. Alternatively, the directions might require that only mothers with children between nine and eleven years of age living within a certain area are eligible to participate.

In some cases it may be necessary to question potential participants with a brief screening instrument to ascertain whether they qualify for participation. Such questionnaires are neither as elaborate nor as formal as a typical survey instrument. Prospective participants might only be asked to indicate a few basic demographic characteristics, but they may also be questioned very briefly about their views or experiences. For example, only those familiar with the issues or topics of interest to the sponsor might be eligible while all others may be disqualified and politely dismissed from further participation.

Participation and payment

Survey respondents are only rarely paid for their participation, and then only under special circumstances. But responding to a survey questionnaire ordinarily takes very little time and effort. By contrast, taking part in a focus group discussion typically requires the person to visit a special facility at a specific time, to spend an hour or so there, and to participate much more actively with the others in the group. Consequently, focus group members often either receive monetary compensation for participating or they're given a substantial gift or premium for doing so.

Compensation is something of a two-edged sword: On the one hand, selection bias and error are reduced by compensation because desirable participants who would otherwise refuse can be induced to attend and participate. On the other hand, compensation might also increase bias and error. If they're given too much, it might encourage too favorable an attitude toward the issues, topics, or sponsor than would normally exist among those in the population to be surveyed. It might also result in greater representation of those who most need or want the money or gift, despite their actual lack of qualification or essential interest in the inquiry. To increase the positive effects and decrease the negative effects of compensating focus group participants, the sponsor or researcher should choose a level and type of compensation that's *proportionate* to the task. The value should be commensurate with both the availability of the desired participants and the degree of effort they have to put forth or inconvenience they must tolerate.

There's one group of potential focus group participants who definitely *shouldn't* be selected—those who have ample time on their hands and greatly enjoy taking part in many such discussions. They may have participated many times in the past and make themselves readily available to the facility recruiting focus group participants. So, they become "professional" participants, and the more experience they gain, the greater their opinions, views, and reactions will vary from those of ordinary people in the population. If their participation isn't strictly prohibited, recruiters are likely to simplify their task by accepting one or several such easily identifiable and readily available "regulars."

The ideal number of focus group participants ranges from six or eight to as many as ten or twelve. Fewer people provide fewer opinions and less diversity, so the cost per item of information is increased. If only a few participants are present, there may be too few to encourage frank, open discussion. Each may see him- or herself as too obviously the center of attention, while a somewhat larger group affords some degree of anonymity to the individual. On the other hand, groups that exceed about a dozen people become difficult for the moderator to manage: They often become fractionated and the shier members become reluctant to express themselves before so many others. In addition, focus groups of eight or ten people are so common that most facilities are arranged to accommodate only about that number: Smaller groups would appear to be underpopulated or underattended while larger groups may severely crowd the space or cramp the facilities.

About ten or fifteen percent of candidates who are recruited and selected probably won't show up (on time) to participate. It depends partly on the amount of compensation offered. Consequently, more participants are ordinarily solicited than will actually be required to compensate for the "no-shows." If, by some happenstance, all or nearly all those invited do show up for the focus group, it's best to exclude the excess, compensate them, and dismiss them rather than including too large a number in the focus group session.

FOCUS GROUP MODERATORS

The single most important individual involved in a focus group is the moderator. The accuracy, utility, and value of the information obtained is directly dependent on the moderator's skill and ability. At first glance, the focus group moderator's job looks fairly simple and easy. In fact, it's deceptively difficult and exceedingly demanding. Even among very experienced moderators, only the best of them really do it well. To make matters even more difficult, a well-trained and very capable moderator might conduct one focus group very successfully, yet the same person might be completely inappropriate for a different group of participants and an agenda focusing on a different set of topics and issues.

Personal Attributes

A focus group moderator's potential depends in part on the nature of the personality. There are some personality traits that most or all effective moderators share and others that are virtually always absent in a good moderator. Yet the biographic characteristics of the best moderators tend to differ very markedly from one to the next—some are men, others women; some young, some elderly, and some middle-aged; some obviously glib and sophisticated, but others of the "salt-of-the-earth" type. There's a good reason for this diversity among focus group moderators.

Biographic characteristics

Moderators tend to be more effective at obtaining information from the focus group members when they share many of the same biographic characteristics as most of the participants. The reasons are about the same as those for selecting participants with common socioeconomic or demographic characteristics: People are vastly more comfortable and at ease, and thus more candid and open, with people who are similar to themselves than with those who are quite different.

Even though some potential moderators might be exceptionally skilled and capable, their ability and experience would hardly compensate for perceived differences between them and the groups that were their demographic opposites. If necessary, it's best to sacrifice some degree of skill and experience in order to get a fairly close match between the demographic characteristics of the group members and those of the moderator—*providing the moderator possesses the basic qualifications.*

Personality and temperament

The best and most effective focus group moderators tend to be fairly open, out-going people. They're usually fairly bright, though they certainly shouldn't appear to be intellectual types. The more friendly and charismatic they are, the better, yet they shouldn't have a celebrity's demeanor. The more they're seen as "just one of the guys or gals," the more effective they're likely to be, unless, of course, the focus group participants are themselves an exceptional group. Good moderators appear to be more curious and inquisitive than they do knowledgeable or authoritative.

The most effective television talk show hosts maintain a certain naiveté—something of a "little boy" or "little girl" mentality. They show an ability to be intrigued or even dismayed. It allows the audience to identify with them, despite their celebrity status and years of association with famous and talented guests. The best focus group moderators have a similar image and demeanor. They have just enough authority to direct and control the flow of conversation but without directly affecting its content. They can engender enough trust so they don't threaten or embarrass the participants, but not so much familiarity that they lose respect or control.

Experience and Skill

The best and most effective moderators aren't necessarily the most experienced. Yet experience does count, and it takes a substantial amount of it for moderators to try different approaches and perfect their style and technique. The prospective moderator's track record is often the single most important indicator of skill and ability. Prospective focus group moderators should be able to provide the researcher with a client list identifying the types of research sponsors they have served, the nature of the focus group topics, and the recency of the experience. Confidentiality and the proprietary nature of research information may prohibit them from identifying each individual client firm. Yet they should be able to provide the identity of former client firms not competitive with the potential client together with the name and location of individuals within those firms who might be contacted for a recommendation. Sponsors or researchers who were former clients are vastly more reliable sources of information about prospective moderators than are the recommendations of data collection agencies, with whom they may be affiliated. Potential moderators may also be interviewed in person or by telephone, especially if they're to moderate several focus groups.

Figure A–2 contains a list of 24 key skills and attributes of an effective focus group moderator. These are the things to look for when interviewing prospective moderators. It's also advisable to evaluate moderators on these same factors after they've been hired and conduct a focus group. That way, moderators who perform well can be coached and advised so that they can improve their performance even further. Those who fail to meet acceptable standards can be avoided in the future. The moderator's level of performance can be taken into consideration when evaluating the accuracy and validity of the information obtained from the focus group.

Figure A–2   *Focus Group Moderator Skills*

Appear relaxed and comfortable	Politely control dominant members
Avoid alienating dislikable members	Prevent undue consensus formation
Avoid favoritism among participants	Probe to learn underlying factors
Avoid revealing own opinions	Pursue unanticipated avenues well
Build rapport with others quickly	Recognize socially desirable answers
Cover every agenda topic and issue	Recognize when a topic is exhausted
Encourage spontaneous reactions	Sense members' moods effectively
Enjoy the company of the group	Show genuine interest in responses
Follow a logical agenda sequence	Successfully obtain minority opinions
Listen attentively to speakers	Treat sensitive issues gently
Never threaten or intimidate members	Use self-disclosure effectively
Obtain comments from quiet members	Use simple, conversational speech

FOCUS GROUP INTERPRETATIONS

The final aspect of focus groups to be considered is the interpretation of the information they generate. Survey *data collection* generates only "raw data" that must undergo substantial manipulation, analysis, and interpretation before it's usable—before it's transformed into *information* that's applicable. Focus group inquiries are quite different in that respect. Much of the "data" obtained is *directly* applicable to the task of survey planning, with little or no intervening manipulation or interpretation.

Monitoring and Recording

Focus groups are often monitored directly by researchers and perhaps by survey sponsors as well. That's especially true when only one or two groups are conducted within a short period of time in the same or in nearby locations. Direct observation provides more vivid and memorable impressions of the participants' reactions and comments. The "live" show conveys more immediate, detailed information and gives those attending a greater appreciation of the nuances and subtle cues inherent in the group discussion. In addition, the research analyst and information seekers can make suggestions and give direction to the moderator during a break in a session or between consecutive focus group sessions.

Audio recording

The most simple and inexpensive method of recording focus group sessions is merely to record them on audio tape cassettes. Often only one microphone is needed. It and the recording equipment should be as inconspicuous as possible, so it doesn't inhibit the responses of participants—especially those who are more shy or reserved or who hold "minority" opinions on the issues.

Audio tapes can be transcribed verbatim or condensed into brief, written reports, but they seldom are. Written reports contain only the words of participants, but not the manner in which they were spoken. Most of the time, the *way* something is said contains as much or more information as *what* is said—as the words themselves. So, research analysts and information seekers benefit most from hearing the actual voices of participants. The recordings may be auditioned in their entirety, or they may be edited so the audio report contains only the most meaningful and relevant excerpts.

Video recording

The *advantage* of video recording is that it captures and conveys much more information than just audio recording. However, the *disadvantages* may sometimes outweigh the benefits: Video taping is more expensive, involves more equipment, and requires a camera operator, but those aren't the critical factors. The biggest disadvantage of video taping is the *intrusiveness* of the process. Participants may be a little shy about a microphone for audio taping, but they get used to it rather quickly and usually just forget it's there. Not so with a video camera.

Most people respond *very* differently if they notice a camera is focused on them. Yet it may be difficult to conceal the video camera and equipment in operation, except in special facilities where the camera is in an observation room. Even in that case, there may be technical problems unless there are two cameras or special seating arrangements.

Video tapes let the survey research analyst, staff, and information seekers go back and review the entire focus group or the most relevant parts as they're formulating survey information needs and planning the survey process. So, they have some *very important* benefits. On the other hand, if a camera operator is walking around the room, zooming in on speakers as they contribute to the discussion, the results may be worse than useless! They may be downright misleading. So, the general rule is to video tape focus groups only when it can be done *unobtrusively*.

Analysis and Application

Survey sponsors and information seekers can gain much by attending and observing focus groups or watching and listening to the recordings. However, the research analyst normally has much more experience with focus group inquiries. The analyst can enhance the meaning and value of the information by providing a written or oral commentary that explains and interprets the focus group results.

The simple picture of "where people stand" on the topics and issues on which the group focused is often fairly obvious in the recording of the sessions. However, it's much more difficult for information seekers with little or no training and experience regarding focus groups to identify the relevant relationships between various aspects of the participants' responses. Consequently, the research analysts who analyze and interpret the information often concentrate on comparing and contrasting various opinions and reactions among individuals with different characteristics. The interpretive commentary should highlight the most relevant and indicative similarities and distinctions the focus group discussion reveals.

An effective focus group agenda will include both the "what" and the "why"—both what the participants think, feel, and do, and also why they respond that way. The search for the feelings, beliefs, and assumptions that underlie verbal opinions is a key aspect of the analysis and interpretation of focus group responses. The analyst should identify prototypical response patterns, then relate them to the factors or conditions that underlie each identifiable pattern.

Figure A–3   *Applying Focus Group Information*

Area Affected	Questions to be Answered
Information Needs	What are the *key* issues or considerations in the minds of respondents? How do they think about these matters? What *feelings* do they have? How *important* are these things to them? What *belief* patterns, *experiences*, or *assumptions* will they bring to the response task?
Sampling Design	How much *diversity* is there in their thinking on these issues? How will that *variance* affect *sample size* and *reliability*? Must certain groups be represented? Does this suggest a *stratified* sample? Can they be reached and will they respond readily?
Instrumentation	What *vocabulary*—what *words or phrases*—did participants use when they spoke about each topic? How does this affect the *wording* of questions? What *range* or *spectrum* of opinions was revealed? What kind of *scales* does that imply? How much *instruction* will be needed?
Data Collection	*Can* and *will* these people respond to a self-administered, mail questionnaire? Will they require *personal* contact? *Telephone* contact? How much *probing* will they need? Will it be easy or difficult to build *rapport*? What kinds of *interviewers* would be best for this group?
Data Processing	Can the *range, diversity,* and *depth* of response be reflected *numerically?* How much *verbal* response will be needed, if any? What methods should be used to reveal *patterns* of response? How should the *associations* between variables be measured?
Report Generation	What report mechanisms are likely to portray survey responses from this group most effectively? Will a written report suffice? Would these *information seekers* respond better to an *oral presentation?* How much *graphic* material should be anticipated in the report?

Focus groups provide *preliminary, qualitative* information to help sponsors and information seekers get a better grasp of the problem and formulate the research questions more precisely. The researcher's goal is to learn more about the survey respondents' general perspective on the issues—about their frame of reference, way of thinking, and typical vocabulary when dealing with the topics to be covered in the survey. An effective focus group inquiry can provide the research analyst and staff with insights regarding *all six* steps in the survey research process. The areas affected and the relevant questions the researcher should ask when applying focus group information to the survey process are listed in Figure A–3. It certainly doesn't constitute an exhaustive list, but it does suggest many of the most important ways and means of applying the information gained in focus groups to the planning and execution of a reliable, valid survey.

SUMMARY

Focus Group Inquiries

A. Focus groups are a *popular* form of *preliminary, exploratory* research inquiry because they're *fast, flexible,* and *easily understood.*

B. With so few respondents, focus groups are *not* an adequate substitute for field surveys of a substantial sample of respondents.

C. Focus groups require *special expertise* and perhaps special facilities, so they're rather expensive and several of them may be required.

D. The vast majority of focus groups are conducted at *special facilities or centers* designed for that purpose.

E. Focus groups are guided by an *agenda* of the *key issues and topics,* and it must be fairly *flexible,* rather than rigid.

F. *Agenda questions* fall into three broad categories: *essential information, important information,* and *supportive information.*

G. The *flow of discussion* on each major topic should be organized to move *from the general to the specific* questions and reactions.

H. Participants should be screened so the group will be *demographically homogeneous* but *heterogeneous regarding individual views.*

I. Effective group moderators are of *various demographic backgrounds* but they *share many special personality traits.*

J. The role of the *moderator is critical* and the task requires a great deal of *skill and experience* to perform effectively.

K. Focus group sessions can be *observed directly* by sponsor representatives, and they should be *audio or video recorded* and summarized in a commentary report.

L. Focus group results are applicable to *all six* main steps or phases of the survey research process.

Appendix B

Statistical Tables

Example B–1 *Using a Random Number Table*

To Pick a Random Sample From a Population of 5,000				
37722	55794	14636	05148	54505
43339	65689	76539	27909	05467
92925	92124	92634	35681	43690
01172	*46045*	46991	33804	80006
33304	*57975*	03985	21566	65796
11838	**10433**	21564	51570	73558
40098	*97962*	89845	28392	78187
43370	**28007**	06779	72402	62632
37738	**24849**	70722	71859	83736
06435	*52758*	45685	90151	46516
40359	**28723**	15364	69125	12609
90648	**24362**	83314	00014	19207
38790	*53626*	93780	18629	68766
51935	**05711**	09799	79077	88159
28598	*70013*	63794	53169	97054

1. Pick a spot *at random* at which to begin. (e.g., *4604*)
2. *Randomly* choose the direction to move—up, down, left, or right. (e.g., **down**)★
3. Accept the first four-digit number less than or equal to 5000. (e.g., *4604*)
4. Continue drawing acceptable numbers. (e.g., **1043, 2800, 2484, . . .**)
5. Ignore any numbers greater than the population size. (e.g., *9796, 5275*)
6. Numbers selected here are 571, 1043, 2436, 2484, 2800, 2872, and 4604.
7. Continue to end of column or row, then advance to the next in the table.

★Since numbers are random, they may be selected by group or choosen across columns or up or down rows, ignoring groups.

Table B–1   *Table of Random Numbers*

02711	08182	75997	79866	58095	83319	80295	79741	74599	84379
94873	90935	31684	63952	09865	14491	99518	93394	34691	14985
54921	78680	06635	98689	17306	25170	65928	87709	30533	89736
77640	97636	37397	93379	56454	59818	45827	74164	71666	46977
61545	00835	93251	87203	36759	49197	85967	01704	19634	21898
17147	19519	22497	16857	42426	84822	92598	49186	88247	39967
13748	04742	92460	85801	53444	65626	58710	55406	17173	69776
87455	14813	50373	28037	91182	32786	65261	11173	34376	36408
08999	57409	91185	10200	61411	23392	47797	56377	71635	08601
78804	81333	53809	32471	46034	36306	22498	19239	85428	55721
82173	26921	28472	98958	07960	66124	89731	95069	18625	92405
97594	25168	89178	68190	05043	17407	48201	83917	11413	72920
73881	67176	93504	42636	38233	16154	96451	57925	29667	30859
46071	22912	90326	42453	88108	72064	58601	32357	90610	32921
44492	19686	12495	93135	95185	77799	52441	88272	22024	80631
31864	72170	37722	55794	14636	05148	54505	50113	21119	25228
51574	90692	43339	65689	76539	27909	05467	21727	51141	72949
35350	76132	92925	92124	92634	35681	43690	89136	35599	84138
46943	36502	01172	46045	46991	33804	80006	35542	61056	75666
22665	87226	33304	57975	03985	21566	65796	72915	81466	89205
39437	97957	11838	10433	21564	51570	73558	27495	34533	57808
77082	47784	40098	97962	89845	28392	78187	06112	08169	11261
24544	25649	43370	28007	06779	72402	62632	53956	24709	06978
27503	15558	37738	24849	70722	71859	83736	06016	94397	12529
24590	24545	06435	52758	45685	90151	46516	49644	92686	84870
48155	86226	40359	28723	15364	69125	12609	57171	86857	31702
20226	53752	90648	24362	83314	00014	19207	69413	97016	86290
70178	73444	38790	53626	93780	18629	68766	24371	74639	30782
10169	41465	51935	05711	09799	79077	88159	33437	68519	03040
81084	03701	28598	70013	63794	53169	97054	60303	23259	96196
69202	20777	21727	81511	51887	16175	53746	46516	70339	62727
80561	95787	89426	93325	86412	57479	54194	52153	19197	81877
08199	26703	95128	48599	09333	12584	24374	31232	61782	44032
98883	28220	39358	53720	80161	83371	15181	11131	12219	55920
84568	69286	76054	21615	80883	36797	82845	39139	90900	18172
04269	35173	95745	53893	86022	77722	52498	84193	22448	22571
10538	13124	36099	13140	37706	44562	57179	44693	67877	01549
77843	24955	25900	63843	95029	93859	93634	20205	66294	41218
12034	94636	49455	76362	83532	31062	69903	91186	65768	55949
10524	72829	47641	93315	80875	28090	97728	52560	34937	79548
68935	76632	46984	61772	92786	22651	07086	89754	44143	97687
89450	65665	29190	43709	11172	34481	95977	47535	25658	73898
90696	20451	24211	97310	60446	73530	62865	96574	13829	72226
49006	32047	93086	00112	20470	17136	28255	86328	07293	38809
74591	87025	52368	59416	34417	70557	86746	55809	53628	12000
06315	17012	77103	00968	07235	10728	42189	33292	51487	64443
62386	09184	62092	46617	99419	64230	95034	85481	07857	42510
86848	82122	04028	36959	87827	12813	08627	80699	13345	51695
65643	69480	46598	04501	40403	91408	32343	48130	49303	90689
11084	46534	78957	77353	39578	77868	22970	84349	09184	70603

Example B–2 *Cross-Tabs and the Significance of Chi-Square*

Typical Cross-Tabulation Table					
Count Exp.Val. Row Pct. Residual	1	2	3	4	Row Total
1	8 5.1 26.7% 2.9	9 6.3 30.0% 2.7	10 9.0 33.3% 1.0	3 9.6 10.0% −6.6	30 30.0%
2	5 5.8 14.7% −.8	6 7.1 17.6% −1.1	7 10.2 20.6% −3.2	16 10.9 47.1% 5.1	34 34.0%
3	4 6.1 11.1% −2.1	6 7.6 16.7% −1.6	13 10.8 36.1% 2.2	13 11.5 36.1% 1.5	36 36.0%
Column	17	21	30	32	100
Total	17.0%	21.0%	30.0%	32.0%	100.0%

Chi-Square 14.07257   df = 6   Prob. = ? ★
Minimum Expected Frequency = 5.100

1. Refer to the row in the table for 6 degrees of freedom.
2. Chi-Square (14.07) is *larger* than 10.645 so p *less* than 0.20.
3. Chi-Square is *larger* than 12.592 so p *less* than 0.10.
4. Chi-Square is *larger* than 12.592 so p *less* than 0.05.
5. Chi-Square is *smaller* than 14.449 so p *greater* than 0.025.

★Actual computed chi-square probability = .02884

Table B–2 *Critical Values of Chi-Square*

df	Right-Tail Area					
	0.20	**0.10**	**0.05**	**0.025**	**0.01**	**0.001**
1	2.706	3.841	3.841	5.024	5.412	6.635
2	4.605	5.991	5.991	7.378	7.824	9.210
3	6.251	7.815	7.815	9.348	9.837	11.345
4	7.779	9.488	9.488	11.143	11.668	13.277
5	9.236	11.070	11.071	12.833	13.388	15.086
6	10.645	12.592	12.592	14.449	15.033	16.812
7	12.017	14.067	14.067	16.013	16.622	18.475
8	13.362	15.507	15.507	17.535	18.168	20.090
9	14.684	16.919	16.919	19.023	19.679	21.666
10	15.987	18.307	18.307	20.483	21.161	23.209
11	17.275	19.675	19.675	21.920	22.618	24.725
12	18.549	21.026	21.026	23.337	24.054	26.217
13	19.812	22.362	22.362	24.736	25.472	27.688
14	21.064	23.685	23.685	26.119	26.873	29.141
15	22.307	24.996	24.996	27.488	28.259	30.578
16	23.542	26.296	26.296	28.845	29.633	32.000
17	24.769	27.587	27.587	30.191	30.995	33.409
18	25.989	28.869	28.869	31.526	32.346	34.805
19	27.204	30.144	30.144	32.852	33.687	36.191
20	28.412	31.410	31.410	34.170	35.020	37.566
21	29.615	32.671	32.670	35.479	36.343	38.932
22	30.813	33.924	33.924	36.781	37.659	40.289
23	32.007	35.172	35.173	38.076	38.968	41.638
24	33.196	36.415	36.415	39.364	40.270	42.980
25	34.382	37.652	37.653	40.646	41.566	44.314
26	35.563	38.885	38.885	41.923	42.856	45.642
27	36.741	40.113	40.113	43.194	44.140	46.963
28	37.916	41.337	41.337	44.461	45.419	48.278
29	39.087	42.557	42.557	45.722	46.693	49.588
30	40.256	43.773	43.773	46.979	47.962	50.892

Example B-3 *ANOVA and the Significance of F*

	Analysis of Variance				
Source	Sum of Squares	D.F.	Mean Squares	F-Ratio	F Prob.
Between Groups	8.4805	2	4.2043	4.2268	?*
Within Groups	97.3095	97	1.0032		
Total	105.7900	99			

1. Refer to the *first* page of the table, for the F-distribution for .05.
2. Refer to the column for the *numerator* df of 2.
3. Refer to the row with the closest value (120) for the *denominator* df of 98.
4. F-ratio value (4.2268) is *larger* than 3.07 so p *less* than 0.05.
5. Refer to the *third* page of the table, for the F-distribution for .01.
6. Refer to the column for the *numerator* df of 2.
7. Refer to the row with the closest value (120) for the *denominator* df of 98.
8. F-ratio value (4.2268) is *smaller* than 4.79 so p *greater* than 0.01.

*Actual computed F-ratio probability = .0174

Table B–3–a *Critical Values of the F Distribution—Level of Significance = .05*

df Denominator	Numerator Degrees of Freedom								
	1	2	3	4	5	6	7	8	9
1	161.00	200.00	216.00	225.00	230.00	234.00	237.00	239.00	241.00
2	18.50	19.00	19.20	19.20	19.30	19.30	19.40	19.40	19.40
3	10.10	9.55	9.28	9.12	9.01	8.94	8.89	8.85	8.81
4	7.71	6.94	6.59	6.39	6.26	6.16	6.09	6.04	6.00
5	6.61	5.79	5.41	5.19	5.05	4.95	4.88	4.82	4.77
6	5.99	5.14	4.76	4.53	4.39	4.28	4.21	4.15	4.10
7	5.59	4.74	4.35	4.12	3.97	3.87	3.79	3.73	3.68
8	5.32	4.46	4.07	3.84	3.69	3.58	3.50	3.44	3.39
9	5.12	4.26	3.86	3.63	3.48	3.37	3.29	3.23	3.18
10	4.96	4.10	3.71	3.48	3.33	3.22	3.14	3.07	3.02
11	4.84	3.98	3.59	3.36	3.20	3.09	3.01	2.95	2.90
12	4.75	3.89	3.49	3.26	3.11	3.00	2.91	2.85	2.80
13	4.67	3.81	3.41	3.18	3.03	2.92	2.83	2.77	2.71
14	4.60	3.74	3.34	3.11	2.96	2.85	2.76	2.70	2.65
15	4.54	3.68	3.29	3.06	2.90	2.79	2.71	2.64	2.59
16	4.49	3.63	3.24	3.01	2.85	2.74	2.66	2.59	2.54
17	4.45	3.59	3.20	2.96	2.81	2.70	2.61	2.55	2.49
18	4.41	3.55	3.16	2.93	2.77	2.66	2.58	2.51	2.46
19	4.38	3.52	3.13	2.90	2.74	2.63	2.54	2.48	2.42
20	4.35	3.49	3.10	2.87	2.71	2.60	2.51	2.45	2.39
21	4.32	3.47	3.07	2.84	2.68	2.57	2.49	2.42	2.37
22	4.30	3.44	3.05	2.82	2.66	2.55	2.46	2.40	2.34
23	4.28	3.42	3.03	2.80	2.64	2.53	2.44	2.37	2.32
24	4.26	3.40	3.01	2.78	2.62	2.51	2.42	2.36	2.30
25	4.24	3.39	2.99	2.76	2.60	2.49	2.40	2.34	2.28
30	4.17	3.32	2.92	2.69	2.53	2.42	2.33	2.27	2.21
40	4.08	3.23	2.84	2.61	2.45	2.34	2.25	2.18	2.12
60	4.00	3.15	2.76	2.53	2.37	2.25	2.17	2.10	2.04
120	3.92	3.07	2.68	2.45	2.29	2.18	2.09	2.02	1.96
∞	3.84	3.00	2.60	2.37	2.21	2.10	2.01	1.94	1.88

Table B–3–a   *(Concluded)*

Numerator Degrees of Freedom								df Denominator		
10	**12**	**15**	**20**	**24**	**30**	**40**	**60**	**120**	**∞**	
242.00	244.00	246.00	248.00	249.00	250.00	251.00	252.00	253.00	254.00	1
19.40	19.40	19.40	19.40	19.50	19.50	19.50	19.50	19.50	19.50	2
8.79	8.74	8.70	8.66	8.64	8.62	8.59	8.57	8.55	8.53	3
5.96	5.91	5.86	5.80	5.77	5.75	5.72	5.69	5.66	5.63	4
4.74	4.68	4.62	4.56	4.53	4.50	4.46	4.43	4.40	4.37	5
4.06	4.00	3.94	3.87	3.84	3.81	3.77	3.74	3.70	3.67	6
3.64	3.57	3.51	3.44	3.41	3.38	3.34	3.30	3.27	3.23	7
3.35	3.28	3.22	3.15	3.12	3.08	3.04	3.01	2.97	2.93	8
3.14	3.07	3.01	2.94	2.90	2.86	2.83	2.79	2.75	2.71	9
2.98	2.91	2.85	2.77	2.74	2.70	2.66	2.62	2.58	2.54	10
2.85	2.79	2.72	2.65	2.61	2.57	2.53	2.49	2.45	2.40	11
2.75	2.69	2.62	2.54	2.51	2.47	2.43	2.38	2.34	2.30	12
2.67	2.60	2.53	2.46	2.42	2.38	2.34	2.30	2.25	2.21	13
2.60	2.53	2.46	2.39	2.35	2.31	2.27	2.22	2.18	2.13	14
2.54	2.48	2.40	2.33	2.29	2.25	2.20	2.16	2.11	2.07	15
2.49	2.42	2.35	2.28	2.24	2.19	2.15	2.11	2.06	2.01	16
2.45	2.38	2.31	2.23	2.19	2.15	2.10	2.06	2.01	1.96	17
2.41	2.34	2.27	2.19	2.15	2.11	2.06	2.02	1.97	1.92	18
2.38	2.31	2.23	2.16	2.11	2.07	2.03	1.98	1.93	1.88	19
2.35	2.28	2.20	2.12	2.08	2.04	1.99	1.95	1.90	1.84	20
2.32	2.25	2.18	2.10	2.05	2.01	1.96	1.92	1.87	1.81	21
2.30	2.23	2.15	2.07	2.03	1.98	1.94	1.89	1.84	1.78	22
2.27	2.20	2.13	2.05	2.01	1.96	1.91	1.86	1.81	1.76	23
2.25	2.18	2.11	2.03	1.98	1.94	1.89	1.84	1.79	1.73	24
2.24	2.16	2.09	2.01	1.96	1.92	1.87	1.82	1.77	1.71	25
2.16	2.09	2.01	1.93	1.89	1.84	1.79	1.74	1.68	1.62	30
2.08	2.00	1.92	1.84	1.79	1.74	1.69	1.64	1.58	1.51	40
1.99	1.92	1.84	1.75	1.70	1.65	1.59	1.53	1.47	1.39	60
1.91	1.83	1.75	1.66	1.61	1.55	1.50	1.43	1.35	1.25	120
1.83	1.75	1.67	1.57	1.52	1.46	1.39	1.32	1.22	1.00	∞

Table B–3–b *Critical Values of the F Distribution—Level of Significance = .01*

df Denominator		Numerator Degrees of Freedom							
	1	2	3	4	5	6	7	8	9
1	4052	5000	5403	5625	5764	5859	5928	5981	6022
2	98.5	99.0	99.2	99.2	99.3	99.3	99.4	99.4	99.4
3	34.1	30.8	29.5	28.7	28.2	27.9	27.7	27.5	27.3
4	21.2	18.0	16.7	16.0	15.5	15.2	15.0	14.8	14.7
5	16.3	13.3	12.1	11.4	11.0	10.7	10.5	10.3	10.2
6	13.7	10.9	9.78	9.15	8.75	8.47	8.26	8.10	7.98
7	12.2	9.55	8.45	7.85	7.46	7.19	6.99	6.84	6.72
8	11.3	8.65	7.59	7.01	6.63	6.37	6.18	6.03	5.91
9	10.6	8.02	6.99	6.42	6.06	5.80	5.61	5.47	5.35
10	10.0	7.56	6.55	5.99	5.64	5.39	5.20	5.06	4.94
11	9.65	7.21	6.22	5.67	5.32	5.07	4.89	4.74	4.63
12	9.33	6.93	5.95	5.41	5.06	4.82	4.64	4.50	4.39
13	9.07	6.70	5.74	5.21	4.86	4.62	4.44	4.30	4.19
14	8.86	6.51	5.56	5.04	4.69	4.46	4.28	4.14	4.03
15	8.68	6.36	5.42	4.89	4.56	4.32	4.14	4.00	3.89
16	8.53	6.23	5.29	4.77	4.44	4.20	4.03	3.89	3.78
17	8.40	6.11	5.18	4.67	4.34	4.10	3.93	3.79	3.68
18	8.29	6.01	5.09	4.58	4.25	4.01	3.84	3.71	3.60
19	8.18	5.93	5.01	4.50	4.17	3.94	3.77	3.63	3.52
20	8.10	5.85	4.94	4.43	4.10	3.87	3.70	3.56	3.46
21	8.02	5.78	4.87	4.37	4.04	3.81	3.64	3.51	3.40
22	7.95	5.72	4.82	4.31	3.99	3.76	3.59	3.45	3.35
23	7.88	5.66	4.76	4.26	3.94	3.71	3.54	3.41	3.30
24	7.82	5.61	4.72	4.22	3.90	3.67	3.50	3.36	3.26
25	7.77	5.57	4.68	4.18	3.85	3.63	3.46	3.32	3.22
30	7.56	5.39	4.51	4.02	3.70	3.47	3.30	3.17	3.07
40	7.31	5.18	4.31	3.83	3.51	3.29	3.12	2.99	2.89
60	7.08	4.98	4.13	3.65	3.34	3.12	2.95	2.82	2.72
120	6.85	4.79	3.95	3.48	3.17	2.96	2.79	2.66	2.56
∞	6.63	4.61	3.78	3.32	3.02	2.80	2.64	2.51	2.41

Table B–3–b   *(Concluded)*

10	12	15	20	24	30	40	60	120	∞	df Denominator
			Numerator Degrees of Freedom							
6056	6106	6157	6209	6235	6261	6287	6313	6339	6366	1
99.4	99.4	99.4	99.4	99.5	99.5	99.5	99.5	99.5	99.5	2
27.2	27.1	26.9	26.7	26.6	26.5	26.4	26.3	26.2	26.1	3
14.5	14.4	14.2	14.0	13.9	13.8	13.7	13.7	13.6	13.5	4
10.1	9.89	9.72	9.55	9.47	9.38	9.29	9.20	9.11	9.02	5
7.87	7.72	7.56	7.40	7.31	7.23	7.14	7.06	6.97	6.88	6
6.62	6.47	6.31	6.16	6.07	5.99	5.91	5.82	5.74	5.65	7
5.81	5.67	5.52	5.36	5.28	5.20	5.12	5.03	4.95	4.86	8
5.26	5.11	4.96	4.81	4.73	4.65	4.57	4.48	4.40	4.31	9
4.85	4.71	4.56	4.41	4.33	4.25	4.17	4.08	4.00	3.91	10
4.54	4.40	4.25	4.10	4.02	3.94	3.86	3.78	3.69	3.60	11
4.30	4.16	4.01	3.86	3.78	3.70	3.62	3.54	3.45	3.36	12
4.10	3.96	3.82	3.66	3.59	3.51	3.43	3.34	3.25	3.17	13
3.94	3.80	3.66	3.51	3.43	3.35	3.27	3.18	3.09	3.00	14
3.80	3.67	3.52	3.37	3.29	3.21	3.13	3.05	2.96	2.87	15
3.69	3.55	3.41	3.26	3.18	3.10	3.02	2.93	2.84	2.75	16
3.59	3.46	3.31	3.16	3.08	3.00	2.92	2.83	2.75	2.65	17
3.51	3.37	3.23	3.08	3.00	2.92	2.84	2.75	2.66	2.57	18
3.43	3.30	3.15	3.00	2.92	2.84	2.76	2.67	2.58	2.49	19
3.37	3.23	3.09	2.94	2.86	2.78	2.69	2.61	2.52	2.42	20
3.31	3.17	3.03	2.88	2.80	2.72	2.64	2.55	2.46	2.36	21
3.26	3.12	2.98	2.83	2.75	2.67	2.58	2.50	2.40	2.31	22
3.21	3.07	2.93	2.78	2.70	2.62	2.54	2.45	2.35	2.26	23
3.17	3.03	2.89	2.74	2.66	2.58	2.49	2.40	2.31	2.21	24
3.13	2.99	2.85	2.70	2.62	2.54	2.45	2.36	2.27	2.17	25
2.98	2.84	2.70	2.55	2.47	2.39	2.30	2.21	2.11	2.01	30
2.80	2.66	2.52	2.37	2.29	2.20	2.11	2.02	1.92	1.81	40
2.63	2.50	2.35	2.20	2.12	2.03	1.94	1.84	1.73	1.60	60
2.47	2.34	2.19	2.03	1.95	1.86	1.76	1.66	1.53	1.38	120
2.32	2.18	2.04	1.88	1.79	1.70	1.59	1.47	1.32	1.00	∞

Example B–4 *Paired t-Test and the Significance of T*

t-Test Breakdown Table				
REACTION	**COUNT**	**MEAN**	**STD. DEV.**	**STD. ERROR**
Variable 1	100	2.0600	.814	.081
Variable 2	100	2.2400	.726	.073
Difference	100	−0.1800	.783	.078

t-Value = .−2.30   d.f. = 99   2-tail Probability = ?★   1-tail Probability = ?★★

For a Two-Tail Test (Variable 1 < or > Variable 2)

1. Refer to Abs. table for the *Student t* distribution.
2. Refer to the row with the closest value (120) to the df of 99.
3. Abs. t-value (2.30) is *larger* than 1.289 so p is *less* than 0.20.
4. Abs. t-value (2.30) is *larger* than 1.658 so p is *less* than 0.10.
5. Abs. t-value (2.30) is *larger* than 1.980 so p is *less* than 0.05.
6. Abs. t-value (2.30) is *smaller* than 2.358 so p is *greater* than 0.02.

★Actual computed two-tail t-value probability = .024

For a One-Tail Test (Variable 1 < Variable 2)

7. Refer to the row with the closest value (120) to the df of 99.
8. Abs. t-value (2.30) is *larger* than 1.289 so p is *less* than 0.100.
9. Abs. t-value (2.30) is *larger* than 1.658 so p is *less* than 0.050.
10. Abs. t-value (2.30) is *larger* than 1.980 so p is *less* than 0.025.
11. Abs. t-value (2.30) is *smaller* than 2.358 so p is *greater* than 0.010.

★★Actual computed one-tail t-value probability = .012

Table B–4   *Student* T *Distribution*

	Level of Significance for One-Tailed Test					
	0.100	0.050	0.025	0.01	0.005	0.0005
	Level of Significance for Two-Tailed Test					
df	0.20	0.10	0.05	0.02	0.01	0.001
1	3.078	6.314	12.706	31.821	63.657	636.619
2	1.886	2.920	4.303	6.965	9.925	31.599
3	1.638	2.353	3.182	4.541	5.841	12.924
4	1.533	2.132	2.776	3.747	4.604	8.610
5	1.476	2.015	2.571	3.365	4.032	6.869
6	1.440	1.943	2.447	3.143	3.707	5.959
7	1.415	1.895	2.365	2.998	3.499	5.408
8	1.397	1.860	2.306	2.896	3.355	5.041
9	1.383	1.833	2.262	2.821	3.250	4.781
10	1.372	1.812	2.228	2.764	3.169	4.587
11	1.363	1.796	2.201	2.718	3.106	4.437
12	1.356	1.782	2.179	2.681	3.055	4.318
13	1.350	1.771	2.160	2.650	3.012	4.221
14	1.345	1.761	2.145	2.624	2.977	4.140
15	1.341	1.753	2.131	2.602	2.947	4.073
16	1.337	1.746	2.120	2.583	2.921	4.015
17	1.333	1.740	2.110	2.567	2.898	3.965
18	1.330	1.734	2.101	2.552	2.878	3.922
19	1.328	1.729	2.093	2.539	2.861	3.883
20	1.325	1.725	2.086	2.528	2.845	3.850
21	1.323	1.721	2.080	2.518	2.831	3.819
22	1.321	1.717	2.074	2.508	2.819	3.792
23	1.319	1.714	2.069	2.500	2.807	3.768
24	1.318	1.711	2.064	2.492	2.797	3.745
25	1.316	1.708	2.060	2.485	2.787	3.725
26	1.315	1.706	2.056	2.479	2.779	3.707
27	1.314	1.703	2.052	2.473	2.771	3.690
28	1.313	1.701	2.048	2.467	2.763	3.674
29	1.311	1.699	2.045	2.462	2.756	3.659
30	1.310	1.697	2.042	2.457	2.750	3.646
40	1.303	1.684	2.021	2.423	2.704	3.551
60	1.296	1.671	2.000	2.390	2.660	3.460
120	1.289	1.658	1.980	2.358	2.617	3.373
∞	1.282	1.645	1.960	2.326	2.576	3.291

Example B–5   *Rank Correlation and the Significance of Rho*

Rank Correlation Breakdown Table					
REACTION	**COUNT**	**MEAN**	**STD. DEV.**	**MIN.**	**MAX.**
Variable 1	20	3.00	1.45	1	5
Variable 2	20	3.10	1.25	1	5

N-par r = .4495 n = 20 2-tail Probability = ?* 1-tail Probability = ?**

For a Two-Tail Test (r ≠ 0)

1. Refer to the table for the *Critical Values of Rho*.
2. Refer to the *row* with the value closest to *n* (20).
3. Abs. Rank r (.4495) is *larger* than 0.377 so p is *less* than 0.10.
4. Abs. Rank r (.4495) is *smaller* than 0.450 so p is *greater* than 0.05.

*Actual computed two-tail t-value probability = .047

For a One-Tail test (r > 0) [OR (r < 0)]

1. Refer to the table for the *Critical Values of Rho*.
2. Refer to the *row* with the value closest to *n* (20).
3. Abs. Rank r (.4495) is *larger* than 0.377 so p is *less* than 0.05.
4. Abs. Rank r (.4495) is *smaller* than 0.450 so p is *greater* than 0.025.

**Actual computed one-tail t-value probability = .023

Table B–5   *Critical Values of Rho* — Rank Correlation Coefficient*

n	Level of Significance for One-Tailed Test			
	.05	.025	.01	.005
	Level of Significance for Two-Tailed Test			
	.10	.05	.02	.001
5	0.900	—	—	—
6	0.829	0.886	0.943	—
7	0.714	0.786	0.893	—
8	0.643	0.738	0.833	0.881
9	0.600	0.683	0.783	0.833
10	0.564	0.648	0.745	0.794
11	0.523	0.623	0.736	0.818
12	0.497	0.591	0.703	0.780
13	0.475	0.566	0.673	0.745
14	0.457	0.545	0.646	0.716
15	0.441	0.525	0.623	0.689
16	0.425	0.507	0.601	0.666
17	0.412	0.490	0.582	0.645
18	0.399	0.476	0.564	0.625
19	0.388	0.462	0.549	0.608
20	0.377	0.450	0.534	0.591
21	0.368	0.438	0.521	0.576
22	0.359	0.428	0.508	0.562
23	0.351	0.418	0.496	0.549
24	0.343	0.409	0.485	0.537
25	0.336	0.400	0.475	0.526
26	0.329	0.392	0.465	0.515
27	0.323	0.385	0.456	0.505
28	0.317	0.377	0.448	0.496
29	0.311	0.370	0.440	0.487
30	0.305	0.364	0.432	0.478
>30	Use the table for the standard, normal distribution, z.			

*For small samples of 30 or less.

Example B–6 *Normal Distribution and the Significance of z*

Significance of Differences Between Means					
Population Mean	**Sample Mean**	**Diff. in Means**	**Sample Std. Dev.**	**Number**	**z–Value**
500.0	507.8	7.8	20	100	1.94

2-tail Probability = ?   1-tail Probability = ?

For a Two-Tail Test (Sample Mean ≠ Population Mean)

1. Refer to the table for the areas under the *Normal Curve.*
2. Refer to the *row* for the *first two digits* of the value of *z* (**1.9**4).
3. Refer to the *column* for the *third digit* of the value of *z* (1.9**4**).
4. Note the proportion under the curve in the intersecting cell (0.4738)
5. Subtract: 0.5000 − 0.4738 = 0.0262 = Probability of difference.

For a One-Tail Test (Sample Mean > Population Mean)

6. Refer to the table for the areas under the *Normal Curve.*
7. Refer to the *row* for the *first two digits* of the value of *z* (**1.9**4).
8. Refer to the *column* for the *third digit* of the value of *z* (1.9**4**).
9. Note the proportion under the curve in the intersecting cell (0.4738)
10. Subtract: 0.5000 − 0.4738 = 0.0262 = *Two-Tail Probability*
11. Divide: 0.0262 / 2 = 0.0131 = *One-Tail* Probability of difference.

Table B–6 *Areas Under the Normal Curve*

Z	0.00	0.01	0.02	0.03	0.04	0.05	0.06	0.07	0.08	0.09
0.0	0.0000	0.0040	0.0080	0.0120	0.0160	0.0199	0.0239	0.0279	0.0319	0.0359
0.1	0.0398	0.0438	0.0478	0.0517	0.0557	0.0596	0.0636	0.0675	0.0714	0.0753
0.2	0.0793	0.0832	0.0871	0.0910	0.0948	0.0987	0.1026	0.1064	0.1103	0.1141
0.3	0.1179	0.1217	0.1255	0.1293	0.1331	0.1368	0.1406	0.1443	0.1480	0.1517
0.4	0.1554	0.1591	0.1628	0.1664	0.1700	0.1736	0.1772	0.1808	0.1844	0.1879
0.5	0.1915	0.1950	0.1985	0.2019	0.2054	0.2088	0.2123	0.2157	0.2190	0.2224
0.6	0.2257	0.2291	0.2324	0.2357	0.2389	0.2422	0.2454	0.2486	0.2517	0.2549
0.7	0.2580	0.2611	0.2642	0.2673	0.2704	0.2734	0.2764	0.2794	0.2823	0.2852
0.8	0.2881	0.2910	0.2939	0.2967	0.2995	0.3023	0.3051	0.3078	0.3106	0.3133
0.9	0.3159	0.3186	0.3212	0.3238	0.3264	0.3289	0.3315	0.3340	0.3365	0.3389
1.0	0.3413	0.3438	0.3461	0.3485	0.3508	0.3531	0.3554	0.3577	0.3599	0.3621
1.1	0.3643	0.3665	0.3686	0.3708	0.3729	0.3749	0.3770	0.3790	0.3810	0.3830
1.2	0.3849	0.3869	0.3888	0.3907	0.3925	0.3944	0.3962	0.3980	0.3997	0.4015
1.3	0.4032	0.4049	0.4066	0.4082	0.4099	0.4115	0.4131	0.4147	0.4162	0.4177
1.4	0.4192	0.4207	0.4222	0.4236	0.4251	0.4265	0.4279	0.4292	0.4306	0.4319
1.5	0.4332	0.4345	0.4357	0.4370	0.4382	0.4394	0.4406	0.4418	0.4429	0.4441
1.6	0.4452	0.4463	0.4474	0.4484	0.4495	0.4505	0.4515	0.4525	0.4535	0.4545
1.7	0.4554	0.4564	0.4573	0.4582	0.4591	0.4599	0.4608	0.4616	0.4625	0.4633
1.8	0.4641	0.4649	0.4656	0.4664	0.4671	0.4678	0.4686	0.4693	0.4699	0.4706
1.9	0.4713	0.4719	0.4726	0.4732	0.4738	0.4744	0.4750	0.4756	0.4761	0.4767
2.0	0.4772	0.4778	0.4783	0.4788	0.4793	0.4798	0.4803	0.4808	0.4812	0.4817
2.1	0.4821	0.4826	0.4830	0.4834	0.4838	0.4842	0.4846	0.4850	0.4854	0.4857
2.2	0.4861	0.4864	0.4868	0.4871	0.4875	0.4878	0.4881	0.4884	0.4887	0.4890
2.3	0.4893	0.4896	0.4898	0.4901	0.4904	0.4906	0.4909	0.4911	0.4913	0.4916
2.4	0.4918	0.4920	0.4922	0.4925	0.4927	0.4929	0.4931	0.4932	0.4934	0.4936
2.5	0.4938	0.4940	0.4941	0.4943	0.4945	0.4946	0.4948	0.4949	0.4951	0.4952
2.6	0.4953	0.4955	0.4956	0.4957	0.4959	0.4960	0.4961	0.4962	0.4963	0.4964
2.7	0.4965	0.4966	0.4967	0.4968	0.4969	0.4970	0.4971	0.4972	0.4973	0.4974
2.8	0.4974	0.4975	0.4976	0.4977	0.4977	0.4978	0.4979	0.4979	0.4980	0.4981
2.9	0.4981	0.4982	0.4982	0.4983	0.4984	0.4984	0.4985	0.4985	0.4986	0.4986
3.0	0.4987	0.4987	0.4987	0.4988	0.4988	0.4989	0.4989	0.4989	0.4990	0.4990

Report Presentations

WHY DO A PRESENTATION?

Business and organizational presentations of all kinds have become increasingly popular in the past few years. Despite the cost, time, and effort an effective presentation requires, there are many sound reasons for doing oral presentations in addition to conventional written reports. By far the most compelling and important reason is simply that people recall a *vastly* higher percentage of what they see *and* hear than what they only see *or* hear.

The entire objective of survey research is to create and convey *information!* That means literally *informing* sponsors and information seekers about the findings of the project. Oral presentations lend themselves exceedingly well to reporting survey research results. But that's *not* to say they're always required or even always appropriate. Many times, a written report and perhaps a brief, informal meeting or conference are completely adequate. Each situation has to be evaluated, keeping the advantages and disadvantages of a formal presentation firmly in mind.

Presentation Advantages

The "pro's and con's" of doing an oral presentation of survey research results are outlined in Figure C–1. The principal advantage—the tendency for sponsors and information seekers to retain more information for a longer time—was noted earlier. The fact that they bring everyone together in the same room at the same time is nearly as important. It would be almost impossible to establish the information needs for a survey at the beginning of the process without meeting or conferring extensively by telephone. A report presentation at the end of the project is a neat parallel that brings closure to the effort. Thus, the process "comes full circle," in a manner of speaking.

Presentation Disadvantages

The cost of report presentations is their main disadvantage. Their complexity and the demands they place on the research analyst and staff are close behind, and sometimes even

Figure C–1 *Pro's and Con's of Report Presentations*

Pro's	Con's
● Presentations *dramatize* the results of a survey, so they're recalled more vividly and in greater detail than written reports.	○ Report presentations are *costly* i̶n̶ ̶t̶e̶r̶m̶s̶ ̶o̶f̶ money, researcher time and effort, and the information seekers' time.
● They're *interactive,* so the presenter can listen to questions, ask for clarification, and respond immediately.	○ They're *perishable* (when they're over, they're gone) so they're always *extra* or *supplementary* to a written report.
● They provide audience *feedback,* so the presenter can be sure sponsors and information seekers understand results.	○ They're *demanding* on the researcher's expertise, not only on technical matters, but also at speaking before a group.
● They address a *group* of information seekers simultaneously, allowing audience members to converse with one another.	○ They're *time and location specific,* so they may require rigid scheduling and travel by the researcher or information seekers.
● They're *compelling* because the information can't be readily ignored, while written reports are often set aside.	○ They're *complex* and *difficult to control,* so there are many opportunities for something to go wrong or go badly.

more serious. Almost all the main threats to an effective presentation can be controlled by careful planning and preliminary work. They *can* be, but they *won't* all be. The vision of a *prospective* report presentation is virtually always more positive than the view in *retrospect*.

PLANNING AND PREPARATION

The complex, demanding nature of a report presentation shouldn't discourage the researcher. Rather, it should prompt greater attention and advance effort. There are some aspects of a report presentation that are clearly beyond the researcher's control. Occasionally, serendipity will prevail. Both the information seekers and research staff may benefit from some fortuitous break. More often, however, a truly successful report presentation is the result of careful planning and preliminary work. That includes consideration of the many contingencies that might arise and how they will be handled.

One of the best ways to cope with unexpected circumstances or events during a presentation is to play "What if . . . ?" with colleagues. The game is akin to a *negative* brainstorming session. It's a simple but highly effective device. The lead analyst merely assembles a few others and asks them to envision *every possible, PLAUSIBLE thing* that might happen to diminish or disturb the report presentation. It isn't necessary to answer the "What if . . . ?" questions at the time, but they should be noted for later reference. Later, the person responsible for the presentation can examine the list, eliminate things regarded as implausible, and plan a strategy or tactic for handling the remaining threats or contingencies. This process will reduce the risks dramatically.

Oral presentations require more careful planning than written reports because they're "live." Written reports can be edited and reworked as many times as necessary to be sure they're accurate, complete, and effective. By contrast, once an oral report begins, what's said, done, and shown can't be recaptured and corrected. In effect, one can't "unring" the bell. There is one thing that can be done to be sure the presentation goes well. Every experienced speaker knows about it. Every effective speaker does it. Unfortunately, most inexperienced presenters are reluctant to do it. *It* is simply *rehearsal!* That means going through the entire presentation from start to finish *exactly as it will be done for the audience.* There's no substitute for thorough rehearsal.

Selecting Content

Written reports are in three phases: An *introductory* overview, followed by the *body* of the report, concluded by a brief *summary* of the findings. Oral presentations are rarely that repetitive or thorough because of the time limitations. The information needs dictate what should be in both the written report and the oral presentation. Originally, during the planning phase described in Chapter 2, the information needs were classified into three levels of importance: (1) *absolutely essential,* constituting the main reason for the project, (2) *highly valuable* for making important decisions, and (3) *supportive data* to enhance the understanding of decision makers and clarify the picture portrayed by the survey results.

The written report should be composed before the oral presentation is prepared. It includes all three levels of information. An oral presentation typically follows the same sequence as the written document, but only the first two levels of information priority are ordinarily included—*absolutely essential* and *highly valuable* information. Supportive data usually appear only in the written report.

Written reports virtually always include both narrative text and numeric tables. They often include graphs and charts as well. During report *presentations,* the information is usually *projected* onto a screen for all the audience to view simultaneously. So, the presentation often consists almost entirely of two forms of display: *graphics* and *bullet charts.* Reading text that's projected onto a screen is *very tedious!* Reading tables that way is almost as difficult unless they're exceedingly simple. Consequently, the most effective presentations use very few numbers and words and a lot of pictures. Figure C–2 contains three typical frames[1] for a survey report presentation. The guidelines for preparing bullet charts and graphic slides or transparencies are provided in Guidelists C–1 and C–2, respectively.

Choosing Presenters

Occasionally an entire survey research project is conducted by only one researcher. If only one person is responsible for the project, except for so-called outside services by external agencies, there won't be any question about *who* or *how many* people should present the information. However, most research projects are conducted by a project *team* or by a *lead* analyst or investigator with the help of a resident research *staff.* If that's the case, there may be questions about *who* should make the report presentation and how others might participate, if at all.

---

[1] A "frame" is one slide or transparency. A *frame* is to a presentation what a *page* is to a written report.

Figure C–2   *Typical Report Frames for Projection*

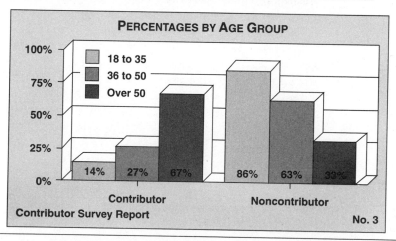

GUIDELIST C–1

For Preparing Bullet Charts

● **Limit the Content**
  ○ Limit the number of . . .
    ◗ Words in each bullet
    ◗ Bullets in each section
    ◗ Sections on each frame
■ **Organize the Material**
  ❏ Always move from the . . .
    ▮ Most to the least important
    ▮ General to the specific
✱ **Chart Format**
    ✳ Keep it clean and simple
    ✳ Use large, bold type
    ✳ Indent to show levels
    ✳ Use bullets to show levels
    ✳ Use little or no punctuation
    ✳ Title each chart frame
    ✳ Number each chart frame

One presenter

There are some advantages, but also some requirements that must be met, if one person from the project team is to make the report presentation to the sponsor and information seekers. The main advantages of using a single presenter are *consistency, continuity,* and *concentration* of responsibility. The presentation is likely to be more consistent throughout if only one person is reporting. There won't be any transitions from one presenter to another, so the *continuity* is almost automatic. If more than one person are doing the presentation, that requires more supervision to be sure everyone—*every one*—has prepared and rehearsed thoroughly. With only one presenter, the responsibility is concentrated in that person, and the individual is likely to be keenly aware of his or her responsibility.

When one person has the sole responsibility for making the actual presentation, that individual has to be completely familiar with every aspect of the report, and preferably with every aspect of the entire project. Even if the presenter knew the report content thoroughly and completely, it would be impossible to answer questions about sampling, data collection, or analysis unless he or she had firsthand knowledge of what was done and why. So, using only one presenter to do the entire job alone may put too much responsibility on one individual.

Multiple presenters

Some survey research presentations call upon as many as five or six people to present various aspects of the project or different parts of the results. More than that would be inadvisable,

GUIDELIST C–2

For Preparing Graphics for Projection

1. Choose a clean, simple, *standard* format for every slide or transparency (frame), including a border, presentation title, and frame title format and location.

2. Limit the number of graph *elements*—bars, segments, lines, or slices—that are included in each frame.

3. Add *value labels* to graph elements when it's feasible to show the actual numbers without projecting tables.

4. Use distinctive shading or cross-hatching to make individual elements easily distinguishable from one another.

5. Use a sufficiently large *type size* and bold print for words and numbers so they can be read easily at a distance during projection.

6. Use shape, size, space, and location to portray quantities and relationships as clearly and accurately as possible.

7. Include enough "white space" to make the figures and labels stand out from the background of each frame.

8. It's better to use many, simple frames shown in sequence than to use fewer, more complex frames with too many elements on each.

9. Add color, depth, and pictures for a more dramatic effect *only* when they can be used *consistently, expertly,* and *attractively.*

10. Prepare a *title frame* identifying the presentation, sponsor, survey project, and presenter, to be projected prior to or at the beginning of the presentation.

11. Prepare "handouts" for the audience showing each frame in miniature so they don't have to write down the information that's projected.

12. When the final frames are complete, write notes for explanation of each one and *project them during rehearsal* to be sure everything is correct.

and usually fewer take part in the presentation. The main advantage is that each may offer special expertise, background, or experience regarding a particular aspect of the project or findings. The disadvantages are the difficulties in controlling consistency, continuity, and concentration or responsibility, noted earlier.

One plus others

Often the best of both alternatives cited here can be obtained by having one person do the presentation while one or more others from the project team attend and participate during discussion or Q & A. That puts fewer demands on the main presenter, since he or she can defer to a colleague to respond to technical questions beyond the presenter's familiarity or expertise.

If one person is *principally* responsible for making the presentation, who should it be? If the project director or lead analyst is also the most articulate and comfortable with speaking to a group, the problem is solved. Often that's not the case. It may be advisable to select the person who has the most poise and presence when making a presentation of this kind. If that's the choice, there are two conditions that apply: First, the person should be *reasonably knowledgeable* and technically capable regarding the project in particular and survey research in general. One wouldn't want to hire a professional master of ceremonies for the job, or pick someone from the project team who is only marginally qualified save for his or her skill at public speaking. Second, those who accompany the presenter and assist in answering questions must be thoroughly knowledgeable about their area and completely prepared to respond when needed.

Organization and Timing

There are usually three or perhaps four parts to a survey report presentation: *Introduction, body* of the presentation, *conclusions* by the analyst, and often a *question and answer* (Q & A) session. The total duration of the presentation should be set by the sponsor in advance. It's the analyst's or presenter's responsibility to stay within the time allotted and to be available to respond during a Q & A session if that's desirable. Since almost everything takes longer than expected, the presentation should be planned and created to take only about *two-thirds* of the actual time allocated.

Report introduction

It's always advisable to create a title frame to project on the screen just prior to and during the beginning of the presentation. Usually a sponsor representative will introduce the presenter (or the *lead* presenter if more than one person will present the information). After greeting the group, the presenter should take a minute or so to outline the project *very briefly*. That will refresh the memory of those who worked with the project earlier. There may also be others in the audience who aren't at all familiar with the survey project.

This introductory sketch should indicate: (1) The main *reason* for the survey or the principal research *question* or *issue* the survey information obtained will help to resolve. (2) Who in the sponsoring organization arranged for or contracted for the project. (3) Approximately *when* the project began and *when* the data were collected. (4) *What population* was surveyed, together with how they were *sampled,* how the data were *collected,* how many were *sampled,* and how many *responded.* Reference to the actual questionnaire and the items within it should be reserved for later discussion. At the discretion of the presenter, one or two frames may or may not be projected to outline the information provided in the introduction. Their appropriateness is directly related to the formality of the meeting, complexity of the project, and size of the audience.

Audience handouts

What written material should be given to the audience, and *when* should it be provided? Although they may seem inconsequential, those are questions that deserve some consideration. Some speakers prefer to give the audience *nothing in advance.* They want the audience's undivided attention. They want to control the pace of the presentation and they don't want people to be looking ahead. A less rigorous approach is to give the audience copies of blank questionnaires or the *response summary questionnaire* (discussed in Chapter 12) at the beginning of the presentation.

Ultimately, those who attend the presentation should receive copies of a *response summary questionnaire,* miniature reproductions of the slide or transparency content, and perhaps copies of the entire written report (if the sponsor approves its distribution). Most experienced presenters who have good command of audience attention prefer to distribute any handouts in their entirety at the beginning of the presentation. Alternatively, they can be handed out by the presenter or a colleague *in sections* during the course of the presentation. It's usually not advisable to distribute such material well in advance of the presentation. That tends to diminish enthusiasm for the presentation, and such things are almost never ready until the last minute anyhow.

The body of content

Presenting the main substance of the report should occupy about two-thirds to three-quarters of the time allotted to the entire presentation. The presenter projects each frame in sequence, identifying the main features of each graph or plot and "fleshing out" the brief phrases on bullet charts. Very simple, straight forward graphs such as those in Figure C–2 usually require only 20 or 30 seconds of explanation by the presenter and examination by the audience. More complex graphs or plots and more lengthy bullet charts may take two or three minutes of study and discussion.

Some experienced speakers and presenters believe in what's known as "The Four-Minute Rule." It stipulates that audience attention and interest in any one topic or visual image drops *precipitously* after four minutes—more or less regardless of what the topic or image is! In other words, the limitations on audience attention span are *in the audience,* not in the content that's presented. This rule does appear to have some substance. If so, the presenter wouldn't want to approach that duration, let alone exceed it. None of the frames presented should be so complex as to require more than two or three minutes to explain and comprehend. Information requiring more extensive study should be broken into segments or conveyed in detail in the written report.

Audience reactions

Whether questions, reactions, and discussion by the audience should be expressed *during* the body of the presentation or at the conclusion depends on sponsor preference and the nature of the material presented. It's important to note that *questions of clarification* should always be welcomed and answered *during* the presentation—at any point at all. These are questions about what's being said or shown. For instance, if someone in the audience is unsure whether a set of values is frequencies or percentages, they should be encouraged to ask immediately. Similarly, if they want to know if the entire sample or only part of it is included on a chart, they should ask. If they're not sure where the question was asked in the questionnaire, they must be free to inquire right away. They need that information to understand what's being presented at the moment.

Questions about *why* this group responded as they did or about *what the sponsor should do* given this information are quite another matter. Those are questions of *substance,* not clarification. Most presenters would prefer to approach such questions only after the entire body of information has been presented. Their reasons are several: Discussing such issues during the presentation may take so much time it will require rushing through the remainder of the information. The answers to such questions may become more clear after subsequent information has been presented. Some, and perhaps most of the audience, may want to move on rather than pause to discuss this particular issue. Dealing with the issue may result in discussion *among the audience* that would best be reserved for a later conference in the absence of the presenter or research staff.

If *substantial* questions are to be reserved for the conclusion or Q & A session to follow the presentation, the presenter should remind the audience that they can return to any particular frame or section, later. They should be encouraged to make a note of their question or comment, referring to the section or frame number, so the issue won't be neglected later. *They* should make note of it, since it's usually awkward for the presenter to pause and do so during the presentation.

Summary and Q & A

It's customary for the presenter to provide a *very brief* summary of the main results and implications after the last of the body of information content has been presented. It's often effective to express such concluding material on one or two bullet charts that highlight each fact. After thanking the audience for their attention, the presenter would open the discussion to questions from the audience, if a Q & A session was planned and if time allows it. Guidelist C–3 offers several tips for enhancing one's credibility during both the presentation and the Q & A session.

If the slides or transparencies have been organized, labeled, and numbered carefully, it won't be difficult to refer back to the frame containing the information in question during the Q & A. It's best to take the few seconds required to identify and project the appropriate frame unless the question is either very *quick* or extremely *general,* so it related to no *one* frame or section. When responding to questions of substance, and especially if they deal with *why* a certain response resulted, there are some basic rules presenters may find it beneficial to observe: First, there are times when the presenter or research can't be expected to *know* why. So, it may call for an admission that there's nothing within the data or the researcher's background or expertise that would provide an explanation.

The second rule is that sponsors and information seekers may *speculate* all they want. The researcher may *not.* There are few things more embarrassing in such situations than to move further and further out on a limb, only to eventually either have it sawed off or to break of one's own weight. In addition, to offer an opinion that proves to be patently unsound will jeopardize the credibility of the *entire presentation.*

Rule three for responding to Q & A issues is to ask if additional data analysis might answer the question. For example, someone may want to know, "Why do you think one in five people responded in such-and-such a way?" An experienced researcher might frame that question very differently—in research terms: "*Who* are these people? How does this variable *relate* to other variables in the survey?" Thus, the researcher might suggest conducting some additional *measures of association* between this and other items to shed more light on the question.

Lastly, the researcher is forbidden to reveal specific information learned from other surveys. It was funded and it belongs to other sponsors—it's proprietary—and can't be released without written permission. But this certainly doesn't preclude researchers from bringing their professional background and expertise to bear on the question. It simply means the explanation should be couched in general terms. For example, mail surveys typically result in relatively low response rates—astoundingly so to many sponsors. Information seekers may want to know, and *should* want to know, what kind of nonresponse bias can be expected. They may ask how the response rate for this study compares with others.

Those are legitimate, appropriate, and intelligent questions. They can't be answered

---

GUIDELIST C–3

For a More Credible Demeanor

1. *Show confidence, but not arrogance.* Relax, smile, and converse with the audience as you would with a group of friends.

2. *Dress in business attire.* Even if the audience is dressed more casually, those in business suits or dresses gain respect and credibility.

3. *Don't wander about.* The presenter is almost always standing, but shouldn't be *walking* unless there's a reason to do so.

4. *Don't fidget!* Whether speaking or listening, your hands should either rest lightly on the lectern (not gripping it) or *hang at your sides. (This takes practice!)*

5. *Don't play with things.* If using a pointer, *put it down* when not in use. Keep pencils, pens, keys, and so on in pocket or purse where they belong.

6. *Keep your hands off your face.* Never, ever speak with your hand over your mouth. Don't play with your hair, rub your head, or stroke your chin, either.

7. *Stop and listen intently!* When someone speaks or interrupts, *stop*. Face them. Look *directly* at their face. Listen carefully and *wait* until they've finished.

8. *Pause before responding.* Don't be too quick to answer questions or respond to comments. Take *several seconds* to *think* before speaking in response.

9. *Restate what they say.* By repeating what you heard, you and they can be sure you understand. Only then should you reply to a question or comment.

10. *Don't use big words.* Talk as you would to a friend in a *social* situation, not as you would to a colleague on your project team.

11. *Don't be defensive.* Even if challenged rudely, it's better to respond with an understanding smile and quiet assurance than with a strident rebuttal.

12. *If you don't know, say so.* Don't ever try to "fake it" if you're puzzled or confused. Admit openly you don't know but will find out, then go on.

---

definitively, but they can and should be answered tentatively. The researcher might explain how this response rate compares with others, based on professional experience or familiarity with other studies of this kind. Based on his or her background and expertise, the researcher may explain that *typically* those who are *most positive* or *most negative*—those with *extreme views or reactions*—respond at higher rates than those "in the middle." Similarly, those with more involvement in the issues and with more time respond at higher rates, and so forth. Thus, researchers should be encouraged to share their knowledge and expertise with those less familiar with the survey research process and the results that it typically obtains.

PRESENTATION TECHNOLOGY

The *basic* characteristics of an effective report presentation have remained the same over many years. However, the *technology* for creating and projecting audio-visual information has developed at an astounding pace. Constant exposure to highly sophisticated communication and information systems in their business and organizational lives also elevates audience expectations for a report presentation. The biggest contributions to presentation technology come from desktop computer systems, including both hardware and software, but video and audio devices also offer additional capability for more sophisticated presentations.

Presentation Software

Several types of desktop computer programs are capable of generating graphs, plots, diagrams, and bullet charts for presentations. Many statistical analysis programs, spreadsheets, charting and graphing programs, so-called draw and paint programs, word processing programs, and page processing or desktop publishing programs have such features. It depends on the individual program, the volume and complexity of the information, the nature of the frames to be produced, and the projection medium to be used—slides, transparencies, or the computer display screen itself.

In recent years, a new class of software has developed to meet the need for creating and manipulating presentation material. These programs are called "presentation managers." They're dedicated primarily or exclusively to creating and manipulating a series of frames for projected presentations. Presentation manager programs allow the user to create a presentation within the program or to "import" data from spreadsheets, graphing or charting programs, drawing or painting programs, and word processing or page processing programs.

Figure C–3 *Presentation Manager Program Features*

Modes of "View"

Slide view	One frame at a time, much as it would appear when projected, with a "toolbox" and other features for creating and manipulating the image.
Outline view	Words and numbers in a typical outline format with a "major" heading for each frame title and minor headings for its contents.
Sorting view	All frames in *miniature* form, so frames can be *dragged* from one place to another in the sequence, using the cursor and a "mouse."
Notes view	One frame at a time, about half normal size, with space beside or below it for inserting speaker notes to accompany the frame.
"Master" views	Views for creating "master" formats for frames, note pages, and handout pages that will apply to *all* the frames and pages created.
Magnification	Shows a display screen in *actual* size, magnified two, four, or eight times for close work, or in fractional sizes showing the entire frame on screen.

Output Formats

Slide shows	Displays one frame at a time, *exactly* as it would be printed, in timed sequence, on signal, or go to a frame's number, with special *transitions*.
Print slides	Sends each frame in sequence to an output device in the specified format—35mm slides, transparency, or special formats.
Print notes	Sends one page per frame to the printer, containing the reduced frames and notes to accompany each one.
Print handouts	Sends pages to the printer with reduced or miniature images of each frame, two, three, six, or eight frames per page.
Print outline	Sends as many pages as required to the printer, containing the frame contents in outline format, usually without graphic material.

They allow the user to display the words and pictures and work with them in different "view" modes and to print in various formats, described in Figure C–3.

All the special *presentation manager* programs have what are usually called "slide show" routines. When running the "slide show," the screen displays only the actual frame. It doesn't show other, normal screen content such as scroll bars, menus, or tool boxes. These routines let the user project the frames of the presentation in sequence, moving from one to the next on a signal from the keyboard or after a preset time for each. They also allow the presenter to go to any frame in the presentation by number. This is especially useful during a *discussion* or *Q and A* session, when it may be necessary to refer back to frames that were shown earlier in the presentation.

Presentation manager programs provide special *transition* formats for moving from one frame to another. The old or new frame may "slide in" from any direction, fade from one to the next, shrink or explode, and so forth. When projecting bullet charts or graphs, each "new" line or bar may appear in sequence. Presentations that use such special transition effects are time-consuming to produce and require considerable skill, but they're extremely dynamic and colorful. Despite their attractiveness, they probably don't add substantially to the audience's *understanding* of the information reported. They're more appropriate for *persuasive* programs, such as sales presentations, than for more *informative* presentations.

Projection Equipment

There are several devices for projecting survey report presentations. Usually the projector is at the facility where the presentation will take place, such as a conference room at the sponsor's offices. Research organizations that regularly make presentations may have their own projection equipment, but most presenters don't provide their own because projectors are expensive and bulky to carry.

Overhead projectors

The simplest and by far the most common kind of projector is an *overhead transparency projector*. The ordinary kind is fairly bulky and not very portable. It also has a fan to cool the bulb, so it may be rather noisy in a small room. There is also a simpler, quieter, more portable, and much more expensive version of the overhead projector. It has no fan, makes no noise, and it can be folded fairly flat, so it's very transportable. Unfortunately, the bulb is rather fragile and has a relatively short life span. Either form of overhead projector is quite satisfactory for small- to medium-size rooms and audiences. Most such projectors don't provide enough illumination for a large room where those in the back of the audience are some distance from the screen.

The overhead transparencies themselves are quite easy and relatively inexpensive to produce. *Heat-resistant* blank transparencies are readily available from office supply and copy shops. They can either be printed directly on a laser printer or transparency *masters* can be printed on plain paper. The masters can then be copied to transparencies on most copy machines. This method produces black and white transparencies only. Transparencies can also be printed on inkjet color computer printers, but they require a special kind of transparency that accepts color ink without running or streaking. They're made and sold by most of the same companies that make and sell the black and white variety, but they're much more expensive.

Slide projectors

At present, only those who routinely make report presentations are likely to use 35mm slides. As the technology for making slides from a desktop computer continues to develop, they'll become less difficult and time consuming to create and less expensive to produce. Slides almost always use color. The graphics can include many, dramatic special effects to make the presentation more interesting and attractive. Whether such refinements contribute to the information seekers' *understanding* of the survey results is open to question, however. Nonetheless, slides may be required for large rooms and audiences because their level of illumination is much greater than that from overhead projectors.

Color slide presentations are usually created on a computer with a color monitor and color-capable software. Presentation manager programs and graphics programs have special data output formats for the completed slide presentation. Slides can be "printed" on regular 35mm color slide film by special output devices. The film can then be processed at a local photo lab. For those who don't have such a device, there are several electronic graphics studios that specialize in processing, printing, and mounting slides from electronic media. Either a diskette can be sent to them, or, more commonly, the data are sent to them electronically via modem. Finished slides are often in hand the same day or the following day.

Projection LCDs

It would be ideal if the presenter could project images directly from the computer to the audience for the report presentation. That way, the presenter can use the "slide show" feature of a presentation manager to good effect, whether the presentation is in color or black and white, and whether or not the special *transition* effects are used. If there are only a few people in the audience for a report presentation, they may be able to watch the presentation on the computer display screen itself. But if there are more than a few in the audience, some form of projection will probably be necessary.

Perhaps the easiest way to project images directly from a computer is with a *projection liquid crystal display (LCD)*. A projection LCD is a flat box that sits on top of an ordinary overhead projector. When it's coupled into the computer, it displays whatever the computer's monitor shows. An overhead projector provides the light source and projects the images to a screen, just as it would from a transparency. Some projection LCDs also have a cooling fan and may also plug into a wall socket for power. Some only project in black and white, but most are color displays. They're much more portable than an ordinary overhead projector, and they're fairly simple and easy to use. They need only be focused and adjusted prior to the presentation.

There are several other ways to display or project visual or audio-visual material directly from a computer. With the right equipment, several computer displays can be coupled to the host computer running the presentation program. There are also hardware and software devices that allow the computer to display information to video monitors, television screens, or projection television sets. Technology provides almost limitless possibilities, but the research analyst or presenter must be aware of one, *cardinal* rule: *The probability of problems increases exponentially with the increase in complexity!*

MAKING THE PRESENTATION

Much of what the presenter needs to know and do are implied in the recommendations for preparation and rehearsal. Guidelist C–4 contains an extensive set of suggestions and recommendations about what to do just before the presentation, at the beginning, during the presentation, during the discussion or Q & A session, and at the conclusion. There are three additional aspects of the presentation that deserve brief consideration: How to cope with *presentation anxiety,* use *notes* effectively, and control the *pace* and *timing* of the presentation.

Presentation Anxiety

There are a few—*very* few—who are quite comfortable speaking to a group of people they don't know. Almost all presenters, including even the most experienced, feel a little anxiety as the time to begin approaches. That's to be expected, but if the presentation has been well planned and *rehearsed* and the presenter is well prepared, any nervousness will almost certainly wane and disappear within a few minutes into the presentation.

So, the most important thing for the presenter to do to avoid anxiety and stress is to prepare thoroughly and rehearse—again and again. Sheer repetition is a potent enemy of anxiety. It's much easier to stay calm if one knows *exactly* what he or she will say and do at every point. The confidence gained from the experience of rehearsal will also lend a great deal of credibility to the presenter and the presentation. Guidelist C–4 lists several tips that will both reduce presentation anxiety and help ensure a fluid, effective presentation.

Using Notes Effectively

A presenter who needs no notes whatsoever is a rare exception. Most presenters depend on notes of varying detail to guide them while speaking. Yet probably the main guideposts for a report presentation are the visual frames that are shown or projected. The best way to write and organize notes for a presentation is to take each frame in order and jot down a *few* words or phrases that are *cues* or *reminders* of what should be said about each. The notes should be *very brief.* More elaborate notes or actual *scripting* too often encourages the presenter to *read* from them. That's anathema to an interesting and informative presentation. The audience will hate it. If the presenter is sufficiently familiar with the material and has rehearsed thoroughly, he or she won't need more than an occasional glance or quick reference to the notes to bring the next topic to mind as a new frame of the presentation is shown.

Pacing and Timing

One might mistakenly assume a presentation's pace should be determined almost exclusively by the time allotted and the material to be presented. In fact, that equation should have been achieved before the presentation was prepared. If the sponsor specified how much time was

For Making an Effective Presentation

Before the Presentation

1. Ask the principal sponsor contact how many will attend and who they are. Learn as much as possible about the audience, and especially the "key" people.

2. Check the venue for the presentation in advance. Know how to get there, where to park, how to enter, and move any equipment and make it operational.

3. Check out the room where the presentation will be made in advance. Go to the lectern or place the presenter will stand and view the room from there.

4. If using overhead transparencies, try to arrange the seating or have it arranged so the projector isn't between the screen and anyone in the audience.

5. Several minutes before it's time to begin, check out the equipment one last time to be sure everything is adjusted, set, and working as it should.

6. *Don't* review notes or "go over" the material mentally while waiting to start. Instead, sit back, relax, and chat with others, preferably about other topics.

At the Beginning

7. Greet the audience, introduce yourself if you weren't introduced, and thank them for attending. Then, *begin immediately* in a pleasant, matter-of-fact way.

8. If anxious or nervous, *don't apologize or comment on it*. If it shows, they'll know it. If it doesn't, don't tell them. They *all* know *they* would feel that way anyhow.

9. Keep your mind on the *material*—on the *information* you want to convey, without thinking about *how* you're doing it or how you've done so far.

During the Presentation

10. Follow the suggestions in Guidelist C–3 to maintain credibility. Be especially careful *never* to argue or be defensive.

11. f using a projector, avoid, if possible, standing front of the projected image or blocking any-
    view. If it's unavoidable, move to the side
    ly.

12. Face the audience when speaking. If it's necessary to look at the projection screen, pause, do so, then turn and again speak to the audience.

13. If using an overhead projector, view the images from the transparency, not the screen. Point to items on the *transparency,* itself, using a pencil, not a finger.

14. If using transparencies, *keep them in order* after showing them by stacking them neatly, face down, so they can be easily located by number later, if needed.

15. If using a slide projector, point to items on the screen with a light pen or a long pointer, but not with hand and arm. (An ordinary yardstick will suffice.)

16. Check a clock or wristwatch often. Strive to stay on schedule, and if the audience delays, remind them politely that there's more to cover.

During the Discussion or Q & A Session

17. Gauge the time and keep your responses as brief as possible. Rarely should they require more than about 30 seconds. Don't say more than what's required.

18. Observe the suggestions in Guidelist C–3. Remember, you aren't expected to have all the answers. If you don't know, say so!

19. When questions arise that require more study or analysis, make notes of *what's* to be investigated and *who* in the audience wants to know.

20. If audience members converse among themselves, suggest *they* meet later, reserving *this* time for questions *you* can address (unless there's plenty of time).

At the Conclusion

21. Note any additional study or analysis that will be done and tell the audience *what* you will do, about *when* it will be done, *how* you'll report, and to *whom*.

22. Thank the sponsor and audience for the opportunity to do the study and make the presentation, and especially for their interest, attention, and participation.

available, the presentation should have been geared to that duration. If the sponsor left it up to the researcher, the analyst should have estimated the time required and notified the sponsor. Typically, those arrangements are worked out in conversation between sponsor and researcher well in advance. Even so, it's impossible to anticipate precisely how long a presentation will take.

When a written survey report is read from the printed page, the pace is controlled entirely by the reader. Readers can move quickly or slowly, reviewing or scanning ahead at will. By contrast, *presentations are externally paced* from the audience's point of view. The presenter sets and maintains the pace. If the presentation moves too quickly, much of the material will escape the comprehension of the audience, or at least its slower members. If it moves too slowly, some are likely to lose interest and become distracted. So, the goal is to find a pace where *most* of the audience has sufficient time to comprehend the material.

By watching the audience carefully for cues at the beginning of the presentation and any time the nature of the content changes significantly, the presenter can usually tell when it's time to move on, when to pick up the pace a little, and when to go more slowly. *Flexibility* is important! Sometimes inexperienced report presenters adopt a *rigid* time schedule—in the worst case, a certain number of seconds or minutes for *each frame* of the presentation. That's absurd because some frames will obviously require more study than others. There's nothing wrong with calculating time to give to each frame on the *average,* but the emphasis here is on the *average* time. That should be only a *rough* guide to keeping pace and staying on schedule.

The two main threats to a well-timed presentation are *rambling presenters* and *digressing audience members.* If there's more than one presenter, *every one* must be assigned a *very specific* time, beyond which they *must not go!* If they do, the lead research analyst or presenter should politely but firmly ask them to summarize and finish their portion. If not, those who come later won't have sufficient time to present their material. All too often, one or more members of the audience will digress from the information at hand or want to discuss some issue of special interest to them. Unless it's the sponsor's chief representative, the presenter is well advised to remind the person or people that there's much yet to be covered and that there will be ample opportunity, *later,* to discuss such matters.

Concluding the Presentation

It's incumbent on the lead researcher or presenter to respect the sponsor's and audience members' time—to stay within the time limits set by the sponsor. It's also important to recognize that *everything, always* takes longer than expected. *Everything* and *always* are strong generalizations. They make room for *no* exceptions. That's because there *are* no exceptions. Every experienced presenter knows that. So, it's vitally important to plan the presentation exactly as though there were only about two-thirds of the actual time allocated. That "extra" time must *not* be consumed during the early part of the presentation. The pace must be maintained. Inevitably, there will be sufficient questions, comments, and discussion by the audience at the end of the presentation. In the exceedingly unlikely event the presentation ends early and there's nothing more to say, certainly nobody would object in the slightest. There may be serious objections, however, if time runs out or the end comes late.

The sponsor's chief representative will usually signal when it's time to end the discussion of the project and terminate the meeting. They ordinarily don't just conclude it themselves. Rather, they give the presenter or participants a verbal cue that's usually easy to recognize. It's the presenter or lead presenter's job to recognize the cue and *promptly* conclude by thanking the sponsor for the opportunity to do the project and make the report. Then the presenter should turn to the audience and thank them cordially for their participation, interest, and comments.

As the report conference breaks up and people begin leaving, there may be some audience members who approach the researchers individually. They may even ask for a special meeting or report. That's not unusual, but it's a sensitive issue. In such circumstances, the researcher is well advised to seek the sponsor's chief representative or liaison and include him or her in the conversation and arrangements. Additional contact of this sort may or *may not* be welcome or acceptable to the sponsor.

SUMMARY

Making Report Presentations

A. Consider the pro's and con's. Some projects *require* a report presentation and they're of great value to others, but sometimes they're inappropriate or impractical.

B. Plan and prepare *carefully*. Typically, 99 percent of the work and as much of the value is in the planning and preparation; one percent in doing it.

C. Select only *major* content. The most salient aspects of the survey results should be presented, but the detailed information should be in written form.

D. Choose an *effective* presenter. If there's a project team, it's often best to have one make the presentation while others attend and respond to questions.

E. *Logically* organize the material. Introduce the presentation, provide handouts, present the body of the report, and be prepared for discussion or Q & A.

F. Explore computer software options. *Presentation manager* programs are the most capable, but other programs can be used instead.

G. Check projection equipment needs. Overhead projectors are the most simple and common, but slide projectors or projection LCDs may also be appropriate.

H. Remember the cardinal rule: *THE PROBABILITY OF PROBLEMS INCREASES EXPONENTIALLY WITH THE INCREASE IN COMPLEXITY!*

I. Expect presentation anxiety. Almost all speakers and presenters initially feel some anxiety, but it *can* be reduced and it should dissipate quickly.

J. Use notes effectively. They should be brief, providing only cues about what to say, and they should *never* be read verbatim.

K. Watch the pace and timing. The pace should be geared to time needed for audience comprehension; timing to the period allocated by the sponsor.

L. Conclude promptly and courteously. The sponsor usually signals the end of the conference, when the presenter should thank everyone and terminate.

Glossary

absolute frequency   The number of cases or respondents appearing in each category of a frequency distribution or in each cell of a cross-tabulation table.

absolute value   The value of a number, ignoring the plus or minus sign.

accessibility bias   One type of selection bias during sampling, where some respondents in the population are over- or underrepresented because they are more accessible or are less accessible than others.

acquiescence bias   Agreement or consent by respondents to what they believe an interviewer or sponsor would like them to think or say rather than giving their real opinion or reaction.

action component   One of the three basic components of an attitude, indicating the person's consistent tendency to take action regarding the topic or to remain passive about it.

adjective checklist   A scaling device that lists a series of adjectives that might be used to describe some person, place, or thing and asks the respondent to check any adjective that applies.

affiliations   The network of durable, formal, and informal associations an individual has with family, relatives, friends, and acquaintances.

affinity bias   A form of interviewer bias resulting from interviewers showing preference for certain types of people for whom they have an affinity, such as respondents who are similar to them or that they find attractive, and including them in the sample at higher rates than others.

aided recall   A form of questioning respondents about what they remember, where their memory is aided by presenting or describing the things they might recall.

all-inclusive categories   Response categories defined to ensure that every feasible answer will fit into a category; that there will be a category for every possible answer.

alpha level   The critical value, or probability level above which a relationship between variables will not be regarded as statistically significant because it is too likely that it could result only by chance from sampling error if the variables were actually not related in the population as a whole; also refers to the probability of a Type I error in academic research.

alphanumeric variable   A variable whose "values" are characters (words or letters) rather than numeric values.

alternative hypothesis   The proposition that some condition or relationship exists, accepted in scientific or academic research, if the results fail to support the "null hypothesis" that it does not exist.

analysis of variance (ANOVA)   A statistical measure of the association between a categorical independent variable and a continuous, numerical, dependent variable from an interval or ratio scale, used to assess the significance of differences among means for different groups.

area sampling   A form of cluster sampling where the region of the population is first divided into areas, some are randomly selected, and then respondents within those areas are randomly selected.

attitude   Relatively durable, psychological predispositions of people to respond toward or against an object, person, place, idea, or symbol, consisting of three components: their knowledge or beliefs, their feelings or evaluations, and their tendency toward action or passivity.

attitude scale   A scale used to measure attitudes, usually focusing on the respondents' feelings or evaluations toward one or more objects or topics.

auspices bias   The tendency for respondents to react toward the survey sponsor, if they know who the sponsor is, rather than providing their own, honest reactions to the survey questions themselves.

average   A measure of central tendency that represents the most typical case, usually referring to the arithmetic mean, but also applying to the median and the mode.

banner   A method for showing several cross-tabulations in one, condensed table in order to save space or facilitate comparison, ordinarily used only when one varable is cross-tabulated against several others.

bar chart   A graphic portrayal of several quantities, such as frequencies or percentages, where the length of the horizontal or vertical bars represents the relative magnitudes of the values.

behavior   The actions of people or objects in the past or at the present.

bias   The tendency for some extraneous factor to affect the answers to survey questions or the survey results in general, in a systematic way, so that results are "pushed" or "pulled" in some specific direction.

bimodality   The existence of two modes or peaks in a distribution of response, rather than a single modal value, often caused when the sample contains two, distinct populations or groups with differing reactions.

bipolar adjectives   A pair of adjectives, such as those used in a semantic differential scale, that represent the polar extremes on one dimension or continuum.

bivariate relationship   A relationship between only two variables.

bivariate statistics   The statistics used to measure the relationship between only two variables and assess its statistical significance.

bottle scale   A pictorial scale showing a series of bottles filled to varying levels, sometimes used when surveying those who may not always understand verbal or numeric scales, such as young children or those with reading impairments.

breakdowns   A data analysis procedure that computes and reports the mean, standard deviation, and number of cases for a continuous numeric variable for each level of a categorical variable, ordinarily using analysis of variance to measure the statistical significance of differences in mean values.

callbacks   The second and subsequent attempts to contact respondents by telephone or in person when they were not present to respond to the first attempt to contact them.

case   A set of data obtained from one completed questionnaire or one respondent that serves as a single unit for analysis.

categorical data   Nominal data where the values of the variables are merely the names of discrete, independent categories and the numeric magnitudes have no meaning or stand in no fixed relationship, as opposed to continuous data.

categorical item   A survey question coded with values that are merely the names of categories, so that the values do not represent magnitudes or stand in any ordered relationship with one another.

causality   The potential influence or effect that one item or variable has on another.

ceiling effects   The truncation or "chopping off" of the high side of a distribution because respondents' answers could go no further up the scale.

census   Counting or taking measurements from all members of a given population, rather than sampling only a portion to represent the whole.

central systems   Computer systems that do the actual processing at some central location accessible by communication to several operators or users.

central tendency measures   Statistical averages that describe the most typical value or case, such as the mean, median, and mode.

chi-square   A value, usually obtained from cross-tabulation of two items in survey research, that can be compared with the values of the chi-square distribution to obtain a probability for assessing statistical significance.

chi-square distribution   The particular form of a distribution derived from a set of computations and defined by the number of "degrees of freedom," often listed in statistical reference tables.

classification variables   Survey items, such as demographic variables, that are used to classify respondents into groups or categories for comparison.

closed-ended questions   A structured survey question where the alternative answers are listed so that respondents must ordinarily pick only from among them.

cluster   One group of individuals or sampling units that have proximity with one another within the sample frame in some respect, such as those within a given area.

cluster bias   A form of selection bias resulting when a cluster sampling design selects respondents who are too closely related to one another within a cluster, so that they tend to give similar responses.

cluster sampling   A technique often used in surveys to save travel or long-distance toll charges where the population is divided into clusters and a few clusters, each containing many respondents, are randomly selected.

codebook   The entire set of codelists for several variables from one survey.

codelist   The list of code values and category labels for a single survey variable that is generated by postcoding and used during analysis and reporting.

coding   The process of assigning code values to the various alternative answers to survey questions, either when constructing the questionnaire (precoding) or after the data collection (postcoding).

coefficient of determination   The square of the correlation coefficient, indicating the proportion of "shared" variance for correlation or the proportion of variance in the dependent variable that was "explained" by the independent variable in regression.

comparative scale   A scale using one entity as the standard by which one or more others are judged or evaluated.

computer hardware   The physical devices and components of computers, including both the central processing unit and the peripheral devices for inputting, storing, and outputting data.

computer software   The programs and coded instructions to the computer, including both the operating system that provides general control and the applications programs that perform specific computations.

conditional branching Instructions or "go-to" statements in a questionnaire indicating the interviewer or respondent should skip items that don't apply, based on answers to previous questions.

confidence interval The range around a numeric statistical value obtained from a sample, within which the actual, corresponding value for the population is likely to fall, at a given level of probability.

confidence level The specific probability of obtaining some result from a sample if it did not exist in the population as a whole, at or below which the relationship will be regarded as statistically significant.

continuous variable A variable that represents a continuum without any breaks or interruptions, so the numeric values could potentially take on an infinite number of values expressed in whole numbers and fractions.

convenience sample A sample selected more on the bias of the researcher or data collection team's convenience than on the requirements for random selection with a known probability of inclusion and representation.

correlation analysis A measure of the relationship or association between two continuous numeric variables that indicates both the direction and degree to which they co-vary with one another from case to case, without implying that one is causing the other.

correlation coefficient The value computed with correlation analysis, ranging from zero to indicate no systematic relationship to plus or minus one, indicating a perfect linear relationship, where the positive or negative value shows if the relationship is direct or inverse, respectively.

correlation matrix The correlation coefficients between each pair, for several variables, arranged so that each variable is identified on each row and on each column, with the coefficient listed in the cells defined by the rows and columns.

critical value The probability level above which a relationship between variables will not be regarded as statistically significant because it is too likely that it could result only by chance from sampling error if the variables were actually not related in the population as a whole.

cross-tabulation Plotting two categorical variables in the form of a matrix so that the values of one variable define the rows and the values of the other define the columns, with the cells containing the frequency of cases with a given value for each of the two items and from which a chi-square value can be computed to assess the statistical significance the relationship.

curvilinear A line or distribution of values that is continuous, but forms an arch, rather than a straight line.

data Most often numbers, but also letters or words that symbolize or represent quantities, entities, or categories of things.

data analysis The manipulation of numbers, letters, or symbols in order to suppress the detail and reveal the relevant facts or relationships.

data collection The process of communicating questions and obtaining a record of responses from a sample, either by mail, telephone, or personal interviewing.

data field The location and number of columns in a data file record required to contain the largest number of digits for any code value for a particular variable.

data point   A datum, or one, single entry of a number, letter, or symbol, usually for one variable and one case or respondent.

data processing   Submitting the survey data to computer programs and routines in order to perform the statistical analysis and to generate reports, as opposed to hand tabulation of the data.

decisions   The process and/or results of individual evaluations, judgments, and choices among alternatives.

degrees of freedom (d.f.)   A parameter most often based on the number of cases or respondents, but slightly reduced to adjust for some earlier computations and used when checking reference tables or computing probability to assess statistical significance.

demographics   A set of conditions or attributes of people, often including age, sex, marital status, education, employment, occupation, and income, among others, usually measured in surveys to determine the types of people represented by the sample and to make comparisons of other results among demographic groups.

dependent variable   The variable that is viewed as being potentially influenced, affected, or determined by some other variable in a cause-and-effect relationship, based on the logic and meaning of the things represented by the variables.

depicted scale   Any scale that cannot be included within the survey question, so that it must be shown in the form of numbers, words, or pictures representing response alternatives.

descriptive research   Research that is designed primarily to describe rather than to explain a set of conditions, characteristics, or attributes of people in a population, based on measurement of a sample.

descriptive statistics   Statistics such as averages and measures of spread, used to suppress the detail in data files and to condense and summarize the data to make facts more visible, as well as to indicate the degree to which the sample data are likely to represent the entire population.

desires   Expressed wishes or conscious urges of respondents that may be a topic for survey research measurement within the broader topic category of "needs."

desktop systems   Computer systems that do some or all of the processing right at the operator's desk or work station.

diagram scale   Any form of scale that uses a diagram to depict the response options or to obtain or collect the answers to survey questions.

dichotomous question   A question with only two response alternatives, such as a yes/no question or an item that can either be checked or ignored.

discrete variable   A categorical variable yielding nominal data, where all of the answers must fall within a category and the code values stand in no ordered relationship to one another.

discriminant analysis   A statistical measure of the relationship between a continuous, numeric independent variable from an interval or ratio scale and a categorical dependent variable defining two or more groups, used both to assess statistical significance and also to compute the discriminant function, used to predict or classify new cases into groups.

discriminant function   The prediction or classification equation obtained from discriminant analysis, used to predict or classify new cases into groups when only the value of the independent variable is known.

dispersion   The range and degree of spread or variance in the distribution of data for a survey variable.

editing   The process of examining questionnaires or data against some set of criteria, to be sure the content is correct or appropriate.

executive summary   The first section of the final report, including only an outline of the major highlights of the results.

expected cell frequency   A value computed during or after cross-tabulation, based on the proportion of the data represented by the entire row and column on which the cell resides.

explicit scale   Any scale that is directly expressed or stated, either verbally or visually, as opposed to those that are only implied by the question.

extreme case   A response that is an outlier, with a value so extreme it is far distant from any other response, which may sometimes suggest there has been an error while recording or transferring the data.

extremity   The extreme or terminal point, limit, or part of something, such as the upper or lower limit of a scale or distribution of scores.

F-distribution   The particular form of a distribution derived from a set of computations and defined by two numbers of "degrees of freedom," often listed in statistical reference tables.

F-ratio   The ratio of a numerator and denominator value consisting of variance expressed as "mean squares," or the "sum of squares" divided by the degrees of freedom for each, usually computed with analysis of variance and compared to the F-distribution in a statistical reference table to assess statistical significance.

feeling component   One of the three main components of attitudes, consisting of the evaluations and judgments of the topic by the individual holding the attitude.

fixed sum scale   A particular type of scale where the respondent is asked to list the number of times each of a set of alternatives occurred or apply, out of a given total, so that the sum of the values must equal the total.

floor effects   The truncation or "chopping off" of the low side of a distribution because respondents' answers could go no lower on the scale.

forced ranking scale   A type of scale, yielding ordinal level data, where the respondents are instructed to rank a series of items in sequential order, with no "ties" or equal rankings allowed.

formatting   The design or a particular arrangement for words, numbers, or symbols, specifying their order or sequence, physical location, relative distance or proximity, and general form, often used in reference to the location of data fields within a file record.

frequency distribution   The number of cases that contain each of the scale values for a particular survey item or variable.

frequency table   A tabular presentation of the frequency distribution, often including percentage distributions based on the frequencies and the sample size, the number of valid cases, and the cumulative number of valid cases.

goals   Specific objectives or ends sought by respondents that may be a topic for survey research measurement within the broader topic category of "needs."

go errors   An error that results when a decision maker goes ahead with a course of action and it proves to be costly or unsatisfactory.

grand mean   The arithmetic mean of the dependent variable for *all* of the cases in an analysis of variance, as opposed to the "group means," including only the cases in each category of the independent variable.

graphic data description   Portrayal of data distributions for individual survey variables with charts, graphs, or data plots rather than numeric tables.

graphic scale   Any scale with scale points portrayed as pictures or diagrams, rather than numbers, letters, or words.

hand tabulation   The statistical computations and analysis of survey data without the use of computer analysis routines, usually confined to frequency tables, cross-tabulation tables, and the statistics that can be obtained from them without the processing of continuous numeric variables with many scale values.

happy-sad face scale   One form of pictorial scale showing a series of simple sketches of faces with the mouth of each turned up in a smile to show pleasure or down to show displeasure in varying degrees, often used for surveying young children who may not be able to understand numeric or verbal scales.

histogram   A horizontal bar chart showing the frequency or percentage distribution of response for a survey item in graphic form, often generated by computer analysis routines if requested.

homoskedasticity   The required condition of a scatterplot of data for regression analysis, where the data points are spread around the regression line in approximately equal amounts at any given point on the line, forming an even corridor of data, as opposed to heteroskedasticity, such as a "funnel shaped" pattern of data round the regression line.

hostility bias   Opposition, resentment, or resistance to an interviewer, survey sponsor, response task, or situational factor that negatively affects answers to one or more specific survey questions.

hypothesis   A conjectural statement about the value of some variable or the relationship between variables that will be tested and ultimately accepted or rejected on the basis of statistical analysis of survey results, most often used in formal scientific or academic research.

images   The generalized or synthesized picture representation of some object, person, or idea held in the minds of people, based on partial information from previous experiences, perceptions, or evaluations, and often one of the major topics of survey research.

implicit scale   Any scale that need not be explicitly stated in the question or presented verbally or visually to respondents because they automatically understand how they are to respond, such as asking one's age with the implicit understanding that it will be expressed in years since birth.

independence   The condition between two variables or measurements where information about one gives no indication of the likely value of the other because they are unrelated.

independent variable   The variable that is viewed as influencing, affecting, or determining the values of another variable when they are regarded as being in a potential cause-and-effect relationship.

inferential statistics   Any statistical measure that can be used to make inferences or generalizations about a population, with a known level of probability, based on the values or conditions of a sample.

information needs   The specific categories of information required by those sponsoring pragmatic survey research, in order to make decisions or choices or to set policy, or required by those conducting academic research to test a theoretical or conceptual hypothesis and enhance some body of knowledge or literature.

instrumentation   The survey questionnaire and other devices, such as cover letters, rating cards, and the like, used to obtain data from respondents.

instrumentation bias   The tendency for some aspect of the survey instruments to cause respondents to answer in a particular way or systematically "push" or "pull" the survey results in some given direction, thus reducing the survey validity.

instrumentation error   The tendency for some aspect of the survey instruments to randomly affect the data in such a way that they are not true representations of the respondent opinions or conditions, but there is no specific direction or systematic influence, so that survey reliability is reduced.

integer   A whole number, as opposed to a fractional or decimal value.

interpretation error   Error that results when interviewers are asked to interpret responses during the interview or make judgments about the responses.

interrogation error   Errors that occur when questions are expressed differently from one respondent to the next.

interval scale   Any scale where the intervals between scale points are equal, even though there may be no zero value or zero does not represent a complete absence of the thing measured, such as the Fahrenheit scale.

interviewing bias   The tendency for some aspect of the interviewing to cause respondents to answer in a *particular way* or systematically "push" or "pull" the survey results in some given direction, thus reducing the survey *validity*.

interviewing error   The tendency for some aspect of the interviewing to randomly affect the data so they don't truly represent the respondents' opinions or conditions, thus reducing survey *reliability*.

judgment sample   A sample selected on the basis of the researcher's judgment about what units or respondents should and should not be included, as opposed to random selection.

knowledge component   One of the three main components of attitudes, consisting of the facts or beliefs the individual holds about the topic of the attitude.

kurtosis   A statistical measure of the shape of a distribution that indicates whether the curve is more peaked or more flat than a normal, bell-shaped curve and how much so.

level of confidence   The specific probability of obtaining some result from a sample if it did not exist in the population as a whole, at or below which the relationship will be regarded as statistically significant.

lifestyle   The general pattern of daily behavior, activities, choices, and preferences for an individual or family that might be used to characterize them and distinguish them in meaningful ways from those following a different pattern.

Likert scale   A type of scaling where the respondents are presented with a series of statements, rather than questions, and asked to indicate the degree to which they agree or disagree, usually on a five-point scale.

linear, numeric scale   A scale used when items are to be judged on a single dimension and arrayed on a scale with equal intervals, providing both absolute measures of importance and relative measures, or rankings, if responses among the various items are compared.

mail data collection   The mailing of questionnaires and their return by mail by the designated respondents.

maximum   The highest value for a variable that was actually obtained from a sample, often reported by analysis routines and used by analysts to assess range and likelihood of outliers or ceiling effects.

mean   The most common average or measure of central tendency, providing an indication of the most typical or representative value for the sample and the population as a whole, within a given confidence level.

mean squares   A value usually computed for analysis of variance to form an F-ratio to assess statistical significance, consisting of the total of the squared deviations from the mean for each data point, or sums of squares, divided by the number of cases or degrees of freedom.

measures of spread   Statistical indications of the dispersion of the data around the central point, such as the standard deviation.

median   An average or measure of central tendency, consisting of the value the middle case would take on if the cases were arrayed from lowest to highest value for the variable and the scale represented a continuum or could include an infinite number of points, used in preference to the mean for ordinal level data and often preferred to the mean for distributions that are highly skewed to one side or have outlying values.

mental set   The existing frame of mind, point of view, or train of thought adopted by a respondent at a given moment, used to judge a series of survey questions or items.

midpoint   The middle point on a scale with an odd number of scale points, sometimes reflecting neutrality on the spectrum of response.

minimum   The lowest value for a variable that was actually obtained from a sample, often reported by analysis routines and used by analysts to assess range and likelihood of outliers or floor effects.

minimum expected cell frequency   The lowest expected cell frequency in a cross-tabulation table, that must be at least five for valid use of the chi-square statistic to assess the significance of the relationship, computed by identifying the smallest row frequency and column frequency, multiplying the two, and dividing by the total frequency for the table.

mode   The only average appropriate to indicate the most typical case for a distribution of nominal data, consisting of the category with the highest frequency, and also representing the location of the peak or high point in a distribution of continuous numeric data with many scale values.

motives   The impetus or urge causing a person to take some action, that may be a topic for survey research measurement within the broader topic category of "needs."

multiple rating list   A survey item format used to save space and response time, designed so many items can be rated on the same scale.

multiple rating matrix   A survey item format used to save space and response time, designed so the same scale is used to rate multiple items on several dimensions.

multiple regression   Linear regression that uses a single dependent variable and two or more independent variables in the same analysis, in contrast to simple, linear regression using only one independent variable, so that both the effect of each independent variable and the effects of interactions among independent variables can be gauged.

multiple response item   A structured, multiple-choice survey question that allows the respondent to choose as many response categories as apply.

multivariate analysis   Statistical analysis techniques to assess the relationships or patterns among more than two variables simultaneously, including such methods as multiple regression, factorial analysis of variance, analysis of covariance, factor analysis, cluster analysis, multidimensional scaling, and the like.

mutually exclusive categories   Response categories defined to ensure a unique association between any given answer and only one category or alternative, so no response can fit into two or more categories.

namelist   A listing of names and addresses, often used for mail surveys, that may be accumulated or acquired from one of many namelist brokerage firms who accumulate and manage such lists for people with particular characteristics or in certain locations.

nay-sayer   An individual or respondent who persistently tends to respond in the negative more often than others, regardless of the questions.

nay-sayer bias   The tendency for a set of survey results to be generally and artificially negative on a series of items because all items are inclined in the same direction, toward the positive or toward the negative, and negative responses to the earlier items were generalized to the remaining ones, thus reducing the validity.

need   A persistent or fundamental requirement of the individual in order to maintain physical, psychological, or social well-being, usually fluctuating over time in its degree of satisfaction, and often a topic for survey research measurement.

no-go errors   Errors that result when a decision maker either fails to take some action that would have positive results, or ignores an alternative that would be more positive, choosing some less positive course.

nominal scale   A scale that uses numbers, letters, or symbols only as the names of independent categories, so that the scale values do not stand in any ordered relationship to one another.

nonprobability sampling   A nonrandom sampling design such as convenience sampling, where the probability of selecting a given sampling unit from the population is neither known nor equal to the probability of selecting any other unit.

nonrespondents   Those in the population who were included in the sample but failed to respond because they refused or could not be reached, or for some other reason.

nonresponse bias   A systematic effect on the data reducing validity that results when those with one type of opinion or condition fail to respond to a survey more often than do others with different opinions or conditions.

normal curve   Any distribution that conforms exactly or very closely to a normal distribution.

normal distribution   A continuous, symmetrical distribution that forms a curve with a particular shape defined by a mathematical equation, often referred to as a "bell-shaped" curve, valuable as a statistical reference because the precise areas under the curve can be computed or obtained from statistical tables.

N-size   A commonly used term for the sample size or the number of cases included in an analysis or tabular report.

nth name sampling   A sampling design where the number of units in the sample frame is first divided by the desired sample size to obtain the value of *n,* a value between one and *n* is randomly selected as a starting point or first case to be selected, and then every *n*th name or unit is selected, yielding a random sample.

null hypothesis   The hypothesis stipulating there will be no significant relationship between two variables, which can be tested with survey or other data and rejected in favor of the alternative hypothesis if the relationship proves significant, and most often used in scientific or academic research.

numeric item   Any survey item with scale numbers that are meaningful and stand in an ordered relationship to one another, such as those from ordinal, interval, or ratio scales.

open-ended question An unstructured survey question that does not include a list of alternative answers, so that respondents must answer in their own words.

order bias The tendency for the order in which survey items are listed to affect respondents' answers in some systematic way, reducing validity.

ordinal scale A particular type of scale where the response alternatives define an ordered sequence, so the first is less than the second, the second less than the third, and so on, yielding ordinal level data where the intervals between scale points are not known or necessarily equal.

outlier An extreme case or data point that stands well above or well below its nearest neighbor and is highly atypical of the distribution as a whole.

paired comparison scale A type of scale that presents respondents with one pair of alternatives at a time, instructing them to pick just one from each pair, yielding dichotomous, nominal data.

paired t-test A technique for assessing the statistical significance of differences in mean values when both are obtained from the same respondents, and are therefore paired with one another.

panel data collection A survey of a group of preselected respondents who agreed to be panel members on a continuous basis for a given period of time and provided initial demographic data, allowing selection of special groups and permitting the use of surveys to monitor responses over time.

parameter A coefficient or value for the population that corresponds to a particular statistic from a sample and is often inferred from the sample.

percentage distribution table A table listing the percentage of respondents selecting each response category or scale point.

percentile An indication of the position of a case or value within a distribution, based on the number of cases with a lesser value out of a total of 100 cases.

peripheral devices Units of computer hardware, other than the central processing unit, used to input, store, and output data or information.

personal interview Data collection accomplished with the interviewer in the presence of the respondent, so that they have visual contact, as opposed to telephone interviewing.

pictorial scale Any scale with scale points portrayed as pictures or diagrams rather than numbers, letters, or words.

pie chart A method for portraying survey results graphically, consisting of a circle divided by lines from the center to the perimeter, so that the angles between the lines and therefore the size of the "pieces" represent proportions.

pilot survey A brief preliminary survey, often using a small, convenience sample, conducted to test the survey instruments and data collection method before the project details are finalized and the larger, formal survey conducted.

population The definition of all those people or elements of interest to the information seekers and from among whom the sample will be selected.

population parameters Values or coefficients such as the mean or variance that describe the distribution of a variable in the population, often estimated or inferred based on the corresponding values of *sample statistics*.

postcoding The process of examining completed survey questionnaires, choosing response categories for items not precoded, assigning code values to them on the documents, and recording codes and category labels in a codelist.

precision   The range of the confidence interval at a given level of probability, expressed in absolute terms or as a percentage of the mean value.

precode   Assigning code values to the categories of structured questions and listing them for printing on the questionnaire prior to data collection.

preferences   Predetermined choices by respondents from among alternative goods, that may be a topic for survey research measurement within the broader topic category of "needs."

prestige   A condition of superior status, rank, or distinction relative to one's peers or society in general, constituting a basic human need, sometimes causing respondents to react to questions in ways they perceive to be more prestigious.

pretest   Preliminary trial of some or all aspects of the sampling design, survey instrumentation, and data collection method, to be sure there are no unanticipated difficulties or problems.

primary data   Data collected for a particular project to meet specific information needs, as opposed to data that already exist for general use or as the result of inquiries for other purposes.

probability sampling   Any sampling design where every element in the population has either an equal probability of selection, as with random sampling, or a given probability of being selected that is known in advance and used in analysis to assess significance.

process editing   Examining survey data with computer processing routines to be sure the data conform to the data file format and that all values are expressed in the proper form and are within the range of the scale for each item.

product-moment correlation   The statistical method of correlation that requires interval or ratio level data and is not appropriate for ordinal scale data, which require rank correlation.

qualification   The process of inspecting or interrogating potential resondents to be sure they are qualified to respond or that they fit the quota specifications for a particular interviewer.

qualitative research   Research obtaining data in the form of words or other indications that do not lend themselves to quantitative analysis and whose analysis and interpretation depend on subjective judgments by experts.

quantitative research   Research obtaining data in a form that can be represented by numbers, so that quantities and magnitudes can be measured, assessed, and interpreted with the use of mathematical or statistical manipulation.

questionnaire   The basic survey instrument containing instructions, questions, or items, response alternatives where appropriate, and specific means for recording responses.

quota   A set number or proportion of respondents with given characteristics or attributes sought in a sample or assigned to specific interviewers or fieldworkers.

quota sample   Any sampling design that requires a set number or proportion of respondents with given characteristics or attributes.

quota specification   The listing of quota requirements for the entire sample or for specific interviewers, including identification of the characteristics that define the quota, the manner in which they are to be ascertained, the method of qualification of respondents, and the number or proportion of respondents who are to have each attribute or combination of attributes.

random digit dialing   A sampling system for telephone surveys where all telephone numbers in households or all that have one of a given set of three-digit telephone number prefixes are regarded as the sample frame, and seven-digit or four-digit numbers are generated and dialed manually or automatically to obtain the sample.

random error   The result of extraneous factors, such as sampling error, affecting the survey results in no systematic pattern, so that answers are not consistently pushed or pulled in one specific direction.

random sampling   A sampling design that seeks to select respondents from the population or sample frame in a completely random fashion, so every respondent has an equal probability of being selected.

range   A measure of the spread in the distribution of data for a variable, defined as the maximum minus the minimum, plus one.

rank correlation   The statistical method of correlation appropriate when one or both of the variables are from only ordinal level scales, sometimes called Spearman rank correlation.

rank order scale   A scale essentially the same as the forced ranking scale.

rating card   A card or sheet containing a rating scale that is handed to or shown to respondents during personal interviews and from which they pick their response alternatives by number or letter.

rating scale   Any scale from which respondents choose values that represent their responses, ordinarily yielding interval or ratio level data.

ratio scale   Any scale that has the same characteristics as an equal interval scale, plus the fact that zero represents the complete absence of the thing being measured, so that a ratio of one scale value to another has a meaningful and legitimate interpretation.

raw data   Data that has not been transformed or processed, although it may have been edited and transferred from one medium to another.

recode   The process of systematically assigning new code values to variables, based on the original values, usually done in order to group data into larger categories to obtain fewer code values.

record format   The specification of where the data field for each variable is to be keyed or recorded in a data file, including both the column(s) and the record numbers within a single case.

recording error   Error that may occur when interviewers are required to write down verbal answers by respondents, typically caused by unsatisfactory abbreviation when there is insufficient time to record entire verbatim answers.

regression analysis (simple linear regression)   A statistical measure of the effect of one interval or ratio level variable on another, used both to indicate the statistical significance of the relationship and to generate an equation to predict or estimate the value of the dependent variable for a new case, based only on the known value of the independent variable.

regression equation   The equation generated by linear regression analysis, expressed as a coefficient that can be multiplied by the value of the independent variable for a new case and a constant to be added to predict the unknown value of the dependent variable.

relative frequency   A term that is sometimes used to refer to the percentages listed in a frequency table, indicating the proportion of the sample in each category.

reliability   The degree to which the survey results are free from random error, as opposed to systematic bias, often expressed in terms of confidence intervals or confidence levels.

report generation   The process of arranging and condensing tabular survey results and expressing the written interpretations of the findings to provide information to those seeking it.

responding sample   The number of cases with valid responses to the survey or to an individual survey item, as opposed to the total sample size.

response bias   The tendency for some aspect of the response task, such as annoyance or a desire to please the interviewer, to cause respondents to answer in a particular way or systematically "push" or "pull" the survey results in some given direction, thus reducing the survey validity.

response error   The tendency for some aspect of the response task, such as boredom, inattention, or fatigue, to randomly affect the data in such a way that they are not true representations of the respondent opinions or conditions, but there is no specific direction or systematic influence, so that survey reliability is reduced.

response option error   Error resulting because interviewers read the alternative answers to respondents when they shouldn't do so or fail to read them when they should.

response rate   The percentage of those included in the sample who responded to the survey and provided usable, completed questionnaires.

r-square (r², Rsq)   The coefficient of determination obtained during regression analysis, indicating the proportion of variance in the dependent variable that is "explained" by the values of the independent variable.

runs test   A statistical process used in connection with regression analysis to determine the probability that the data are actually linear or arrayed evenly around a straight line if the data were plotted, by counting the "runs" of successive data points that are all on one side of the regression line.

sample   The number and/or identification of respondents in the population who will be or have been included in the survey.

sample frame   A listing that should include all those in the population to be sampled and exclude all those who are not in the population.

sample selection bias   Any form of bias resulting from the selection of respondents in a manner that deviates from random selection, so that some types of respondents are over- or underrepresented in the sample.

sample unit   The smallest unit of the sample to be surveyed or the unit that will constitute one case for analysis, ordinarily one respondent or questionnaire.

sampling design   The specification of the sample frame, sample size, and the system for selecting and contacting individual respondents from the population.

sampling error   The degree to which the results from the sample deviate from those that would be obtained from the entire population, because of random error in the selection of respondent and the corresponding reduction in reliability.

scale interpretation error   Error associated with the use of rating cards where respondents answer with the name of a category, rather than its number or code, and the interviewer records the wrong code value because the category names are not listed on the questionnaire.

scatterplot   A graphic plot of the data points for two variables, usually generated on request by analysis routines during regression analysis, so that each data point is plotted horizontally according to the value of the independent variable and vertically according to the value of the dependent variable.

secondary data   Data initially acquired for general use or for some purpose other than the information requirements of the project at hand.

selection bias   A systematic effect on the data resulting from selection of respondents in a manner that deviates from random selection, so that some types of respondents are over- or underrepresented in the sample.

self-selection bias   A systematic affect on survey results because some respondents voluntarily participate while others decline or refuse, so that those with certain opinions or conditions are under- or overrepresented in the sample.

semantic differential scale   A scaling device that lists several pairs of bipolar adjectives, usually separated by a seven-point scale, and instructs respondents to rate the topic or object on each, ordinarily used to measure image and provide a profile.

semantic distance scale   A scale listing several adjectives or phrases, where respondents are instructed to indicate how well each describes some object or topic based on a linear, numeric scale, often used to measure image and obtain a profile in much the same manner as the semantic differential scale is used.

sequential sample   A sampling design that requires the collection of data in increments with a relatively small sample at each stage, so that analysis can be performed after each stage to determine when the sample is large enough to provide the required level of confidence or reliability.

shape   The form or outline of a data distribution arrayed from lowest to highest value, portrayed in a data plot or described by statistical values such as the coefficients of skewness and kurtosis.

sight–edit   The visual examination of the completed questionnaires immediately after data collection to determine if they are sufficiently complete and usable.

significance level   The probability that the magnitude of the relationship might result in a sample of that size purely from sampling error if, in fact, it did not exist in the population.

simple random sample   A sampling design that seeks to select respondents from the population or sample frame in a completely random fashion, so every respondent has an equal probability of being selected, and no clustering or stratification methods are used.

single response item   A structured, multiple-choice survey question that requires the respondent to choose only *one* response category, such as one that represents the "best" or "favorite."

skewness   A designation of the shape of a distribution, indicating the degree of symmetry or the degree and direction that the mode or peak "leans" toward one side, with only a few values extending well out toward the tail on the other.

slope   In regression analysis, the "rise over the run" when the dependent variable is plotted on the vertical axis of a scatterplot, or the amount of increase or decrease in the units of the dependent variable for each unit of the independent variable, indicated by the regression coefficient.

social desirability   The tendency for respondents to give answers to survey questions that are consistent with what the society believes is right, proper, correct, or acceptable, creating bias in the results whenever the true answers are suppressed to meet social norms.

spread   The range and degree of dispersion or variance in the distribution of data for a survey variable, often described by the *standard deviation* of the distribution.

stair–step scale   One type of pictorial scale graphically showing the scale points as a series of steps, appropriate for use with young children or other respondents who might have difficulty understanding a numeric or verbal scale.

standard deviation (S.D.)   A computed measure of spread or dispersion in a distribution of data, based on the squared deviations of each point from the mean, that can be used to indicate the proportion of data within certain ranges of scale values when the distribution conforms closely to the normal curve.

standard error (S.E.) of the estimate   A computed value in regression analysis based on sample size and variance around the regression line, determining the confidence interval around a predicted value of the dependent variable at a given probability.

standard error (S.E.) of the mean   A computed value based on the size of the sample and the standard deviation of the distribution, indicating the range within which the mean of the population is likely to be from the mean of the sample at a given level of probability.

statistic   Some value computed from sample data that may also be used to make inferences about the corresponding value or "parameter" for the whole population.

statistical analysis   The process of computation and manipulation of sample data in order to suppress the detail and make relevant facts and relationships more visible and meaningful, and to generate statistics in order to make inferences about the population as a whole.

statistical inference   The process of generalizing information from a sample to the population as a whole by estimating population parameters, based on their corresponding statistical values from the sample.

statistical significance   An explicit assumption by the analyst that a relationship revealed in the sample data also exists in the population as a whole, based on the relatively small probability that it would result only from sampling error if it did not exist in the population.

stratified sampling   A sampling design that divides the population into specific strata containing certain types of respondents, then selects subsamples of the required size for each strata.

stratum   The singular form of "strata," indicating one level of a stratified sampling design.

structured question   Any question that lists or prescribes the response alternatives from which respondents must choose, such as multiple-choice or true/false questions and items accompanied by rating scales.

subsample   One part of an entire sample that is singled out for special attention or analysis, often defined in terms of a demographic characteristic.

sum   The total of a series of values or the process of adding them.

sum of squares (S.S.)   A value computed for several forms of statistical analysis, such as computing the standard deviation, analysis of variance, regression analysis, and the like, where some mean is subtracted from each data point, this deviation is squared, and the squared values are added for all the cases.

survey   A research technique where information requirements are specified, a population is identified, a sample selected and systematically questioned, and the results analyzed, generalized to the population, and reported to meet the information needs.

systematic   A relationship or effect that is not random, but rather one that is consistent or in a given "direction."

systematic bias   A redundant term, since bias is defined as a systematic effect, but commonly used to emphasize the nonrandom nature of a bias or to distinguish bias from random error.

systematic sampling   Another term for *n*th name sampling, where the number of units in the sample frame is first divided by the desired sample size to obtain the value of *n,* a value between one and *n* is randomly selected as a starting point or first case to be selected, and then every *n*th name or unit is selected, yielding a random sample.

system hardware   Any mechanical or electronic device linked in a computer system, including the central processing unit and "peripheral" devices such as printers and external disk drives.

t-distribution   A symmetrical statistical probability distribution, slightly flatter and wider than the standard, normal distribution, often listed in statistical reference tables and used to determine the significance of paired t-tests.

telephone interview   Interview data collection using the telephone to contact respondents, as opposed to personal interviewing where respondents are in the presence of the interviewer and have visual contact.

termination bias   Bias resulting when respondents of a certain type or with a certain orientation prematurely terminate their participation in a continuing study, such as a panel study, at greater rates than others.

threat   A source of bias or resistance resulting when respondents find survey items or topics intimidating or threatening, such as questions about financial matters, or instructions, questions, or scales that are confusing, suggesting the respondent is ignorant or incompetent.

t-test   A statistical method of assessing the significance of differences between two mean values for the same variable, as opposed to a paired t-test of values for two different variables for the same cases, yielding the same basic information as an analysis of variance with only two categories for the independent variable.

Type I error   In academic or scientific research (as opposed to pragmatic research), the probability of rejecting the "null hypothesis" that no relationship exists, and, therefore, accepting the "alternative hypothesis" that there is a relationship, when, in fact, no relationship exists in the population as a whole.

Type II error   In academic or scientific research (as opposed to pragmatic research), the probability of not rejecting the "null hypothesis" that no relationship exists, and, therefore, rejecting the "alternative hypothesis" that there is a relationship, when, in fact, a relationship does exist in the population as a whole.

unaided recall   A form of questioning respondents about what they remember, where the facts, objects, or events are not listed or presented to them to aid their recollection, as with aided recall.

unbiased   Free of bias or unaffected by any extraneous factor that would systematically affect the values or results.

unbiased estimate   A statistical term that indicates the value of a particular statistic, such as the mean, obtained from the sample, will be exactly equal to the corresponding value of the population parameter, on the average over an infinite number of such samples.

unconditional branching   Instructions that control the "path" of interrogation by directing all respondents who reach a specific place in the questionnaire, such as the end of a special section, to go to another location in the questionnaire, rather than merely continuing from that point.

unimodal   Having only one modal value for a distribution of categorical data or only one peak or mode for a continuous distribution.

univariate analysis   The statistical description or the analysis of just one variable at a time.

unstructured question   An "open-ended" survey question where the alternative answers are not listed and respondents must provide the answers in their own words.

validation   A term commonly but incorrectly used by survey researchers and data collection agencies to indicate "verification" of responses.

validity   The degree to which the survey data or results are free from both systematic bias and random error.

variable A measurement unit that can be taken on several different values, usually used to refer to the distribution of data for one survey item.

variance A statistical term referring to the sum of the squared deviations of each data point from the mean (the sum of squares), divided by the number of cases or degrees of freedom (the mean squares), and also the value from which the standard deviation is computed by extracting the square root.

verbal frequency scale A particular type of verbal scale where the frequency of an event to be indicated by the respondent is expressed verbally, ordinarily with the words "Always, Often, Sometimes, Rarely, and Never," rather than in numeric quantities.

verbal scale Any scale whose points are expressed in words or whose numeric code values are labeled throughout the scale with words.

verification The process of checking with respondents after they have been interviewed to be sure the person was actually interviewed and that the interview was done correctly and completely when and where it was supposed to be, and commonly but incorrectly called "validation."

visibility bias One form of selection bias, where a particular type of respondent is over- or under-represented in the sample because they are more visible than others with different characteristics.

yea-sayer An individual or respondent who persistently tends to respond in the affirmative more often than others, regardless of the questions.

yea-sayer bias The tendency for a set of survey results to be generally and artificially positive on a series of items because all items are inclined in the same direction, toward the positive or toward the negative, and positive responses to the earlier items were generalized to the remaining ones, thus reducing the validity.

Index